The literary career of Thomas Nashe reflects the Elizabethan ambivalence about singularity, which could be defined either as originality or as idiosyncrasy. Nashe began as an eloquent spokesman for orthodoxy, associated with the court humanism of Archbishop Whitgift, but ended his career as a heterodox renegade, his works banned by the same bishop. In each of his works, Nashe struggled to express a compromise between the traditional ideals of Elizabethan society and the social changes that called those ideals into question. His works were also a series of failed attempts to create a niche for himself as an author with a general readership at a time when the role of vernacular literature was still being defined. Such was the overarching paradox in Nashe's career.

Stephen Hilliard uses that paradox as a context to discuss the thematic oppositions, structure, and style of the major texts. Included in this discussion is a new, detailed account of the complex literary quarrel between Nashe and Gabriel Harvey. Both Nashe's satiric comments on Elizabethan society and the Nashe-Harvey controversy raise questions about the literary idealism and putative harmony of the "golden age" of Elizabethan England.

Stephen Hilliard is assistant dean of arts and sciences and professor of English at the University of Nebraska–Lincoln.

THE
Singularity
OF
Thomas Nashe

BY
STEPHEN S. HILLIARD

UNIVERSITY
OF
NEBRASKA PRESS
LINCOLN AND LONDON

Copyright 1986 by the
University of Nebraska Press
All rights reserved
Manufactured in the
United States of America
The paper in this book meets
the guidelines for permanence
and durability of the
Committee on Production
Guidelines for Book
Longevity of the Council
on Library Resources.
Publication
of this book
was aided by
a grant from
The Andrew W. Mellon
Foundation.

Library of Congress
Cataloging in Publication Data
Hilliard, Stephen S., 1939–
The singularity of Thomas Nashe.
Bibliography: p.
Includes index.
1. Nash, Thomas, 1567–1601—
Criticism and interpretation.
I. Title.
PR2326.N3H55   1986   828'.309   85-16538
ISBN 0-8032-2326-9 (alk. paper)

To Terry and to the patience of my friends

Contents

A Note on Sources and Quotations / ix
Introduction / 1

1
The Paradox of Nashe's Career / 5

2
Nashe's Orthodoxy / 25

3
The Devil's Orator: *Pierce Penniless* / 62

4
Self-Effacing Authorship / 90

5
This Fantastical Treatise: *The Unfortunate Traveler* / 121

6
Quarreling in Print: The Harvey-Nashe Controversy / 169

7
Nashe as Ironist: *Nashe's Lenten Stuff* / 221

Works Cited / 243
Index / 255

A Note on Sources and Quotations

As scholarship and criticism proliferate, the art of citation has become so complex that the notes to a monograph can sometimes threaten to engulf the text. To avoid this, citations here have been kept to a minimum. Space will not be used to argue with the views of other writers except where matters of fact are in dispute. I owe a general debt to all the Nashe scholars who have preceded me, especially to Ronald B. McKerrow for his edition of Nashe's works. The parenthetical references to Nashe's text in this book are to the volumes and page numbers of his edition. In the absence of a modern edition, references to Gabriel Harvey's works are to microfilms and facsimiles of the original texts. References to the Marprelate Tracts are to the edition edited by William Pierce. Several of the anti-Martinist tracts were reprinted by McKerrow in his edition of Nashe, although only *An Almond for a Parrot* is now attributed to Nashe. Quotations from early texts retain original spellings and punctuation, except that modern typographical conventions are observed in the use of *i* and *j* and *u* and *v*, proper names have been changed from italic, and archaic contractions have been expanded.

Introduction

In 1589, near the start of his literary career, Thomas Nashe was employed by Richard Bancroft and Archbishop Whitgift to defend the established church against the pseudonymous satirist Martin Marprelate; in 1599 his career was ended when Bancroft and Whitgift cosigned an order banning all his works. These facts define the scope and central theme of this study of Nashe's literary career. In his works he presents himself as a latter-day humanist defending Elizabethan society against innovation, but he was perceived as a renegade who epitomized the presumption he attacked. Midway in his career he lamented, "Let me but touch a peece of paper, there arise such stormes and tempestes about my eares as is admirable" (2:186).

Nashe was a malcontent in spite of himself, or so it would appear from his presentation of himself in his works and the reactions of other Elizabethans to him. Because of the scarcity of biographical information about the historical Thomas Nashe, the Nashe we know is very much his own creation, the outspoken persona that he develops in a series of works. This Tom Nashe is a compelling figure who invites imaginative speculation, as a recent full-scale biography by Charles Nicholl witnesses. The problem is that Nashe is by his own admission a trickster like his creation Jack Wilton; the self-presentation in his works is often self-dramatizing or outright subterfuge. Nevertheless, this study will speak of Nashe as if he were a figure we could know and will even indulge in biographical

Introduction

speculation of its own. But it does not do so in all innocence.

It is hard not to speak of Nashe rather than the text because so many of the texts ask their reader to consider the remarkable case of Thomas Nashe. They represent their author as trapped between the traditional system he idealized and the exploitative urban life he despised. This persona's experience of London is the animus for bitter satire in the name of a vague set of traditional beliefs that become increasingly tenuous in the works. Although he professes orthodoxy, he depicts an Elizabethan England that falls far short of its ideal self-image and begins to expose these discrepancies as essential flaws in the system. Insight into urban life and a biting style subvert the orthodoxy that is his essential point of departure.

This confict between orthodox values and a cynical perception of injustice and exploitation cuts across Nashe's decade-long career, complicating each work and even adding tension to particular phrases and images. At all levels of discourse there is a split between the manifest rhetorical purpose and the latent anarchy of the language: at times chaos is barely contained. No wonder Nashe has attracted the interest of present-day "poststructuralist" critics, most notably Jonathan V. Crewe. Nashe asserts the humanist faith in the power of rhetoric to maintain order yet undercuts it by his own excesses. As Crewe shows, rhetoric in Nashe's hands becomes "mere rhetoric" in the pejorative sense and authorship a scandal that can still provoke distaste in some modern readers. Without any such intention, Nashe gives the lie to idealized conceptions of literature and society. Those of us who are logocentric, believing in the power of language and rhetoric to communicate verifiable truths, can be disturbed by the anarchistic undercurrents in Nashe's works.

More a historical critic of literature than Crewe, I prefer to situate Nashe more firmly in the 1590s, insofar as we can know the 1590s. The split in Nashe's works may reflect an essential division between rhetoric and logic, but in more local terms it was caused by the uncertain status of vernacular literature in Elizabethan England. What should be the role of printed works in English and what was that role in fact? The answers to these questions were complicated by the divisions in Elizabethan society, in particular the widening gap between the ideal and the actual that Nashe tried to bridge with satire and wit. From one angle the feudal order was giving way to bourgeois hegemony; from another, traditional communal values were being supplanted by a fragmented, modern ethic. Whatever terms one uses, all coherence was in question, if not yet gone. Perhaps, as Neil Rhodes has argued, Nashe inaugurated a tradition of Elizabethan grotesque that continued to order reality for him and others in an acceptable if melancholic fashion.

In sixteenth-century terms, Nashe's controversial standing as an author reflects Elizabethan ambivalence about "singularity," a quality both prized and condemned. To be singular was to be different and original, estimable characteristics in literature and on the streets of London to the point that they threatened to become disruptive to the traditional social order. Nashe's singularity was both a literary goal and a condition forced on him by his estranged status. He was part of a new world of isolated individuals, even though his allegiances were to the hierarchical community of Tudor ideology. He was quick to condemn unorthodox beliefs and behavior in others; others were as quick to condemn his outspoken pamphlets. Nashe's humanistic conception of the exalted social role of the poet justified his own singularity to him, but his critics saw him as a presumptuous hack writer. At issue was not his personal character so much as the effect of his pamphlets on their readers. Like many other Elizabethan writers, he resorted to complex rhetorical contortions in his efforts to be original without appearing arrogant or idiosyncratic.

Nashe's works do not show a very developed understanding of the social and economic conditions of their production. The anxiety that propels the prose forward insures that the works are flawed by ambiguities and careless writing. The works would not necessarily be better if they were more reflective and better organized; rather, they acquire a special importance because Nashe's imaginative response to adversity impelled him to write works that reveal the contradictions of

Elizabethan society rather than the idealized myth. Like Shakespeare, Nashe in his lesser fashion manages to encompass aspects of life excluded by prevalent idealistic literary modes. At their best his works show the emergent urban life of his time with a clarity and force that surpass their limitations.

CHAPTER
1

The Paradox of Nashe's Career

WHAT is known of Thomas Nashe's life indicates that he was one of the many Elizabethan intellectuals who found that the limited upward mobility permitted by the social hierarchy often led to estrangement rather than preferment. Born in 1567 at Lowestoft, where his father was a minister, he matriculated at St. John's College, Cambridge, in 1582. Although rumored to be an indifferent student, he received a bachelor's degree and began the master's degree that might have assured him a career. But after some seven years at Cambridge his studies were cut short, presumably by financial difficulties caused by his father's death. In 1588, "yet altogether raw, and so consequently unfitte for any calling in the Common wealth" (1:37), he betook himself to London, the manuscript of his first work, *The Anatomy of Absurdity*, in hand.

Writing barely existed as a profession, but Nashe was fortunate at first: the popular Robert Greene allowed him to write a preface to one of his romances, *The Anatomy* was published, and he was employed by the ecclesiastical authorities to write propaganda against Martin Marprelate. His activities from the ending of the anti-Martinist campaign in early 1590 through the summer of 1592 are unknown, but he suggests that he managed a precarious living by ghostwriting and undertaking minor projects, such as the preface he wrote for an edition of Sir Philip Sidney's *Astrophil and Stella*. The disreputable part of his career is represented for us by "The Choice of Valentines," a pornographic poem he wrote about this time. Although it circulated only in manuscript, it tainted his reputation.

In September of 1592 he achieved his greatest success with *Pierce Penniless His Supplication to the Devil*, a controversial pamphlet that used his experience of poverty as a basis for a satiric account of the sins and follies of England. In spite of the work's audacity, he received the support of a most orthodox patron, the archbishop of Canterbury, for whom he wrote his one surviving play, *Summer's Last Will and Testament*. A critical passage on Richard Harvey in *Pierce Penniless* marked the beginning of his famous controversy with Gabriel Harvey, who wrote a pamphlet defending his brother. Nashe answered him in *Strange News*, written late in 1592. During 1593, his most productive year, he wrote a short treatise on apparitions, *The Terrors of the Night*, *The Unfortunate Traveler*, and an emotional religious tract entitled *Christ's Tears over Jerusalem*. For a few months he received hospitality from Sir George Carey on the Isle of Wight at a time when a major outbreak of the plague made it unsafe to be in London. But shortly he was back in the city, facing a variety of criticisms of his work and another damaging attack by Gabriel Harvey. The popularity of *Pierce Penniless* had turned to notoriety; it and his other works were searched for topical allusions and condemned as arrogant. He never again received regular patronage or achieved a popular success.

His publishing career was in decline. In 1594 his name appears as co-author on the title page of Marlowe's *Dido—Queen of Carthage*, but it is doubtful that he did more than edit the text. He worked in some capacity for John Danter, a marginal printer who himself had a short and troubled career (Hoppe, *The Bad Quarto*). In 1596 he published *Have with You to Saffron Walden*, the belated second reply to Gabriel Harvey which includes an admission that he was again eking out a living by ghostwriting. In 1597 his contribution to the writing of a lost satiric play, *The Isle of Dogs*, forced him to flee London while the investigator and torturer Richard Topcliffe searched his papers by order of the Privy Council for evidence of sedition. Nashe found refuge in Yarmouth, where the kindness of the town inspired his last work, *Nashe's Lenten Stuff*, a mock encomium of Yarmouth's main product, kippered herring. It was published in 1599, shortly before the scandalous controversy with Harvey caused the bishops to ban all his works. The circumstances of his death shortly thereafter are unknown, but it can be conjectured that the chronic poverty that threatened him all his life was a factor. Certainly he never had the means or leisure to write the kinds of serious literature he himself esteemed.

THE WRITER IN THE WORK

Nashe's travails as a writer are often his subject, explicitly in *Pierce Penniless* and the pamphlets answering Harvey and indirectly in most of his other works. His personal plight as a masterless man seeking a place in the social order is presented as symptomatic of the decay of humanistic ideals. Nashe saw his failure to find steady employment for his talents as an indictment of his age, particularly when he considered the uneducated merchants and second-rate writers who were being handsomely rewarded. The autobiographical references in his works were not egocentric for Nashe because they were the central evidence in his quarrel with society. Because he is presenting himself as a typical case, it is difficult to know how closely the image he presents corresponds to the actual Tom Nashe, but the fictionalized Nashe or Pierce Penniless of the pamphlets is a constant element in his career.

That career impresses us first with its diversity. The attitudes expressed in his works are not fixed, nor is there a progressive development from work to work. Restlessness and dissatisfaction are the hallmarks of his style; he often changes direction within a particular work, such as *The Terrors of the Night*, or even within a single paragraph or sentence. The works are also original in form, at times to the point of being idiosyncratic, as in *Christ's Tears over Jerusalem* or *Nashe's Lenten Stuff*. When his works are in an accepted genre, they bend its rules: *Summer's Last Will and Testament* is a combination of court entertainment, rustic pageant, and sophisticated comedy that fits uneasily into any history of the development of English drama. In the dedication to *The Unfortunate Traveler* Nashe explains that friends have pressed him to write "in this kind," but critics remain uncertain about what genre or subgenre includes this "fantastical treatise." *Nashe's Lenten Stuff* has been seen as an example of "pure" literature with only the most tenuous relationship to the external world; it has been compared to *Finnegans Wake* and other modernist works.

Nashe's corpus as a whole and many an individual work appear to be hodge-podges or gallimaufries, to use Elizabethan terms, but there is a program underlying the sequence of works. At the simplest level, the biographical one, Nashe's purpose was to find employment. Except for brief periods he failed. His writings were popular, but it was not possible to live on publisher's fees; he needed the regular employment a patron could insure him (E. Miller, *The Professional Writer*). His first published work, the outspoken "Preface to *Menaphon*," was successful if it did in fact lead to his employment as an anti-Martinist and the subsequent patronage of Archbishop Whitgift. The archbishop's support, Sir George Carey's, and any by other patrons, was only temporary, and often Nashe's dedications met with no response. One reason, then, that the works are so diverse is that they usually failed to please those above Nashe in the social hierarchy, even when they amused the general reader. *Pierce Penniless* went through several editions, but the mysterious Amyntas to whom it was dedicated apparently did not reward Nashe's efforts, so the promised sequel was never written. *Christ's Tears over Jerusalem* did not lead to Nashe's reemployment as a religious controversialist. If the earl of Southampton had responded to the dedication to *The Unfortunate Traveler*, Nashe might well have attempted another work of fiction.

The need to find employment became a subject of his works as well as the occasion of their publication. Predecessors like Gascoigne, Lyly, and Spenser had discreetly used literature to promote their own careers; Nashe's works also call attention to his talents and availability, most obviously in *Pierce Penniless*. The "Preface to *Menaphon*" and *The Anatomy of Absurdity* are patent self-advertising, and *The Terrors of the Night* includes a digression on his failure to find patronage and his hopes of the generosity of Sir George Carey. *Christ's Tears over Jerusalem*, which professes a new policy of self-effacement, includes an argument that the authorities should employ writers with a classical education to prevent the spread of atheism and worldliness. Even the pamphlets attacking Harvey are in part demonstrations of Nashe's rhetorical ability.

Nashe's failure at establishing a career animates the anger that fuels his satire: the ideals of the previous generation of humanists were being betrayed by self-indulgent and exploitive individuals; the myth of a golden age, so close to realization, was being forestalled by a presumptuous middle class, seditious Puritans, and indolent aristocrats. As his prospects faded, Nashe became more disillusioned: his earlier writings exhibit a firm belief in traditional values and the social order; in later works he is more cynical about the justice and openness of his society. His disillusionment was not unusual; the 1590s seemed to many Elizabethans a period of confusing disintegration of a golden age. Nashe's shift from apologist to malcontented fugitive epitomizes his culture facing its own limitations.

As overwhelming as his personal disappointment must have been, Nashe could not let his works become overt self-expression. At times he may seem to be exhibiting his personal opinions or showing off his rhetorical prowess, but the readers he esteemed would expect him to show his skills in a serious and socially useful endeavor. The meaninglessness and pure play modern critics have seen in Nashe would have also offended his contemporaries. The purpose of Nashe's major works was to persuade his readers to be good citizens of the commonwealth, although as a satirist most of his effort went into attacking abnormalities, rather than advancing a positive position. His works for the most part were directed at the same people who read Greene's romances on the one hand and popular ethical tracts on the other. He did not attempt fine aesthetic effects or deal with courtly themes; he wanted to appeal directly to the middle class and sway them to his orthodox view of society. *Summer's Last Will and Testament* was written for private performance, and "The Choice of Valentines" makes no claims for itself, but in his other works he is basically a moralist and social critic: F. P. Wilson aptly termed Nashe's works "lay sermons" (*Elizabethan and Jacobean*, 6). In the late works, however, Nashe's increasing pessimism about society blunts and displaces his persuasive purpose.

Although Nashe mentions in *Pierce Penniless* that he hoped one day to write a work in Latin for an international audience (1:215), his existing works are very much vernacular literature written for the relatively uneducated reader. Writing in English was an increasingly serious endeavor, and after 1575 eloquence was prized because of its beneficial effect on the language, but English was still seen primarily in terms of education and rhetorical persuasion rather than as a vehicle for serious discourse or original thought (R. Jones, 32–67). As we shall see, Nashe's intention was to popularize the court humanism that was the semi-official ideology of Elizabethan government. The hold of that ideology on the country was incomplete and insecure: in the London that became the center of Nashe's activities it was threatened by puritanism and by unthinking worldliness. Nashe's task was to compete with the first group for the souls of the second, to win the disorganized and worldly lower middle class to the civic religion of court humanism rather than let the Puritans convert them to a more radical social stance. Nashe's inventive style and the rhetorical originality of his works are in part ploys for reaching this intended audience, an audience as disposed to be amused as instructed (E. Miller, *Professional Writer*, 27–62; Louis Wright, 81–118).

The ideal reader of his pamphlets was one of the displaced young men of the city, perhaps a literally masterless man, disrespectful of authority and prone to disruptive behavior. In the 1590s such people became a major social problem (Beier). Partly as a strategy and partly because of his own experience, Nashe became a spokesman for the unemployed and underemployed "Pierce Pennilesses" who undermined the security of Elizabethan London. His purpose was to articulate the dissatisfactions he shared with them, then lead them into a reaffirmation of the traditional social order. He ran into difficulties on two fronts. His championing of court humanism is not as convincing as his expression of social discontents. Moreover, he was highly critical of the economic structure of

London life, not understanding its essential relationship to the national political order that he idealized.

This is why Nashe's literary career also became a series of skirmishes with censorship. Elizabethan censorship was erratic because the control over printing was imperfect and because no one was sure what the effect of the printed word was on the beliefs of the people (E. Miller, *Professional Writer*, 171– 202; Siebert, 21–104). Nashe's works were frequently criticized because of topical allusions and were condemned as a disruptive social influence. *Pierce Penniless* was thought to gird at prominent figures and insult Denmark, then an ally. *Christ's Tears over Jerusalem* offended the London authorities; Nashe was forced to soften a passage. *The Isle of Dogs* was suppressed by the Privy Council while Nashe fled London. Finally, the quarrel with Harvey led to the banning of all Nashe's works. Such difficulties with censorship were internalized in the works themselves, as in the provocative "Tale of the Bear and Fox" in *Pierce Penniless* or the elaborate baiting of the reader in *Nashe's Lenten Stuff*. Not only did Nashe fail to lead his readership back in the shaky new Anglican fold; he became in the eyes of the authorities one of the renegade wolves himself.

Nashe's literary career has an interest greater than the intrinsic value of the particular works because its permutations trace a sea change in his society's conception of literature. The perspective Nashe offers on the social dynamics and personal disappointments of the period are a corrective to the more idealized vision of the great Elizabethan poets and playwrights. Nashe closed with the Blatant Beast while Spenser kept to the highlands of Mount Acidale. He was the writer who first confronted the new social unrest that gave the lie to the myth of a golden age. His brave effort to extract humor from his confusion and desperation became an example for Jonson and Shakespeare. They achieved a deeper understanding of the forces dividing society, but no one felt the divisions more intensely or realized them in prose as vividly.

THE SOCIAL ROLE OF LITERATURE:
THE ANATOMY OF ABSURDITY

As the first heir of Nashe's invention, *The Anatomy of Absurdity* establishes the basic attitudes he was to develop in later works, while posing the literary and rhetorical problems that are the context of his career. In particular it introduces his belief that literature was at the heart of a nation's culture and that writers were therefore unacknowledged social arbiters. The *Anatomy* was written while he was still a student at Cambridge, steeped in traditional humanism and angered by the Puritans who dominated his own college, St. John's, and the university. Published in 1589, it attracted little attention, in part because it is an unsuccessful attempt to apply the courtly eloquence of late humanism to the social concerns that so inflamed the Puritans. Little esteemed by Nashe's great editor, called "drearily dull" by a modern biographer, the *Anatomy* fails to find a style of its own, is largely derivative of other men's books, and is only intermittently satiric (D. Allen, *"The Anatomie"*; Hibbard, 11; McKerrow, 4:1–2). It is, nevertheless, the prolegomenon to Nashe's literary career.

The purpose of the work becomes clearer if it is placed in the context of the two previous anatomies it imitates. It is a variation on the tradition of stylized, courtly literature popularized ten years earlier by John Lyly's *Euphues: The Anatomy of Wit*. Nashe later confessed his admiration for Lyly's work: "*Euphues* I readd when I was a little ape in Cambridge, and then I thought it was *Ipse ille*" (1:319). Although he denied imitating Lyly, *The Anatomy of Absurdity* is euphuistic in its use of verbal schemas and classical allusions. One passage echoes *Euphues*, and Nashe borrows extensively from Gosson's *Ephimerides of Phialo* and Melbanke's *Philotimus*, two earlier imitations of Lyly (McKerrow, 4:12, 483; ibid., "Supplement," 1–7). The elaborate, euphonic style called euphuism confined the rhetorical training of humanism to the ends of elegance and wit (Croll, 237–95; Hunter, *John Lyly*, 257–80). For all that its harmonies were mechanical and its analogies from nature artificial and fabulous, euphuism was in accord with the analogical and hierarchical cosmology that justified the social order. Even when used satirically, its mild irony and decorous wit fitted it to the needs of the complex role playing and protective discretions of court life. In adopting the euphuisitic style, Nashe was trying to identify his work with the courtly phase of humanism and the social and literary attitudes of court circles. He probably hoped to call attention to his talents and obtain preferment as Lyly had done, but euphuism was passing from favor.

While *The Anatomy of Absurdity* uses the style of *The Anatomy of Wit*, it is a response to Phillip Stubbes's very different *Anatomy of Abuses*. This puritan criticism of Elizabethan society was unusually popular, going through three editions by 1585. Carefully revised in each edition, it uses a dialogue format, allusions to contemporary events, and a vivid "plain style" to direct its message to a wide audience, not merely to the learned or to magistrates (Pearson). Unaware of or not sufficiently appreciative of the economic factors causing social change, Stubbes and other Puritan critics saw change as the result of pride and various forms of self-indulgence. According to this anatomy, pride was the root of all social ills. It led to the breakdown of social order, as in Stubbes's vision of every man "crying with open mouth: I am a Gentleman, I am worshipful, I am Honourable, I am noble" (sig. B7r). He was particularly critical of those private vices that influenced people to such presumption; for example, he saw pride of apparel as worse than pride of heart and pride of mouth because it caused others to become presumptuous. This social perspective on vice underlies his criticisms of drama and wicked books, which both encourage antisocial behavior:

> And yet, notwithstanding, whosoever wil set pen to paper now a dayes, how unhonest soever, or unseemly of christian eares his argument be, is permitted to goe forward, and his woork plausibly admitted and freendly licensed, and gladly imprinted without any prohibition or contradiction at all: wherby it is growen to this issue, that bookes & pamphlets of scurrilitie and baudrie, are better esteemed and more vendible then the godlyest and sagest bookes that be. (sigs. P7r–P7v)

Such debased books "corrupt mens mindes, pervert good wits, allure to baudrie, induce to whordome, suppresse vertue & erect vice" (sig. P7r). Stubbes, of course, spoke for the Puritan movement and expressed concerns that troubled the authorities as well as zealots (Fraser; Knappen, 466–80; Sasek).

Nashe begins his anatomy by agreeing with the Puritans that debased books are threatening the good order of the commonwealth, but he focuses more narrowly on the ignorance of popular writers: "It fareth nowe a daies with unlearned Idiots as it doth with she Asses, who bring foorth all their life long; even so these brainlesse Bussards, are every quarter bigge wyth one Pamphlet or other" (1:9). He also objects to writers who encourage lust and cater to women readers, flattering them with general encomiums. In answer to such "blazing of Womens slender praises," Nashe launches into a misogynist diatribe. He is especially critical of the "Homer of Women," who is apparently Robert Greene, to judge by a pun: "See how farre they swerve from theyr purpose, who with Greene colours, seeke to garnish such Gorgonlike shapes [as those of women]" (1:16). McKerrow could not reconcile this pun with Nashe's friendship for Greene, but Greene would not have been much offended: shortly he was to disown his own romances (McKerrow, 4:7–10; Pruvost, 320–23). In a conventional manner, Nashe saw the praise of women as a reversal of the ethical hierarchy and an encouragement of sensuality. The Puritans favored a plain style and had a higher opinion of women, but otherwise the opening pages of Nashe's text could be those of a Puritan tract.

Then, Nashe unexpectedly turns the argument back on the Puritan social critics and on Stubbes in particular. Just as profane pamphleteers and romance writers abuse the press, so do those "who make the Presse the dunghill whether they carry all the muck of their mellancholicke imaginations, pretending forsooth to anatomize abuses and stubbe up sin by the rootes" (1:20). Uneducated men like Stubbes are not qualified to be social critics; they are guilty of the pride and ignorance they attack: "Their ignoraunt zeale wyll presumptuously presse into the Presse, enquiring most curiouslie into every corner of the Common wealth, correcting that sinne in others, wherwith they are corrupted themselves. To prescribe rules of life, belongeth not to the ruder sorte; to condemne those callings which are approoved by publique authoritie, argueth a proude contempt of the Magistrates superiority" (1:21). The Puritans contribute to the disorder they criticize by being models of presumption: "Each trifling Pamphlet to the simpler sorte" seems "a most substantiall subject, whereof the wiser lightly account, and the learned laughing contemne" (1:22). Moreover, "these men inveigh against no new vice," but simply repeat traditional invectives (1:20).

Nashe's account of what literature should be is itself traditional and rather idealistic, given the conditions he would himself face in the next decade. In the dedicatory epistle, art is seen as the answer to absurdity since its traditional wisdom is a corrective for the self-centered follies that beset society. A well-written tract by a trained humanist such as himself could offset stupidity and corruption. He distinguishes serious authors from hacks who publish for money: "What wyl they not faine for gaine? Hence come our babling Ballets, and our new found Songs and Sonets" (1:23). Poetry should praise the virtuous, but ignorant praise "rather breedes detestation then admiration" (1:24). The true poet is learned, and good poetry akin to philosophy. Bad poetry is all too common, but Nashe cannot agree with the "preciser censure" of those who account "Poetrie impietie, and witte follie" (1:27). They are confusing the abuse of poetry with its proper function as an adjunct of learning.

Both in the arts and in life, learning "ought to be the Levell, whereby such as live ill, ought to square theyr crooked waies" (1:49). This emphasis on learning reflects Nashe's hope that his university degree would find him employment, but it also is in accord with the humanism of Ascham and Cheke. "It is learning and knowledge which are the onely ornaments of a man, which furnisheth the tongue with wisedome, and the hart with understanding, which maketh the children of the needy poore to become noble Peeres, and men of obscure parentage to be equall with Princes in possessions" (1:34). Through art, learning mitigates the absurdities humanity is prone to because of the Fall. Since the emphasis is on the persuasion of fallen humanity to virtue rather than the discovery of new truths, rhetoric is essential. "Amongst all the ornaments of Artes, Rethorick is to be had in highest reputation, without the which all the rest are naked, and she onely garnished" (1:45). But even this self-evident truth is oppugned.

In this way Nashe, like many a modern social critic, traces absurdities back to the educational system. Through the debasement of learning and unsound innovations and by neglecting and corrupting training in rhetoric, the universities have disabled their graduates. The Puritans are again partly to blame, since they seek the rapid production of preachers at the expense of classical studies. Sound education is also threatened by the shortcuts of the Ramists, who were favored by the Puritans. Nashe's attitude is that of a latter-day Ascham, lamenting the decay of learning and abandonment of humanistic ideals. He wants to reject the innovations of "impudent incipients in Arts" such as Ramus and return to traditional studies. Such a reform would benefit the whole of society, since university graduates would resume their proper role in persuading the commonwealth to eschew absurdity.

At the start of his career, Nashe thought of the world in literary and rhetorical categories. Although there are references to oratory, the emphasis is on books, which had become the center of the nation's culture and a major influence on how people lived their lives. Romances, for example, influenced women and their male friends to reverse the proper ethical order. Puritan tracts caused hypocritical and self-centered behavior to replace traditional charity. Ignorant poets caused readers to scorn rather than respect the virtues they intended to praise. The solution was a sound literature that applied traditional wisdom to contemporary issues in a rhetorically effective fashion; literature should persuade readers to become useful members of the commonwealth. Nashe is particularly concerned with two wayward groups, as his title page announces: those "who live more licentiously" and those "addicted to a more nyce stoicall austeritie." If the *Anatomy* reached neither the worldly nor the Puritans, it was because Nashe himself was not rhetorically adept enough to persuade unwilling readers to change their attitudes.

Euphuism was dated, and Nashe's mastery of it was mediocre compared to Lyly's eloquence. The *ethos* or authorial presence in the work is indistinct and the voice imprecise; who is this person who sounds like an angry John Lyly? Nashe's scorn for uneducated writers does not sit well with his own secondhand learning, and his criticism of writers like Stubbes for presumption raises questions about Nashe's own qualifications as a social critic. Nashe tries to anticipate this charge in the dedication to Sir Charles Blunt: "What I have written, proceeded not from the penne of vain-glory but from the processe of that pensivenes, which two Summers since overtooke mee" (1:5). Nevertheless, the twenty-year-old Nashe had no authority to write an account of contemporary social absurdity. The *Anatomy* is too much a self-serving demonstration of the talents of its author to pass itself off as a disinterested humanist tract. It partakes too much of the singularity it denounces. Nashe claims to have adopted a "satyrical disguise," but the satire is occasional and does not emanate from a central persona. Nashe could not protect himself with the persona or ethos of this work the way that he could with Pierce Penniless, Jack Wilton, or even the later Tom Nashe.

THE RHETORICAL STANCE: NASHE'S PREFACES

The Anatomy of Absurdity shows the extent to which the problems Nashe faced at the start of his career were rhetorical. First, he needed a way of presenting himself with a respectable ethos or of masking himself behind a persona that would give coherence and credibility to his works. He also needed a way of including his reader in the work that would reach the relatively uneducated readers of vernacular printing. Finally, he needed a style that would bridge the gap between the implied author and the implied reader, a way of writing that would entertain and convince. His formal training and allegiance to the humanism of Ascham meant that he saw his problems in terms of classical rhetoric. Later his awareness of the "preemptive power of contingencies" would undermine his faith in the efficacy of rhetoric and the truth of language itself, but in his early works he shares the assumptions of his age about the possibility of direct communication (Crewe, 21–26). Rhetoric was subordinate to logic and received truth; he had not yet abandoned the tenets of English Ciceronianism (Vos; see also Ong, *Rhetoric*).

Classical rhetoric, developed to serve the ends of oratory, was imperfectly suited to the needs of the printed book (Ong, *Rhetoric*, 23–47). Like an orator, vernacular writers were trying to persuade their readers to proper beliefs and courses of action, but because a readership is unseen and fragmented they could not appeal to the group dynamics of an assembled audience. At the same time the author was unseen by the readers; everything depended on developing an ethos that was attractive and compelling within the confines of the printed text (Kennedy, 1–19). Delivery and a credible personal presence were no longer relevant to the rhetorical task. Nashe's problem was compounded by his lack of any personal authority other than his university training, which he exploited as best he could. He needed to develop a style that was plausible and a repertory of rhetorical devices that would create a semblance of the personal contact possible in oratory. He tried from the start of his career to write in a style that would justify itself by the sheer brilliance of its wit, but he did not master such a style until he had learned from the Marprelate controversy how to attach the wit to a rhetorical fabrication that represented himself or to an imagined spokesperson within the text itself. He further learned to include a representation of his imagined reader so that he could simulate some of the give-and-take of oratory.

Like *The Anatomy of Absurdity*, the "Preface to *Menaphon*" lacks an effective rhetorical strategy, but it shows again his rhetorical attitude towards literature. In the form of an epistle "to the gentlemen students of both universities," it is incongruously prefixed to one of Robert Greene's popular romances. Although its ostensible purpose is to recommend *Menaphon* as an example of the kind of artful literature that should prevail over the debased books in demand, it gives only passing praise to Greene's style. At one point it appears to ridicule Greene's affected classical allusions (McKerrow, 4: 445). The view of literature Nashe advances is in fact antithetical to the main features of Greene's own career, yet Greene presumably invited the epistle as a gesture of friendship to a fellow Cantabrigian newly arrived in London (E. Miller, "The Relationship of Robert Greene and Thomas Nashe"). Published before the *Anatomy*, the "Preface to *Menaphon*" is an outspoken assault on the Elizabethan literary scene. It is extraordinary that Nashe should elect and be permitted to begin his literary career with such a bold, albeit obscure manifesto.

Nashe extends his attack on bad literature to include criticism of ignorant dramatists and actors. He also names specific authors and hints at others, to the delight and confusion of modern critics. The decrying of bombastic drama echoes views expressed by Greene, but Nashe could hardly use writers of popular romances as an example of debased literature as he had done in the *Anatomy*. The terms of the attack are Nashe's: playwrights are "ideot Art-masters, that intrude themselves to our eares as the Alcumists of eloquence, who (mounted on the stage of arrogance) thinke to out-brave better pennes with the swelling bumbast of bragging blanke verse" (3:311). This criticism of Marlovian drama was general enough that Nashe could later claim Marlowe himself as a friend he had never abused (3:131). Another passage seems more clearly an insulting allusion to Thomas Kyd, but the exact meaning of Nashe's comments on contemporary dramatists, including his tantalizing reference to an early version of *Hamlet*, continues to elude critical inquiry (5:315–16; on Kyd see Freeman, 30–55).

The comments on drama are part of Nashe's more general concern with the detrimental effect of inflated rhetoric on the common people. Unlike the Puritans, he is not particularly disturbed by immoral or seditious content in plays. His objection to whatever early version of *Hamlet* he saw was not that it promoted a revenge ethic, but that it was bombastic and plagiarized from Seneca. His praise of George Peele as a playwright is similar in its focus on rhetoric: "I dare commend him unto all that know him, as the chiefe supporter of pleasance now living, the Atlas of Poetrie, and *primus verborum Artifex*: whose first increase, the arraignement of Paris, might pleade to your opinions his pregnant dexterity of wit, and manifold varietie of invention; wherein (*me iudice*) he goeth a steppe beyond all that write" (3:323). In *Pierce Penniless* history plays are praised as models of human behavior, but at this point Nashe saw drama as a verbal structure and a branch of poetry that was primarily rhetorical.

The rest of the literary criticism in the "Preface" also focuses on the rhetorical success or failure of the works in question. As in the *Anatomy* bad writers are castigated for their lack of academic training: "How is it then such bungling practitioners in principles should ever profit the Common-wealth by their negligent paines, who have no more cunning in Logicke or dialogue Latine then appertaines to the literall construction of either?" (3:318). Nashe again expresses his loyalty to Cheke, Ascham, and the other Cambridge humanists, particularly those associated with his own college (Arnold). St. John's is, however, no longer "that most famous and fortunate Nurse of all learning" because of the "Divinitie Dunces, that strive to make their pupills pulpit-men before they are reconciled to Priscian" (317, 318). Some few humanistic translators and poets survive with difficulty in an age when they are discouraged by "the upstart discipline of our reformatorie Churchmen, who account wit vanitie, and poetry impiety" (321). As in the *Anatomy* Nashe sees the humanism he championed as under attack by a Puritan movement that scorned the classical arts of language.

The "over-racked Rhetoricke" of bad writers corrupted the common reader by encouraging a specious, inflated view of the world that could lead to disorder and sedition. He notes "that every mechanicall mate abhorreth the English he was borne too, and plucks, with a solemne periphrasis, his *ut vales* from the inkehorne" (3:311), but he blames this presumption on the tragedians and their poets who set bad examples. Shopkeepers are to be praised for a native wit that is superior to dry scholasticism: "Oft have I observed what I now set downe: a secular wit that hath lived all dayes of his life by What doe you lacke? to be more judiciall in matters of conceit then our quadrant crepundios, that spit *ergo* in the mouth of every one they meete" (314). Unfortunately, such talented common people "are so affectionate to dogged detracting, as the most poysonous *Pasquil* any durty mouthed Martin or Momus ever composed is gathered up with greedinesse before it fall to the ground" (315). The popular interest in rhetoric has split from the proper use of rhetoric in humanistic arguments in support of the commonwealth. Instead, "the minde of the meanest is fedde with this folly, that they impute singularity to him that slaunders privily, and count it a great peece of Art in an inkhorne man, in any tapsterly termes whatsoever, to expose his superiours to envy" (315). By a sort of Gresham's law of language, bad rhetoric drives out good and corrupts the minds of the common people.

Bombastic playwrights and insolent prose writers like Martin Marprelate have substituted the false eloquence of outspoken conceit for the true eloquence of the trained humanist. For Nashe the solution is more sound secular writing, not the renunciation of literature. "The private truth of my discovered Creede in this controvesie is this, that . . . I deeme him farre unworthy the name of a scholer, and so, consequently, to sacrifice his endevours to Art, that is not a Poet, either in whole or in part" (3:321). The idealism is reminiscent of Sidney, but the difference between Nashe's "Preface" and *The Defense of Poetry* show the limitations of both critics. Nashe never makes a case for his allegiance to a humanistic conception of literature; he simply asserts his "creed." Sidney, on the other hand, develops an eloquent defense of the value of poetry without answering the specific complaints of the puritan critic about its detrimental effects. Nashe is closer to the actual marketplace of popular ideas and opinions, where superficial cleverness and wit outweight substance, where "two-pennie Pamphlets" count for more than the "excellent translation of Maister Thomas Watsons sugred *Amintas.*"

The middle style Nashe attempts with mixed success is appropriate to the give-and-take of the popular literary scene. Sidney's *Defense* is in the form of a classic oration, and it was intended for manuscript circulation in upper-class and intellectual circles. Nashe's epistle is prefaced to a best-selling romance, so he tried to suit his style to the general reader, for all that it is nominally addressed to university students. Quintilian had argued that an extemporal style was best for *ad hoc* political situations (Quintilian, 4:127–51). He had in mind the styles and breaking of decorum, appeal to the presumptuous tendencies of the people. The tradition established by the Cambridge humanists of the mid-century has been carried forward by a few writers of neo-Latin verse and by some vernacular writers, above all Sidney and Spenser, but the demands of actors for sensational scripts and the popularity of uneducated poets and pampleteers "have made Art bankerout of her ornaments, and sent Poetry a begging up and downe the Countrey" (3:324). The Puritans would suppress all secular literature because of such abuses, but for Nashe the solution must be the arrival of new writers who can use a singular style to promote orthodox values. Nashe clearly has himself in mind, but already his singularity is being seen as arrogance rather than originality.

CHAPTER

2

Nashe's Orthodoxy

APPROACHED in isolation from their historical context, Nashe's works seem more modern and "themeless" than they do when they are cross-referenced with the works that make up their "background." That historical background, like the life of the author, is in part our construct, built by selecting texts that support our theses about the Elizabethan period. Moreover, as in a painting, the foreground defines the background: Nashe's literary career shapes an attitude toward the Elizabethan literary scene. It invites us to see Elizabethan orthodoxy as an ideology in need of defense, rather than as a comfortable set of beliefs. This impression is confirmed by the career of Nashe's first patron, Archbishop Whitgift, who was an ideologue, if that term fits any Elizabethan. Another modern term, *propagandist*, describes Nashe's role in the anti-Martinist campaign. Even the festive entertainment he wrote for the archbishop, *Summer's Last Will and Testament*, has an ideological function. Later in his career Nashe departed from orthodoxy, although he continued to profess allegiance to it, but his early works are firm in their support of the dominant system of conformity promoted by the archbishop.

When Nashe arrived in London in 1588, two events symbolized the precarious situation of the Elizabethan government: the defeat of the Spanish Armada off the southern coast and the clandestine printing of the first Martin Marprelate tract just outside London. The fortunate destruction of the Armada seemed to Elizabethans only the first encounter in a long struggle against an international Catholic threat. The sense of danger was exacerbated by an indigenous Catholic population, both an old guard and newer malcontented converts. Many of these recusants remained loyal to the queen, although they had been officially absolved of that duty by the Papal Bull of 1570. The Marprelate tracts were an extreme expression of danger to the Elizabethan compromise from radical Protestantism. Puritan asceticism and the new morality represented by Stubbes's *Anatomy of Abuses* were the popular arm of a Puritan movement that was also political. Although the Puritans sought only ecclesiastical reform, particularly the elimination of the office of bishop, their campaign seemed seditious to the Anglican establishment. The defensive stance of orthodox Anglicanism was a response to real dangers, not paranoia.

An official version of the "natural truth" about social life was actively promulgated by the government, and opposing views were as vigorously suppressed. Through patronage and the silencing of dissent, Elizabethan institutions were kept within a framework of acceptable beliefs (Hurstfield, 63–70). Literature and publishing were not exempt: books favorable to the Elizabethan social system were promoted, others discouraged or censored (Bennet, 56–86; Rosenberg, 3–18). When Nashe's works seemed to support the system of conformity, they were encouraged; when their exposure of abuses and outspoken singularity implicitly questioned the system, they were ignored or censored. Nashe's depiction of the discrepancy between the ideal and the actual dynamics of London life was too sharp to be tolerated for long. Elizabethan society's idealized self-image shrank from too strong a light.

This ideological justification of Elizabeth's government was well argued and has continued to color subsequent evaluations of her reign, in part because the system does seem superior to much that went before or came afterwards, but the very need for vigilant defense is evidence that the government's control of ideas was imperfect. Compared to the thought control in modern totalitarian states, the ideological programs of the Elizabethans were very much an amateur effort. The queen herself allowed rather un-Machiavellian sentiments like religious piety to blunt her political shrewdness. Her council displayed a mixture of loyal service, political contrivance, and personal ambition—often tendencies uneasily combined in a single councillor like Leicester or Raleigh. There was no agreement about what policies would best insure domestic tranquility. Elizabethan government, like the society as a whole, was a mixed bag of conflicting loyalties and beliefs, barely contained by an ideological framework that was in constant need of adjustment.

Fortunately we do not need to untangle the whole complex system of beliefs or trace its historical origins to understand its importance to Nashe's career (see J. Allen; Morris; E. Smith; Talbert). He himself accepted the orthodoxy of his day without questioning its origin, and his pamphlets do not deal with political questions. Nashe's belief in conformity led him away from any examination of existing social institutions; reform for him was a matter of encouraging people to live up to the ideals of society rather than changing anything. Vernacular printing and the popular stage should function as means of socialization, bringing the common person into line with Tudor values, not as vehicles for reexamining values. In spite of such traditional beliefs, Nashe could not contain himself within the orthodox system. In particular, his inchoate conception of individuality, both as he attacks it as a form of presumption and as he embodies it in his own singularity, can be understood in terms of the ideological insistence on obedience and the subjugation of the self.

THE IDEOLOGY OF CONFORMITY

As a student in the 1580s Nashe encountered the increasingly bitter division between those who supported the Elizabethan religious settlement and those who wished to reform it further (Collinson, 122–30; Curtis, *Oxford and Cambridge*, 165–226; Hibbard, 4–8). The reformers, who were unsystematically lumped together as Puritans, thought the ecclesiastical structure of the church hindered the spiritual restructuring of the minds of the people. Nashe's own college, St. John's, was at the center of the Puritan campaign to replace the hierarchical governance of the church with a system of community control. At issue in this presbyterian or "disciplinarian" movement was the nature of the social order. Although most Puritans never intended to question the political order, they had a limited respect for the effectiveness of the traditional social hierarchy as a form of social control. Order must be maintained, but the willfulness of the individual could best be channeled into useful social behavior by local supervision (Hill, 219–58). In particular Puritans questioned the office of bishop, the means by which Elizabeth and her government tried to control the life and thought of local parishes.

The court itself was divided on the issue of further reform. In the late 1570s Archbishop Grindal had refused to carry out the queen's wish that he suppress the "prophesizings," or local Bible study groups, which were precursors of a presbyterian organization. In anger she deprived him of power, although she could not remove him from office. The theocratic tendencies of the movement were unacceptable to her; she could not tolerate a system where she and her magistrates would be subject to ecclesiastical correction. Several members of her Privy Council were either less perspicacious about the dangers or willing to take the risk; Leicester, Walsingham, Knollys, and at times Burghley were sympathetic with the reformers. The House of Commons also became a battleground over proposed changes in the established church, but the queen adamantly opposed further reformation, particularly if it might in any way abridge her perogative or weaken the social hierarchy of which she was the head (Neale, *1559–1581*, 417–20; Neale, *1584–1601*, 198–99, 216–32).

The vociferousness of Puritanism during Grindal's enforced sequestration suggests the importance of the office of archbishop to Elizabeth's control of the church. Upon Grindal's death in 1583, she found a willing instrument for her policy in her choice of John Whitgift as the new archbishop of Canterbury. His success in suppressing the early stages of the Puritan movement at Cambridge recommended him for the appointment. He was the adversary of Thomas Cartwright, the leading spokesman for the reformers, and as master of Trinity and vice-chancellor of the university had used his power of passing on appointments to discourage those unsympathetic with the established church. He was an ideal choice from the queen's point of view, since he was an able administrator who relentlessly opposed Puritanism without being vituperative or vindictive. He soon became the queen's agent in an inflexible and at times cruel campaign against the Puritans. When the inquisition-like rigor of his High Commission was opposed by Burghley and other members of the Privy Council, he reminded them forcefully that his authority came directly from the queen (see Collinson, 243-48; Dawley; Read, 294-98; Strype).

Whitgift figures prominently in the career of Nashe. As the former master of a college, influential past vice-chancellor, privy councillor, and archbishop, Whitgift remained a major force in the political and intellectual life of Cambridge. Through his own writings and his patronage of religious writers like Richard Hooker, he sustained and toughened the ideology that justified the existing religious, political, and social order (Almasy; Little, 135-47). He defended that order by controlling the press and by driving dissenters out of the colleges and church. Whitgift's double-edged program of strengthening the dominant ideology while discrediting and at times destroying opposition would have powerfully influenced Nashe's thought, even if Nashe had never become directly involved with the archbishop's campaign against Martin Marprelate.

As an undergraduate at the notorious St. John's, Nashe might well have become a Puritan; instead he aligned himself with the humanist tradition at St. John's and supported the existing order (Caspari, 132-56). Ascham, Cheke, and the other Cambridge humanists of the mid-century were his heroes rather than the more radical and contentious contemporaries who set the tone at the Cambridge of the 1580s. His early works are quite explicit in their rejection of the Puritans and like-minded educational reformers. He rejects Ramism, because Ramus's devaluing of Ciceronianism undercut the conception of office or duty and the accompanying formal rhetoric that legitimized subservience to a central authority. Ramism was popular with the Puritans because it simplified rhetoric and because it made the order of the commonwealth more a matter of human agreement and less a reflection of universal order (Kearney, 46–70). Nashe was no Hooker and would probably have been hard pressed to defend his beliefs, but he was nevertheless passionate in his devotion to humanism and the traditional order it supported.

His humanism was the English strain fostered during the Henrician period and given a somewhat rigid cast during the social and political upheavals of the mid-century (Kearney, 34–45). Cheke and Ascham were pragmatic in their approach to government service; the Puritans were heirs to the more independent, idealistic elements of earlier humanism. Such court humanism stressed obedience to the monarchy and other institutions of government. It valued persuasive skills more than philosophic inquiry; the development of speaking and writing skills and the cultivation of an engaging personal presence would secure a courtier or civic servant a position and render him an effective agent of authority. Success as an instrument of power could lead to rapid advancement, as Tudor history so often witnessed. A person like Nashe, without background or personal fortune but with a university education and rhetorical skills, could hope for such advancement, particularly with the help of a patron. The probabilities of success were perhaps slim, but the appeals of government service outweighed those of the major alternative, the humble life of a clergyman such as Nashe's father had lived.

The court humanism supported by Whitgift and espoused by Nashe advanced a pattern of conformation rather than the pattern of reformation favored by the Puritans (Little, 147). Its central doctrine was obedience, obedience not so much to personal authority as to the traditional institutions of society. The queen and her magistrates were also circumscribed by duty and law. The value of such a doctrine to the government is so obvious that one could make the mistake of seeing it as political expediency, but it would not have worked if it had been a cynical ploy. The doctrine of obedience offered the subject security from political disorder and economic deprivation in an age when the margin for survival was slim. He or she was obedient not because authority could not be wrong but because a private person's judgment was worth little and could be dangerous. In this way the doctrine was linked to the Christian ideal of humility and the abhorrence of pride, the primal sin. Subjects were frequently reminded of Saint Paul's dictum: "Let everie soule be subject unto the higher powers: for there is no power but of God: & the powers that be, are ordeined of God" (Geneva Bible, Romans 13:1; see E. Smith, 19). Puritans and Anglicans differed over what the proper external authority should be, but both sides denounced the egalitarianism and anarchy they thought had prevailed during the domestic peasant rebellions and Continental Anabaptist uprisings.

Post-Burckhardtian students of the Renaissance often see the age as one of emergent individualism and a new bourgeois ethic, but the age itself saw such tendencies as undesirable. Singularity, presumption, ambition, and arrogance were all destructive branches of pride. Individualism, as a code of values centered on the private person, did not yet exist; individuation, in the sense that people experienced themselves as alone and particular, did, and it was frightening to the person as well as threatening to society. Some tension between the individual and society is characteristic of all human cultures; the all-encompassing community of the Middle Ages is probably a nostalgic myth. Still, the Reformation, the emergence of the centralized modern state, and the urbanization of London exacerbated the sense of isolation, at least among the audience for whom Nashe wrote. The Puritans recorded their misgivings about their own pride in their diaries and tracts, but their fear of themselves was shared by the Anglicans and secular-minded as well (Bercovitch, 1–34; see also Esler). Marlowe comes close to affirming a value in individuality, but his fear of his own boldness finds eloquent expression in the anguish of Dr. Faustus and in Edward II's tragic loss of self.

The doctrine of obedience was promulgated incessantly, both as a matter of government policy and as an expression of the belief of particular authors. A succinct statement of it can be found in the notes for a sermon delivered by Whitgift on the Queen's Accession Day in 1583, shortly after he became archbishop. Grounding his argument on the Bible, he complained that obedience was particularly necessary "in these our corrupt days, so full of disobedience; in the which they that preach obedience to princes are counted men-pleasers and time-servers!" (Whitgift, 3:586). Obedience frees the subject from fear of the anarchy that would prevail without magistrates. When every man does what he lists, confusion follows. Moreover, "equality of persons engendereth strife; which is the cause of all evil" (588). The disobedient are divided into three classes: "papists, anabaptists, and our wayward and conceited people." The third group are the Puritans, who set themselves up against the authority of the bishops and are thus "wayward and conceited fellows who do not 'condemn' magistrates, but 'contemn' and despise magistrates" (593). They are contentious and slanderous for all that they profess faith and purity. "All evil-speakers are contentious persons. Contentious persons are disobedient" (595). Obedience must take precedence over any inclination a subject might have to be critical of authority.

Obedience was more than an abstract injunction; in practice it was subdivided and formalized into a complex system of duties and functions. Whitgift reminded his audience that "the rule of obedience, that is betwixt the magistrate and the subject, holdeth betwixt the husband and the wife, the father and his child, the master and the servant" (590). The potentially dangerous ego of the Elizabethan was circumscribed by a network of familial, occupational, social, civic, and religious obligations and expectations. The self was secure only when it was a subject, obedient to God by being obedient to the queen and the social order she headed. The formal nature of the order was emphasized in the complex system of laws, the rituals of church and civic life, and the requirements of decorum. That decorum extended to the clothes one wore and the language one used. Sumptuary legislation and censure by preachers attempted to prevent people from dressing in the manner reserved for higher classes (Baldwin, 192–247; Hooper). Nashe was just one of many writers, including Shakespeare and Jonson, who ridiculed the attempt of the common people to dress, speak, write, or live in a style appropriate to their betters. Elizabethan England was not a caste society—the laws and ridicule would not have been necessary if everyone had kept to his or her station—but social mobility and private space were a source of distrust and fear.

That distrust and fear centered on certain stereotypes: the prodigal apprentice, the masculine woman, the atheist or epicure, but especially on the masterless man and the malcontent (Lyons, 17-21; Walzer, 9-13, 199-204). The masterless man could be a rogue or a vagabond, and he was likely to be a malcontent, although a malcontent could also be a person dissatisfied with his social role because of ambition, melancholy, or underemployment. Such people were potentially seditious; moreover, their very existence called into question the good order of the commonwealth. Often malcontents were in effect underground masterless men, who pretended to love and duty while scheming for personal gain. For Whitgift and Nashe, Puritans were malcontents who pretended to idealistic values in a hypocritical fashion. They were motivated by envy of those who had the power and status they coveted. The self-proclaimed "Church millitant heere upon earth" is, Nashe wrote, "a company of Malecontents, unworthy to breath on the earth" (1:22). Like Whitgift, Nashe emphasizes that the Puritans are contentious, malicious, and given to backbiting. Ultimately they are treasonous, since their program of "reforms" threatens the traditional order of society.

Conformity was also sought through a skillful appeal to nationalistic sentiments. The pope's anathematizing of the queen and the defeat of the Armada created a patriotic fervor that was used to discredit the recusants and the aspirations of the Puritans. Central to this promotion of nationalism was the growth of printing and the spread of literacy (Ebel; Eisenstein, 1:117-18; 358-67). Along with court rituals, pageantry, drama, and sermons, printed books in the vernacular contributed to the dominance of the court, in part by promoting Tudor mythology. When the potential utopia was threatened, either by the recusants and Jesuits or by the Puritans, printing became a front-line defense of the commonwealth. Throughout Elizabeth's reign the presses were kept busy publishing religious controversy, views opposing the government's often being published abroad or by clandestine presses (Bennett,

74–86, 113–29). These tracts and pamphlets tried to win adherents to their cause by the skillful deployment of rhetoric. The religious controversies of the Reformation were the crucible of modern prose, even if their influence has not been studied as closely as that of classical rhetoric.

Nashe's rhetorical approach and his personal style were derived more from these vernacular predecessors than they were from classical or Continental models. I have argued that *The Anatomy of Absurdity* is an imperfect amalgamation of the courtly style of Lyly with the polemical concerns of Phillip Stubbes, even though it was written when Nashe was still a student, presumably immersed in the study of Latin literature. The works written after his arrival in London reveal even more clearly their native roots. In particular, his style was forged by his involvement in the Marprelate controversy. That famous battle of the wits was his postgraduate education as a pamphleteer, as well as the reason for his association with Whitgift. The Puritan movement was anathema to Nashe, but he used it both as a point of reference to define his orthodox beliefs and as a source for the style that made him famous.

THE MARPRELATE CONTROVERSY

Nashe's actual role as a propagandist for Bancroft and Whitgift is unknown, but later tradition held that he played an important role in "quelling" Martin Marprelate, and Nashe's own comments substantiate that he was an anti-Martinist. It is uncertain whether the propagandists recruited by Richard Bancroft to counter Martin's popularity worked as a group or subdivided the task. A convincing case has been made, though, that Nashe wrote *An Almond for a Parrot*, the penultimate pamphlet in the anti-Martinist series (Hibbard, 36–48; McGinn, "Nashe's Share"). His actual role is less important than the influence of the controversy, including Martin's tracts and those of his adversaries, on Nashe's career. Martin gave Nashe the rhetorical stance and repertory of devices that enabled him to link wit and style to an ironic persona in imaginary oral discourse (Summersgill). From the anti-Martinists he learned how to make *reductio ad absurdum* into a continuous rhetorical strategy that ridiculed an opponent in an almost nihilistic fashion. Their dramaturgical use of rhetoric undercut Martin's serious purpose just as he had undercut the preeminence of the bishops.

The short career of Martin Marprelate is an abstract and brief chronicle of an ideological conflict that led to civil war and the end of the English Renaissance (Carlson; McKerrow, 5:34–65; Pierce). Whoever wrote the Marprelate tracts was driven to assume his pseudonymous fool's coat by Whitgift's success at checking the growth of Puritanism. Progress in Parliament had been stymied by Whitgift and the queen, Puritan ministers were being deprived of their livings by Whitgift's oath of supremacy, and Whitgift's High Commission was hounding the leaders of the movement into silence, prison, or exile. Those who helped Martin—John Penry, Job Throkmorton, Robert Waldegrave, and the others—had failed on different fronts of the movement. Penry, whom the author of *An Almond for a Parrot* thought to be Martin, was one of a number of articulate pamphleteers and preachers who had argued for reform only to find their words suppressed or confuted in what seemed to them unfair attacks on their integrity. Throkmorton, who probably was in fact Martin, had been unable to get legislation favorable to the Puritans through the House of Commons (Carlson). Waldegrave had printed tracts by Penry, Udall, and others, and for his pains had his type defaced and his presses smashed.

Such was the group that began clandestinely printing pamphlets in 1588, shortly after the defeat of the Armada. The argument against episcopal church government was not new, nor were the Marprelate tracts the first Puritan works printed anonymously and in secret. What was new was the Martin Marprelate persona and the colloquial satiric style, which used imaginary scenes of oral discourse as a way of involving the reader and ridiculing the bishops. Martin is imagined in a variety of ironic roles, arguing with one or another of the bishops in front of an assembled audience of his readers. Although he changes his stance, sometimes playing the fool, sometimes a rustic clown, his various selves all seem facets of one flexible personality. Martin cleverly uses asides, either incorporated in the text or in the margins, to create the effect of oral give-and-take. He also uses slang and grotesque imagery to make his opponents seem venal pigmies, masquerading in the pompous robes of ecclesiastical office. Martin's satire is functional to his purpose and integral to his Calvinist view of the fallen nature of humanity. The self-mockery of his assumed name—a martin was an ape—and his own lack of stylistic pretension contrasted sharply with the claimed dignity and preeminence of the bishops (Anselment, 33–60; Coolidge).

Although the tracts present three personas—Martin himself and his two sons Martin Senior and Martin Junior—all were presumably created by a single author, so they are treated as a single phenomenon. Martin is self-consciously in the tradition of popular buffoonery associated with fictionalized figures like Scogan and Will Summers and with comedians, particularly Richard Tarlton. Like these antecedents, Martin makes a profession of irreverence, arrogating to himself the traditional license of the Lord of Misrule and the professional jester. By presenting himself theatrically in a variety of roles he manages to suggest that the office of bishop is also a kind of performance.[1] Aylmer or Whitgift is presented as playing at being the doughty bishop, just as the unknown author plays at being Martin. The byplay between Martin and his sons adds to this theatrical effect. This approach has barbed implications, since the traditional defense of weak bishops and uneducated ministers was that the role was greater than the imperfect individual who filled it.

Seen as exercises in frustration and as belated contributions to the tedious debate about episcopacy, the Marprelate tracts are often dismissed as by-products of history, a failed attempt to revitalize a defeated cause. They did not affect policy and discredited the Puritans more than they helped them. The presbyterian movement ceased to be a central part of Puritan-

---

1. In a little-known tract, Nashe's adversary Phillip Stubbes advanced a similar argument, ostensibly against Roman Catholic bishops: "And in this playerly manner doth this hystrionical bishop play his part amongst the rest, making the temple of the Lord a stage or theater, themselves players, and the people stark fooles in beholding their fooleries" (*Theater,* sig. E2r).

ism in the 1590s; when it did return in the seventeenth century, the memory of Martin played a minor role. Martin Marprelate was a failure in terms of his own goals: his press was seized, his confederates were arrested and tortured, and he himself was discredited. If Martin was Job Throkmorton, he had enough influence to escape physical punishment, although he was troubled with an indictment and published abuse. Martin's own misgivings about the wisdom of his proceedings gives a special poignancy to the last tract, *The Protestation*. He remains defiant, but he had been defeated in the mad game of words he played with the bishops.

The causes of his failure suggest his importance as a figure in the cultural history of the period. He had hoped that his bold persona and lively style would win adherents to his cause. His defaming of the bishops both as a group and as fallible individuals was intended to discredit their office and destroy their argument for preeminence. Such tactics left him open to the charge of dealing in personalities rather than issues. From an orthodox point of view, Martin was a symbol of presumption, of a private person daring to set his fallen understanding of what the world should be against the traditional wisdom of society. His attack on the private persons who filled the office of bishop was proof that he saw society from a dangerously individualized perspective, rather than as a system which was perhaps arbitrary and historically contingent but to be preferred over the anarchy of human willfulness. Martin seemed to substantiate the Anglican fear that the limited goals of the Puritans were a prelude to sedition, revolution, and anarchy (Anselment, 54–60).

The Marprelate tracts began as an answer to John Bridges's *Defense of the Government Established in the Church of England* (1587), a long-winded installment in the controversy over the existence of bishops. Seizing on Bridges's occasional resorts to invective, Martin claims his satiric answer is a response in kind: " 'May it please you' to give me leave to play the dunce for the nonce, as well as he; otherwise dealing with Master Doctor's book, I cannot keep *decorum personae*" (Marprelate, 17). Martin will treat the bishops and their supporters with the same lack of respect they have shown the Puritans. "I jested because I dealt against a worshipful jester, Dr. Bridges, whose writings and sermons tend to no other end than to make men laugh" (118). This is Martin's excuse for mixing ridicule of the bishops in with his serious arguments against episcopacy. Bridges and a few notoriously venal bishops made easy targets.

In their first responses to Martin, the bishops refrained from lowering themselves to his level. There is some scorn but little levity in Bishop Thomas Cooper's *Admonition to the People of England: Wherein are answered, not onely the slaunderous untruethes, reprochfully uttered by Martin the Libeller, but also many other Crimes by some of his broode, objected generally against all Bishops* . . . (1589). The aging Cooper, who was probably picked to answer Martin because of his accrued dignities, gives us an unzealous picture of how the controversy appeared to the supporters of the Elizabethan religious compromise. He concedes that the common people are disdainful of religion: "When I call to my rememberance, the loathsome contempt, hatred, and disdaine, that the most part of men in these dayes beare, and in the face of the worlde declare towarde the Ministers of the Church of God, aswell Bishops as other among us here in Englande my heart can not but greatly feare & tremble at the consideration thereof" (sig. B1r). Many ministers are in fact "farre from that rule that Christian perfection requireth," but people should respect priests in spite of the weakness of some people who fill the office.

Cooper thus grounds his criticism of Puritan arrogance on a pessimistic rather than an idealistic portrayal of the social order. Catholicism has been weakened, but the Reformation has barely taken hold; in such a volatile political situation the Puritan attack on the bishops cannot be well-intentioned:

> If right zeale, with conscience and detestation of evil, were the roote of these invectives . . . , surely, the same spirit would moove them to breake out into like vehement lamentations against the evils and vices, which shew themselves in a great number of the Realme: I meane, the deepe ignorance and contempt of God in the midst of the light of the Gospell, the heathenish securitie

in sinne and wickednesse, the monstrous pride in apparell, the voluptuous riot and sensualitie, the excessive buildings and needelesse nestes of mens treasures, which bee as cankers consuming the riches of this Realme. (sigs. D3r–D3v)

In such a disordered time, obedience to what order does exist takes precedence over reform. Martin and other Puritan pamphlet writers contribute to disorder by "distracting the mindes of the Subjects," which helps divide them into factions and increases "the number of Mal-contents, and mislikers of the state" (sig. F2r). Given that "the schoole of Epicure, and the Athiests, is mightily increased in these days," the church needs to preserve a united front. The attacks of the reformers have discredited religion as well as church government. Cooper is a conservative pragmatist who wants to shore up the church as it is, not undertake major repairs in the face of secular indifference and hostility.

In his specific criticisms of Martin Marprelate, Cooper struck the note that was to dominate the anti-Martinist campaign: Martin is a libeller motivated by envy rather than zeal. What pretends to be a limited call for ecclesiastical reform is a prelude to an assault on the civic order as well. Cooper sees this in Martin's style as well as in his programs: "When there is seene in any Common wealth such a loose boldenesse of speech, against a setled lawe or State, it is a certain proofe of a loose boldnesse of minde. For, *Sermo est index animi.* that is, Such as the speech is, such is the minde." Boldness and contempt like Martin's are "the very roote and spring of discorde, dissention, uprores, civill warres and all desperate attempts" (sig. F2v). Martin's program is no more misguided than that of his predecessors, but his method of arguing—the use of a persona and personal attacks on the bishops—was a dangerous innovation. He was a model of arrogance in a society already prone to presumption.

Martin defended himself in *Hay Any Worke for Cooper*, the title of which puns on a London street cry. His style is not evidence of a disorderly mind, but a strategy:

I am not disposed to jest in this serious matter. I am called Martin Marprelate. There be many that greatly dislike my doings. I may have my wants I know, for I am a man. But my course I know to be ordinary and lawful. I saw the cause of Christ's government, and of the Bishops' antichristian dealing to be hidden. The most part of men could not be gathered to read anything written in the defense of the one and against the other. I bethought me, therefore, of a way whereby men might be drawn to do both; perceiving the humours of men in these times (especially of those that are in any place) to be given to mirth. (Marprelate, 238–39).

But it would be a mistake to see Martin's style as merely a rhetorical strategy, a *decorum personae,* since his character is closely related to the programs he advances. Because of his Protestant interest in the private person, Martin was willing to deal in personalities and exploit the comic persona he invented for himself. The Puritans were painfully aware of human shortcomings, but they nevertheless wanted to shift the focus to the individual soul. Martin thought of himself, his readers, and the bishops as private persons rather than in terms of traditional social roles (Richmond).

Martin's presentation of his own unorthodox role in heroic terms has been part of his enduring appeal. Partly in an effort to protect his coconspirators, he claims, "I am alone. No man under heaven is privy, or hath been privy, unto my writings against you. I use the advice of none therein" (246). With joking bravado, he mocks the fact that he is a hunted man in danger of the gallows. It is hard not to admire his courage: "Whether I be favoured or no, I will not cease, in the love I owe to her Majesty, to write against traitors, to write against the devil's bishops" (256). In the last tract, after his main press had been seized and many of his supporters arrested, Martin pauses to examine his own motives in good Puritan fashion: "These events I confess do strike me and give me just cause to enter more narrowly into my self to see whether I be at peace with God, or no" (397). He concludes that he is and that he is willing to be martyred for the truth as he sees it. "And as for myself, my life, and whatsoever else I possess I have long ago set up my rest" (404-5).

The anti-Martinists did not, however, find this stance heroic or appealing. Bishop Cooper had looked foolish trying to answer Martin seriously; Bancroft's propagandists focused instead on responding in kind to Martin's persona. Modern critics, sympathetic with Martin, have faulted the anti-Martinists for avoiding the substantive issues to indulge in invective, but the anti-Martinists felt that the libel and scurrility began by Martin had to be met with the same weapons. Whitgift, Bridges, Cooper, and others had long since mounted an official answer to the presbyterian arguments; what was new was Martin's introduction of personality into what had been a theological and political debate. The authoritarian and orthodox anti-Martinists were reluctant to deal with ecclesiastical issues in any case; rather, their task was to expose Martin as a seditious hypocrite. Their own resort to invective bothered some of them and was criticized by neutral observers, but slandering a renegade like Martin was of a different order than slandering a bishop.

The anti-Martinist tracts proper are those published under pseudonyms and without a publisher's name, in imitation of Martin's own procedure. Presumably all were written by the popular writers recruited by Bancroft and were sponsored unofficially by the government. Another group of subsidiary publications continued the theological debate with the Puritans. The pseudonymous anti-Martinists all adopt belligerent personas who in one way or another challenge Martin to combat, often using metaphors of physical violence. All resort to innuendo, suggesting that Martin is covertly seditious, greedy for church wealth, envious of the bishops' status, and even lecherous. Martin is also used as a brush to tar the whole Puritan movement; the term "Martinist" is bandied about as if it were the name of an actual sect. The humor of the pamphlets is, as is often charged, scurrilous: in particular their delight in the prospect that Martin will be tortured and executed offends a modern sensibility.

The doctrine of obedience is a central tenet of the anti-Martinist creed. In one of the secondary tracts, Leonard

Wright reduces it to a rather naked, if traditional, formula: "Whoever resisteth power, resisteth the ordinance of God" (sig. D3v). Pasquil, the most theoretical of the anti-Martinist personas, sees religion as essential to the maintenance of political order. It is not power that keeps the people obedient to the queen, but the legitimization of her rule provided by religion. "If we search it till the worlds end, we shall find no other cause of this sweet harmonie of peoples harts, that remaine faithful and flexible to the shaking of her princely finger, but only this, the Religion of the Land" (in McKerrow, 1:78). A subsequent comparison of Martin with Savonarola as described by Machiavelli shows that Pasquil is thinking in political rather than theological terms. He reminds his readers "howe inclinable the simpler sort of the people are to rowtes, ryots, commotions, insurrections, and plaine rebellions, when they grow brainsicke, or any new toy taketh them in the head: they neede no Travars nor Martin to encrease their giddines" (81). Pasquil's conclusion epitomizes the anti-Martinist position: "Therefore I would wysh the whole Realme to judge unrightly, who deserves best to be bolstred and upheld in these dangerous times, either they that have religiously & constantly preached obedience to her Majesties loving people, or they that with a maske of Religion discharge them of theyr obedience?" (82). The answer is obvious: the hierarchical structure of the church is "a thing glorious in gods eyes, because he is the GOD of order" (91).

From such a perspective Martin must needs appear a mad dog or charlatan. Marphoreus, the author of *Martin's Month's Mind*, sees Martin's focus on the personalities of the bishops as seditious: "And to be short, never better lawes, nor wiser Magistrates; yet never such libertie in speaking, impudencie in writing, nor mischiefe in working, both privatelie against particuler persons (and those of the best) for their defacing, and publiquelie for the undermining of the Church, and overthrowe of the common wealth as now" (sigs. A4r–A4v). All the Elizabethan anxiety about disorder is focused on Martin as Marphoreus waxes eloquent in a long sentence:

But verie fitlie have they taken their name of *Marring;* that professe nothing else but *marring:* both the names of men, and quiet of the common wealth, and peace of the Churche, and livings of the Church, and Churches themselves: and the rewards of learning, and places of learning, and degrees of learning, and learning it selfe: and the lawes of the land, and the authoritie of the Prince, and last of all (for what can be lefte after for the Divell himselfe) sacrements, Ministers, praiers, yea the Lordes praier; and so set their brasen faces against heaven, and bend their forces against the Lord himselfe. (sigs. C3r–C3v)

Given this extreme view, Marphoreus is unsparing in his grotesque account of the hoped-for death and funeral of Martin Marprelate.

The anti-Martinists attempted to discredit Martin by exposing his envious motives and seditious goals and by separating the comic persona from the real person who was risking his life. In the tracts Martin manages to make a buffoon of himself without compromising his serious intent; by reducing the controversy to mere buffoonery the anti-Martinists try to make Martin seem only a clown. This is the tactic used by John Lyly, whom we know to be the author of *Pap with an Hatchet.* Like Marphoreus, he emphasizes the ludic element in the Marprelate tracts to suggest they are a mere game or rhetorical contest. Apologizing for the abusiveness of his pamphlet, he says of his opponents, "Seeing then either they expect no grave replie, or that they are settled with railing to replie; I thought it more convenient, to give them a whisk with their owne wand, than to have them spurd with deeper learning" (*Works*, 3:396). Accordingly, *Pap with an Hatchet* is an exercise in invective and scandalous innuendo. If the whole Marprelate controversy sometimes seems to degenerate into a tongue-in-cheek flyting or mere war of words, it is not because of Martin, who is clearly in earnest for all his japes, but because the anti-Martinists deliberately ignore Martin's sincerity.

Lyly uses the metaphor of role playing, introduced into the controversy by Martin in order to discredit the bishops, as a way of suggesting that Martin's objectives are as much play-acting as his style and comic devices. Throughout his pamphlet, Lyly reminds us that his railing, for all its nastiness, is a performance: "Now comes a biting speach, let mee stroake my beard thrice like a Germain, before I speak a wise word" (406). His theatrical persona shifts roles constantly, clowning like Martin, swaggering outrageously, pontificating. Lyly, the professional dramatist and wit-about-town, advises Martin, "If thy vain bee so pleasant, and thy wit so nimble, that all consists in glicks and girds; pen some playe for the Theater, write some ballads for blinde David and his boy, devise some jestes, & become another Scogen" (412). If Martin sets himself up as a clown to make the bishops seem clownish, Lyly dramatizes himself as a belligerent ruffian in an attempt to make Martin seem arrogant. Such a dramatic use of a fictive persona is no innovation for the creator of Euphues.

Pap with an Hatchet was criticized by Gabriel Harvey because of the potentially disruptive effect of its theatricality. Harvey's "An Advertisement for Pap-hatchet and Martin Mar-prelate" was written in 1589 to answer an insult directed at him in Lyly's pamphlet, although it was not published until 1593 as part of *Pierce's Supererogation*. Harvey understands that Lyly's raillery is intended as a response in kind to Martin but does not think this excuses "the carrion of thy unsavory, and stinking Pamflett" (sig. I4v). The deliberately arrogant style will appeal "onely to roister-doisters, and hacksters, or at-least to jesters, and vices" (K1r). Though Lyly's persona is like a Lord of Misrule intended to bring order to the disorderly, Harvey fears that Lyly is merely reinforcing the bad example set by Martin. "If the world should applaude to such a roisterdoisterly Vanity, (as Impudency hath beene prettily suffered to sett-upp the creast of his vaineglory:) what good could grow of it, but to make every man madbrayned, and desperate; but a generall contempt of all good order, in Saying, or Dooing; but an Universal Topsy-turvy?" (sig. K2v). Lyly's theatricality is the problem. "He hath not played the Vicemaster of Poules, and the Fool master of the Theater for naughtes; himselfe a mad lad, as ever twangd, never troubled with any substance of witt, or circumstance of honestie" (sig. R4r). Harvey accuses

Lyly of fabricating scandalous anecdotes of Puritan concupiscence, then presenting them as fact. The anti-Martinists have joined Martin in subverting the social order by suggesting it is a theatrical fiction and by encouraging the sort of egocentric belief and assertive behavior that dare challenge that fiction.

Cutbert Curry-knave, who was probably Nashe himself, combines the tactics of Martin and the previous anti-Martinists in *An Almond for a Parrot*. His persona is as belligerent as Lyly's, although not as obsessively abusive. Like Marphoreus and Lyly, he accentuates the theatricality of the controversy, particularly in his mock dedication to "that most Comicall and conceited Cavaleire Monsieur du Kempe, Jestmonger and Vice-gerent generall to the Ghost of Dicke Tarlton" (Nashe, 3:341). At the same time he is like Pasquil in his attempt to join issue seriously with the Puritans. And he is like Martin in his style and in his use of journalistic facts, in this case, to expose the hypocrisy of the Puritans. By the time *An Almond* was published in 1590, Martin's main press had been seized and most of the assistants arrested, so the work broadens its attack into a general indictment of the Puritan movement. As in *The Anatomy of Absurdity*, the hypocrisy of the Puritans particularly incenses the author; this is the implicit excuse for the work's resort to scandalmongering. Unlike the allusive and probably fictive libel of *Pap with an Hatchet*, the accounts of Puritan misdeeds in *An Almond* are specific and often documented.

Like Martin himself, Cutbert Curry-knave wants to expose his opponents as knaves pretending to sanctimony for selfish motives. This muckraking can be amusing, as when that champion of Puritan asceticism Phillip Stubbes is accused of trying to seduce a widow with the pledge of a Geneva Bible. John Penry is traduced in an extended mock biography that depicts him as an arrogant man who espouses unorthodox opinions in an effort to aggrandize himself. Evidence is gathered to suggest that Penry is Martin. He embodies the singularity of the Puritans, their tendency to value and promote their private opinions to the detriment of good order in the commonwealth. Cartwright is accused of being the source of such presumption: "What childe doth not see into the pride of his heart, that first entertained the impudency of controlling antiquity, and preferd the poison of his owne perverse opinions before the experience of so many Churches, counsails, and fathers?" (3:60). Once introduced, Puritanism has attracted a host of malcontents and hypocrites: "I am more then halfe weary of tracing too and fro in this cursed common wealth, where sinfull simplicitye, pufte uppe with the pride of singularity, seekes to perverte the name and methode of magistracy" (358).

Cutbert Curry-knave's account of Puritanism adheres to the official view of Whitgift and Bancroft. He extolls obedience in the name of Christian humility and decries arrogance as the child of Satan. Puritanism has caused "the utter impoverishing of allegeance of the communality" and has promoted treason in the name of reform. As for Martin himself, how could anyone believe "this myrie mouthed mate a partaker of heavenly inspiration, that thus aboundes in his uncharitable railings?" (347). Cutbert sees himself as a champion fighting Martin in single combat. "Thou art the man, olde Martin of Englande, that I am to deale withall, that strives to outstrip all our writers in witte, and justle our governement forth of doores with a jest" (349). Martin's new-forged weapons of controversy are turned against him with a vengeance.

Marphoreus and Lyly easily outdid Martin in railing because for him railing was secondary to a serious purpose while for them it was the essence of the controversy. Their reduction of the dispute to a shouting match was effective at making Martin seem contentious but at the expense of making the anti-Martinists and their sponsors seem petty and contentious as well. The author of *An Almond* keeps to a slightly higher road by discussing substantive issues, but his attempts to expose the hypocrisy of the Puritans through specific attacks on their peccadilloes makes him seem spiteful and mean-spirited also. Moreover, his focus on the discrepancy between the pretensions and the private lives of the Puritans, like Martin's similar account of the bishops, threatened to make the whole religious and social order seem a theatrical contrivance. Cutbert's attempt to outclown Martin suggested that both parties in the dispute were playing out an irreverent comedy.

This is the point of Francis Bacon's objection to "this immodest and deformed manner of writing lately entertained, whereby matters of religion are handled in the style of the stage" (76–77). A theatrical role is artificial and assumed by a performer, but a social role in a traditional society is intended to have a reality of its own and be greater than the fallible human who fills it. The legitimacy of the ecclesiastical hierarchy was particularly important, since it legitimized so many other social institutions. Lyly's quip "Well, either religion is but policie, or policie scarce religious" was dangerous to the extent that the Elizabethan church was a matter of policy (Lyly, 3:407; see also J. Allen, 178–81). Martin undermined the political and social order by shifting attention from the performance to the actor. If the bishop of London was only greedy John Aylmer, a dwarfish thief in giant's robes, what might follow about Lord Burghley or the queen? The Puritans denied any such implications, but subsequent history shows that they questioned more than the ecclesiastical hierarchy.

The number of anti-Martinist works projected but never published, the apologetic tone of Pasquil's last tract, and the comments of observers like Bacon and the Harveys show that the pseudonymous campaign against Martin was cut short because it reflected badly on the government and encouraged the dissension it was intended to suppress. Puritan leaders publicly disowned Martin's method of arguing; the bishops could not long condone the use of the same methods by the anti-Martinists, even in secret. The ideological position of Lyly, Nashe, and the others was militantly orthodox, but the fictitious spokesmen they invented and their employment of invective meant that their appeal to readers was closer to that of Martin than that of the dignified bishops. They were trapped between two decorums: the requirement that they write a style in accord with the gravity of the topic and their desire to fight Martin on his own terms and reach the readers he delighted. They erred in tacitly granting that the controversy was a theatrical performance in which they themselves, Martin, and, by implication, the bishops all played roles like actors.

These radical implications of the Marprelate controversy would have been rejected by most Elizabethans, including the participants in the quarrel. But Nashe was to continue to explore the theatrical metaphor with its implication that social roles were artificial. In the pamphlets he published during the next decade he adapted Martin's use of a persona to his purposes and mastered the colloquial style Martin popularized. He continued to reject the arrogance of the Puritans, but his own writings became more singular as he drifted away from orthodoxy. Writing itself was increasingly a performance and rhetoric not a tool but a contrivance. Martin lost his battle against episcopacy, but in the case of Nashe and probably many others, he undercut naive faith in the social order. From a traditional point of view his effect was insidious, since it induced a basic shift in perspective even among his opponents. The efforts of the Harveys to link Nashe and Martin reflect a truth: Nashe may have helped "quell" Martin, but Martin destroyed Nashe's innocence and set his literary career on an unknown course away from orthodoxy.

ENTERTAINING THE ARCHBISHOP:
SUMMER'S LAST WILL AND TESTAMENT

Summer's Last Will and Testament was written for performance before Archbishop Whitgift, his household, and his guests in his country palace at Croydon in the autumn of 1592. A major outbreak of the plague kept the archbishop and his entourage from returning to London. The audience was dominated by Whitgift himself, the patron or employer of most of those present, including Nashe and the actors. Both the plague and the audience put constraints on Nashe and the actors, since both threatened to nullify the festive spirit they sought to create. The context of the plague needed to be acknowledged and the nature of the audience confronted if the play was to achieve the holiday spirit appropriate to the archbishop's harvest-home celebration. Nashe does so by reaffirming the orthodox values of his audience as the best attitude to take towards the plague while satirizing the beliefs of the Puritans, particularly their opposition to popular entertainments like the play itself. The archbishop's presence as chief spectator and a symbol of the established church made it possible to do this without being so explicit as to give offense, but Nashe's indirection means that his script loses part of its complexity when read outside the context of its original performance.

The play represents itself as no more than a festive entertainment—"nay, 'tis no Play neyther, but a shewe," as the presenter Will Summers puts it (3:235, line 75; hereafter cited by line numbers). Performed at least in part by boys, interspersed with music and dance, it is a series of spectacles and set pieces only loosely connected by its plot: the allegorical figure Summer calls his servants and potential heirs to a final reckoning before making his will and dying. Any attempt to sustain a dramatic illusion is undercut by the fool Will Summers, who remains on stage throughout, always ready to lighten the proceedings by mocking the author or the imperfect artifice of the actors. Since C. L. Barber's account of the play, it has been recognized as a masterpiece of festive comedy, all the more so because it was written in time of plague. Critics have also noted its anti-Puritan bias, but they have not explored how the occasion of performance links the anti-Puritanism with both the plague and the festive spirit (Hibbard, 87–105).

The play is discreet in its allusions to the conflict between the archbishop and the Puritans because a direct discussion of politics or sharp satire would have been inappropriate to the occasion. The prologue warns the audience not to expect topical allegory: "Deepe reaching wits, heere is no deepe streame for you to angle in. Moralizers, you that wrest a never meant meaning out of every thing, applying all things to the present time, keepe your attention for the common Stage: for here are no quips in Characters for you to reade" (64–69). This disclaimer is disingenuous, as is often the case with Nashe. Puritan asceticism, an issue that angered Nashe in his pamphlets, is central to the concerns of the play. Although the play intends to entertain the archbishop and his guests, not instruct them on social issues, the occasion required that he set the entertainment in a context of the plague and the Puritan disapproval of such endeavors as his "shewe."

The nature of the audience is integral to the play's effect and meaning. The script stresses the play's special relation to its chief spectator, the archbishop, presenting him as a figure of awesome authority. Entering with his coat half on, Will Summers chats with the audience until he notices the archbishop: "God forgive me, I did not see my Lord before. Ile set a good face on it, as though what I had talkt idly all this while were my part" (17–19). Attention is again focused on Whitgift when Will Summers complains that a long speech must be a diversionary tactic "of some that have a messe of creame to eate, before my Lord goe to bed yet" (586–87). At the end of the play he tells the little boy who gives the epilogue, "Be not afraide; turne thy face to my Lord" (1896–97). The audience present at Croydon would have included other formidable figures, perhaps Bancroft or Richard Hooker. Nashe described what must have been Whitgift's household when he answered Gabriel Harvey's charge that he was a dissolute Bohemian: "For the order of my life, it is as civil as a civil orenge; I lurke in no corners, but converse in a house of credit, as well governed as any Colledge, where there bee more rare quallified men and selected good Schollers than in any Noblemans house that I knowe in England" (1:329). This accords with a description by Whitgift's contemporary biographer, who says that the archbishop maintained many poor scholars out of charity: "There were also divers others, that for learning, languages, and qualities, were fit to be employed by any Prince in Christendome. Insomuch as his house, for Lectures and scholasticall exercises therein performed, might justly be accounted a little Academie" (Paule, sig. L1v; Hibbard, 89).

Throughout the play Will Summers jokes on behalf of the author and players about their possible rejection by the archbishop's "little academy." We do not know the nature of Nashe's relationship to the archbishop; aside from the play the major piece of evidence that Whitgift was for a time his patron is a complaint against Whitgift written in 1597 about earlier events which refers to "his Nashe gentleman" (McKerrow, "Supplement," 5:74). Nashe's later complaint about his inability to find sustained patronage is evidence that the archbishop's support was temporary. Probably Nashe was too profane and outspoken to last long in an archbishop's employ. This is also evident in Nashe's insecurity about the reception of the play. Will Summer's mockery of "the Idiot our Playmaker," who "like a Foppe & an Asse, must be making himselfe a publike laughing stock, & have no thanke for his labor" (23–24) presages the actual course of Nashe's literary career.

Before such an audience the very intention to perform a play takes on ideological overtones. The Puritans disapproved of drama and other popular entertainments because they at best wasted time that would be better spent in godly exercises and useful labor and at worst encouraged worldliness and vice. The authorities were never as explicit about why they favored or tolerated drama, but presumably, aside from their enjoyment of plays, they regarded popular entertainments as harmless recreation that kept people away from worse behavior. Nashe himself had advanced such a temporizing defense of drama earlier in the year in his *Pierce Penniless*. Whitgift's own attitude is not recorded, but Nashe obviously judged him receptive to a performance of a play. Since it was a private performance, the play would not have been as offensive to the Puritans as one at a public theater, but in 1592 any performance of a play under the auspices of the archbishop was implicit defiance of the Puritans (Chambers, 4:236–68). We do not know if the Puritans reacted to this performance, or even if they knew of the play's existence, but Nashe and his audience would have been aware that the event was anathema to their opponents.

The play also implicitly defied the Puritans in its celebration of traditional popular entertainments such as the Morris dance, May rituals, Christmas festivities, and the harvest-home holiday of which it was a part. Nashe's adversary Phillip Stubbes decried such popular rituals, which he saw as residues of pagan worship and the occasion of vice. In the play, Ver's introduction of the hobby-horse and attendant Morris dancers suggests Nashe was aware of the folk connection between the hobby-horse and its pagan symbolism of death and rebirth in the winter and spring (Brissenden, 9). The play is also explicit in its support of traditional attitudes towards Christmas and its scorn for Puritan desires to reform the holiday. A play so thoroughly rooted in the traditions of popular entertainments and exuberant in its portrayal of folk rituals functioned as a deliberate rejection of the Puritan position.

If the archepiscopal presence at a play that celebrates popular festivals was offensive to the Puritans, his sponsorship of such a play during a major epidemic of bubonic plague would have seemed blasphemous. To the Puritans the awesome depredations of the plague—the outbreak that began in 1592 was to kill an estimated 23,000 Londoners—seemed preternatural and evidence of extraordinary anger on the part of God (Mullett, 62–104; F. Wilson, *Plague*). They came to see the plague as a scourge on the social abuses they denounced in their tracts and sermons. Among these were the growth of drama, the continuing indulgence of the people in folk entertainments that perpetuated pagan customs, and the ecclesiastical neglect that left the people in ignorance. The audience at Croydon would have seen Whitgift not as part of the problem but as the proper leader in the spiritual battle against the plague. The traditional ceremonies of the church, as codified in *The Book of Common Prayer*, were sufficient remedies and consolation for the plague; the epidemic was perhaps punishment for the sins of England, but it was not evidence of any special need for social or ecclesiastical reform. The often repeated plague order, first issued in 1578, made it clear that the government was concerned that fanatical insistence on the primary cause of plague, God's anger, would interfere with precautions about the secondary causes in the order of nature (Mullett, 96–97; K. Thomas, 85–89). Within a year, in *Christ's Tears over Jerusalem*, Nashe himself became apocalyptic about the social abuses that brought on the plague, but he blamed exploitation and venality rather than plays, popular festivals, or the retention of bishops in the church.

The play presents the plague as an example of the mortality inherent in the human condition rather than as evidence of special providence. Occasional references keep the plague in the minds of the audience without letting its grim reality undermine the holiday spirit of the play. As in the *Decameron*, festivity is given an elegiac cast by the excluded yet threatening epidemic. At the outset, Will Summers casually remarks that "the plague raignes in most places in this latter end of summer" (80–81). When the allegorical figure Summer first enters, a dirge is sung that reminds the audience that misery and mortality are part of a natural cycle:

> Fayre Summer droops, droope men and beasts therefore:
> So fayre a summer looke for never more.
> All good things vanish, lesse then in a day,
> Peace, plenty, pleasure, sodainely decay.
>   Goe not yet away, bright soule of the sad yeare;
>   The earth is hell when thou leav'st to appeare.
>   (105–10)

This sad note quickly gives way to clowning and festive dance, but mortality remains a constant theme.

Nashe's famous lyric "Adieu, Farewell Earth's Bliss" is the most effective reminder of the plague in the play. The last line of its refrain, "Lord have mercy on us," echoes *The Book of Common Prayer* and was the phrase posted as a warning on the doors of the infected (F. Wilson, *Plague*, 61–64). Even the rhythm of the poem is measured and liturgical, producing a solemn, ceremonial tone (Amis). The lyric's theme—that mortality exposes the vanity of worldly desires—is thoroughly traditional, yet it can be seen as an answer to the Puritan contention that the plague represents the special providence of God:

> Adieu, farewell earths blisse,
> This world uncertaine is,
> Fond are lifes lustfull joyes,
> Death proves them all but toyes,
> None from his darts can flye;
> I am sick, I must dye:
>   Lord, have mercy on us.
>   (1574–80)

Mortality is an unavoidable part of nature: "All things to end are made," and "Brightness falls from the ayre" (not just from the hair of beautiful queens). There is no suggestion that death from the plague is a punishment for specific sins. The acceptance of death as the context of life and the final answer to human vanities leads away from a concern with social reforms.

Once more at the end of the play, a song brings the audience back to the circumstances of the performance and the 1592 epidemic that the comedy had temporarily allowed them to forget:

> Autumne hath all the Summers fruitefull treasure;
> Gone is our sport, fled is poore Croydens pleasure:
> Short dayes, sharpe dayes, long nights come on a pace,
> Ah, who shall hide us from the Winters face?
> Colde dooth increase, the sicknesse will not cease,
> And here we lye, God knowes, with little ease:
> From winter, plague, & pestilence, good Lord, deliver us.
> (1872–78)

The second stanza is explicit about the effects of the plague on London ("Trades cry, Woe worth that ever they were borne") and on the exiles at Croydon ("Long banished must we live from our friends"). The single line refrain is adapted from the Litany in *The Book of Common Prayer;* the substitution of "winter" for the original "famine" links death from the plague with the natural ravages of the season.

Nashe uses the simple allegorical structure of the cycle of the seasons to suggest that the plague is part of the natural order and not an extraordinary visitation. As in traditional seasonal pageants or in Spenser's *Shepheardes Calender* or "Mutability Cantoes," the cycles of nature are used as an allegory for a view of life that stresses the naturalness of mortality. This analogy between nature and human life was questioned by Puritans and the harbingers of modern science. Ramus had inspired a deemphasis of Aristotle's analogous cosmology. Richard Hooker was in the process of defending the traditional view as the justification for Elizabethan civic and religious hierarchies. Thus the thematic core of Nashe's allegory is in accord with the view of human life Whitgift was reaffirming in the face of Puritan opposition.

But the seasonal pageant, while essential to the play's allegorical center, is only part of the stage business. Nashe uses the interactions between the various allegorical figures as a frame for a series of set pieces that are more academic in their appeal than the pageantry. These formal speeches, which are derived from the debates, paradoxes, and mock encomiums of academic exercises, are self-consciously rhetorical in ways likely to amuse people themselves in the profession of persuasion. The outer frame of Will Summer's comments also provides occasion for wit and for urbane mockery of the rustic elements in the plot. Himself the product of a long tradition of court foolery, Will Summers is used in a paradoxical way that anticipates and perhaps influenced Shakespeare's fools (Barber, 61–67). His good-natured ridicule of the clownish behavior of the lower classes helps to integrate the buffoonery and rustic pageantry with the academic wit and ironies of the set speeches (Hibbard, 101–5). For the archbishop and his little academy, these more sophisticated comic elements would have been a sort of busman's holiday, an amusing exercising of their wits as a respite from the serious deployment of rhetoric in defense of the established church.

Several of the set speeches are satiric comments on the dispute between Whitgift and the Puritans. Ver's defense of prodigality and Bacchus's justification of intoxication raise the question of the best attitude towards common vices. However much Nashe himself may have favored cakes and ale, these speeches are ironic in context, examples of false logic and the abuse of rhetoric. There is, nevertheless, a spirit of toleration towards Ver's hedonism and Bacchus's drunkenness at odds with Puritan asceticism. We know from his other works that Nashe, the "beggerly poet" as Will Summers calls him, was sympathetic with Ver's scorn for those who over value securing wealth: "The earth yelds all her fruites together, and why should not we spend them together? I thanke heavens on my knees, that have made mee an unthrift" (319–21). Bacchus's praise of wine also suggests toleration: "There is no excellent knowledge without mixture of madnesse. And what makes a man more madde in the head then wine?" (994–95). The play's indulgent attitude towards common sins is linked with its patronizing but affectionate attitude towards the common people. This can be seen in the treatment of Harvest, the one retainer of Summer who has served his master faithfully. He is characterized as a typical honest yeoman in the midst of celebrating "harvest home." Although he has drunk too much posset and is too feisty for his humble role, he acquits himself well and earns Summer's praise. Puritan asceticism was more critical of the everyday vices and entertainments of the lower classes.

Winter's long speech in dispraise of learning includes a more direct satire on the Puritan position as it was understood by Nashe and his audience. While strong advocates of literacy and Bible study, the Puritans were thought to be opposed to humanistic learning; for example, the influential William Perkins wrote that natural wisdom was a curse without spiritual wisdom (Knappen, 477). This Puritan suspicion of secular learning was easily exaggerated, as in *The Pilgrimage to Parnassus* (1598 or 1599), where the Puritan Stupido tells the play's heroes, "Studie not these vaine artes of Rhetorique, Poetrie, and Philosophie: there is noe sounde edifying knowledg in them; why, the[y] are more vaine than a paire of organs, or a morrice daunce" (*Three Parnassus Plays*, 113). Nashe criticizes Puritan indifference to traditional education in *The Anatomy of Absurdity*. In *An Almond for a Parrot* Puritans are mimicked: "What is Logicke but the highe waie to wrangling, contayning in it a world of bibble babble. Neede we anie of your Greeke, Latine, Hebrue, or anie such gibbrige, when wee have the word of God in English?" (3:350). Sections of Winter's diatribe are similar in spirit:

> In briefe, all bookes, divinitie except,
> Are nought but tales of the divels lawes,
> Poyson wrapt up in sugred words,
> Mans pride, damnations props, the worlds abuse.
> (1417–20)

Satire on the Puritans is only one element in this egregious mock dispraise of learning.

The Puritan position is more explicitly satirized in Winter's son, Christmas. Christmas was the most festive of Elizabethan holidays, but the Puritans wished to make it more dignified by purging it of pagan and medieval customs. Phillip Stubbes complained that at "Christmas tyme there is nothing els used but cards, dice tables, masking, mumming, bowling & such like fooleries" (*Anatomie*, sig. O6v). Nashe's Christmas is established as a Puritan by his entrance:

Summer.	Christmas, how chaunce thou com'st not as the rest,
	Accompanied with some musique, or some song?
	A merry Carroll would have grac't thee well;
	Thy ancestors have us'd it heretofore.
Christmas.	I, antiquity was the mother of ignorance: this latter world, that sees but with her spectacles, hath spied a pad in those sports more then they could.
Summer.	What, is't against thy conscience for to sing?
Christmas.	No, nor to say, by my troth, if I may get a good bargaine.

(1623–31).

Christmas's last line quoted here is a slur suggesting that Puritans will overcome their compunctions about oaths if profit is involved. The frequent charge that Puritans were seditious and mercenary is summed up in Christmas's statement, "I respect no crownes but crownes in the purse" (1663–64).

Christmas rejects the traditional ideal of hospitality, seeing it as an excuse for gluttony. In *The Anatomy of Absurdity* Nashe had seen niggardliness as a Puritan characteristic: "When men shall publiquelie make profession of a more inward calling, and shall waxe cold in the workes of charitie, and fervent in malice, liberall in nothing but in lavishe backbyting, holding hospitalitie for an eschewed heresie, and the performance of good workes for Papistrie, may wee not then have recourse to that caveat of Christ in the Gospell, *Cavete ab hipocritis*" (1:22). This attitude is reflected in Summer's rebuke:

> Christmas, I tell thee plaine, thou art a snudge,
> ....
> It is the honor of Nobility
> To keepe high dayes and solemne festivals:
> Then, to set their magnificence to view,
> To frolick open with their favorites,
> And use their neighbours with all curtesie;
> When thou in huggar mugger spend'st thy wealth.
>
> (1722, 1725–30)

The occasion of the play was, of course, just such an exercise in hospitality and display of magnificence on the part of the archbishop; such princely behavior by the bishops was an issue in the Marprelate tracts. Whitgift was particularly noted for his hospitality at Christmas, as his biographer reported: "At Christmasse, especially, his gates were alwayes open, and his Hall set twice or thrice over with strangers" (Paule, sig. L3r). Whitgift's own view found expression a few years later when he criticized the archbishop of York for using the Puritan expression "Christ's tide" instead of Christmas in an official letter (Collinson, 431).

Back-winter, a return of winter late in the season, is represented in the play as the ultimate repudiation of the order of nature and cycle of the seasons. While destructive Winter is part of the necessary cycle, Back-winter, if he had his way, would bring chaos to the world and destroy humanity:

> Earth, if I cannot injure thee enough,
> Ile bite thee with my teeth, Ile scratch thee thus;
> Ile beate downe the partition with my heeles,
> Which, as a mud-vault, severs hell and thee.
> Spirits, come up; 'tis I that knock for you,
> One that envies the world farre more then you:
> Come up in millions; millions are to few
> To execute the malice I intend.
> (1773–80)

The lavish backbiting and fervent malice of Back-winter and his evocation of chaos make him an objectification of the Elizabethan fear of anarchy. The Puritans also abhorred disorder, but Whitgift's polemicists argued that the Puritan attack on the hierarchy of the church would lead to an attack on the social and political order and then to anabaptistical confusion. They argued that the apparent piety of the Puritans was a cover for envy and malice. In this way Back-winter's comic rage as he falls on the floor and bites and claws at the earth reflects the prejudice of the audience about their opponents.

The anarchy the Puritans would unleash on the commonwealth could be prevented, in the view of the Croydon audience, by loyal obedience to the queen and the hierarchical society she headed. As a symbol of order she was elevated in Elizabethan ideology to the status of a sacred figure, spoken of in the language of adoration. She was the link between the ideal order of the universe and the social order that imperfectly mirrored that ideal. Elizabeth's popularity and effectiveness as a monarch were trump cards in the ideological battle between the defenders of the established church and the Puritan reformers, but the intense loyalty of the orthodox shows that faith in the queen was part of their creed, not mere propaganda or flattery. The Puritans were inclined to be as loyal, but occasionally an extremist like Penry would question the queen's authority and give substance to the charge that Puritans were seditious. Whitgift himself had additional reasons to be loyal to the queen, since he was her protégé as archbishop and a personal friend.

Queen Elizabeth is seen as a figure who transcends the mutable world of the seasonal cycle both times she is evoked in *Summer's Last Will and Testament*. At the start of the play, Summer says that he would have already died,

> But that Eliza, Englands beauteous Queene,
> On whom all seasons prosperously attend,
> Forbad the execution of my fate,
> Untill her joyfull progresse was expir'd.
> (133–36)

Before Winter does die at the end of the play, he names the queen in his will, again seeing her as above the natural order, a secular saint:

> Unto Eliza, that most sacred Dame,
> Whom none but Saints and Angels ought to name,
> All my faire dayes remaining I bequeath,
> To waite upon her till she be returnd.
> Autumne, I charge thee, when that I am dead,
> Be prest and serviceable at her beck,
> . . . .
> And, Winter, with thy wrythen frostie face,
> Smoothe up thy visage, when thou lookst on her;
> Thou never lookst on such bright majestie:

A charmed circle draw about her court,
Wherein warme dayes may daunce, & no cold come.
            (1841–46, 1850–54)

A subsequent invocation of the queen seemed a direct address and evidence that Elizabeth was present to Nashe's editor, R. B. McKerrow, and revision of an earlier text has been proposed, but if she had been at Croydon the prologue and epilogue would surely have been addressed to her and not to "my Lord" (McKerrow, 4:416–19; Best). She is evoked as if present because she was the symbolic center of the social structure being defended by the archbishop as well as the actual source of his power and wealth. "How is't? how is't? you that be of the graver sort, do you thinke these youths worthy of a *Plaudite* for praying for the Queene, and singing of the Letany?" (1886–88). Will Summer's appeal for applause calls attention to the play's reaffirmation of loyalty to the queen and to the church in defiance of the physical threat of the plague and the ideological threat of the Puritan movement.

Just as the plague is kept at bay, so is the sature on the Puritans kept gentle. We know that Nashe could be more outspoken when he wished to attack openly, just as we know from his difficulties with the suppressed satiric play *The Isle of Dogs* and the banning of all Nashe's works by Bancroft and Whitgift in 1599 that satire could easily become offensive. Thus the satire in the play is subordinate to the play's affirmation of traditional values and to its holiday mood.

Will Summer's appeal for applause, like his other apologies and disclaimers, reveals that Nashe and his players feared that the play, as mild as it is, would prove offensive to their grave and powerful audience. The epilogue says on behalf of the players, "Your Graces frownes are to them shaking fevers, your least disfavours the greatest ill fortune that may betide them" (1925–27). Nashe's subsequent career is evidence that the "beggerly poet" had as much reason as the actors to fear frowns and disfavors. He was never able openly to acknowledge Whitgift as a patron, even when it would have been a powerful argument for his respectability in the controversy with Gabriel Harvey. Moreover, Whitgift's support may not have amounted to much; Nashe was to complain within a year that Sir George Carey's hospitality was the only satisfactory treatment he had ever received from a patron. We do not even know if *Summer's Last Will and Testament* was actually performed, since it is possible that Whitgift refused to sponsor a drama that amounted to a direct repudiation of the popular ethic the Puritans advanced. If it was performed, the archbishop and his guests may have been cool towards a play that was mainly festive entertainment, or at least apprehensive that the offense given to others would reflect on their probity.

Many moderates, including courtiers and church officials, sympathized with Puritan ethics while rejecting their call for ecclesiastical reform. Asceticism had its point: there is an unreconcilable difference between Carnival and Lent, between the irreverence and indulgence of holidays and the harsh realities of everyday life. In a preindustrial economy progress is likely to depend on some self-denial. The Elizabethan festive tradition could be wasteful and it could be seditious, although it was not necessarily so. The irreverence of Nashe's comedy is harmless enough, but the play's delight in manipulating the framework of theatrical illusion and its playing with the conventions of rhetoric are an implicit challenge to high seriousness. The final stanzas of the lyric "Adieu, Farewell Earth's Bliss" assert that earth is but a player's stage, a conventional concept in context but one that could take on skeptical implications. The play's melancholic awareness of mortality can be an argument for piety or for hedonism; the rejection of Puritanism, an argument for orthodoxy or for license. As so often in Nashe, the play both affirms and negates through irony. Will Summers adds elements of a put-on or imposition with his obtrusive deference and complex ironies. The play is Nashe at his most orthodox, but even in front of an archbishop his orthodoxy begins to mock itself.

CHAPTER
3

The Devil's Orator:
Pierce Penniless

A SUGGESTION of how Nashe's career appeared to his contemporaries exists in a fictionalized portrait in *The Three Parnassus Plays,* a sequence of comedies performed at Cambridge around the turn of the century. Ingenioso, who barely survives on the fees he collects from his printer John Danter (Nashe's printer), alternately fawns and rails at the misers to whom he dedicates his works and the fops for whom he ghostwrites erotic poems. He curses his bad fortune and his failure to find a liberal Maecenas, but he does not blame himself. He tells his companions:

> Nay sighe not men, laughe at the foolish worlde:
> They have the shame, though wee the miserie.
> (211)

Like Ingenioso, Nashe projects his failures on the injustice of the world rather than doubting the wisdom of his course. Except for brief periods, he never achieved the support he thought was his due; instead he remained a marginal author, outside the order he defended. His satire was intended to serve orthodoxy, but his bitterness and sharp eye for social abuses tempted him to arrogance and excess.

Nashe's frustrations are depicted in *Pierce Penniless His Supplication to the Devil* (1592), a satiric pamphlet about the despair and anger of the title character at the unjust society that rejects him. It was a remarkably successful work, going through at least five editions by 1596. Part of its appeal was Nashe's bold reversal of the popular prodigal formula (Helgerson, 1–15). Although Pierce has wasted his youth in folly and surfeited his mind with vanity, he has repented and applied himself to mending his fortunes. "But all in vaine, I sate up late, and rose earely, contended with the colde, and conversed with scarcitie: for all my labours turned to losse, my vulgar Muse was despised & neglected, my paines not regarded, or slightly rewarded, and I my selfe (in prime of my best wit) laid open to povertie" (1:157). Unlike a prodigal, Pierce blames society rather than himself: "I grew to consider how many base men that wanted those parts which I had, enjoyed content at will, and had wealth at commaund" (158). Despair and anger at fortune give way to a review of Elizabethan England in terms of its failure to live up to its own ideals.

The short first section of *Pierce Pennilness* introduces Nashe's persona and the situation that prompts him to pen a supplication to the devil. Pierce's search for a messenger to convey his supplication is the occasion for some preliminary satire on the devil-like operation of the merchant exchange and the law courts. The longer second section is the supplication itself, which is not so much an appeal to the devil as a complaint about how the seven deadly sins are manifested in contemporary England. In the third section the devil's messenger, a knight of the post (or professional perjurer) who is a devil in disguise, discourses on the nature of spirits in response to Pierce's asking whether they are imaginary. After the messenger has departed, Nashe speaks for himself and concludes with a rambling apology for the work's deficiencies which turns into a belated epistle to the reader and a dedication. The whole is held together by Pierce's personality and by its lively free-flowing style, which reflects Pierce's stance as a sometimes bitter, sometimes exuberant observer of the London life that excludes him from a significant role.

AUTHOR AND PERSONA

Nashe's invention of Pierce Penniless, the impecunious university wit who mixes personal bile into his satire, allowed him to anchor his extemporaneous style to a fictional persona and give order to his diffuse thinking about society. Pierce is also presented with an irony that enables Nashe to distance himself from his character's more controversial statements. When Gabriel Harvey criticized the arrogance of *Pierce Penniless*, Nashe could excuse "the Methode of my demeanour": his "principall scope" in the work was a "most livelie anatomie of sinne," so, to give the satire a source, "I introduce a discontented Scholler under the person of Pierce Pennilesse, tragicallie exclaiming upon his partial-eid fortune, that kept an Almes boxe of compassion in store for every one but him-selfe" (1:306). Pierce initially functions as a comic exaggeration of his author's emotions and attitudes: "(In a malecontent humor) I accused my fortune, raild on my patrones, bit my pen, rent my papers, and ragde in all points like a mad man" (157). But later the persona becomes a transparent mask through which Nashe can express his own views. Pierce Penniless rapidly became Nashe's nickname in an age given to sobriquets; in later works he used Pierce as a fictional name for himself without any suggestion that Pierce is in some sense a separate character.

Nashe's use of a persona reflects Elizabethan self-consciousness about social roles and the age's uncertainty about the nature of authorship. In ceremonial social interactions, imaginary roles concealed real intentions; a well-known example is the Duke d'Alençon's courtship of Queen Elizabeth, in which political issues were masked in a charade of courtly love. In the tournaments that were a regular part of court life the participants assumed chivalric names that were intended to reflect aspects of their characters and their social roles. This use of sobriquets shaded into its literary counterparts: Sir Philip Sidney was Philisides or Astrophil in his works and in the imaginations of his admirers. Gabriel Harvey invented a number of personas that expressed potential versions of himself, such as Axiophilus the poet, Angelus Furius the man of action, Eutrapelus the rhetorician, and Eudromus the pragmatist (Stern, 175-90). The fact that these personas were known only to the few who could decode them in Harvey's marginalia is evidence that the social and literary custom of assuming roles had a psychological dimension. In practice the social, literary, and psychological uses of personas merged in complex ways: Sidney's Astrophil is a product of literary conventions, of the courtship games of Elizabeth's court, and probably of Sidney's own ambivalence about erotic love.

In literature a writer assumed the role of author, a role most often validated by the professional authority of the writer or by his subordination of his views to the authorities he cited. But the growth of a popular readership changed the nature of authorship; there was an increased interest in the personal voice or ethos of a writer aside from any question of his credentials. The conventions of genre and decorum were powerful, but traditional rhetorical conceptions of authorship were yielding to a more expressive conception of literature that saw works in terms of the opinions and personalities of their authors.[1] Implicit was the fragmenting of received wisdom and an increased emphasis on the individual as the source of his or her social roles. Thus Harvey can conflate John Lyly with his personas: "Surely Euphues was someway a pretty fellow: would God, Lilly had alwaies bene Euphues, and never Pap-hatchet" (*Pierce's Supererogation*, sig. I4r). This denial of the fictional status of Lyly's personas is a reversal of Lyly's denial of Martin Marprelate's sincerity. Pierce Penniless's fictional status in relation to Thomas Nashe troubled contemporaries and is not finally resolvable. In *Four Letters* Harvey hoped that Pierce was just a disreputable persona adopted by the proper young man Nashe because of Greene's bad example; later in *Pierce's Supererogation* he decides Pierce is Nashe and becomes more personal in his criticisms.

To some extent Pierce was a literary persona, a "satyricall disguise" modeled on the precedent of classical satirists. Partly because of a false etymology, the Elizabethans thought of classical satire as the donning of the mask of a satyr—that is, as adopting a rough, crude, and often obscene persona. This view of satire seemed to account for the difficulties of Juvenal

---

1. The view that the satirist's persona is conventional was argued by Mack, "The Muse of Satire," and developed for the Elizabethan period by Alvin Kernan in *The Cankered Muse*. This view of the persona as a literary device is questioned by Ehrenpreis, Gill, and Lecocq.

and Persius and for the rustic elements in works like *Piers Plowman,* the ultimate source of Pierce's name. Nashe himself cites classical precedents since that was the respectable thing to do, particularly since his adversary was the classicist Gabriel Harvey, but his claim that he imitates them is not borne out by evidence of their influence. Only by the most general analogy was Nashe a "young Juvenal." Harvey was closer to the truth when he accused Nashe of deriving his style and authorial stance from Martin Marprelate and Lyly, and from Tarlton and Greene. The general influence of the Elizabethan conception of classical satire must be given its due, but Pierce's origins and popularity are better understood by examining his domestic antecedents.

As Tarlton's name suggests, Pierce is not exclusively literary in origin. Richard Tarlton perpetuated on the stage a tradition of irreverent buffoonery, similar to the license of the professional jester. He was famous for his witty improvisation—he often said more than was set down for him—and for his rapport with his audience. Like the Lords of Misrule who reigned during holiday celebrations, Tarlton voiced the complaints of the subordinate ranks of society in an acceptable comic fashion (Bradbrook, 162–77; Weimann, *Shakespeare,* 185–92). He was cocky and feisty in an exaggerated manner that mocked his own pretensions. To the traditional role of the clown he added a personal element that made him the most popular actor of his day. His style was imitated by Martin Marprelate, by the anti-Martinists, and by Nashe, who also says Tarlton consulted him on matters of wit (1:319). In particular, his imitators followed his practice of breaking frame and violating the decorum of a performance. This the pamphlet writers accomplished by the use of asides to the reader, often printed as marginal comments. As on the stage, these printed asides engage the audience, but they also suggest that the main performance of the persona or character is a mere act. The device is analogous to a wink directed at a third party in a conversation.

Like a wink, Tarlton's asides enhanced his characterization as Tarlton the clown even if they distracted from the verisimilitude of the specific dramatic role he played. His stage personality became conflated with his roles and with his private self. His public personality became like that of the professional jester in that it was a continuous performance made up of lesser bits of comic role playing. Martin Marprelate also created the effect of a central personality holding together the egregious routines he used to bait his opponents. Nashe joined the other anti-Martinists in denying Martin's sincerity, but he adapted Martin's techniques to his own purposes in *Pierce Penniless* and perfected them in the pamphlets he wrote against Harvey. From Tarlton (and Martin) he learned to mock his own "tragical exclaimings" and break the coherence of his performance with asides: "Marke these two letter-leaping Metaphors, good people" (1:181). Role playing for Tarlton and his imitators was a matter, not of consistent impersonation, but of a set of interlocking routines that meshed into a credible overall personality.

After his death Tarlton's persona lived on in anecdotes, jest books, and even on the signs of inns. Such an afterlife as a legend had been achieved by earlier clowns and jesters such as Scogan and Will Summers. These legendary folk heroes joined a number of fictional characters in the popular imagination as symbols of a sort of enlightened roguery. Like Puck and Robin Hood, they violated social decorum in ways that were ultimately just, even if their motivation was questionable. The immorality of these legendary heroes was not an issue in itself but a way of exposing their ethical and social betters to ridicule and laughter. Scogan, Summers, and Tarlton became imaginary folk heroes who cut eccentric trajectories across the too rigid frame of order.

Robert Greene, with his university degrees, moved such irreverent roguery up the social scale, much to the disgust of his critics. His romances seem innocuous enough to modern readers, and his rogue pamphlets claim to expose criminality, but to his contemporaries Greene's career was a scandal. Apparently his notoriety derived in part from the figure he cut in the world of London taverns. In his repentance pamphlets he confesses that he has been a reprobate and an atheist, but his repentance is not very convincing and the last pamphlet attributed to him, *Greene's Groats-worth of Wit* (1592), included libelous allusions to Marlowe, Shakespeare, and others. Greene's various works were popular well into the 1590s; his was still a name to conjure with long after his death. Harvey was to argue that Greene was Nashe's master and the source of a strain of corrupt writing that polluted the press and misled the youth of London.

Greene's notoriety contrasts with that of Martin or Lyly in that its literary component is based on an ethos who is frankly Greene, rather than a persona. He spoke for himself, rather than masking his thoughts with a traditional figure like Tarlton the clown or Colin Clout the shepherd. This is particularly true of his repentance pamphlets, which contribute to the characterization of Pierce Penniless as a reformed prodigal who still cannot find employment. But Nashe was more influenced by Greene's career and his conception of himself as an author than he was by specific works. He came to see Greene's life as a valid although not admirable response to the hostile conditions young intellectuals encountered in London. Like Harvey, Nashe saw Greene's life as symbolic, but for him Greene's dissolution was a result, not a cause, of social disorder.

Greene and Nashe were not the only displaced academics about town, although evidence about the "university wit" as a social type is anecdotal. These "good fellows," as they were called, had the status of their educations but lacked suitable careers. Several tried their hands at writing, but few achieved even the limited success of Lyly, Greene, or Nashe. Often malcontented without being seditious, their lives were irregular without being criminal like those of lower-class rogues. Their lot was not as destitute as that of the uneducated, masterless men who congregated in the city looking for employment, but poverty is relative to expectations, and the bitterness of failure is likely to find expression in cynicism and hostility. Greene saw his own lapse into profligacy and skepticism as typical of contemporary prodigality. The characterization of Pierce Penniless reflects the experience of this new class of alienated intellectuals (Curtis, "Alienated Intellectuals"; Helgerson 22–24).

Although Pierce is in this sense a spokesman for the 1590s, there is also substance in Harvey's view that Pierce is an expression of Nashe's own discontents. Discounting any irony, Harvey links the persona with Nashe himself, Greene's inwardest companion "cruelly pinched with want, vexed with discredite, tormented with other mens felicitie, and overwhelmed with his owne miserie; in a raving, and franticke moode, most desperately exhibiteth his supplication to the Divell" (*Four Letters*, sig. D3v). Harvey saw Nashe's pamphlet as the latest example of the arrogance that infected printing because of the Marprelate controversy and Greene's bad influence. Like his predecessors, Nashe advances his egocentric opinion without humility: "Every Martin Junior, and Puny Pierce, a monarch in the kingdome of his own humour: every pert, and crancke wit, in one odd veine, or other, the onely man of the University, of the Citty, of the Realme, for a flourish or two: who but he, in the flush of his overweening conceit?" (sig. H1v). Nashe objected to this literal reading of his text, but Pierce is in many ways Nashe, and his satire does verge on arrogant self-assertion.

In the first section of the pamphlet Pierce is a comic exaggeration, and in the last section Nashe speaks as author to apologize for the work's deficiencies and dedicate its good qualities to a patron. He uses Pierce to excuse the long section on spirits: "I bring Pierce Penilesse to question with the divel, as a yoong novice would talke with a great travailer." If the discussion becomes tedious, "impute it to Pierce Penilesse that was importunate in demanding" (1:240). But this ironic distance is not maintained in the long supplication, where the personal pronouns often refer to Nashe rather than to Pierce, as in the attack on Richard Harvey. In his response to Gabriel Harvey, Nashe undercuts his own argument that Pierce is a fictional persona when he lapses into the first person: "I expostulated, why Coblers, Hostlers, and Carmen should be worth so much . . . , and I, a scholler and a good-fellow, a begger" (323). In short, Pierce is an exaggerated version of Nashe, not an objectified character with opinions and attitudes of his own.

Although Pierce merges into Nashe during the course of the pamphlet, Nashe's projection of his satiric impulses onto a persona does free him to express his anger in a way acceptable to his readers. If Nashe cannot hide behind Pierce, he can at least use the persona as a way of softening his arrogance by self-mockery. Without Pierce, he would have no defense against the accusations of both Richard and Gabriel Harvey that he sets himself up as a critic of the folly of others. By expressing discontent, a satirist ran the risk of encouraging discontent in others, but this danger was mitigated when the satirist presented himself as a comic character. Thus Jaques in *As You Like It* thinks the motley of a fool will free him to expose sin and folly. *Pierce Penniless* is an improvement on *The Anatomy of Absurdity* in part because the inclusion of the satirist in the text as a comic character gives the satire a center and helps dissipate its inherent presumption.

Pierce's irony represents a new personal stance; he is not just a literary device. He overcomes his despair through the exercise of his own wit. Rather than seeking to reform himself, he exhorts his readers to amend their ways. The wit is functional to the exhortation, but it also allows him to translate his own frustration and anger into humor. There is nothing about the consolations of philosophy or religion, but there is consolation of a sort in the free play of wit. Pierce through his supplication and Nashe through Pierce use wit and irony as a way of exorcising despair as well as appealing for reform. In later works Nashe appears to have incorporated this ironic projection of himself back into his self-image; at least the ethos of "Nashe" in the later pamphlets continues to exhibit the ironic stance introduced in Pierce.

PIERCE'S SUPPLICATION AND TOPICAL SATIRE

Pierce Penniless is also an improvement on *The Anatomy of Absurdity* in its depiction of social vices and in the sharpness of its satire. Nashe's experience of London life fleshes out his polemics; he achieves *copia,* or richness in style, by piling up satiric details rather than by the schemas and allusions of euphuism. Since the details are exaggerated and frequently grotesque, the effect is analogous to Flemish art or Rabelais. Nashe's account of London life is "realistic" if one takes realism to mean verbal references to the everyday stuff of life. Because of this, Renaissance scholars have mined Nashe's works as a source of information about Elizabethan culture. This verisimilitude accounts for the continuing appeal of *Pierce Penniless*, but the journalistic details do not add up to a realistic portrayal of Elizabethan life in the sense that we associate with novels. A realistic novel claims that its plot and characters have a referential truth similar to that of its details, but the kinds of vice Nashe describes and his framework of the seven deadly sins have a "reality" that precedes and is not dependent on personal experience. Literary conventions and the categories of human experience were "real" like the hierarchy of nature, not a matter of human contrivance subject to revision (Manley, 106–33). Nashe was an empiricist in his shrewd observation of London life, but he did not develop new hypotheses on the basis of what he saw. On the contrary, his emphasis is always on the discrepancy between the selfish behavior of his contemporaries and the ordered society that *ought* to exist.

The anger and satire focus on violations of the ideal: a cobbler who was worth five hundred pounds violated the proper order of the commonwealth, as did a patron who neglected to reward merit. At times Nashe comments on the economic changes that interest modern historians, but he saw their cause to be the corrupt desires of presumptuous individuals, not new economic conditions. He was similar to his Puritan adversaries in this view that social change was caused by private vice, but for him vice was more a matter of violating norms and less a matter of personal sin (Peter, 60–103). This difference in emphasis is evident in his argument that an unthrift or prodigal is better than an idle glutton caught up in the vice of acquisitiveness because the unthrift acquires wit by seeing plays and associating with poets. "Nowe tell me whether of these two, the heavie headed gluttonous house dove, or this livelie, wanton, yoong Gallant, is like to proove the wiser man, and better member in the Common-wealth?" (1:210). In preferring the young prodigal Nashe challenges the priorities of the Puritans, and he reasserts his commitment to humanism in seeing service to the commonwealth as the goal of virtue. Conversely, evil is antisocial behavior such as the selfish withdrawal of the glutton. Nashe's account of the seven deadly sins is for the most part conventional, but the emphasis is on those vices that disrupt society rather than on private sins.

Always implicit is the unfairness of a situation that allows selfish people to prosper, while true merit, like that of Nashe, lies unregarded. Nashe's assumption of merit outraged Harvey, but it is not as arrogant as it sounds, given Nashe's orthodox emphasis on a person's social role. His claim for a higher status was based on the importance he ascribed to education and his exalted conception of the writer's vocation. The central role he attributed to the poet followed from his idealistic conception of society. If human behavior is a product of the abstract ideas people hold about themselves, then writers, who deal with images of human behavior, are unacknowledged arbiters and perhaps legislators. Persuading readers to virtue and shaming them from vice required great rhetorical skill, given the recalcitrance of human nature. Thus the account of poetry in *Pierce Penniless* is not really a digression, since literature should be the best way to inspire the populace to greater civic virtue. Unfortunately, poetry is debased by uneducated writers, "so simple they know not what they doe" (1:194), and is under attack by the Puritans. The enmity of "dull-headed divines" is caused by professional jealousy: their own second-hand sermons fail to persuade their auditors to a better life. "Silver-tongued" Smith is an example of an effective preacher who uses the resources of poetry to move the people to repentance. Nashe begins the pamphlet by evoking the memory of Sidney and ends it with praise of Spenser's *Faerie Queene*: these writers embody in their works the sort of heroic, inspirational literature that should be published and that Nashe aspires to write himself.

In a similar vein he defends drama against its critics, a bold undertaking at the time Nashe wrote. Plays are a less vicious pastime than activities such as gaming, drinking, or harlotry. This new pragmatic defense was developed by Chettle and rejected indignantly by the City fathers in their next request to the Privy Council that the theaters be shut down (Chettle, 39–48; Chambers, 4:316–17). But Nashe goes further: "Nay, what if I proove Playes to be no extreame; but a rare exercise of vertue?" (1:212). Like poetry, drama has purified the language of the common people and offered them inspirational models of heroic behavior. The Puritans who object to drama have a narrow and acquisitive conception of virtue: "What do we get by it?" Heroic deeds depicted on the stage stir the audience to emulation, but the opponents of drama respect "onely their execrable luker, and filthie unquenchable avarice" (213). This outspoken defense of drama provoked an angry response from Thomas Bowes in an epistle published as an introduction to a translation of La Primaudaye in 1594: even though "godly learned men, and some that have spoken of their owne experience, have in their bookes that are allowed by authority, termed Stage-playes and Theaters, *The schoole of abuse, the schoole of bawdery, the nest of the devil & sinke of all sinne, the chaire of pestilence, the pompe of the devil, the soveraigne place of Satan,* yet this commendation of them hath lately passed the Presse, that they are rare exercises in vertue" (La Primaudaye, sig. B4v). Bowes calls for pamphlets like Nashe's to be burned in Paul's Churchyard.

The humanistic view of the social order that lies behind these defenses of poetry and drama is also evident in Nashe's praise of the flexibility of the English system. In Denmark all ranks are fixed in a caste system: "None but the son of a Corporall must be a Corporall, nor any be Captaine, but the lawfull begotten of a Captaines body" (1:178). In England, on the other hand, "vertue ascendeth by degrees of desert unto dignitie" (176). The possibility that an ordinary divine may become a bishop, or a common lawyer rise to be a member of the Privy Council, inspires excellence. "You all knowe that man (insomuch as hee is the Image of God) delighteth in honour and worship, and all holy Writ warrantes that delight, so it bee not derogatory to any part of Gods owne worship: now take away that delight, a discontented idlenesse overtakes him" (179). For simple hire, one gets only day labor. Society should be governed by a desire for honor; contention and emulation are the springs of virtuous action, although one should beware of envy.

Ideally the distribution of wealth should reinforce the meritorious social order Nashe envisions; instead, gold is in the hands of the undeserving and the avaricious. The humble are made proud, and those who have a right to honor are humiliated. Affectations—like those of Mistress Minx, a merchant's wife, or of obscure upstart gallants—are external evidence of a distorted value system. Antiquarians squander money on gewgaws: "This is the disease of our newfangled humorists, that know not what to doe with their welth" (183). Italianate Englishmen and epicurean feasts are further evidence of distorted values. The more ostentatious vices of the sort that were covered by the futile Elizabethan sumptuary legislation are fueled by the faulty distribution of wealth and the corrupt values of the people. The solution is a reaffirmation of the proper order of the commonwealth and its decorum of social roles. In his earliest writings Nashe argued for the importance of good literature in reaffirming proper social values and exposing abnormalities; in *Pierce Penniless* he widens his scope to anatomize the social order that needs the better guidance of writers like himself.

The problem for Nashe was to expose the follies of his society without so offending those he criticized that they would harass and discredit him. This is apparent in his circumspection about the aristocracy. The sloth and luxury of some nobles brings them into contempt. "Is it the loftie treading of a Galliard, or fine grace in telling of a love tale amongst Ladies, can make a man reverenst of the multitude? no, they care not for the false glistering of gay garments, or insinuating curtesie of a carpet Peere" (210). In describing the prevalence of lechery he includes the court by a rhetorical trick: "The Court I dare not touch, but surely there (as in the Heavens) be many falling starres, and but one true Diana" (216). At the very end of the pamphlet, when he decries the lack of patrons, he becomes so outspoken that his diatribe threatens to become an attack on the aristocracy:

> We want an Aretine here among us, that might strip these golden asses out of their gaie trappings, and after he had ridden them to death with railing, leave them on the dunghill for carion. But I will write to his ghost by my carrier, and I hope hele repaire his whip, and use it against our English Peacockes, that painting themselves with church spoils, like mightie mens sepulchers, have

nothing but Atheisme, schisme, hypocrisie, & vainglory, like rotten bones lie lurking within them. (242)

Aware that such railing might seem seditious, Nashe immediately qualifies his denunciation: "Far be it, bright stars of Nobilitie, and glistring attendants on the true Diana, that this my speech shoulde be anie way injurious to your glorious magnificence."

The invocation of Aretino is a reminder that Elizabethans had two conceptions of satire, both of which appealed to Nashe. There is little specific borrowing from Aretino in Nashe's works, but he was inspired by the Italian satirist's style and career (Rhodes, 26-36). Thomas Lodge labeled Nashe "our English Aretine." Aretino's frequent resort to invective, however, conflicted with the more humanistic conception of satire. A shibboleth for almost all Elizabethan satirists was that they attacked vice in general, not particular people, but Aretino had made his reputation naming names. His specialty was railing, often in a deliberately scurrilous and obscene fashion. Rather than begging, he extorted support from patrons, as Nashe does when he threatens retaliation against anyone who sends him "away with a Flea in mine eare" (1:195). Both sides in the Marprelate controversy had used invective in the manner of Aretino because they intended to discredit their opponents as well as argue the issues, but personal attacks were reluctantly adopted as a strategy. As an orthodox humanist Nashe was committed to impersonal satire; thus his later claim that he intended *Pierce Penniless* as a lively anatomy of sin and his frequent disavowels of topical allusions. But this idealistic posture does not square with the passages of invective in the pamphlet nor with the patent topical references. Moreover, the tone is often belligerent and sometimes irate; Nashe cannot maintain the ironic distance established at the start by his use of a persona.

The epistle "The Author to the Printer," added in the second edition, indicates Nashe's conflicting sentiments as a satirist. It pretends to be a private letter but was probably intended for publication; the subterfuge is required by the witty device of putting the prefatory material at the end of the pamphlet. In the letter, Nashe first attempts to allay the arrogance of his satire by the common Elizabethan device of confessing the work "to be a meer toy, not deserving any judicial mans view" (153). At the same time he is angered at the knavery of those rumored to be planning an unauthorized sequel to his work. His main purpose in the epistle is to deny any topical content in his satire. He also denies that he is the actual author of *Greene's Groats-worth of Wit*, "a scald trivial lying pamphlet," which was notorious because of its insulting allusions to Shakespeare and others. He warns off topical interpreters of his work, but promises to counterattack if criticized: "Write who wil against me, but let him look his life be without scandale: for if he touch me never so litle, Ile be as good as the Blacke Booke to him & his kindred" (155). Thus he threatens to write personal invective even as he disowns any such intention in the present work.

Pierce Penniless ran into trouble in three different areas: its criticisms of certain classes of people, its putative topical allusions, and its attack on Richard Harvey. In each case Nashe anticipates the difficulty and tries to avoid hostile reactions. Antiquarians were apparently offended by his ridiculing their interest in "worm-eaten Elde," so he claims in the epistle to the printer that the criticism is directed only at a few foolish antiquarians. He also backs off from potentially offensive criticisms in the text itself, as in his qualification of the indictment of English Peacocks among the nobility. Satire on dull-headed Divines is softened by a marginal note: "Absit arrogantia, that this speeche shold concerne all divines, but such dunces as abridge men of their lawfull liberty, and care not howe unprepared they speake to their Auditorie" (192). In one case there is specific evidence that Pierce's satire on a group of people did provoke offense. Robert Beale, clerk of the Queen's Council and bitter opponent of Whitgift, thought he detected political mischief: "That one of these subjects [presumably of Whitgift's] in his book entitled, *A Supplication to the Devil*, so reviled the whole nation of Denmark, as every one, who so bore any due respect to her Majesty and her friends, might be sorry and ashamed to see it" (quoted by McKerrow, 5:142). The motivation and purpose of the lengthy attack on the pride of the Danes are obscure, but Beale thought it dangerous invective.

In spite of his denials, Nashe was also accused of including allusions to specific persons. A letter of April 1, 1593, reports gossip that he had dared criticize Lord Burghley: "In a late pamphlet entytuled *A Suplication to the Divill* he is girded at, thoughe not somuch as in *Mother Hubberd's Tale*" (Petti, "Political Satire," 141). The comparison with Spenser's controversial poem is a reminder that Nashe's interpolated beast fable, "The Bear and the Fox," would have been read as topical allegory by Elizabethans; Harvey so read it, also comparing it to Spenser's poem. Defending himself, Nashe continued to deny that he had set down "the least allusion to any man set above mee in degree, but onely glanc'st at vice generallie" (1:320). He is explicit about the beast fable:

> The tale of the Beare and the Foxe, how ever it may set fooles heads a worke a farre off, yet I had no concealed ende in it but, in the one, to describe the right nature of a bloudthirsty tyrant, whose indefinite appetite all the pleasures in the earth have no powre to bound in goodnes, but he must seeke a new felicitie in varietie of cruelty, and destroying all other mens prosperitie; for the other, to figure an hypocrite: Let it be Martin, if you will, or some old dog that bites sorer than hee, who secretlie goes and seduceth country Swaines. (320–21).

Even in its own terms this disclaimer is not very convincing, since it hints that the fox is a specific person, presumably the arch-Puritan Thomas Cartwright; moreover, the tale itself contains pointed allusions that invite an allegorical reading. It is cautious enough, however, to defy exact interpretation, and it was probably ambiguous for Elizabethans as well. It is introduced by the Knight of the Post as part of a discussion of hypocrisy, which he defines as all "Machiavilisme, puritanisme, and outward gloasing with a mans enemie" (1:220). The tale clearly refers to the Puritan campaign, as when it recounts how the Fox persuaded the simple swains that their honey bees were in fact drones, that nothing was canonical but what he and the Chameleon spoke. We are told, "The Fox can tell a faire tale, and covers all his knaverie under conscience" (226). Such sentences ask for topical application.

If the Fox is an allegory for Thomas Cartwright, Whitgift's adversary, then the Bear may well be Cartwright's patron, the earl of Leicester, whose device was the bear and ragged staff. Since Leicester had died in 1588, Nashe could gird at him with relative impunity, although he was indeed, as Harvey warned him, risking a "parlous Tale." Such an attack on Leicester's sponsorship of the Puritans would not mean that Nashe was a crypto-Catholic, although we have no way of knowing his private beliefs (but see Nicholl, 112–21). Insofar as the tale can be interpreted, it is Nashe's usual vehement anti-Puritanism. More detailed readings of it quickly become speculative (McGinn, "Allegory"; Petti, "Beasts"; Petti, "Political Satire"). There is, however, one piece of previously neglected evidence that does indicate Nashe alluded to Leicester. In 1594, in the epistle to his translation of *The Second Part of the French Academy*, Thomas Bowes attacks the licentious pamphlets of Greene and his followers. I have already quoted his scornful rejection of Nashe's defense of stage plays. That specific reference and a complaint that lewd books have recently gathered "under the devils banner" are evidence that Nashe was very much on his mind. So he probably believed that the Bear was a reference to Leicester when he wrote, "Are they not already growen to the boldnes, that they dare to gird at the greatest personages of all estates and callings under the fables of savage beasts, not sparing the very dead that lie in their graves?" (La Primaudaye, sig. B4v). An alternate view, that this line is a reference to Lodge's *Catharos* (1591), has much less to recommend it (A. Walker, 266–67).

The quotation from Bowes also shows how scandalized the Elizabethans were by topical satire. As the charges and countercharges of the Marprelate controversy show, libel was a serious offense, involving personal honor as well as the respect due to social classes and offices. Libel was a relatively new offense, since it depended on the growth of printing, so it was often handled by the Star Chamber rather than by the lower courts. The Star Chamber was regarded as an "arm of sovereignty" whose charge it was to punish "errors creeping into the Commonwealth, which otherwise might prove dangerous and infectious diseases" (Holdsworth, 1:504). As printed defamation, libel could be a simple tort handled under common law, but libel of a public person was seen as seditious. Even libels of private persons were regarded as punishable crimes, since they tended to provoke breaches of the peace. Neither the truth of the libel nor the death of the person defamed were defenses in the Star Chamber. So if Nashe could have been proved to have libeled Burghley or Leicester, he would have faced severe penalties, as he did when the Privy Council forced him to flee London for his part in *The Isle of Dogs* a few years later. The Star Chamber was, after all, authorized to use torture in its investigations, and in the 1590s it was increasingly concerned with libel (Holdsworth, 5:205–12; Sisson, 6–11, 186–88).

The third controversy surrounding *Pierce Penniless*, which opened Nashe to the charge that he was more an Aretino than an Erasmus, was his attack on Richard Harvey. Since Nashe could not deny that it was personal invective, he introduces it as only an example of railing, a sample of his quality as a rhetorician. He asks his readers to "put case (since I am not yet out of the Theame of Wrath) that some tired Jade belonging to the Presse, whom I never wronged in my life, hath named me expressely in Print" (which Richard Harvey had done in *The Lamb of God*). "To shewe how I can raile, thus would I begin to raile on him" (1:195). Nashe concludes the detailed lambasting of Richard Harvey by returning to the ironic claim that the invective is merely a demonstration of his skills: "*Redeo ad vos, mei Auditores,* have I not an indifferent prittye vayne in Spurgalling an Asse? if you knew how extemporall it were at this instant, and with what hast it is writ, you would say so. But I would not have you thinke that all this that is set down heere is in good earnest, for then you goe by S. Gyles, the wrong way to Westminster: but onely to shewe howe for a neede I could rayle, if I were throughly fyred" (199). The impudence of this evasion and the exuberance of the style during the passage of invective cannot mask Nashe's cruelty and vindictiveness.

The title page of *Pierce Penniless* calls attention to the inclusion of "conceipted reproofes," suggesting that the attack on Richard Harvey was important to the pamphlet's popularity. However much the Elizabethans said that satire should reprehend vice but not criticize individuals, in fact they appreciated another tradition that saw the satirist's task as more personal and destructive. The ancient satirist Archilochus was said to have provoked the suicides of his victims Lycambes and his daughter. This and other stories of the power of satire sanctioned the view that satire attacked specific people in a vindictive manner (Elliott, 257–75). For example, Nashe threatens to attack anyone who writes against him or patrons who scorn his efforts. Throughout his career he was accused of concealing topical satire in his works, and of course, in his controversy with Gabriel Harvey invective became his central purpose. Thus his reputation as encapsuled in an epigram after his death:

> Nash had Lycambes on earth living beene
> The time thou wast, his death had bin al one,
> Had he but mov'd thy tartest Muse to spleene,
> Unto the forke he had as surely gone:
>   For why there lived not that man I thinke,
>   Usde better, or more bitter gall in Inke.
>   (Nashe, 5:153)

Elizabethans appear to have delighted in vituperation even though they disapproved of it as a violation of Christian charity.

Gabriel Harvey uses Nashe's lapses into personal satire to discredit *Pierce Penniless.* In his *Four Letters* he acknowledges Nashe's talent, but lectures him that the best use of poetry is in praising virtue:

> Good sweete Oratour, be a devine Poet indeede: and use heavenly Eloquence indeede: and employ thy golden talent with amounting usance indeede: and with heroicall Cantoes honour right Vertue, & brave valour indeede: as noble Sir Philip Sidney, and gentle Maister Spencer have done, with immortall Fame: and I will bestow more complements of rare amplifications upon thee, then ever any

bestowed uppon them: or this Tounge ever affoorded; or any Aretinish mountaine of huge exaggerations can bring-foorth. (sig. F4v)

Harvey's rejection of personal satire as a mode (even as practiced by his friend Spenser in *Mother Hubberd's Tale*) is based on a conception of literature similar to Nashe's own. Both saw the poet as someone who should contribute to the good order of the commonwealth, primarily through the celebration of virtue. Harvey argues that invective and libel only contribute to disrespect and disorder: "Honour is precious: worship of value: Fame invaluable: they perillously threaten the Commonwealth, that goe about to violate the inviolable partes thereof" (sig.B1r). Because a spirit of contradiction reigns in "this Martinish and Counter-martinish age," it is better to remain mute than resort to railing. "Aretine, and the Divels oratour might very well bee spared in Christian, or Piliticke [*sic*] Comonwealthes: which cannot want contagion inough, though they bee not poysened with the venemous potions of Inckhorne witches" (sigs. E3r–E3v). Harvey sees Nashe as a "backbiter" who writes "gross scurility and impudent calumny," not as a humanistic reformer of vice.

The other complaints about *Pierce Penniless* mentioned earlier support Harvey's contention that the work contains too much personal satire to pass muster as a humanist tract. It lapses into personal attacks that are tangential to any corrective purpose the work has, and much of the satire seems to reflect the resentment of Thomas Nashe, for all that it is filtered through the persona of Pierce. In claiming that the work is an "anatomy of sin," Nashe was pretending to an objectivity that is belied most obviously by the attack on Richard Harvey, but also by other passages of invective, such as the beast fable or the railing on stingy patrons. The satire often becomes vituperative and destructive rather than charitable and reformist, although the work is too good-humored to become sour. Potential patrons like "Amyntas" were probably reluctant to associate themselves with Nashe's boldness, even if they were entertained by his wit. To the extent that patrons purchased credit and a reputation for service to the commonwealth,

Nashe had little to offer. Harvey was biased, but his rejection of Nashe's claim that *Pierce Penniless* is humanistic satire is compelling. Moreover, such criticisms must have stung Nashe, since his scandalous pamphlet hardly fit his own exalted conception of the function of literature.

THE DEVIL: CREDULITY AND SKEPTICISM

After the long supplication has been read, Pierce asks the Knight of the Post to draw on his experience as a devil and acquaint him "with the state of your infernall regiment: and what that hel is, where your Lord holdes his throne" (1:217). The Knight of the Post's account of spirits and demons has been seen as an irrelevant interpolation, added to pad out *Pierce Penniless*. Most of it is a translation, with some paraphrase, omissions, and a few minor additions, of an obscure Latin demonological tract by Georgius Pictorius, published in 1563. Copying from a single source without acknowledgment is hardly scholarship, even in an age where originality was not prized, but Nashe was not simply filling space while his invention flagged. A mock supplication to the devil was potentially offensive at a time when devils were still believed to be threatening presences. As a popular pamphlet writer and friend of Greene and Marlowe, Nashe took a risk in joking about traffic with the devil, even though there was a literary tradition of mocking the devil, as can be seen in a number of Tudor interludes. The passage on devils, as dull as Nashe himself admits it to be, serves as an avowal of orthodoxy. It may be secondhand, but he could hardly draw on his own experience or make it up out of whole cloth.

In calling Nashe the "Devil's Orator," Gabriel Harvey sought to portray him as a writer who served the devil's ends, however much he professed orthodoxy. Harvey evokes the ghosts of Aretino, Tarlton, and Greene in admonishing Nashe not to play wantonly "with the highest and deepest subjectes of spirituall contemplation: Heaven, and Hell, Paradise, and Purgatory." There is enough in the world to engage Nashe's invention without his offering "vayne Hyperboles of the reverende mysteries of God" (*Four Letters*, sigs. F4r–F4v). Harvey is probably pretending to a greater concern with irreverence than he feels in an effort to discredit Nashe, but the charge was serious at a time when Puritans believed Satan was using profane books to undermine religion. Harvey also represents himself as seeking Nashe's personal salvation in his effort to reform his mode of writing. His accusation that the work is diabolical may be a result of deliberate misreading or a critical judgment that the work is in fact unorthodox.

The accusation was damaging enough to provoke Nashe's *Strange News*, which was retitled *The Apology of Pierce Penniless* in a 1593 reissue. In addition to denying that Pierce is simply himself or that he included topical allusions, Nashe denies that his work is a "diabolicall Discourse," except in the sense that it treated the nature of spirits; "in that far fetcht sense may the famous *defensative against supposed Prophecies* and *the Discoverie of Witchcraft* be called notorious Diabolicall discourses, as well as the *Supplication*, for they also intreate of the illusions and sundrie operations of spirits" (1:308–9). Both of these works were in fact important documents in the growth of rationalism. Henry Howard, earl of Northampton, wrote *A Defensative Against the Poison of Supposed Prophecies* (1583) in an effort to discredit all spurious predictions of future events. The work was written because Howard's ancestors had been disastrously misled by prophecies, but it was published because of the "great disorder" caused by Richard Harvey's *Astrological Discourse*, "chiefly among the simple and unlearned people." [2]

---

2. McKerrow doubted that the work was a reply to Richard Harvey (5:166–67), and Don Cameron Allen saw it as a reply in a general sense (*Star-Crossed Renaissance*, 112–16). Although most of *The Defensative* was written before Richard Harvey published his predictions, the title page alludes to the recent controversy. Near the end of the book Howard writes, "I could adjoyne the pregnant follies of some other freshe in memorie . . . saving that it is the part of no good nature, eyther to insulte on those, that are alreadye overthrowne with shame, or to agravate, affliction and miserye" (sigs. 2G4v-2H1r). Howard notes that he has been collecting material for his book since he was fifteen, but is now forced into publication by circumstances (sig. 2K1r). Thus, there may be an ironic edge to Nashe's mentioning this book in a pamphlet answering Gabriel Harvey, although Gabriel himself had reservations about his brother's astrology.

Nashe, who had ridiculed Richard Harvey's predictions himself, shared Howard's skepticism about astrology and borrowed frequently from *A Defensative* (Harlow, "A Source"). Reginald Scot's *Discovery of Witchcraft* (1584) is unique for its time in its wholesale rejection of witchcraft as a fraud and delusion. Scot's work is in fact so skeptical that it was judged a diabolical discourse by its many opponents (Anglo).

In *Pierce Penniless*, the discussion of devils and spirits is introduced as a refutation of skepticism. Pierce asks the Knight of the Post whether hell is the place of legend, where the userer has to drink molten gold and the glutton eat nothing but toads, or "whether (as some phantasticall refyners of philosophie will needes perswade us) hell is nothing but error, and that none but fooles and Idiotes and Machanicall men, that have no learning, shall be damned" (1:218). In this way Nashe contrasts credulity with skepticism, before offering a middle way with his translation of Pictorius's pseudoscientific demonology. The Knight of the Post discounts imaginative speculation about the nature of hell, then explains how the skeptical view can reduce devils to moral allegories: "Some men there be that, building too much upon reason, perswade themselves that there are no Divels at all, but that this word *Daemon* is such another morall of mischeife, as the Poets Dame Fortune is of mishap . . . so that the Divell (as they make it) is onely a pestilent humour in a man, of pleasure, profit, or policie, that violently carries him away to vanitie, villanie, or monstrous hypocrisie" (219–20). This rationalistic explanation of moral or "earthly" devils is presented as a useful descriptive approach to human behavior, but Nashe follows Pictorius in rejecting its skeptical implications.

Demonology was a vexing problem for the Elizabethans, an area where conflicting opinions were more the rule than a firm set of beliefs. The Reformation had sought to purge religion of magic: both Puritans and Anglicans were scornful of the more superstitious aspects of medieval folk religion. Purgatory was dismissed as a myth, the saints were reduced to heroes, and ceremonial remissions of sin were abandoned. The Puritans wanted yet further reformation, but at the same time they had a vivid sense of the devil's imminence and active role in human life, so were fearful of witchcraft. Tracts on witchcraft and demons advanced a variety of opinions, ranging from Scot's skepticism to the rather credulous accounts of witchcraft trials. Most Protestant works tried to assert that devils were real and witchcraft possible but that the devil worked more through illusions than through miraclelike interventions. Occultists and Neoplatonists sought to incorporate demons into their cosmologies in pseudoscientific fashion (West, 15–53).

This intellectual debate over the nature of demons intersected with traditional folk beliefs and superstitions. Whatever his role in Christian theology, in village life the devil served to explain apparently preternatural happenings, particularly untoward misfortunes. An inexplicable illness or a crop failure might be evidence of witchcraft, particularly if there was a malevolent old woman in the neighborhood who bore a grudge against the victim. Village witchcraft was more a matter of black magic than of heresy, and as such it was part of a complex system of superstitious magic that was often quite tangential to Christian doctrine. Theologians saw all such magic as trafficking with the devil, although in practice the devils involved were the semicomic figures of folk myth rather than that embodiment of evil, Satan (K. Thomas, 435–583). Puritans and Anglicans alike were as interested in exorcising such superstitions as they were in exorcising devils. Nashe himself made a minor contribution to the effort in his *Terrors of the Night*, which questions folk superstitions.

Caution was necessary, though, because the devil was considered theologically necessary, even if belief in his existence was cluttered with superstitions. Sir Thomas Browne put it succinctly in the next century: "I have ever beleeved, and doe now know, that there are Witches; they that doubt of these, doe not onely deny them, but Spirits; and are obliquely and upon consequence a sort, not of Infidels, but Atheists" (29). King James accused Reginald Scot of Sadduceeism, a heresy that denied spirits, and was reported to have ordered all copies of *The Discovery of Witchcraft* burned. Scot himself was careful to assert his orthodox belief in the existence of spirits, although he defined them as being incapable of any interaction with the physical world. But his position was unusual: most Elizabethans apparently experienced the devil as a personal threat. Through witchcraft and magic, possession and temptation, Satan and his cohorts played an active role in Elizabethan life. Mocking the devil was courageous, if foolhardy; mocking belief in the devil would have been doing the devil's work: "It is a policy of the Devil to persuade us that there is no Devil" (K. Thomas, 476).

Since *Pierce Penniless* was written in English in a popular format, it ill behooved Nashe to let his mockery of "the high and mightie Prince of Darknesse, Donsell dell Lucifer" seem to be scoffing at belief in the devil. The passages from Pictorius are included to offset any such implication. Nashe's labors as a translator were also necesary because his conception of evil does tend to be rationalistic rather than diabolical. The image of London life in *Pierce Penniless* is more a matter of "wit's misery and the world's madness" than of "discovering the devils incarnate of this age"—to quote the title and subtitle of a 1596 work by Thomas Lodge which also tries to amalgamate a theological and rationalist explanation of evil. Pierce's supplication is a complaint that people have usurped the devil's role as a source of evil: he tells the devil that a number of uncharitable cormorants have "incurd the daunger of a *Praemunire* with medling with matters that properly concerne your owne person" (1:165). Nashe is being witty, but his conception of vice is of a humanly motivated malignancy.

The medieval format of the seven deadly sins in *Pierce Penniless* is used in ways that anticipate social psychology. The emphasis is on how a perturbation of the mind like envy or wrath causes men and women to pervert or abuse their social roles. The effect can be subtle and perceptive, as in the description of a typical young prodigal:

> A yoong Heyre or Cockney, that is his Mothers Darling, if hee have playde the waste-good at the Innes of the Court or about London, and that neither his Students pension, nor his unthrifts credite, will serve to maintaine his Collidge of whores any longer, falles in a quarrelling humor with his fortune, because she made him not King of the Indies, and sweares and stares, after ten in the

hundreth, that nere a such Pesant as his Father or brother shall keepe him under: hee will to the sea, and teare the gold out of the Spaniards throats, but he will have it, byrlady. (1:170–71).

Such passages anticipate the vogue of Theophrastian characters, which, in their emphasis on the individual playing social roles, were more psychological than medieval "estates" satire (Boyce, 69–71). The specific details quite naturally entice readers into supposing that an actual person is intended; in this case Thomas Lodge has been proposed by modern critics (McKerrow, 4:100; Nicholl, 59–60; Tenney, 130–31).

Pierce Penniless is rationalistic in its emphasis on how people through folly or hypocrisy make themselves into social stereotypes; even viciousness is likely to be an extreme affectation in Nashe's London. In such a world the devil's role is secondary; people are more free agents than agents of the devil. Pierce asks Satan: "You goodman wandrer about the world, how doe yee spende your time, that you do not rid us of these pestilent members? you are unworthy to have an office, if you can execute it no better. Behold another enemy of mankinde, besides thy selfe, exalted in the South, Philip of Spaine" (1:184). Nashe was hardly a philosopher and probably would have been unable to account for any discrepancy between his orthodox beliefs and his perception of the way people act in society. At issue are complex questions about how the devil is manifested in the world that are not to Nashe's purpose. His tendencies toward rationalism were a product of common sense and alienated cynicism rather than philosophical inquiry. For all that he paraded his learning, he was street wise, to use a modern term, rather than book wise. He presumably had no personal difficulty in squaring his orthodoxy with his secularized attitudes towards social behavior.

Nashe was not a systematic thinker, but skepticism was fashionable, and many of its attitudes met his needs. Barnaby Rich commented scornfully on the way young gentlemen affected "to be curious in cavilling, propounding captious questions, therby to shew a singularitie of their wisedomes: for the helping whereof, they diligently studie bookes for the purpose, as Cornelius Agrippa, *de vanitate scientiarum,* and other like" (sigs. H1v–H2r). Marlowe and Greene, as well as Raleigh and his circle, all dabbled in this fashionable skepticism without being full-fledged Pyrrhonists or forming a "school of night." From Agrippa's *Of the Vanity and Uncertainty of Arts and Sciences,* one of his most quoted books, Nashe acquired an easy cynicism about other people's learning. He even knew a translation of Sextus Empiricus (Sprott). Nashe would have disavowed any heterodox intentions, but the attitudes of skeptical authors found their way into his works. The account of spirits in *Pierce Penniless* claims to be a refutation of skepticism and of those who build too much on reason, but this encapsuled expression of orthodoxy cannot offset the playful skepticism of the rest of the pamphlet.

This playfulness, the impudency, and the singular style have a melancholic undertone, although Pierce's discontent is initially presented in a comic fashion. Nashe tries to distinguish Pierce's irony from the estrangement of the true malcontent, a social type who receives one of his earliest portraits in this work. The malcontent starves himself so he can dine once or twice a term at an expensive ordinary and affects "a scornfull melancholy in his gate and countenance." He talks "as though our common welth were but a mockery of government, and our Majestrates fooles, who wronged him in not looking into his deserts, not imploying him in State matters, and that, if more regard were not had of him very shortly, the whole Realme should have a misse of him, & he would go (I mary would he) where he should be more accounted of" (1:170). At the start of the pamphlet Pierce also threatens to exile himself in his discontent. Pierce is more ironic and orthodox in his beliefs, but he is also a malcontent. Scornful melancholy and a feeling of personal grievance show through in spite of Nashe's efforts to use his persona to diffuse his anger.

Pierce Penniless is not a diabolical discourse, except in the eyes of Gabriel Harvey and of those Puritans who regarded all profane pamphlets as the devil's work. For the most part it is too conventional and playful to pose much threat to the orthodoxy of its readers. But not all of its satire was directed at approved targets, and often the destructive potential of the mode shows through as anger and envy (Lecocq, 299–315). Moreover, Nashe's mastery of Pierce is incomplete: instead of being a comic character, Pierce becomes a spokesman for discontent with Elizabethan society. Elizabethan ideology was uncomfortable with any criticism, particularly criticism disseminated among the lower ranks of society. Thus, the charge that Nashe was the devil's orator was damaging, although overstated. When the Harveys linked him with Martin Marprelate and the traitor Babington, they were being grossly unfair to his manifest orthodoxy, but *Pierce Penniless* was too outspoken and singular to be entirely safe, or to gain Nashe the respectability he needed if he was to receive sustained patronage.

CHAPTER
4

Self-Effacing Authorship

THE reception of *Pierce Penniless* shows how vulnerable Nashe was in a society that valued authority more than authorship. The defensive epistle to the second edition is evidence of this, as are Nashe's efforts to justify himself in *Strange News*, although it is also a rather arrogant work. Basic to his difficulties was that rhetoric was suspected to be an art of lying, particularly when it was self-conscious and ostentatious (Crewe, 21-44). Nashe's singularity and extemporaneous style violated the prevailing Ciceronian sense of decorum. Moreover, Nashe was not self-effacing and humble enough, except in the prefaces to his works and there not very convincingly. He projected a self-assured authorial presence that contrasted with his actual marginal status as a writer. Whatever the style and beliefs of the historical Nashe, his creation, Pierce Penniless, is irreverent and arrogant. Denying his own prodigality, he asserts his right to criticize society and to be specific like Aretino. The popularity of the work suggests Harvey was right in his fear that Pierce would appeal to the discontented and contentious elements in Elizabethan society.

Nashe's arrogance was to find its apotheosis in *The Unfortunate Traveler*, where fiction protected him, and in the quarrel with Gabriel Harvey, where it did not. Here we are concerned with two potentially controversial works, *The Terrors of the Night* and *Christ's Tears over Jerusalem*, and the strategies they use to avoid seeming objectionably arrogant. Caution was necessary because both works deal with "subjects of spiritual contemplation," topics Harvey had warned Nashe to avoid. Like *Pierce Penniless, The Terrors of the Night* raises questions about diabolical intervention, although it is cautious that its skepticisms about witchcraft and visions not seem to deny the devil's existence. The authorial voice of this slim pamphlet is self-effacing in the manner of an essayist: the work pretends to no consequence and is allusive rather than outright in its questioning of superstition.

Although written in 1593, *The Terrors of the Night* was not published until 1594, probably because Nashe feared controversy. His insecure relationship to orthodox values—hammered home for him by Harvey's criticisms and the horrors of the 1592–93 epidemic—caused a crisis in Nashe's literary career. The disapproval of arrogant satire threatened his career externally and presumably internally in the form of self-doubts. Those self-doubts would have been aggravated by his tenuous situation: the temporary patronage of Whitgift and George Carey gave him the freedom to write the five works that followed *Pierce Penniless* in a two-year period, but the controversial reception of his more outspoken satire undermined his support. The context was relentlessly debilitating poverty: Nashe's taunt that Harvey was holed up in London during the worst days of the plague while he enjoyed the hospitality of his patrons reflects back on the precariousness of Nashe's own situation. In fact Nashe was soon back on the streets of London, scratching out a living with his pen.

His fear of frowns and disfavor motivated an artistic about-face in *Christ's Tears over Jerusalem,* a long religious tract published in the late summer of 1593. It is both his most self-effacing and most arrogant work; in it he disowns the ethos of his former works and takes on the persona of Christ. As conventional literature *Christ's Tears* is dreadful, but as a failed experiment in an extreme style and a new polemic mode, it reveals much about the context of Nashe's career. Nashe substitutes a highly emotional rhetoric for his usual witty, improvisational style, renouncing satire in favor of an overwrought, pathetic appeal that is sensationalistic and at times hysteric. It tries to override the limitations of rhetoric and work directly on the emotions of its readers. The hysteria invites conjecture that

Nashe had undergone or was in the midst of an emotional crisis, but the complete conversion from his former self that he professes is perhaps more a rhetorical than a psychological change. When *Christ's Tears* proved unsuccessful, Nashe quickly enough reverted to his former style and, according to Harvey, to his former personal demeanor. It is an excursus from the main direction of Nashe's career, but its renunciation of satire, its rhetorical excesses, and its criticisms of Elizabethan society provide another perspective on Nashe and his perception of the flaws in the orthodox ideology.

SUPERNATURAL SOLICITATIONS: *THE TERRORS OF THE NIGHT*

Nashe again trod the fine line between credulity and skepticism in *The Terrors of the Night*, a short pamphlet occasioned by the diabolical vision of a dying man and by humanity's perennial fear of things that go bump in the night. As in the demonological section of *Pierce Penniless*, Nashe tries to distinguish between the rational world of cause and effect, the discredited realm of miracles and magic, and the overarching framework of doctrinal truth. Again he asserts his belief in the existence of the devil while mocking anecdotal reports of his machinations. Nashe's position is orthodox but rationalistic: the devil should be advanced as an explanation for phenomena only after all natural explanations have been exhausted. These include the various ways the mind can be fooled both by its own melancholia and by the chicanery of others. Such an approach requires an empirical sifting of data. What are the circumstances surrounding a supernatural event that support or question its validity? Nashe is much influenced by those two great skeptics Agrippa and Reginald Scot and by the more moderate rationalism of Henry Howard, earl of Northampton. *The Terrors of the Night* is too modest to have a place in the development of secular thought, but these few pages of skepticism about the supernatural nevertheless reflect the decline of magic in the face of rationalistic explanation (K. Thomas; D. Wallace).

The essay format of *The Terrors of the Night* results from

Nashe's need to present his topic gingerly. By keeping his prose casual and self-effacing he avoids the appearance of arrogance. For example, the text begins with disarming insouciance: "A Litle to beguile time idlely discontented, and satisfie some of my solitary friends heere in the Countrey, I have hastily undertooke to write of the wearie fancies of the Night, wherein if I weary none with my weak fancies, I will herafter leane harder on my penne and fetch the petegree of my praise from the utmost of paines" (1:345). The work makes no claims for itself or its author. In casual asides Nashe keeps his readers conscious of the work as an extemporal performance without any serious purpose or pretentious import. His success at being inconsequential kept the work from attracting adverse attention, but it has also made it easy to dismiss the work as a fugitive performance. McKerrow regarded it as having "so desultory a character that any attempt at analysis would be useless" (4:197). G. R. Hibbard saw that "the work is meant as an attack on superstition and credulity," but he also claimed that it is "one of the first, if not the first, prose works in English that exists for no other end than to give the pleasure a discriminating reader can find in a difficulty overcome, the difficulty in this particular case being that of making something out of nothing by sheer literary artifice" (113, 118).

But the extemporal style and casual structure of the work are a defensive strategy, not an exercise in spinning out words. Though the pamphlet is subtitled *A Discourse on Apparitions*, it is not really a discourse or treatise but an essay. For want of the term Nashe is at a loss what to call it; at one point he compares it to "an old Praeface" (1:382). To account for its "botched up" structure, he compares it to a dream: "To say the troth, all this whole Tractate is but a dreame, for my wits are not halfe awaked in it: & yet no golden dreame, but a leaden dreame is it" (360–61). As in a dream, the progression of ideas is associational rather than strictly logical. Its more tangential digressions are excused by the fact that its form is like that of its subject: "Come, come, I am entraunced from my Text, I wote well, and talke idlely in my sleepe longer than I should" (361). The text is also like its subject in its emotional effect on the reader, who may be subject to nightmares because of the pamphlet, and on the author, who becomes too involved in what he is writing:

> Fie, fie, was ever poore fellow so farre benighted in an old wives tale of divells and urchins. Out upon it, I am wearie of it, for it hath caused such a thicke fulsome Serena to descend on my braine, that now my penne makes blots as broad as a furd stomacher, and my muse inspyres me to put out my candle and goe to bed: and yet I wyll not neyther, till, after all these nights revells, I have solemnly bid you good night; as much to saye as tell you how you shall have a good night, and sleep quietly without affrightment and annoyance. (384)

The explanation that the work is like an old wives' tale or a dream is Nashe's justification for a format that did not yet exist as a literary genre. Like an essay, the pamphlet is loosely organized and lacks a well-defined topic; rather, it is a series of thoughts occasioned by an event and linked through the ethos of the writer. Its art is clearer if it is seen in terms of the rhetorical problem Nashe faced. The main purpose is to discredit the foolish terrors of the night without appearing to be so skeptical as to be unorthodox. The reception of *Pierce Penniless* meant Nashe had to guard against any suggestion that he was taking it on himself to promote either credulity or skepticism. He needed no more controversy, particularly at a time when he was trying to secure the patronage of the respectable Carey family.

The essay format and casual style also allow Nashe to be personal without being obtrusive or arrogant. After reporting the superstitious views of "aged mumping beldams," he can comment, "When I was a little childe, I was a great auditor of theirs, and had all their witchcrafts at my fingers endes, as perfit as good morrow and good even" (1:369). He can be as personal about the process of writing the pamphlet: "I have rid a false gallop these three or foure pages: now I care not if I breathe mee, and walke soberly and demurely halfe a dozen turnes, like a grave Citizen going about to take the ayre" (368). The first-person pronouns are employed with unusual frequency for an Elizabethan work. As in Montaigne's essays, which were not yet translated nor evidently known to Nashe, we are conscious of a topic being presented to us as it exists in another person's consciousness. Yet the effect is not quite one of meditation, since the other consciousness is depicted as someone addressing an audience of readers. The ethos that Nashe develops in *The Terrors of the Night* is deferential and open-minded, not arrogant like Pierce Penniless or defiant like the Nashe of *Strange News*.

Because the work is indirect and ironic, it is difficult to tell when it is serious and when it is mocking. Often seriousness slides into mockery in the manner of a tall tale. For example, the work begins with a serious account of the devil's affinity for the night, then goes on to affirm that there are hosts of subordinate devils under Lucifer. The exaggerated description of their number is tongue-in-cheek without being openly skeptical: "There is not a roome in anie mans house, but is pestred and close packed with a campe royeall of divels." At what point does the grotesque picture of a world crowded with devils become ludicrous? "Infinite millions of them wil hang swarming about a worm-eaten nose" (349). The exaggeration undercuts folk superstitions about devils and perhaps calls their very existence into question: "Not so much as Tewksburie mustard but hath a spirit in it or els it would never bite so" (350). Nashe himself was probably not certain where his belief in the reality of devils parted company from old wives' tales of their intervention in the world.

Nashe also tests the credulity of his readers in a digression on the wonders of Iceland that casts doubt on witchcraft fables. He reports a prevalent belief that in Iceland "(as I have read and heard) spirites in the lykenesse of ones father or mother after they are deceased, doo converse with them as naturally as if they were living" (359). His skepticism about this example of witchcraft becomes clear as he reports other "facts" about Iceland that are increasingly preposterous and apparently of his own devising. There is "the bottomlesse Lake Vether, over which no fowle flies but is frozen to death, nor anie man passeth but he is senselesly benummed like a statue of marble." If his readers believe that of Iceland, will they believe that "they have Ale that they carry in their pockets lyke glue, and ever when they would drinke, they set it on the fire and melt it" (360)? The account of Iceland concludes with an apology for digressing, but the actual effect is to set tales of witchcraft in a context of other tall tales. Nashe does not draw firm lines between superstitions and orthodox belief, but his comic exaggerations elicit skepticism from all but the most naive of readers.

Nashe's doubts about fables of witchcraft and the omnipresence of devils create a skeptical context for the main topic, the significance of dreams and apparitions. He rejects the notion that dreams are supernatural in origin or content. Just as extreme cases of melancholia lead to hallucinations, so does everyday melancholy engender dreams: "A dreame is nothing els but a bubling scum or froath of the fancie, which the day hath left undigested; or an after feast made of the fragments of idle imaginations" (355). This rationalistic explanation of dreams is adapted from Henry Howard's *Defensative against the Poison of Supposed Prophecies* (Harlow, "A Source"). Since dreams are "but the Eccho of our conceipts in the day" (356), without occult properties, the interpretation of dreams is a variety of penny-ante magic and the academic study of them, a pseudoscience: "Those that will harken any more after Dreames, I referre them to Artimidorus, Synesius, & Cardan, with many others which onely I have heard by their names, but I thanke God had never the plodding patience to reade, for if they bee no better than some of them I have perused, every weatherwise old wife might write better" (361). Nashe also follows Howard in discounting any prophetic content in dreams, except in the special cases of visions recorded in the Bible or ancient texts.

Nashe sums up his view of dreams and the central thesis of his pamphlet in a sentence: "When all is said, melancholy is the mother of dreames, and of all terrours of the night whatsoever" (357). For an Elizabethan, this is a bold dismissal of superstition and the occult. Nashe further risks offending his readers in his description of how self-proclaimed "wise men" take advantage of the credulity first of simple people, then of courtiers. "Our chiefe noted Augurers and Soothsayers in England at this day" are charlatans whose magic serves only to pick men's purses. Whether or not the details of the account are topical, the blanket rejection of traffickers in the occult is audacious. It is caused by doubts that the devil involves himself directly in human affairs. Nashe claims, "The divell of late is growen a puritane, and cannot away with anie ceremonies" (367). In ancient times, "I will not gainsaye but hee was wont to jest and sport wyth countrey people, and play the good fellowe amongst kitchin-wenches, sitting in an evening by the fire side making of possets, and come a woing to them in the likenes of a cooper, or a curmogionly purchaser." But "now there is no goodnes in him but miserablenes and covetousnes" (367–68). Behind his joking, Nashe is advancing a view that the devil operates through the workings of sin, not through direct interventions in the lives or dreams of individuals. He is contributing to that gradual redefinition of the devil which would eventually reduce him to a symbolic existence.

This skepticism about magic was controversial: if visionary dreams and apparitions were not caused by the devil or witchcraft but by melancholy, then some very powerful people were caught up in the delusion. The specific visions that occasioned the pamphlet may well have been those experienced by Thomas Cotton prior to his death in 1593, but even if this identification is incorrect, the possibility is a reminder that the pamphlet ran the risk of offending the dead man's heirs. Between the time the pamphlet was written and published, Fernando Stanley, the earl of Derby, who was in all probability both the Lord S. to whom "The Choice of Valentines" was dedicated and the "Amyntas" praised in *Pierce Penniless,* died under mysterious circumstances. The hallucinations he experienced were attributed to witchcraft; Nashe's patron Sir George Carey undertook to apprehend one of the suspected witches (Harlow, "Nashe"). Nashe's skeptical attitude toward such phenomena thus had to be expressed with great delicacy lest he offend people in a position to harm his career.

For this reason the account of the dying man's vision is framed with cautionary statements that witchcraft should not be excluded as an explanation. Even though the pamphlet has ridiculed dream interpretations and prophecies at some length and mocked tales of the devil's intervention in the world—borrowing from Howard and citing Reginald Scot—Nashe backs away from the implicit conclusion in his transition to the tale: "I write not this, for that I thinke there are no true apparitions or prodigies, but to shew how easily we may be flouted if we take not great heed, with our own anticke suppositions. I will tell you a strange tale tending to this nature: whether of true melancholy or true appartition, I will not take upon me to determine" (378). He explains that in February last (1592 or 1593) a country gentleman of good credit fell ill and experienced a number of waking visions which he related to a great man of the land (perhaps Robert Cotton if the gentleman was in fact his father Thomas). Nashe promises to give an objective account of the incident: "beleeve it or condemn it, as you shal see cause, for I leave it to be censured indifferently" (378).

The account is not, however, very objective. In re-creating the visions, Nashe adds ironic details and grotesque images that burlesque what must have originally seemed a frightening example of diabolical temptation. As in the digression on Iceland, the account becomes increasingly incredible. The devils who tempt the dying man with treasures had "faces far blacker than anie ball of Tobacco, great glaring eyes that had whole shelves of Kentish oysters in them, and terrible wyde mouthes, whereof not one of them but would well have made a case for Molenax great Gloabe of the world" (379). Perhaps this is just an attempt to be vivid, but the "goodly lustfull Bonarobaes" that present themselves to the dying man are more a comic act than incarnations of evil: "Then did ther, for the third pageant, present themselves unto him, an inveigling troupe of naked Virgins" who "majestically paced about the chamber, to the end their naturall unshelled shining mother pearle proportions might be more imprintingly apprehended." But the dying man rejects their "impudent profer unto him of theyr lascivious embraces"—"a cold comfort," Nashe comments, "to poore wenches no better cloathed" (380–81). The ill man is temporarily relieved by "a most precious extract quintessence" which causes him to think he sees "all the fore-named Enterluders at once hand over head leap, plunge, & drowne themselves in puddles and ditches hard by." But the cure is temporary: within four hours the man suffered a relapse, and two days later he died.

Nashe claims to be offering an exact report of the event: "God is my witnesse, in all this relation, I borrowe no essential part from stretcht out invention, nor have I one jot abusde my informations; onely for the recreation of my Readers, whom loath to tyre with a course homespunne tale, that should dull them woorse than Holland cheese, heere and there I welt and garde it with allusive exornations & comparisons: and yet me thinks it comes off too goutie and lumbring" (382). In fact he uses the ironic effect of his exaggerated style to guy the narrative even as he relates it (Hibbard, 110–12). His pretense of objectivity is partly a comic pose, partly a defense against seeming to mock belief in diabolic apparitions or offending any powerful friends of the dead gentleman. The use of comic details in this tale and elsewhere in the pamphlet has the effect of deflating the wonders described without denying that they might be real. The "amplifications" Nashe adds exaggerate, not the terror of apparitions, but their foolishness.

There may also be a touch of whistling in the dark in the pamphlet's dismissal of nighttime fears; Nashe writes from a daytime perspective, but his description of how dreams can trouble a melancholic sleeper shows that he takes the effects of dreams seriously, even if he denies them any occult qualities. A case can be made that he had himself in mind, although he never asserts it. In a discussion of lingering agonies, he mentions his own situation: there is no greater misery than a "long depending hope frivolously defeated": "It is a cowardly feare that is not resolute inough to despaire. It is like a pore hunger-starvd wretch at sea, who still in expectation of a good voyage, endures more miseries than Job. He that writes this can tell, for he hath never had good voyage in his life but one" (374). Nashe is referring to the hospitality of Sir George Carey and his family, who were apparently the only people to provide him with sustained patronage. Logically the praise of Carey is a digression included to flatter a patron, but psychologically Carey's support is related to Nashe's own ability to resist the terrors of the night. The conventions of praise do not account for a personal note: "Whatsoever minutes intermission I have of calmed content, or least respite to call my wits together, principall and immediate proceededth from him." He continues: "Through him my tender wainscot Studie doore is delivered from much assault and battrie: through him I looke into, and am lookt on in the world; from whence otherwise I were a wretched banished exile" (375). These are the words of a man who knew the isolation that caused melancholy and bad dreams.

They are also the words of someone who prefers the security of an orthodox social role to the independence of the masterless man. In a sentence Nashe recorded his dependence on the social order: "I acknowledge all redundant prostrate vassailage to the royall descended Familie of the Careys: but for whom, my spirit long ere this had expyred, and my pen serv'd as a puniard to gall my owne hart" (375). His need for a patron was emotional as well as economic. This explains why his dedications are so fulsome that they seem flattery or parody. The dedication of *The Terrors of the Night* ascribes to Sir George Carey's daughter Elizabeth a supernatural perfection: "True Stemme of Nobilitie, out-flourishing your sexe or your age; pure saint-like picture of Sobrietie and Modestie, sacred and immaculate virgin Starre, cleare (if anie living) from the originall sin of thought: give me leave (though contemptible & abject) once more to sacrifice my worthles wit to your glorie" (341). The false note here is not so much a matter of insincerity as of intemperate idealization, motivated by the desperation evidenced in the self-abasement. The religious overtones are not merely metaphoric: for orthodox Elizabethans the social order embodied spiritual values. Elizabeth Carey was not in fact free from original sin, but as a member of a "royally descended" family she represented the traditional values Nashe revered.

Perhaps the exaggerated praise of Elizabeth Carey verges on parody; by the time *The Terrors of the Night* was published Nashe was again experiencing "long depending hope frivolously defeated." He consented to publication after at least a year's delay because, he claims, scriveners had been profiting from the sale of manuscript copies. The epistle "To Master or Goodman Reader, generally dispersed East or West" reveals an antagonism towards critics that contrasts sharply with the eagerness to please in the dedication. By 1594, when the epistle was written, *Pierce Penniless* and *Christ's Tears over Jerusalem* had landed Nashe in considerable difficulty, both with Puritan critics and civic authorities. This is what he has in mind when he writes, "Martin Momus and splaiefooted Zoylus" who formerly "kept a foule stir in Poules Church-yard, are now revived againe: and like wanton Whelpes that have wormes in their tungs, slaver and betouse everie paper they meete withall" (343). He defies their censure: "I will not beg of them neither, go the world never so hard, no not so much as a good word: but if in word or deed I hear they wrong me, Ile meet them right if I can" (344). Still hopeful that he would find a secure patron, Nashe was despairing of the public reception of his works.

The Terrors of the Night is an effort at exorcism, not in the disallowed medieval manner, but in the new rationalistic fashion that culminates for us in psychoanalysis. Like an analyst, Nashe sees dreams acquiring power in proportion to the guilt and the anxiety of the dreamer. Dreams and other threats of the night originate in the mind of the troubled person, not in a supernatural realm. In the case of the dying gentleman Nashe does not deny the possibility of witchcraft, but his ironic account suggests he thinks the "pageants" were hallucinations. Nashe neither affirms nor denies, but the satiric tone of his pamphlet reduces much of demonology and witchcraft to skimble-skamble stuff. The real threat in the watches of the night is not external evil but the troubled conscience of the sleeper. Nighttime terrors are lightly mocked, but Nashe is eloquent about the experience of guilt and despair, perhaps because melancholy was a familiar companion. In writing of this topic, he may well have been exorcising his own private demons as well as those of his readers. But Nashe never says this. Already under attack for personal arrogance, he wrote for readers who did not expect introspection from authors. He could not include his own experience as an example as freely as Montaigne did when he treated similar topics. Without Montaigne as a precedent, Nashe cannot move himself to center stage, any more than he could develop the full implications of his skepticism. These limitations prevent *The Terrors of the Night* from achieving its full potential, but it has merits and charms enough to warrant a better fate than it has obtained.

PERSONATING PASSION: *CHRIST'S TEARS OVER JERUSALEM*

The severity of the plague and the growing distrust of satire inspired Nashe to write *Christ's Tears over Jerusalem*, the serious endeavor he had been promising his readers. His most ambitious work, it attempts nothing less than to "moove secure England to true sorrow and contrition." To accomplish this Nashe puts off his former self and takes on the role of Christ in a lament over the fall of Jerusalem that is intended as a warning to London. Then, as a "mortal," he describes the destruction of Jerusalem in highly charged rhetoric before turning to London and anatomizing its sins. The whole work is a bizarre bid for the respectability that eluded Nashe in his career. Even as he renounces arrogance, he takes it upon himself to offer a controversial explanation of the social sins that caused the epidemic, an explanation that aroused as much protest as his secular works. In assaying divinity he wrought confusion. A few years later when the actors were in trouble he could quip, "The players as if they had writt another Christs tears, ar piteously persecuted by the L. Maior & aldermen" (5:194).

While Nashe's temporary departure from satire may reflect a personal crisis, it more certainly is a response to criticisms of the mode, criticisms to be taken more seriously in time of plague. Both prophecy and satire seek to depict vice and follies vividly in order to move their audiences to repentance, but critics feared satire was tainted by its secular attitudes and by the implicit arrogance of its authors. Under the influence of the Puritans, prophetic tracts with satiric overtones became a minor genre. Some of them, like George Gascoigne's *Spoyles of Antwerp*, were occasioned by the fall of Antwerp in 1576; other examples of this "literature of warning" revived the story of the fall of Jerusalem (Mackerness; Pratt). Related to such specific warnings of impending disaster are the tracts of social criticism such as Stephen Gosson's *School of Abuse* (1579) and Stubbes's *Anatomy of Abuses,* which were as strident in their denunciations of sin but less apocalyptic in their predictions of divine retribution. Playwrights and popular pamphleteers attempted the mode, but clerics and the Puritan social critics regarded writers like Greene, Lodge, and Nashe as interlopers, guilty of presumption in their unauthorized promotion of their private views about what ailed contemporary society. It was the same charge Nashe had made against Stubbes. This jurisdictional dispute between Puritan reformists and the secular satirists was exacerbated by the distrust of satire caused by the Marprelate controversy (Lecocq, 109–19).

An example of the denunciation of satire will clarify why Nashe turned away from the mode to write a jeremiad. In 1592 William Cupper published *Certain Sermons Concerning God's Late Visitation in the City of London,* which anticipates Nashe in its attempt to explain what sins have caused the plague. In an epistle to the reader, Cupper recapitulates the complaints of Edward Dering about the abuse of printing, but adds that a new abuse has been added since Dering wrote in 1572: "I meane those prophane and satirical pamphleters, who have opened their mouths against God, and have blotted not only papers, but heaven and earth with their venemous pens, not sparing to name persons unspotted of the world, and through their sides to give (as much as in them lieth) a deadly wound to the holy religion of God and the glorious Gospell of Jesus Christ" (Cupper, sig. A6r). Cupper also denounces the arrogance of authors who attempt serious topics without any authority. He need not apologize for any deficiencies in his work,

> seeing that so manie private persons, tickeled with vaineglorie, blinded with selfe-love, bewitched with gaine, or such lyke carnall affections, are bold in the pride of their wittes, uppon the reading of a fewe bookes, or the hearing of a fewe Sermons, to thrust forth a Pamphlette into the worlde, neither reverncing the grave censure of learned men, nor fearing the severitie of the judgements of God against such as do take his name in

vaine, but breaking the bounds and venturing uppon those thinges, whereunto, neither their skill, nor calling, will give anie warrant to their consciences. (Sig. A4v)

Cupper later claims such contempt of God and his holy word is one of the causes of the plague.

Whether or not Cupper had Nashe in mind, 1593 was not an auspicious year for satire, nor for a lay person to write a religious tract. In his epistle to the reader, Nashe bids "a hundred unfortunate farewels to fantasticall Satirisme." He confesses that in the satiric vein "I mispent my spirite, and prodigally conspir'd against good houres" (2:12). Apologizing for his previous works and for volumes now under the printer's hand, he promises an "unfained conversion." "Those that have beene perverted by any of my workes, let them reade this, and it shall thrice more benefite them" (13). In addition, he apologizes for any offense he has given and seeks reconciliation with Gabriel Harvey. "Many things have I vainly sette forth whereof now it repenteth me" (12). Like Greene before him, Nashe is capitalizing on his own notoriety—or so it seemed to Harvey, who rejected the offered reconciliation, regarding Nashe's conversion as too abrupt and out of character to be convincing: "Methinkes the raunging Eyes under that long haire, (which some would call ruffianly haire) should scarsely yet be bathed in the heavenly Teares of Christ, or washed in the divine Tears of Penitence" (*A New Letter*, sig. C4v). Report has it that Nashe still frequents taverns in lewd company; Harvey claims to suppress details that give the lie to Nashe's new piety in the hope that he will finally repent in fact. Since it is the custom of pamphlet merchants to "play much upon the advantage of the *time*," he suspects Nashe of expediency. "There is a great distance betwixt Hell, and Heaven: the Divell and God: Rakehells, and Sainctes: the *Supplication to the Divell*, and the *Teares of Christ*: . . . the *Divels Oratour* and *Christes Chauncellour*" (sig. D1r). Aretino is a precedent of a hell-hound incarnate who mixed lewd and blasphemous works with hypocritical religious tracts.

Nashe's motivations are theatrical in a way that justifies Harvey's suspicions. His decision to impersonate the passion of Christ is presented as a willed performance, and the style adopted is hyperbolic—"puffing, or blustering in bombasted terms," as Harvey put it. Harvey prays that "the promised Teares of Repentance, prove not the Teares of the Onion upon the Theater" (sig. D2r). Whether Nashe was being as opportunist as Harvey implies, he is trying on new rhetorical roles, first that of Christ, then that of a penitent prodigal. The strategy of using Christ as a mouthpiece is not unprecedented, but as Harvey protested, it was too presumptuous a leap for the likes of Tom Nashe. Professing humility, Nashe presumes to impersonate Christ in his writing, not merely imitate him in his deeds. In so doing Nashe uses his elaboration on the words of Christ to support his own interpretation of what is wrong in London. This appropriation of the persona of Christ would approach blasphemy, except that he does not attribute to Christ himself any controversial ideas.

The arrogance of the undertaking is confronted squarely in a preliminary section where Nashe invokes Christ's guidance: "Be present with me (I beseech thee) personating the passion of thy love." Nashe dissociates his personal goals from the project in hand: "Farre be from me any ambitious hope of the vaine merite of Arte; may that living vehemence I use in lament onely proceed from a heaven-bred hatred of uncleannesse and corruption." As in the epistle to the reader he emphasizes his distance from his former self: "Mine owne wit I cleane disinherite." Anticipating the doubts of Harvey and presumably others, Nashe tries to convince readers of his sincerity by denying that he is any longer the notorious Tom Nashe. "Now helpe, now direct; for now I trans-forme my selfe from my selfe, to be thy unworthy Speaker to the World" (2:15–16). Even assuming that Nashe sincerely wanted to transcend his former singularity, one could doubt whether such a change could be sustained.

Nashe's changed purpose entailed a change in style: "Newe mynt my minde to the likenes of thy lowlines: file away the superfluous affectation of my prophane puft up phrase, that I may be thy pure simple Orator" (15–16). This statement is extraordinary, considering that the rhetoric he attributes to Christ is among the most ornate in the language. Christ's lament seems frequently to pass over the boundary into parody, as in the following passage: "The fount of my teares (troubled and mudded with the Toade-like stirring and long-breathed vexations of thy venimous enormities) is no longer a pure silver Spring, but a mirie puddle for Swine to wallow in. Black and cindry (like Smithes-water) are those excrements that source downe my cheekes, and farre more sluttish then the uglie oous of the channell. Tis thou alone (ulcerous Jerusalem) that hast so fouled and soyled them" (36). Christ is made to play on words like "stone" and "gather" in drawn-out passages that read like parodies of the sort of worrying of the text found in sermons of the day (Hibbard, 130–33). The style is excessive throughout the pamphlet, but not as strange as this version of Christ.

Harvey, who must have seen the work before he wrote *A New Letter*, saw the style as evidence of unsound intentions. "He is the perfect Oratour, that figureth and representeth every thing in *Art*, as it is in *Nature*: that dispatcheth light points roundly; handeleth weightier matters more substantially; in the gravest subject proceedeth with due reverence; and of faith discourseth faithfully, of heaven heavenly, of divinity divinely, of Christ like Christ. *Dalliance* in the sagest, and highest causes, is an absurdity" (sig. D1v). Nashe answered Harvey and other critics in a new, defiant epistle to the reader which replaced the original conciliatory epistle in 1594. Nashe tacitly admits that the decorum of the work influenced his desire for peace: he had sought to shake hands with Harvey "because I desired to conforme my selfe to the holy subject of my booke" (2:180). The replacement epistle is belligerent in the style of the old Nashe, and it renews the quarrel with Harvey. Nashe also defies objections to *Christ's Tears* from other sources. Some have complained of the work's "puffed up style" and its "prophane eloquence"; other, more exacting critics have objected to his coining of new compounds and Italianate words. "To the first array of my clumperton Antigonists this I answer, that my stile is no otherwise puft up, then any mans should be which writes with any Spirite; and whom would not such a devine subject put a high ravishte Spirite into?" (183). His compound words and new usages are also necessary, he argues, for the persuasive high style he seeks to create.

This new transcendent decorum is in response to the failure of more conventional forms of religious exhortation. In *Pierce Penniless* Nashe had complained of dull-headed divines "that have nothing but the pilfries of your penne, to pollish an exhortation withall: no eloquence by Tautologies, to tie the eares of your Auditorye unto you: no invention but heere is to bee noted, I stoale this note out of Beza or Marlorat: no wit to moove, no passion to urge" (1:192). In *Christ's Tears* he develops his view that the church needs humanistically trained eloquence (such as his own), not the plain style and austere approach of the Puritan ministers. To reach the profane, one must use an appropriate style. "If you count it prophane to arte-enamel your speech to empeirce, and make a conscience to sweeten your tunes to catch soules, Religion (through you) shal reape infamy. Men are men, and with those thinges must be mooved, that men wont to be mooved" (2:124). The Puritan-minded eschewed eloquence as vain ornamentation and were dubious that the unregenerate could be saved by its means (Blench, 168–208). Their austerity reflected a different conception of the way language should communicate. William Cupper, who was quoted above, complained, "Do not the most part preferre wordes before matter, shewe before substance, and foolish affected finesse of speech, figures and allusions, before the sound, wholesome, and right dividing of the word of God?" (sig. A5r). In response to such views, Nashe argues that one should use the full resources of knowledge in religious discourse. "Unworthy are wee of heavenly knowledge, if we keepe from her any one of her hand-maydes. Logique, Rethorique, History, Phylosophy, Musique, Poetry, all are the hand-maides of Divinitie" (2:126). Detailed biblical explication will not reach the unregenerate in the way that eloquence might.

Nashe's argument for an artful style of religious writing and preaching is predicated on his conception of the audience that must be reached. "Ridiculous dull preachers" are partly responsible for a revival of the "scornful sect of atheists" because their sermons are so tedious: "all is voyce and no substance: they deafe mens eares, but not edifie" (2:123). Preachers and writers without humanistic training are powerless against atheists because the expanding heresy particularly bewitches "high wits." Thus it is an especial problem in London and at court. Such people must be answered with intelligence and style. "I am at my wits end, when I view how coldly, in comparison with other Countrimen, our Englishmen write. How, in theyr Bookes of confutation, they shew no wit or courage, as well as learning" (122). Nashe is probably exaggerating the dangers of atheism in an attempt to convince the authorities that they need his writing skills, but scattered evidence from the period suggests that there were a number of skeptical or worldly-minded people (Buckley, 80–92; Strathmann, *Ralegh*, 61–97; K. Thomas, 166–73). There is no evidence they constituted a sect, as he claims, nor that they shared any doctrine of disbelief. Atheism was used as an all-purpose term for simple worldliness or unorthodox religious beliefs: the Puritans often called Catholics atheists, while Nashe includes Puritans as examples of "inward atheists." The "outward atheists" who are his special concern are those who establish reason as their god. He has in mind the skepticism that ridicules the superstitious aspects of religion and doubts the whole enterprise: a well-known example is the collection of skeptical comments attributed to Marlowe by informers (Kocher, 21–68).

Arguments against atheism were popular, whatever the actual extent of the problem. Arthur Golding completed Sidney's translation of de Mornay's *On the Trueness of the Christian Religion*, and a Protestant version of Robert Parson's *First Book of the Christian Exercise* (known as the *Resolution* and mentioned by Nashe) was published (D. Walker; Strathmann "Robert Parson's Essay"). Both works addressed themselves to the reclaiming of atheists, as did Henry Smith's popular tract *God's Arrow against Atheists*. Atheism was perhaps more an intellectual fad than a settled position—Nashe calls it a damnable paradox—but it excited the imagination of Elizabethans and generated concern. In such a pervasively Christian culture true atheism was unlikely; the atheism Nashe describes must have usually been a compartmentalized and temporary position. Greene's description of how an effective preacher shook his lack of faith and of how reading Parson's *Resolution* reclaimed him to religion suggest how ambivalent Elizabethan atheists were. In cases like Greene's, where skepticism was a rationalistic conception superimposed on a more emotional set of beliefs, sudden reconversion was possible, particularly in the face of adversity. Nashe writes, "Tis nothing but plenty and aboundance that makes men Atheists" (2:120). Thus, those who wrote against atheists used primitive emotional appeals along with their rational arguments for the existence of God. Parsons, for example, worked on his readers' fear of retribution through graphic descriptions of the ugliness of sin and the pains of hell. Nashe uses a similar strategy, although as an orthodox Anglican he conceives of the hell of social anarchy in this world as a more immediate horror.

The highly charged rhetoric of *Christ's Tears* and its overblown picture of chaos, first in Jerusalem and now in London, are intended to frighten skeptical readers back into belief. This rhetorical intention is evident in the second section of the pamphlet, which describes the destruction of Jerusalem that Christ foretold. It is an emotional and at times grotesque paraphrase of Joseph Ben Gorion's (or Youssipon's) *History of the Latter Times of the Jews' Commonwealth,* a medieval work that pretends to be a contemporary account. The English translation of Peter Morvyn was frequently reprinted, probably because it is well-narrated with long, lamenting set speeches and lurid details. In retelling the story, Nashe uses all the rhetorical resources he can to strike fear into his readers. He protests that his sentences, as overloaded as they are, give only a shadow of the true horrors of the fall of Jerusalem: "Should I write it to the proofe, weeping would leave me no eyes: like tragick Seneca, I shoulde tragedize my selfe, by bleeding to death in the depth of passion. . . . God forbid I shold be so Luciferous passionative-ambitious, to take upon me the full blast of this *desolative-*Trumpet of Jerusalem" (2:60). The topic requires "that whatsoever I have in witte or eloquence must bee drayned to the delineament of wretchednesse," so he appeals to God to "enlarge myne invention and my memorie, sincerely and feelingly to rehearse the disornamenting of thys mother of Citties" (63).

Describing the effects of famine and pestilence on the beseiged city is a nearly impossible task: "In gyving them sutable phrase, had I the commaund of a thousand singular wits, I should banqroute them all in description" (69). Such lamenting on the insufficiencies of language is a device for snatching a grace, or in Nashe's case a horror, beyond the reach of art.

The miseries of Jerusalem before its fall are epitomized in the story of Miriam, a mother who cannibalized her own son because of famine and despair. Nashe's source also emphasized the gruesomeness of the story, but he heightens the effect still further in his effort to be emotionally overwhelming: "Mothers of LONDON, (each one of you to your selves) doe but imagine that you are Miriam, wyth what hart (suppose you) could ye go about the cooquerie of your own chyldren?" (71). Nashe gives Miriam a long, lachrymose soliloquy on her suffering and horror at the thought of her own deed. After she has killed, "sod, rost, and powdred him," and consumed her fill, the smell of cooked flesh attracts the criminal rulers of Jerusalem to her house, where they demand a share of what they imagine was concealed food. Grotesque details make the account ludicrous rather than pathetic, as when Miriam taunts her oppressors, "Beholde his pale perboyld visage, how pretie-pitteous it lookes. His pure snow-moulded soft fleshe will melt of it selfe in your mouthes: who can abstaine from these two round teat-like cheeks? Be not dainty to cut them up, the rest of his body have I cutte up to your hands" (76). The story of Miriam is the high point in Nashe's effort to use the sufferings of Jerusalem to shock his readers into a reconsideration of the sins of London. Miriam's grisly act acquires an archetypal significance as an extreme example of despair. She accuses the rebel leaders of causing her desperation and "thus mirrouring mee for the Monarch-monster of Mothers" (76).

With our lower toleration for rhetorical ornamentation, modern readers are likely to find *Christ's Tears* excessive and at times ludicrous, but the work was not a failure for all of its original audience. In 1600 an anonymous writer praised the work: "Read, I pray you, Thomas Nashe's book, entitled, 'The Tears of Christ over Jerusalem': which book, if you have any grace in you, will make you to shed tears for your sins" (McKerrow,

4:213–14). It also achieved a second edition in 1613, long enough after Nashe's death to indicate it was liked for its own merits. From our point of view, however, the overblown rhetoric calls itself into question; Jonathan V. Crewe sees Nashe as teetering between "naive hubris and cynical fraud" (60). Christ's words failed to save Jerusalem from destruction, could Nashe's highly mannered elaboration of those words save London from a similar fate? While the plague did pass, Nashe's exhortation to retreat from the "frontiers of sin" had little effect. Old vices continued unabated, and the new vices he feared became more common; some were being converted to virtues. Moreover, his success at transforming himself from satirist to Christ's simple orator was limited. Tongue-in-cheek irony was a saving grace in *The Terrors of the Night*; here, the suggestion of it, as in the account of Miriam, is the mark of the devil's hoof.

LONDON AND THE FRONTIERS OF SIN

If, as Horton Davies has written, the Puritans felt charged with the responsibility of creating the New Jerusalem in England, Nashe in *Christ's Tears* was obsessed with avoiding the fate of the ancient Jerusalem (66). His amateur Christology focuses not on the passions of the cross, but on the passion felt by Christ when he prophesied the destruction of Jerusalem. Nashe's Christ stresses the willfulness and disobedience of its citizens; both traits were manifestations of pride: "I my selfe have no enemy but Pryde, which is the *Summum genus* of sinne, & may wel be a convertible name with the divell, for the divell is nought but pryde, and pryde is an absolute divell" (2:41). The description of the siege of Jerusalem focuses on the social anarchy and on individual acts of desperation. Although the need for love and charity is mentioned, the emphasis is on the need for obedience and political order. In this respect the book is very much what one would expect from a sometime protégé of Archbishop Whitgift.

The verbal pyrotechnics of the first two sections of the book have obscured Nashe's true subject, his account of the social vices that have brought the plague on London. The last two-thirds of the work is an expansion of Pierce Penniless's analysis of contemporary sin, with the emphasis more sharply on London and in a style that is more exhortative than satiric. Nashe is quite explicit in his warning: "As great a *desolation* as Jerusalem, hath London deserved. Whatsoever of Jerusalem I have written, was but to lend her a Looking-glasse. Now enter I into my true Teares, my Teares for London, wherein I crave pardon though I deale more searchingly then common Soule-Surgions accustome; for in this Booke, wholy have I bequeathed my penne and my spyrite to the prosternating and enforrowing the frontiers of sinne" (2:80). The sins of London, particularly the newer ones, are all seen as subdivisions of pride, which is traditionally the root of the other sins. Much of Nashe's account is quite conventional, but he is "more searching," as he claims, than most Elizabethan social critics, and he does focus on the "frontiers of sin." Most religious tracts of the period disappoint the modern scholar because they are so conventional and general, even when a specific event or social problem is the occasion of the work (Louis Wright, 228–96; White). John Stockwood, for example, delivered a sermon similar to *Christ's Tears* in its use of Ben Gorion's account of the fall of Jerusalem, but Stockwood stops short of making the application to contemporary society. Nashe does not want to be topical: "No man in thys Treatise I will particulerly tutch, none I will semovedly allude to, but onely attaint vice in generall" (80). He was, nevertheless, specific enough in his depiction of London vices to incur the wrath of the city fathers.

Nashe's emphasis on pride reflects his fear that the traditional communal bonds were being sundered, that a commonwealth of submissive citizens was giving way to an anarchy of selfishness. This can be seen in his characterization of the children of Pride: the sons Ambition, Vain-glory, Atheism, Discontent, and Contention, and the daughters Disdain, Gorgeous-attire, and Delicacy. Nashe uses these personifications to analyze the form sin now takes in London, its suburbs, and neighboring Westminster. From our point of view it is evident that Nashe's examples of pride are usually manifestations of what a later age would call emergent individualism. By emphasizing the "frontiers of sin" he brings to the fore those new attitudes and behaviors that run counter to the medieval ideal of community or the Renaissance ideal of the commonwealth. In particular he is disturbed by the replacement of feudal bonds with contractual relationships. The humanist ideal of submerging the self in the name of duty is giving way to a selfish ethic that advances the self in the name of profit. The center of these changes is London, so London is especially visited by the plague. The logic of this seemed as irrefutable to Nashe as it did to the Puritans, although his account differed in emphasis from theirs.

Ambition is an obvious example; it is like a great courtier: "Fame hee makes his God, and mens mouthes the limits of hys conscience" (2:81). Absalom, Caesar, and Alexander are evoked, but ambition is also found "in every street in London." Nashe also finds ambition in himself: "Even in thys dilatement against Ambition, the devill seekes to sett in a foote of affected applause and popular fames Ambition in my style" (87). For Nashe the emergence of what we would call individualism is simply pride in the form of ambition: "Over and over I repeate it double and treble, that the spyrite of monarchizing in pryvate men is the spyrite of Lucifer" (91).

Nashe presents avarice as a branch of ambition and usury as the worst form of avarice. If usurers were driven from London, "then it were to be hoped the Plague would cease, els never" (93). Such denunciations of usury were commonplace, but Nashe goes into detail and says he could be even more specific: "What I write is most true, and hath beene practised by more then one or two. I have a whole Booke of young Gentlemens cases lying by mee, which if I should sette foorth, some grave Auntients (within the hearing of Bow-bell) would be out of charity with mee" (95). The reference to Bow bells indicates that the ancients he means are the urban magistrates, particularly the aldermen, who were often prominent merchants and lenders. Usury was worse than petty crime: "It is a hundred parts more hatefull then Conny-catching" (95). The Puritans excuse usury and avarice through the doctrine of justification by faith alone. By contrast, Nashe calls for good works that are the fruits of Christian charity, although he cautions in the margin, "It is not my meaning in all this discourse of good deeds to sejoyne any of them from Fayth" (104). Anticipating some modern accounts of the rise of capitalism, Nashe claims that the Puritans are popular because they advance the value of a barred hutch (strongbox) over the demands of charity:

> Hee that hath nothing to doe with his money but build Churches, we count him one of God-almighties Fooles, or els (if he beare the name of a Wise-man) we tearme him a notable braggart. Tut, tut, Almes-houses will make good stables, and, let out in Tenements, yeelde a round sum by the yeere. A good strong bard hutch is a building worth twenty of those Hospitals and Almes-houses; Our rich Chuffes will rather put their helping hands to the building of a prison then a house of prayer. Our Courtiers lay that on their backs, which shold serve to build Churches and schooles. Those Preachers please best, which can fitte us with a cheape Religion, that preach Fayth, and all Fayth, and no Good-workes, but to the houshold of Fayth. (107)

The substance of Nashe's view can be duplicated in uncontroversial works of the period, but the angry tone and specific details make it read more like invective than wholesome admonition.

The accounts of the other sons and daughters of pride are more conventional, although the emphasis is often on new attitudes and forms of behavior that anticipate individualism. For example, the account of atheism, discussed above, links it with other forms of pride: atheism "is when a man is so timpaniz'd with prosperity, and entranced from himselfe with Wealth, Ambition, and Vaine-glory, that he forgets he had a Maker, or that there is a Heaven above him which controules him. Too much joy of this world hath made him drunke" (114). Like ambition and avarice, atheism entails advancing one's personal existence while ignoring the needs of community and the implications of one's own mortality. Conversely, discontent, the fourth son of pride, is caused by the individual's being unhappy with his personal existence. On the one hand discontent can lead to melancholy and despair, on the other to envy of others. "Every man heere in London is discontent with the state wherein hee lives. Every one seeketh to undermine another" (131–32). Thus discontent can easily lead to contention, the last son of pride. Contention is selfish competition, and it can easily become an end in itself. The contentious person "coveteth not so much to over-come, as contend" (132). This form of pride is a ticklish topic for a reformed satirist: "Were it not that in reproving Contention I might haply seeme contentious, I woulde wade a little farther in thys subject" (134).

The daughters of pride are those forms of egocentricity that Nashe associates with women, including the passive attitudes that underlie or reflect the more aggressive behavior of the sons of pride. Disdain is a superior attitude towards others, "a kind of scorne" (135). The city is a network of contempt: "In London, the ritch disdayne the poore. The Courtier the Cittizen. The Cittizen the Countriman. One Occupation disdayneth another. The Merchant the Retayler. The Retayler the Craftsman. The better sort of Craftsman the baser. The Shoomaker the Cobler. The Cobler the Carman" (135). This disdain and the rivalry it engenders helps cause the taste for gorgeous attire that Nashe classifies as the second daughter of pride. Like Stubbes and other social critics, Nashe emphasizes that over-elaborate styles in clothing reflect a desire to ape a social status above one's station. Clothing becomes costume and social interaction a variety of theatricality: "England, the Players stage of gorgeous attyre, the Ape of all Nations superfluities, the continuall Masquer in outlandish habilements, great plenty-scanting calamities art thou to await, for wanton disguising thy selfe against kind, and digressing from the plainnesse of thine Auncesters" (142). Clothing should reflect status, not become the very stuff of what a person is; Nashe objects that "Tailers, Serving-men, Make-shifts, and Gentlemen . . . are confounded" (142).

Much of what Nashe criticized, including this penchant for extravagant attire, was also denounced in the pamphlets of the Puritan critics, but he stressed economic exploitation more and prodigality less. *Christ's Tears* is outspoken in its criticisms of the financial structure of the city. Like most Elizabethans, Nashe had little understanding of the role of capital in the economy or of the special relationship between London and the rest of society. The city of London was a separate entity encapsulated within the theoretical hierarchical structure of society; it was autonomous, but it dominated the rest of the nation financially and culturally. It gave the queen enthusiastic support in return for royal protection of its independence and its financial hegemony. Few people understood the role of the city fathers in the life of the nation, since their special economic function was not part of the orthodox idealization of the commonwealth (Foster). Thus Nashe's respect for the queen and the nobility was not matched by his feelings for the mayor, aldermen, and the prosperous citizen class from which they were drawn. In his argument that economic exploitation was a cause of the plague, Nashe passed over the boundary between a general account of abuses and specific charges that offended the civic authorities.

Aside from Nashe's own casual reference to the persecution of *Christ's Tears* by the mayor and aldermen, there is no external evidence about what proved offensive in the work. But when *Christ's Tears* was reissued in 1594, one section was changed by means of a cancel sheet (a specially printed replacement page). Because of the cost of cancels, it may well be that other passages were objectionable but that Nashe and his printer hoped to deflect criticism by changing the most offensive passage. Since the original passage is our only evidence for what disturbed the city fathers, it is worth quoting at length. It occurs early in the long peroration to *Christ's Tears*, an emotional appeal to London to reform if it is to escape further ravages of the epidemic:

> London, thou art the seeded Garden of sinne, the Sea that sucks in all the scummy chanels of the Realme. The honestest in thee (for the most) are eyther Lawyers or Usurers. Deceite is that which advaunceth the greater sorte of thy chiefest; Let them looke that theyr ritches shall rust and canker, being wet & dewed with Orphans teares. The Lord thinketh it were as good for him to kill with the Plague, as to let them kill with oppression. He beholdeth from on hie al subtile conveiances and recog-

nisances. He beholdeth how they pervert foundations, and will not bestow the Bequeathers free almes, but for brybes, or for friendship. I pray God they take not the like course in preferring poore mens chyldren into theyr Hospitals, and converting the impotents mony to theyr private usury. (158–59)

This paragraph may be more topical than we know: the management of orphans' accounts by the aldermen was controversial, and suits were not uncommon, so that at any given time a passage such as this might have galled someone's kibe (Foster, 20–21, 87–88).

The passage goes on to describe how young prodigals are entrapped in the city and how Londoners are becoming proverbially cruel in their dealings:

For then Londoners, are none more hard harted and cruell. Is it not a common proverbe amongst us, when any man hath cosend or gone beyonde us, to say, Hee hath playde the Merchant with us? But Merchants, they turne it another way, and say, He hath playd the Gentleman with them. The Snake eateth the Toade, and the Toade the Snaile. The Merchant eates up the Gentleman, the Gentleman eates up the Yeoman, and all three do nothing but exclaime one upon another. (159)

The new version pulls in its horns by softening the tone, omitting specific accusations, and denying any topical allusions. It begins more positively: "London thou are the welhead of the land, and therefore it behoveth thee to send foorth wholsome springs. Suffer not thy channels to overflow like full conduits. Let not gaine outrun godlinesse and honestie." The account of extortions is made more general and is concluded with a disclaimer: "I speake not this for I know any such, but if there be anie such, to forewarne and reforme them." The changes in the second paragraph show that Nashe was taken to be indicting the magistrates as a group, not an unreasonable inference.

Many good men, many good magistrats are there in this City, diverse godly & wise counsellers hath she to provide for her peace, them no part of any reproofe of mine concerneth, how ever it may be otherwise thought. Other wicked livers in it questionlesse there be, which want no ill gotten goods, nor ill mindes to the common wealth. Verie good it were, when they are revealed, they had plague bills set upon their doores, to make them more noted and detestable. The snake eateth up the toade, and the toade the snayle: the Usurer eateth up the Gentleman, and the Gentleman the yeoman, and all three being devoured one of another, do nothing but complaine one upon another. (158–59)

The substitution of "usurer" for "merchant" in the last sentence of the revision shows how fine the line was between safe admonition and dangerous invective.

Nashe's revisions in the attack on magistrates and merchants indicate that his criticisms were too trenchant, not that they were topical. The anxiety caused by the plague made Nashe's diatribe more inflammatory than it would have been in a quieter time, and the city fathers may have been angered by the source of the criticism: words that would have been tolerated from a religious writer may have been unacceptable from the notorious Nashe. Not understanding the role of the city, Nashe criticized London with much less caution than he would have the court. His bitterness betrayed him and confounded his intention to write a work that would avoid controversy. As the book draws to a close, the humble orator for Christ and heart-stricken historian of the seige of Jerusalem has returned to his role as the "English Aretine," scourge of magistrates if not of princes. His reform hardly lasted the length of his manuscript.

Throughout the last part of the book, the anger that fires the prose of Nashe the satirist breaks through and disrupts the moralistic preaching of the penitent prophet. If Nashe's anger got the better of him in the cancelled passage, elsewhere in the book other emotional effects are excessive, as we have seen. The overall effect is one of hysteria, of a person whose emotions are exaggerated and subject to unpredictable changes. The difficulty is in part a matter of faulty rhetoric; *Christ's Tears* is an experiment, an attempt at a new style of religious polemics. It may also reflect a personal loss of control: the 1592–93 plague, which was at its height when Nashe wrote, must have shaken far more sober minds than his. Whatever estimate one uses, the plague more than decimated London, disrupted all the ordinary courses of urban life, and threw the inhabitants back on whatever spiritual resources they had to stave off morbidity. Nashe managed to escape the city during the worse days of the epidemic, but he could not escape the anxiety the plague generated.

The effects of the plague are the subject of the concluding portion of the book, which includes the intemperate passage on economic exploitation later emended. After Nashe has finished the long account of the sons and daughters of pride, he links the two halves of his book by claiming that the plague inflicted on London is similar to the miseries visited on Jerusalem. "How the Lord hath begunne to leave our house desolate unto us, let us enter into the consideration thereof with our selves. At this instant is a generall plague disperst throughout our Land" (156–57). He describes the plight of infected servants, left to die in the fields by callous masters: "In Grayes-Inne, Clarkenwell, Finsbury, and Moore-fieldes, wyth myne owne eyes have I seene halfe a dozen of such lamentable out-casts" (160). Under the pressure of the epidemic, charity has failed and religion become a mockery: "What, is our religion all avarice and no good works?" (161). Plague-stricken London becomes an image of hell for Nashe, a foretaste of far worse eternal punishments. "A confused modell and misty figure of Hell have we, conglomorate in our braynes," which barely approximates the horrors of the true hell (168). Nashe expounds in a traditional fashion on the suffering that awaits the unregenerate. The keeping of God constantly in one's memory is the best way to avoid hell, but purblind London forgets God and itself. Nashe concludes with a prayer that the city be saved.

Christ's Tears claims to renounce satire, but Nashe's penchant for grotesque images and colloquial prose rhythms gives a satiric and iconoclastic edge to his style. This can be disastrous when he is striving for elevated or pathetic effects. His

Christ sounds too much like a distraught rhetorician, while Nashe himself comes across as a sanctimonious Pierce Penniless. His skills as a writer and in all probability the character that gave rise to those skills were antithetical to the intentions of the tract. He may have for a time aspired to Christian humility, and he believed in the submissiveness of the loyal subject, but his anger and scorn reflect his own acquaintance with the sons and daughters of pride. He himself mentions that ambition and a taste for contention tempt him beyond his reformist purposes. The singularity of style and touches of invective betray his assumed ethos; the personal anger of the would-be spokesman for reform shows through.

Nashe's inclinations and talents led him away from what was acceptable to the people he admired into the presumptuous and controversial. The decision to undertake *Christ's Tears* must have been an effort to will himself to write the kind of work that was esteemed by the likes of Whitgift and the Carey family. That intention may well have been sincere, but as an effort of the will it reads like a performance. The problem is not hypocrisy, as Harvey feared, but a need to ridicule and attack rather than admonish or embrace. Derisive laughter was more Nashe's mode than pathetic tears. The flashes of anger and the satiric gibes are also more convincing than the grand effects because they are more in accord with the established ethos of Tom Nashe than the new ethos he tries to impose on his readers. The ethos that protests its humility is perceived as a mask for the more satiric ethos that peeps through from time to time. We react this way because of the compelling power of Nashe in his other works; many Elizabethans must have, like Gabriel Harvey, also read this book as another production of the controversial Tom Nashe. He could renounce "fantastical satirism," but the former self he wanted to leave behind was already public property.

CHAPTER
5

This Fantastical Treatise:
The Unfortunate Traveler

Although unabashedly a fiction, *The Unfortunate Traveler* defies classification: even Nashe was uncertain what he had written. The dedication asserts that it is a new departure: "By divers of my good frends have I been dealt with to employ my dul pen in this kinde, it being a cleane different vaine from other my former courses of writing" (2:201). But Nashe is vague about the nature of his new vein: "All that in this phantasticall Treatise I can promise, is some reasonable conveyance of historie, & varietie of mirth." This diffidence is disingenuous; whatever else the book is, it is another outspoken satire on Elizabethan England. Fiction frees Nashe to develop his criticisms and express his anger more explicitly than before, in part because they are displaced backward in time and across the channel. The narrator, Jack Wilton, functions as a truly independent persona who can express unorthodox views Nashe would have to censure in a conventional tract. The Europe Jack experiences during the reign of Henry VIII is an imaginative extrapolation from the England Nashe knew in the last years of Elizabeth's reign, but fiction helps protect him from the hostile reactions that so often damaged his career.

Nashe's vein is different enough to have confused modern critics and readers. At one time, *The Unfortunate Traveler* was hailed as a progenitor of the realistic novel because of its mundane imagery and colloquial style (e.g., Jusserand, 308–20), but Nashe's lack of interest in verisimilitude and consistency of character made this work seem a failure as a novel. Critics less obsessed with the origins of realism have classified it as a picaresque novel (Bowers, Gohlke), although it is, if anything, too episodic to be an example of that subgenre. In the prototypical picaresque novel, *Lazarillo de Tormes* (1554), the hero progresses through a series of adventures that educates him in roguery while exposing the contradictions of Spanish society. In comparison, Jack Wilton's encounters are random, fantastic, and often grotesque; moreover, Jack learns little except at the very end of his story. Nashe may have read *Lazarillo* (the English translation was reprinted in 1586) and been influenced by its use of first-person narration and an episodic plot, but his work lacks the unity of the anonymous Spanish text.

At first Jack is a rogue telling his adventures in picaresque fashion, but in the last third of the book he becomes enmeshed in a sequence of events governed by a cruel pattern of retribution. Though he does not lose his life, he loses control of it as he witnesses a nightmare that contrasts sharply with the comic episodes that begin the book. To explain this radical change of direction and tone in the book, some critics have argued that it is a formless work, spun out by a careless author with no fixed purpose. According to this "unintentional fallacy," the work is a desultory composition: Nashe began to write a jest book, was deflected by an interest in colorful historical personages, then tempted into various parodies and topics as his fancy led him (Hibbard, 145–79). As he wrote, the interaction between the material and his imagination became increasingly serious in its implications; Jack comes to embody a neurotic and even nihilistic attitude towards life at odds with Nashe's professed idealism and his intention to write a comic work (Lanham, "Tom Nashe"). Such speculations about the composition of the work probably reflect a truth, but they lead away from analysis of the accomplished work. The task is to explain the peculiar power and enduring appeal of *The Unfortunate Traveler*, not to conjecture about how it was written.

Because the rhetorical intentions of the work are obscure and disparate, the work lends itself to modern critical analysis. Jonathan Crewe has argued that Nashe's work in general and this text in particular reflect a crisis point at which rhetoric loses faith in itself. The historic reasons for Nashe's dilemma are of secondary importance to Crewe, since he sees Nashe as an example of the failure of metaphysics and language that Jacques Derrida has argued undermines all Western thought. The peculiar modernity of the text can in this way be explained in poststructuralist terms, or explained by reference to the tradition of the grotesque (Millard; Rhodes; Stephanson), to the concept of play and the author as "maker" (Ferguson), or to other modern critical approaches. Ann Rosalind Jones sees the work as a polyphonic novel that exemplifies intertextuality: "The world it constructs is a jarring confrontation of contemporary discourses" (78). Such attempts to explain the success of the work by means of our own cultural terms are useful, since they illuminate the work and stretch the reach of our critical discourse, which often becomes culture-bound in its own right. This present study only demurs in its belief in the historical context as an essential element in the intertextuality. That context corrects excesses of modern critical approaches, but there is a parallel need to use modern concepts to correct the excesses of historicism.

THE MODE: FICTION FOR AN IRON AGE

The Unfortunate Traveler is antiromantic: its rogue hero drifts from place to place (no more subject to chronology than geography), prevailing or surviving in a series of unheroic encounters with an assortment of dupes and villains. Although Jack pretends to be an earl for a while, he does not discover any concealed nobility in himself nor gain honor through his exploits. The treasure he acquires is ill-gotten, the woman he marries is no maid, and she has saved *him* from a terrible fate. The book is antiromantic rather than parody because it questions the social values that produced the literary conventions it mocks. It prefigures the pessimism that was to animate the satires of Hall, Marston, and Donne and the cynicism of the Jacobean playwrights. Abandoning the idealistic aesthetic of Sidney and Spenser, it subverts the literary and social conventions of the Elizabethan "golden" age. The rejection of idealism is displaced in space and time and filtered through the consciousness of a self-confessed rogue, but the book nevertheless undercuts both the traditional conception of society and the humanistic poetic that Nashe defended in his earlier works.

For Elizabethans, the short life of Sir Philip Sidney was a model of heroism, and his literary remains were representative of the ennobling literature promoted in his *Defense of Poetry*. The *Defense* addresses itself especially to the value of fiction, associating the power of the creative imagination to make fictions with insight into a golden world more ideal than the iron world of history. The world created in fiction is more essential, and it is better; thus, a villain like Sidney's own Cecropia in the *Arcadia* is more absolutely evil than any real villain, but villainy is overcome, as when Cecropia falls from a roof. The positive vision delivered by literature is not simple optimism because the poet's "erected wit" can transcend humanity's fallen state. The "right" poets who are Sidney's main topic are those "which most properly do imitate to teach and delight, and to imitate borrow nothing of what is, hath been, or shall be; but range, only reined with learned discretion, into the divine consideration of what may be and should be" (102).

In contrast, the historian is "tied, not to what should be but to what is, to the particular truth of things and not to the general reason of things" (107). In the iron world of history, fortune often prevails over virtue—the wicked can prosper and the good suffer—but in the golden world of fiction, "poetry ever setteth virtue out in her best colours, making Fortune her well-waiting handmaid, that one must needs be enamoured of her" (111). Fiction is better than history because it reflects a normative hierarchy of values obscured since the fall of Adam. Although freshly put, Sidney's account of the truths embodied in fiction is a modification of humanistic commonplaces about the way poetry, as a branch of rhetoric, persuades its audience to virtue. Meaning in literature is not a function of an author's concerns, nor is it contingent on a particular society; rather, its truths are universal. As we have seen, Nashe's earlier works express similar views, and he aspired to write the kind of literature Sidney advocated, but adverse circumstances and a lack of patronage never permitted him to do so. He was too immersed in "what is" to enter very deeply into "the divine consideration of what may be and should be."

In the *Unfortunate Traveler* Sidney's contrast between fiction and history is turned against idealism. The work retains the contrast between the ideal ordering of human life associated with poetry and the actual working out of human lives in time. In the realm of history, fortune and human irrationality govern events; only through the products of art can the ideal order be seen. Sidney thought the secondary world of art should emphasize the ideal golden world, frequently in the form of romance, but in Nashe's text the iron world of history prevails. Some conflict between the ideal and history is characteristic of all romances and novels, but in this work the iron world is overpowering, and the victory of the ideal in the end is trumped-up and *pro forma*—more a device to end the story than a reaffirmation. While it is suggested that things are ordered better back in England, Jack's narration is focused on his struggles with fortune in the bleak world of the Continent. Ideals are not rejected or ridiculed, but they are presented as separate from the course of historical events and subject to distortion by passion. The egalitarian aspirations of the Anabaptists, Surrey's romantic love for Geraldine, and Cutwolfe's obsession with revenge are all perverse manifestations of an idealism that has become grotesque in its interaction with historical contingencies.

This contrast between the golden and iron worlds is drawn vividly in the juxtaposition of the merchant's banqueting house in Rome with the desolation of the plague beyond its walls. The banqueting house is an artificial paradise that recreates the golden age with lifelike automatons: birds that seem real but move and sing because of elaborate machinery. Jack describes how the machinery is concealed to fool the beholder: "So closely were all those organizing implements obscured in the corpulent trunks of the trees, that everie man there present renounst conjectures of art, and sayd it was done by inchantment" (2:284). Unlike Spenser's Bower of Bliss, the banqueting house has no evil design in its deceit, but its vision of perfection is artificial. Jack describes the other lifelike animals who live in peace in this paradise and lists the ugliness and suffering excluded from it, concluding, "Such a golden age, such a good age, such an honest age was set forth in this banketting house" (285). The values in this architectural wonder are not ridiculed, but they are seen as remote, a matter of contrivance (Hibbard, 165–67; Leggatt, 32–33).

The banqueting house is put in perspective by the plague and civic disorder outside its walls. Nashe was writing at a time when the plague was threatening the civic order of Elizabethan England, the same epidemic he described more emotionally in *Christ's Tears*. In *The Unfortunate Traveler* Jack's cynical voice keeps its distance from the horrors of the plague, either through joking or grotesque exaggeration. "So it fel out that it being a vehement hot summer when I was a sojourner there, there entered such a hotspurd plague as hath not bin heard of: why, it was but a word and a blowe, Lord have mercie upon us, and he was gone" (286). As in the description of the sweating sickness earlier, death is sudden and arbitrary: "Some dide sitting at their meat, others as they were asking counsell of the phisition for theyr friends." The plague and the breakdown of order it causes are the norms of human experience; the banqueting house is an artificial glimpse of a better life.

This ironic ambivalence about idealism is embodied in the earl of Surrey, who is both praised and satirized as an aristocrat, a poet, and a lover. Some readings of the book have emphasized the satire and parody without giving due weight to Jack Wilton's praise of his master (D. Jones; Latham). Jack's admiration is sincere enough, but Surrey does cut a ludicrous figure in the iron world of the story. As an aristocrat, he fails to perform the services to the state that justify noble status. As a poet, he indulges in self-serving erotic lyrics rather than writing useful or heroic literature. As a lover, he loses himself in the complex mixture of affectation, idealism, and eroticism that make up his passion. The poetry that his love inspires reflects the distortion of values that have caused him to deviate from his previous heroic course. On the other hand, his nobility is still evident, even if it is misdirected; in a context of gross fools and villains he deserves Jack's praise and intermittent loyalty. The admirable overtones of Surrey's devotion to Geraldine and to poetry are developed by Michael Drayton in his *Heroical Epistles* (1598), where Nashe's story is purged of its ironic elements, a reversal of the usual sequence, in which the comic version of a story parodies the more romantic original.

Jack's delight at his accidental encounter with his former master is unfeigned, although tinged with irony: "O, it was a right noble Lord, liberalitie it selfe (if in this yron age there were any such creature as liberalitie left on the earth), a Prince in content because a Poet without peere" (2:242). Through his poetry Surrey transcends the iron age, "if there bee anie sparke of Adams Paradized perfection yet emberd up in the breastes of mortall men, certainelie God hath bestowed that his perfectest image on Poets." But while "none come so neere to God in wit" and "none more contemne the world," the world in turn rejects their vision, "so contrarilie of the mechanicall world are none more contemned." Poets are divorced from the everyday world, just as later in the story the banqueting house is isolated from the plague: "Despised they are of the worlde, because they are not of the world: their thoughts are exalted above the worlde of ignorance and all earthly conceits" (242). Jack himself suffers from no such exaltation; hence there is a built-in comedy in his interactions with his master. In short, Surrey is straight out of the pages of the *Arcadia* or *The Faerie Queene*. Jack's praise is exaggerated, but the irony is directed at Surrey's impracticality, not at his heroic values or poetic vocation. He is out of place in Jack's iron world.

Surrey's love for Geraldine pleases Jack, since his formerly grave master "had discarded those nice tearmes of chastitie and continencie" (245). The contrast between master and page becomes especially comic in the Venetian jail, where Surrey, like Shakespeare's Orlando, pretends Diamante is Geraldine and courts her with words, while Jack more practically wins the physical person. "My master beate the bush and kepte a coyle and a pratling, but I caught the birde: simplicitie and plainnesse shall carrie it away in another world. God wot he was Petro Desperato, when I stepping to her with a dunstable tale made up my market" (263). Jack's dunstable, or plain, tale is that Diamante should revenge herself on the jealous husband who has wrongly imprisoned her by making him a cuckold in fact. Surrey meanwhile plays the psychological game of courting Diamante as if she were Geraldine, a strategy unlikely to win either woman. Jack comments, "A holy requiem to their soules that thinke to wooe a woman with riddles" (263). But Jack is a rogue whose view is seldom simply true; earlier he mocks his master's honorable scruples: "Alacke, he was too vertuous to make her vicious; he stood upon religion and conscience, what a hainous thing it was to subvert Gods ordinance" (262). Jack's irony reflects discredit back on his own lack of principles.

Surrey's love is obsessive and masochistic: "Now would he kneele & kisse the ground as holy ground which she vouchsafed to blesse from barrennes by her steppes" (262). The fact that such idolatrous behavior is expended on Geraldine's surrogate, Diamante, who is no better than she should be, underlines Surrey's folly. His playacting shows that his passion is self-generated and contrived, a part of his vocation as a poet. As Jack remarks, "Passion upon passion would throng one on anothers necke, he wold praise her beyond the moone and starres, and that so sweetly and ravishingly as I perswade my self he was more in love with his own curious forming fancie than her face; and truth it is, many become passionate lovers onely to winne praise to theyr wits" (262). Since Surrey's love is a projection of his own imagination, it can be directed to Diamante as passionately as it would be to Geraldine, nor is physical consummation as important to him as it is to Jack.

This "intranced mistaking extasie" finds expression in a poem whose parody of Petrarchan conventions exposes the strange mixture of masochism and obsession underlying Surrey's love. The Elizabethan use of "death" as a term for sexual climax is used for a comic effect that has serious overtones (D. Jones, 50–51):

> If I must die, O, let me choose my death:
> Sucke out my soule with kisses, cruell maide,
> In thy breasts christall bals enbalme my breath,
> Dole it all out in sighs when I am laide.

The linking of death and eroticism capture vividly the folly of seeking immortality through erotic passion.

> Thy eyes lyke searing yrons burne out mine,
> In thy faire tresses stifle me outright,
> Like Circes change me to a loathsome swine,
> So I may live for ever in thy sight.
>   Into heavens joyes none can profoundly see,
>   Except that first they meditate on thee.
> (262–63)

Moved by this sonnet, Jack comments, "Sadly and verily, if my master sayde true, I shoulde if I were a wench make many men quickly immortall."

The poem undercuts the idealism of poetry as well as the idealism of love. Its images of eroticism and death are not products of man's erected wit, Sidney notwithstanding, nor is the world it delivers golden. According to the theories of the Neoplatonists the poet-lover climbs more or less articulated rungs of a ladder, expressing through his verse a purified vision that transcends sexual desire, but Surrey's poem is very much a product of his erotic needs and his psychological state. Surrey's other poems are not parodies, but their imagery is more like the personal conceits of later poetry than like the impersonal eloquence of the historical earl of Surrey's sonnets. Moreover, they are set in the context of Jack's decidedly unplatonic sensibility: "Now I beseech God love me so well as I love a plaine dealing man; earth is earth, flesh is flesh, earth wil to earth, and flesh unto flesh; fraile earth, fraile flesh, who can keepe you from the worke of your creation?" (245). Jack's unregenerate perspective deflates his master's pretensions.

Sidney's values and poetic are also questioned in the description of the tournament Surrey stages in Florence in defense of Geraldine's beauty. The idea for such a tournament and many of the details are derived from Sidney's *Arcadia* (Duncan-Jones; Koppenfels). Of course, elaborate armor and symbolic tournaments were also a part of court life, but Surrey's tournament is more parody than satire. The knights assembled in Florence are a melancholy lot, self-obsessed because of love or adverse fortune and so devoid of fighting skills that Surrey can easily best them. Their actual jousting is a comic scene of misdirected gestures, since none of them can focus on his opponent. They have spent too much of their time designing armor and devising elaborate *imprese* (symbolic devices) to have any skills at fighting. In an effort to achieve *copia,* or abundance of details, as part of the mock epic effect, Nashe gives us too many examples of the comic armor and grotesque *imprese* affected by the knights, but the comedy would have been more vivid for readers who had been asked often enough to take seriously the symbolic language of tournaments.

In addition to *Arcadia,* Nashe draws on Paolo Giovio's book on symbolic devices, *The Worthy Tract of Paulus Jovius,* as translated and introduced by Samuel Daniel (1585). Daniel explains that a true *impresa* was an emblematic image coupled with a *mot,* or slogan, intended "to signifie an enterprise, wherat a noble mind leveling with the aime of a deepe desire, strives with a stedy intent to gaine the prise of his purpose" (sigs. A6r–A7v). They should be "not altogether manifest nor too too obscure, neither yet triviall or common." Interpreting the device was supposed to challenge the wit of the viewer. *Imprese* were to reflect the haughty mind and rarefied intellect of the aristocratic knight, unlike the coat of arms which signified his noble lineage. In the *Arcadia* and in many actual tournaments an *impresa* often signified that a Neoplatonic conception of love or heroic melancholy motivated the heroism of a knight (Strong, 117–62; Yates). In practice *imprese* could be ironic or comic, but they were never ludicrous, as they are in *The Unfortunate Traveler.*

The *imprese* and other devices at Surrey's tournament are ludicrous in several ways. The details of the elaborate armor and trappings are ridiculed: Surrey's own helmet was "round proportioned lyke a gardners water-pot, from which seemed to issue forth small thrids of water, like citterne strings" (2:271). These decorations are often cumbersome: the seventh knight "had, lyke the giants that sought to scale heaven in despight of Jupiter, a mount overwhelming his head and whole bodie" (275). Moreover, they are silly rather than heroic, as in the case of "the knight of the Owle," whose armor was "a stubd tree overgrowne with ivie, his helmet fashioned lyke an owle sitting on top of this ivie" (274). Many of the knights are overburdened with emblematic significance: the Knight of the

Owl has separate mottos for his armor, his trappings, and his shield. Instead of noble minds with level aims and steady intents, we are given a picture of trivial minds with chaotic ideas and emotions that scatter in all directions.

Jack's difficulties in understanding what he sees are caused by the confusion of the knights more than by his own limitations. He puzzles over the shield of the eighth knight:

> On his shield he set foorth the picture of death doing almes deeds to a number of poore desolate children. The word, *Nemo alius explicat*. No other man takes pittie upon us. What his meaning was herein I cannot imagine, except death had done him and his brethren some great good turne in ridding them of some untoward parent or kinsman that would have beene their confusion: for else I cannot see howe death shoulde have bin sayd to doe almes deedes, except hee had deprived them sodainly of their lives, to deliver them out of some further miserie; which could not in anie wise be, because they were yet lyving. (276)

Thus the literalist struggles with allegorical imagery. *Nemo alius explicat* could also mean "no one else can explain." But whatever the *impresa* means, it is fatuous rather than heroic. Like the fictional Surrey's poetic images, the "discontented and amorous devices" of the tournament refer back to the narcissistic concerns of the knights rather than to a superior set of values.

The depictions of Surrey's love for Geraldine and the tournament at Florence question the theory of poetry and the code of values associated with Sir Philip Sidney. For Sidney, the value of poetry is epitomized by the image that links human experience with transcendent values; but Surrey's poetry and the imagery of the tournament are self-serving and personal. Undercut as well are the heroic code of values and the idealizing of the nobility that Nashe himself saw as a central topic of literature in *Pierce Penniless*. Harvey urged Sidney and Spenser on Nashe as models to imitate; Surrey is perhaps his mocking response. *The Unfortunate Traveler* is skeptical about platonic lovers, chivalric knights, and the literary modes that use the passions and adventures of such figures to arrive at a heroic view of human virtues. As Walter R. Davis has put it, "Jack Wilton's experience of reality throughout Europe constantly gives the lie to ennobling formulations of the real, be they literary conventions, intellectual aspirations, or codes of life" (215). Jack is not a simple mouthpiece for Nashe, but an aesthetic and Italianate idealization of life cannot occupy the same textual space as Jack's deflating wit.

Northern European humanism fares somewhat better. Nashe uses Jack's accidental encounters to distinguish between those true humanists who use their wit to improve society and the empty Ciceronians who prize form over substance. He is again criticizing the academic practices of the day, but he is also setting his own work in a context of applied humanism. If Surrey calls into question the aesthetics of Sidney and Spenser, the inclusion of Erasmus, More, Agrippa, and Aretino points to the ironic and satiric humanism Nashe admired. All four are witty men who cope with the world as it is and use rhetoric to shame humanity into better behavior. They are contrasted with the academic humanism of Wittenberg, where learning is empty words and gestures. Jack describes the performance of a Latin play: "One, as if he had ben playning a clay floore, stampingly trode the stage so harde with his feete that I thought verily he had resolved to do the Carpenter that set it up some utter shame. Another flong his armes lyke cudgels at a peare tree, insomuch as it was mightily dreaded that he wold strike the candles that hung above their heades out of their sockettes, and leave them all darke. Another did nothing but winke and make faces" (249). The content of the play is irrelevant, like the content of Vanderhulke's pompous oration. Similarly the theological debate between Luther and Carolostadius is reduced to stances and gestures.

The emptiness of Wittenberg is made evident by Cornelius Agrippa, one of Nashe's favorite sources, who uses his occult powers to reduce academic humanism to a display of superficial magic. The assembled scholars call for visions of the favorite classic authors, until finally Cicero, the idolized Tully, is conjured up at his sophistical worst, pleading so eloquently "that all his auditours were readie to install his guiltie client for a God" (252). The effect of the scene is analogous to the actual Agrippa's debunking account of Cicero's eloquence in *Of the Vanity and Uncertainty of Arts and Sciences*. Because that book was seen as an ironic and paradoxical work, Agrippa had a reputation as a wit; Sidney wrote in *The Defense of Poetry* that "Agrippa will be as merry in showing the vanity of science as Erasmus was in commending of folly" (121). Agrippa was also a legendary magician, but the emphasis in *The Unfortunate Traveler* is more on how he uses his magic to undercut the pretensions and curiosity of his audience. There is an obvious parallel with the Nashe who is writing the book in hand.

An active, involved humanism is also advanced in the digression that brings Surrey and Jack to Rotterdam, "that was cleane out of our waie," so that they can meet up with "aged learnings chiefe ornament, that abundant and superingenious clarke, Erasmus, as also with merrie Sir Thomas Moore" (245). Erasmus and More are planning their respective masterpieces, *The Praise of Folly* and *Utopia*. Both books are "discontented studies," like so many of Nashe's works. Erasmus's book ironically attacks contemporary follies by pretending to praise them; More's book criticizes political exploitation under cover of describing an ideal commonwealth. Both men have the ingenuity and quick wit lacking among the scholars at Wittenberg, who were gross plodders with "some learning and reading, but no wit to make use of it" (251). This account of Erasmus and More is a way for Nashe to cite two precedents for the kind of humanistic satire he aspired to write himself. *The Praise of Folly* uses complex and self-reflexive ironies in ways that anticipate Nashe, while More uses fiction in *Utopia* to present social criticism in an acceptable form. Both works are cautious, potentially controversial, and ambiguous about their stands on the issues they raise. Both make complex use of personas: Folly delivers her own encomium and is sometimes foolish and sometimes wise; Utopia is seen through the eyes of the idealized Raphael Hythloday, who is himself presented in the context of a very pragmatic version of Thomas More.

Nashe also goes "clean out of his way" to include another of his literary heroes, the satirist Aretino, "one of the wittiest knaves that ever God made" (264). Jack praises his brilliant style and his rhetorical powers: "His pen was sharp pointed lyke a poinyard; no leafe he wrote on but was lyke a burning glasse to set on fire all his readers." Again, the praise mirrors Nashe's own program as a writer: "His sight pearst like lightning into the entrailes of all abuses." Particularly impressive is Aretino's political courage: "He was no timerous servile flatterer of the commonwealth wherein he lived" (265). Jack denies that Aretino penned an atheistic work attributed to him and excuses his lascivious works as youthful indiscretions. Aretino's effectiveness is contrasted with the Puritan diatribes of Nashe's own day: "Puritans, spue forth the venome of your dull inventions. A toade swels with thicke troubled poison, you swell with poisonous perturbations; your malice hath not a cleere dram of anie inspired disposition" (266). In this way Nashe links his praise of the Italian satirist with his own program as Aretino's English counterpart.

The Unfortunate Traveler does not include an explicit aesthetic to set against the idealistic theory of literature it parodies, but it does put itself in a context of ironic writers whom Nashe admired. Although the work is a fiction, it suggests that Nashe continued to think of himself as a humanist and a satirist rather than as a writer of narratives. The resources of fiction, such as characterization and verisimilitude, are used for satiric purposes rather than to achieve mimetic effects. The consistency of the work lies in its style and rhetoric, rather than in the self-contained realism we associate with the novel. The label that fits the work best is Menippean satire, although there is no evidence that Nashe was conscious of this genre. Both Erasmus and More were influenced by Lucian, and Nashe followed them even if he does not show any direct knowledge of the ancient satirist. Whether the work is called Mennipean or picaresque, it is, nevertheless, remarkably original and remarkably chaotic for an age when generic expectations usually governed literary form. Literary works always have some antecedents, but the mode of *The Unfortunate Traveler* is highly idiosyncratic, derived more from the sensibilities of Jack Wilton and his creator than from literary tradition.

JACK WILTON AS OUTLANDISH CHRONICLER

Jack Wilton functions both as a character in the story of *The Unfortunate Traveler* and as a persona in the manner of Pierce Penniless or Will Summers. He frustrates the reader raised on novels by being inconsistent as a character and oblique as a narrator. He does not react subjectively to the experiences he relates, except in flippant, unthinking fashion. The narrative progresses from the light comedy of the joke book material to the macabre story of Cutwolfe, but there is no corresponding development in Jack; he is as empty a vessel at the end as he was at the beginning. From one perspective he is merely a peg on which Nashe can hang his style; from another he is a minor character in his own adventure, made to play inconsistent roles as the occasion requires. Jack is often cited as the reason that the narrative fails to qualify as a novel. A protagonist in a novel learns from his or her adventures, or at least interacts with them, but Jack remains a *tabula rasa*. Criticism of *The Unfortunate Traveler* is often querulous; it is the archetypal novel manqué.

Jack's perceived shortcomings reflect a traditional, prepsychological conception of life that does not focus on individual development. From such a perspective, introspection is merely a path to the melancholic terrors of the night, as when Jack fantasizes his own dissection. Extroversion was more useful because the external social reality was the field of activity through which one had to carve a course. This was particularly true for the rogue or masterless man who willy-nilly violated social norms by not having an established role to play. Jack differs from his predecessor Pierce Penniless in his relative acceptance of his rogue status, although he is eager enough to serve Surrey for a time and is frightened back into the chivalric fold at the very end of the story. Like Pierce, though, Jack is impelled by his misfortunes to examine the problems of the world rather than the processes of his own mind. In good Elizabethan fashion, Jack conceives of self-knowledge as a knowledge of how his particular self can fit into external structures. Jack's external search is not articulated in a philosophic manner, nor is there any interest in coming to terms with the psychological effects of the bitterness generated by Jack's alienation.

Jack is an anti-Narcissus who looks into a pool and sees the reeds and the mud rather than his own reflection. Like a hysterical person, he projects his fears and concerns onto the world, living rather than dreaming his idylls and nightmares. His is a distorted world where events and people are transmogrified into grotesques. Of course we are dealing with a literary, not a psychological, artifact; the transmogrification is a product of Nashe's art, not of his character's mind, and conjectures about Nashe's own psychology are unprovable, however interesting they may be. Still, the very rawness of the narration does suggest that Nashe used Jack as an objectification of aspects of his own mind, assigning to his character an unhampered version of his own extemporaneous style and many of his own attitudes and obsessions. Through Jack he constructed a fiction that explores the contradictions between his own orthodox beliefs and his angry perception of social absurdity.

Speculation about Nashe's creative process helps to explain the vague temporal and geographical dimensions of the story. The work is an unsystematic anatomy rather than a mimetic re-creation of a period of time out of a developing character's life. Although the events are ordered sequentially, they are not ordered consequentially, except in the simplest fashion. The sequence is governed, not by the logic of events, nor by Jack's development as a character, but by Nashe's shifting interests. The threat to Jack becomes increasingly serious, but this shift from jests to the macabre is caused by external factors rather than being inherent in the story or in Jack's character. The presence of a central character and the coherence of the style make *The Unfortunate Traveler* a unified experience, even if it lacks the internal unity we associate with novels. As a persona who embodies Nashe's increasingly ironic attitude, Jack is central to the work's success, but as a character he is not psychologically consistent or believable.

Jack's characterization is subordinate to his function as teller of the tale. His narrative stance is set in the Induction, which suggests Jack's social role by postulating an audience of like-minded "dapper Mounsier Pages of the Court," clever pranksters not yet entered into the world of adult responsibilities. Jack is hailed as the king of pages and his story seen as his Acts and Monuments. This mock heroic note is developed in the first sentences of the narrative, where the heroism of the king is contrasted with the disreputable and fortuitous existence of the page:

> About that time that the terror of the world and feaver quartane of the French, Henrie the eight (the onely true subject of Chronicles), advanced his standard against the two hundred and fifty towers of Turney and Turwin, and had the Emperour and all the nobilitie of Flanders, Holand, & Brabant as mercenarie attendants on his ful-sayld fortune, I, Jacke Wilton, (a Gentleman at least,) was a certain kind of an appendix or page, belonging or appertaining in or unto the confines of the English court; where what my credit was, a number of my creditors that I cosned can testifie: *Coelum petimus stultitia,* which of us al is not a sinner? Bee it knowen to as many as will paie mony inough to peruse my storie, that I folowed the court or the camp, or the campe and the court, when Turwin lost her maidenhead, and opened her gates to more than Jane Trosse did. (2:209)

The first sentence descends from the heroic exploits of the king to the catch-as-catch-can trickery of a man of indeterminate origins and uncertain status. Even the syntax unbends and becomes more casual (Kaula, 50). The second sentence moves further into the antiheroic mind of a narrator who uses his wit to reduce events to comic relationships. A heroic victory becomes the occasion for a bawdy analogy. At this point Jack has no particular master and is not even certain why he is in France, except to take advantage of the opportunities for stratagems afforded by an army camp. We are struck from the outset by Jack's vivid, ironic voice; the "character" that is said to generate that voice is an insubstantial figure.

The subsequent opening section of *The Unfortunate Traveler* gives Jack a context but not a background. The format and tone of popular jest books establish Jack as a rouge, a gambler, and a petty confidence man who sometimes plays practical jokes simply to indulge his own talents for knavery. The jokes he relates link Jack with the literary tradition of jest-book heroes, like Scogan, Skelton, Will Summers, and Tarlton. Harvey attacked Greene and Nashe by associating them with jest-book heroes; Nashe's response is to make Jack a veritable hero in a jest book for the first few pages of the story. It effectively identifies him as a rogue who lives by using his wit to exploit the folly of others. It also anchors the style to a traditional form of irreverence; even the use of first-person narration has a precedent in Greene's rogue pamphlet, *The Black Book's Messenger* (1592). Jack is vaguely subversive, like the jest-book heroes or the Ned Browne of *The Black Book's Messenger*: his jokes cause disorder and undermine decorum. It has been suggested that Nashe started out to write a jest book, then became more serious, but it is more likely that he found a jest-book beginning the most effective way of establishing Jack's character and the rhetorical stance of his work (Weimann, "Jest-book").

Jack's wit transforms a miserly victualer into a Baron of Double Beer, then makes his jest at the victualer's expense into a satire on social pretension. To gain the victualer's confidence he treats him as though he were an aristocrat, addressing the same sort of praise to him that Nashe used in his dedications: he tells the victualer of "what entire affection I had borne him time out of minde, partly for the high descent and linage from whence hee sprong, and partly for the tender care and provident respect he had of pore souldiers, that . . . he vouchsafed in his owne person to be a victualler to the campe (a rare example of magnifisence and honorable curtesy)" (2:211). The irony is directed at Jack's victim, but the stress on the victualer's nobility also reflects adversely on the nature of magnificence and honor. "I speake it with teares, too few such noble men have wee, that will drawe drinke in linnen approns" (212). Indirection and ambivalence characterize the satire of *The Unfortunate Traveler*: is Nashe using the code of honor to mock the victualer or the victualer to mock the code of honor? Answering this question is complicated by the double nature of Jack as both hero and rogue. After he has duped the victualer into magnificently showing his nobility by distributing free drink and food to the camp, he is whipped for his "holiday lie," but the whipping is passed over without description, and those who whipped him enjoyed his prank.

Jack's second feat, his jettisoning of a temporary "master" who lived off Jack's profits as a gambler, is based on an appeal to "Captain Gogs-wounds's" heroic self-image. Like the victualer, the captain falls victim to flattery, believing he will show valor and gain reputation by spying on the French. Jack encourages the captain to see himself as a classical hero: "You have read stories, (Ile be sworne he never lookt in booke in his life,) howe many of the Romaine worthies were there that have gone as Spialls into their Enemies Campe?" (220). Jack also praises him for his ability to detect deceit even as he is deceiving him: "No humane braine may goe beyond you, none beguile you; you gull all, all feare you, love you, stoup to you" (222). The captain cannot bring off his imposture when he flees to the French but is spared hanging because he is so obviously a fool. Jack pauses to take pride in his accomplishments: "Here let me triumph a while, and ruminate a line or two on the excellence of my wit: but I will not breath neither till I have disfraughted all my knaverie" (225). He then tells how he impersonated a half-crown wench to cheat a lecherous Swiss captain, and how he made a company of fastidious clerks believe that the camp was invaded so that he could rifle their desks.

The opening jest-book section of *The Unfortunate Traveler* invites us to share in the pleasures of Jack's knavery while hinting that he himself is guilty of the pride he exploits in his victims. The jest books and rogue pamphlets that are Nashe's precedent beg the question of their heroes' immorality by focusing attention on comic victims who evoke no sympathy, but in Jack's jests there is a potential for violence and a sardonic edge to the telling that draws attention back to Jack's character. Jack mentions this in describing the jest directed at the clerks: "My masters, you may conceave of me what you list, but I thinke confidently I was ordained Gods scourge from above for their daintie finicalitie" (226). Being a scourge of God is a dangerous game, as Tamburlaine discovered, particularly when the self-appointed scourge is arrogantly proud of his talents. Describing the army camp as having much chaff mixed with the corn, he boasts: "Amongest this chaffe was I winnowing my wittes to live merrily, and by my troth so I did: the prince could but command men spend their bloud in his service, I could make them spend al the mony they had for my pleasure" (210). The jest-book section creates a moral ambiguity unlike the carefree atmosphere of actual Elizabethan jest books. In his modern edition of Nashe's works, J. B. Steane commented, "I have never found Jack Wilton's jokes quite as mirthful as he himself (and presumably the author) thinks them to be" (31). Jack is ethically problematical in a way that his legendary predecessors are not.

The tension between Jack's amorality and his readers' more ethical response to his knavery is generated in part by the first-person narration. Jack complacently boasts of his own exploits without any touch of repentance. The audience is imagined to be either a group of like-minded pages listening to Jack or a group of readers amused by his knavery. But the nature of the events he relates becomes increasingly serious as his exploitation of others gives way to a desperate effort to save himself from exploitation. Jack continues to be the jest-book hero long after the story ceases to deal with jests and roguery. This discrepancy between Jack's ebullient narration and the reader's increasingly troubled response allows Nashe to question orthodox beliefs while passing off any irreverence as a product of Jack's character. It is not that Jack is a simple stalking-horse; Nashe himself was probably ambivalent about his unorthodox attitudes, and in any case, the effect is complex rather than simple. Jack's indifference to the king's heroic goals in France cannot be reduced to a simple irony whereby either the king or Jack is unambiguously in the wrong.

Critics have been uncertain how to take "serious" passages in the work, like Jack's impromptu diatribe against the Anabaptists or the admonition on the dangers of travel by the banished earl who saves Jack from execution in Rome. For example, Latham believes that the earl's speech would evoke a smile from an Elizabethan reader (89), whereas more recent critics have seen it as a serious statement (Gohlke, 405–6; Leggatt, 40–41). In the context of Nashe's other works the speech is a statement of beliefs important to Nashe, but presented through Jack's roguish perspective it seems as irrelevant as Surrey's idealized love for Geraldine. Jack's iconoclastic style threatens to turn everything into parody.

Jack's main function is rhetorical: he gives a local habitation and a name to a skeptical attitude and an accompanying ironic style developed out of Nashe's own style and attitudes but exaggerated and linked to a tradition of irreverent jest-book heroes and rogues. As a rhetorical device, Jack allows Nashe to consider unorthodox ideas and to express his frustrations and aggression while escaping the consequences by attributing any objectionable implications to his rogue hero. For example, the depiction of Surrey as an enamored aristocrat can be read as a harmless burlesque or as a criticism of the chivalric code of the Elizabethan court. Similarly, the account of Wittenberg can be and was seen as an attack on the academic humanism Nashe encountered at Cambridge, or it can be dismissed as a combination of parody and toothless academic humor. Is Heraclide a heroic victim like Shakespeare's Lucrece, or is she a parody of such maudlin martyrs to the ideal of chastity? In each of these cases our assessment of the character and situation depends on how much we think Jack's roguish consciousness distorts his account. His point of view opens out the range of meanings possible, often confusing rather than clarifying the reader's response. The uncertainty created is partly obfuscation and partly a defensive strategy, but it is also a liberation from the ideology that limits many of Nashe's other works.

This complexity in Jack's point of view is embodied in the flexible style, which combines a diversity of rhetorical modes. Jack has been given the ultimate accolade of being hailed as a progenitor of Falstaff—indeed, at least one "disintegrator" of Shakespeare's texts imagined that Nashe had a hand in the composition of the *Henry IV* plays (Gerrard, 211–46). The style is like Falstaff's in its poetic use of speech rhythms and in the witty imagery that links high and low aspects of Elizabethan life in violation of the usual decorums of the period. Nashe's Jack is also given to comic *ad hoc* role-playing like Shakespeare's Jack, or their common ancestors Dick Tarlton and Martin Marprelate. Both Jacks are masters of burlesque and parody because both are adept at using rhetoric to control situations either for knavish or comic purposes. Wit also has an apparent internal function for both characters; it allows them to cope with their marginal status and the uglier threats of the societies they inhabit.

Looked at more formally, the style of *The Unfortunate Traveler* is a perfected version of the extemporaneous style Nashe had been developing since the "Preface to *Menaphon*." It is similar to the style of *Pierce Penniless* or *The Terrors of the Night*, but less constrained by Nashe's need to censure his arrogance and temper his more controversial views. Because Jack is a rogue, Nashe can ignore decorum and indulge his talent for the "fantastical." The apparent spontaneity may, I suspect, be a product of Nashe's art, but whether or not he labored over his text, he wanted it to be read as an off-the-cuff performance, uttered unreflexively by Jack to a group of similarly irreverent listeners. Like Jack's liberty as a rogue, his spontaneity frees him to express the discrepancies between the idealism of Elizabethan orthodoxy and the more sordid reality of most people's lives. In stylistic terms this leads to a mixture of the idealized high style of heroic amplification with a comic low style that deflates pretensions. Nashe was diverging from the orthodox values he began his career defending, but he was not sympathetic with the values of the newly self-conscious middle class that found a voice in Puritan tracts and in the romances of Thomas Deloney. Nashe's style in *The Unfortunate Traveler* reflects both the freedom and the uncertainty of his movement away from the orthodox ideology.[1]

Although Jack's rhetorical function governs much of his characterization, he is also a character in a story subtitled "The Life of Jack Wilton." It will be argued below that the satire is attached primarily to the fiction that the book is a traveler's account, but Nashe also exploits biographical conventions. At the start he twice calls Jack's story his "acts and monuments," linking *The Unfortunate Traveler* with John Foxe's popular *Book*

---

1. Nashe's style is, of course, a study in itself. Some major discussions are Croston; Friederich; Gibbons; Knights, 301–14. Kaula is useful on Nashe's flexibility; Weimann, on his ideological ambivalence.

of Martyrs, which, like most early biographies and histories, focuses on the heroic exploits of great men rather than on how they became great. Jack is only ironically heroic, but like Foxe, Nashe is interested in how Jack's character stands up to increasingly severe tests, rather than in how he became the sort of witty rogue he is. In Foxe the faith of martyrs is tested; in Nashe Jack's wit is subjected to increasingly difficult tasks. Sometimes he is required to exercise his wit actively, as in his practical jokes or his impersonation of Surrey, but more often he uses his wit passively as a way of coping with an absurd reality that threatens to confuse and daunt him. The work is not schematic, but Jack's use of wit as a form of defense begins to predominate after his arrival in Italy.

This change in emphasis occurs when the prostitute Tabatha the Temptress and her polyglot pimp Petro de campo Frego inveigle Surrey and Jack into their house, then try to suborn the servant to assist them in murdering the master. Since Surrey and Jack have switched roles, the plan fails (Nashe leaves unexplored any implication that Jack might have helped murder Surrey if the tables had been reversed). Surrey and Jack attempt to outtrick the Italians by pretending to acquiesce to the plan and then playacting a discovery as a way of extorting money from the whore and her pimp: Surrey, in his role as servant, pretending to be "striken with remorse of conscience, (God be with him, for he could counterfeit most daintily)," goes "downe on his knees, askt me forgivenesse, and impeached Tabitha and Petro de campo Frego as guiltie of subornation" (257). This variation of the "badger game" seems to work, but the apparently terrified Italians turn out to be more skillful at counterfeiting than the English, paying them off in counterfeit gold that lands them in prison. Jack comments that the experience "planted in us the first Italionate wit that we had" (260), but Jack's playful English roguery is no match for the diabolical villainy of Italy. He must henceforth strain his wit to defend his body from the knife of the anatomist and the lust of Juliana, and his soul from the dismaying examples of human evil and suffering he witnesses.

The dangers that Jack survives in Italy are not presented as retribution for the pride he manifested in earlier sections of the story. Such a pattern of sin and retribution is common in Elizabethan fiction (Helgerson) and is perhaps implicit in Jack's life story, but Jack himself is rarely conscious of any such design, and Nashe does not indicate that it is an important concern. Jack witnesses a play about the prodigal son, but the theme makes no impression on him, nor is it emphasized in the text. Nashe is more interested in the ethics of the society Jack experiences than in the ethics of his hero. Although Jack's alienation from society is like that of a prodigal, Jack is too insubstantial a character to bear much guilt or function as a study in evil. His egocentricity is related to the manifestations of pride he encounters, but he learns little from example or from punishment, except perhaps at the very end of his adventures. Though superficially like Iago, he lacks the inner dimension of Shakespeare's villain. Jack's crimes are glossed over, and his presumption is a source of humor rather than moral insight.

Nevertheless, presumptuous Jack is, and his wanton wit is a topic of *The Unfortunate Traveler*, even if only intermittently (Gohlke). The self-centeredness apparent in the early jests and the exploitation of Surrey's folly correspond to the pride of the people Jack encounters. As in Lyly's *Euphues: The Anatomy of Wit*, Nashe's emphasis is on the intellectual pride that shows itself in arrogant self-confidence and contempt for others. Jack's pride in his own wit never causes him to be vicious, but it does lull him into neglect of his own vulnerability. In northern Europe Jack's egocentricity is overshadowed by the people he meets, people like the pompous academics of Wittenberg. In Italy, "that countrie which was such a curious molder of wits" (255), Jack encounters people who surpass the northern Europeans in viciousness because their code of values is pre-Reformation and focused on externals. If Germans like Vanderhulke tend to be so caught up in themselves that they become fools, the Italians are so obsessed with their reputations that they become knaves. Once in Italy, Jack acquires a courtesan, scorns moral advice, and steals gold from the corrupt mistress of the pope. Yet such sins are insignificant in a context of Esdras and Zachery.

Nashe does not emphasize the sin in Jack's schemes and subterfuges, nor does he explore the moral implications of

Jack's other acts. The banished earl criticizes Jack for being a traveler—a manifestation of his wanton wit, since he has no mission or goal—but Jack's culpability in leaving home is made an issue only late in the narrative. Jack's misuse of his wit is a secondary theme in the work, less important than his admirable use of that same wit to survive in the absurd and vicious world that threatens him. In any case, his actions are unimportant during most of the story; often he functions as a mere observer. For example, his role in the "truculent tragedy" of Esdras and Cutwolfe is accidental, although its outcome has a powerful effect on him. He never achieves the consistency as a character that would elicit a judgment of him as a moral agent.

Jack's wit is more important as an internal process for coming to terms with the realities he encounters. For the Elizabethans, of course, wit was the central intellectual faculty, incorporating the ability to see analogies and make distinctions. Wit did not yet mean primarily verbal ingenuity, although such ingenuity, like the ability to plan knavery or write allegory, was a function of wit. As the individual became more isolated from others and from an all-encompassing tradition that assigned meaning and values, wit became particularized and problematic. In anatomizing wit in his *Euphues* Lyly showed that the individual's private understanding of the world was likely to be distorted by pride and self-deceit. Euphues learns from experience that the wit he is so proud of can be antithetical to true wisdom, because wisdom draws on the experiences of others over time and on revealed truth that transcends experience. Wit becomes a problem when it is too closely tied to an individual perspective: such wit can easily lead to solipsism or villainy.

Gabriel Harvey saw Nashe as an example of wit gone amuck, linking him with Martin Marprelate, Lyly, Greene, and Aretino. Nashe was sensitive to such criticism because he had used similar arguments against Phillip Stubbes, Martin Marprelate, and uneducated popular writers. His dedications frequently show his awareness that his singularity might seem arrogant rather than admirable. Shortly after completing *The Unfortunate Traveler* he disowned it as a trivial work in the epistle to *Christ's Tears* and renounced wit because it was incompatible with Christian humility. But in spite of that temporary and perhaps strategic renunciation, Nashe prided himself on his singular wit and prized the faculty in others. We need look no further than the praise for Aretino in *The Unfortunate Traveler*, which, given Aretino's notoriety, amounted to defiance of the commonplace strictures on wit and singularity (McPherson). Although it is Jack who praises Aretino, there is no suggestion that the praise is to be discounted because of its source.

Like his creator, Jack exhibits the "lateral resourcefulness" that Thomas Greene describes as part of the new flexibility of self in Renaissance literature (241–64). Jack's singular wit allows him to cope with a disorganized and confusing reality where traditional ethical guidelines seem remote. Wit is a way of controlling emotions and ordering reality both for Jack and for Nashe. Pierce Penniless is the transitional figure: the jokes made about poverty by Jack, Pierce, and Nashe in his personal letter to William Cotton are all of a piece. Joking is integral to the wit of character, persona, and author because it helps to restructure reality in a way that channels aggression and deadens pain. Thus, in *The Unfortunate Traveler*, slaughter in battle, the plague, and public executions are presented in a comic fashion tht allows Jack (and Nashe) to face the pain and horror of such events, even if this distancing is often callous. There is a streak of sadism, but at least Jack is not sentimental or myopic about the exploitation and suffering he witnesses. Nashe's accomplishment is obvious if we contrast his accounts of sickness and suffering with the factual accounts in the chronicle histories that were his source, or with the green world of the romances he parodies.

Through the wit Nashe lends him, Jack achieves a complexity lacking in his character. Wit allows him to survive psychologically as well as physically. Early in the book, after his experience of the sweating sickness has forced him to flee England, Jack seeks employment as a mercenary in a battle between the Swiss and French. He wanted to thrust himself "into that Faction that was strongest," but the battle is already underway when he arrives:

It was my good lucke or my ill (I know not which) to come just to the fighting of the Battell; where I saw a wonderfull spectacle of blood-shed on both sides: here unweeldie Switzers wallowing in their gore, like an Oxe in his dung, there the sprightly French sprawling and turning on the stained grasse, like a Roach new taken out of the streame: all the ground was strewed as thicke with Battle-axes as the Carpenters yard with chips; the Plaine appeared like a quagmyre, overspred as it was with trampled dead bodies. (2:231)

The ugliness of death is reduced by grotesque comparisons, while the balanced syntax emphasizes Jack's indifference to the goals of either side. His wit shows itself in the outlandish similes which serve here to discount the heroism usually associated with battle. His contempt for the code of honor is summed up in a pun: "Anie man might give Armes that was an actor in that Battell, for there were more armes and legs scattered in the Field that day than will be gathered up till Doomes-day" (ibid.).

In this fashion Jack's wit allows him to face the terrors of the day, particularly the spectacle of human mortality. "Jack the narrator keeps reality at a distance with his wit, stylistic brilliance, and drink, because reality is simply too horrible to contemplate seriously" (S. Miller, 105). His travels begin as a series of escapades, but they soon become a sequence of ordeals that try his capacity to process the raw material of experience into the tolerable patterns of his own wit. Those patterns are capricious and idiosyncratic, a substitute for a more normative ordering of experience. A less imaginatively agile person might well be defeated by experiences like Jack's, either by succumbing to despair or being reduced to answering evil with evil. At times Jack loses control, as when he cannot face his own dissection at Zachary's hands, but more often his wit triumphs over the grossness of his experience. He finds little consolation in philosophy, as argued at Wittenberg, nor religion, as represented by Luther or the pope, but his imagination makes life tolerable.

At the very end his wit does fail him; he cannot translate the story of Esdras and Cutwolfe into acceptable form. He is not directly threatened, but Cutwolfe's insane revenge and the cruelty of his execution prove too much for Jack: "Mortifiedly abjected and danted was I with this truculent tragedie of Cutwolfe and Esdras. To such straight life did it thence forward incite me that ere I went out of Bolognia I married my curtizan, performed many almes deedes; and hasted so fast out of the Sodom of Italy, that within fortie daies I arrived at the king of Englands campe twixt Ardes and Guines in France, where he with great triumphs met and entertained the Emperour and the French king, and feasted many daies" (327–28). He repents because he sees that murder and revenge are a recurring pattern dominating Italian life and is shocked by Cutwolfe's confession, which emphasizes his blasphemous desire to destroy Esdras's soul as well as his body. Jack is also abjected and daunted by his sense that a providential design predominates over human willfulness and self-importance.

But Jack's reformation is too abrupt to be very convincing: what might be the climax of a serious story of redemption is here wrapped up in two sentences. His performance of many alms deeds before he hastens out of the "Sodom of Italy" is an unlikely sequence of events, while his marriage to Diamante is more like the marriage of Touchstone and Audrey than a love match. The promise of a sequel if the work pleased is evidence that Nashe would have set Jack traveling again if there had been any encouragement. Jack's retreat from Italy is more a device to end his adventures at a comfortable pamphlet length than a resolution of the conflict between his amoral narration and the immorality he describes. Still, if Nashe is not serious about Jack (who is after all a contrivance), he is perhaps more serious about the complex view of the world generated by Jack's perceptions. Jack can be put on the shelf and taken down if needed again, but the world he experiences is, however much exaggerated, a version of the world Nashe inhabited.

TRAVELS IN THE REALM OF FORTUNE

Although a reading of *The Unfortunate Traveler* can be centered on Jack Wilton, the work's coherence emerges best when it is approached as a fictional travel account rather than as a pseudobiography. It may be subtitled "The Life of Jack Wilton," but the emphasis is less on him than on what he witnesses. The main title, *The Unfortunate Traveler*, better represents the work's focus on the relationship between estrangement and the power of fortune. In the Elizabethan period, to travel was to submit oneself to the dangers of misfortune and the ultimate threat of death. Nashe uses these implications of travel to reveal humanity's foolish, noble, and villainous efforts to circumvent fortune. Jack's own life is at first a vain attempt to master fortune through stratagems, then an increasingly grotesque struggle not to succumb to cynicism and despair in response to misfortune. His travels are unfortunate not so much because of what he suffers as because of his experience of suffering and villainy as the human condition.

The episodic structure of the work is like that of popular travel books in its mixture of geographical and historical information with accounts of personal adventures. Like most Elizabethans, Nashe was in fact an armchair traveler, who, as he phrased it, "travelled in histories" (2:266). His book of imaginary travels does not represent itself as a factual account of Europe, nor is it particularly concerned with history as a process or as a source of Elizabethan culture. Instead it uses history symbolically, contrasting its arbitrary and often cruel events with the "golden world" of idealistic literature. The book is no more about travel than it is about Jack, but Elizabethan attitudes towards travel and foreign lands are used as a central analogy in the development of a pessimistic view of human experience.

The Elizabethans' ambivalence about foreign travel was in part an objective response to the reality of European nations and in part a projection of their own preconceptions and stereotypes (Hunter, "Elizabethans and Foreigners"). Their sense of place was symbolic, not factual; they lacked the modern conception of environment and a relativistic awareness of national cultures. In particular theological and political divisions colored their understanding of what countries and peoples were like. Italy and especially Rome acquired an apocalyptic significance because of the belief that the pope was Antichrist locked in battle with England, where true religion was resurgent. Northern Europe was somewhere in the middle symbolically as well as geographically: its Protestantism imperfect and the character of its people prone to national vices. The English character had flaws as well, and the perfection of the English church was in dispute, but compared to foreigners the English were a blessed race. National pride found expression in xenophobia; foreign entanglements were suspect, and resident foreigners were harassed. A few years before *The Unfortunate Traveler* was written, unemployment among weavers caused hostility towards Flemish immigrants. Shortly after Nashe wrote, the alleged conspiracy of the queen's doctor, Roderigo Lopez, a converted Jew of Portuguese origins, caused a surge of anti-Semitism that Nashe anticipated in his portrayal of Zadoch and Zachary (Brown). In short, attitudes towards the Continent were emotional and distorted by Elizabethan ideological needs.

At the same time Europe dominated the culture of Elizabethan England, the more so the further up on the social scale one looked. English culture remained a version of the international feudal culture of the Middle Ages, although it had been naturalized in many ways and modified by the Reformation, itself of European origins. Humanism had also been an international movement, cosmopolitan rather than nationalistic in its assumptions. Style in architecture, clothing, manners, and the like were heavily influenced by Continental practices; this caused increasing conflict between court circles and those Puritans and citizens who followed more indigenous fashions and customs. Literature was also under the shadow of foreign precedents: Spenser set out to excel Ariosto, and Sidney advocated establishing an English vernacular literature. Thus, except for folk customs, English culture of the sixteenth century was still largely a subdivision of European culture. Self-conscious about being "provincial," the Elizabethans were chauvinistic about their incipient national culture and ambivalent about foreign influence. The contradictions often followed class and religious lines; in the next century they contributed to the social fractures that caused the civil war (P. Thomas).

In such a context of stereotypes and prejudices, travel was a controversial undertaking (Fink; C. Howard, 50–71). Roger

Ascham had denounced foreign travel as a source of corruption instead of education; he believed travel to Italy was especially dangerous. His disapproval was widely echoed and augmented, but other writers continued to argue for the educational value of travel, and a tour of the Continent remained a common component in the education of the aristocracy. Returned travelers were ridiculed because of their affected foreign manners and dress—Jack describes his outlandish costume when he first returned to England (2:227). More serious was the fear that travelers would become atheists, papists, or both at once. The physical dangers of travel—shipwreck, disease, treachery—were less significant than the danger to the soul. Ascham's distrust of Italy developed into a national paranoia: all of the Elizabethan fears of foreigners and malcontents became focused on travel to the land of the pope, Jesuits, and Machiavellians. Lord Burghley advised that his grandsons should never cross the Alps, "for they shall learn nothing there but pride, blasphemy and atheism." (Einstein, 160; see also Hunter "English Folly and Italian Vice").

The traveler differed from the voyager, although the terms overlapped in practice (Loiseau). Voyagers venture outward to gain the future benefits of knowledge and riches for themselves and their country; travelers are turned inward and towards the past by their alienating encounter with foreign lands. Voyagers explore new worlds beyond Christian Europe; travelers delve into the traditions of the Old World and into history. Although Nashe was fascinated by Hakluyt's accounts of voyages, Jack Wilton is a traveler who stays well within the bounds of European civilization and whose adventures involve ancient deceptions rather than new, exotic dangers. His transitions from place to place are glossed over in simple phrases: "over Sea with my implements I got me"; "I flew me over to Munster"; "to Bologna with a mery gale we poasted." In *The Unfortunate Traveler* travel is not a movement from place to place but a relationship between a person and a place, the alienated and precarious state of the outsider or stranger. Jack is closer to his listeners or readers than to anyone he encounters on his travels, including his master Surrey, whom he both idolizes and exploits, and Diamante, who is not a confidant or companion. Jack is essentially alone, even when among crowds of people.

These symbolic implications of travel are the burden of the banished earl's admonition to Jack Wilton, after his misadventures have almost brought him to the gallows. The earl reminds him that "the first traveller was Cain, and he was called a vagabond runnagate on the face of the earth" (2:297). Because the traveler lacks any social standing in the countries he visits, he lacks freedom: "It is but a milde kinde of subjection to be the servant of one master at once: but when thou hast a thousand thousand masters, as the veriest botcher, tinker, or cobler freeborne will dominere over a forreiner, and thinke to bee his better or master in companie; then shalt thou finde there is no such hell as to leave thy fathers house (thy naturall habitation) to live in the land of bondage" (297–98). Unprotected by custom or law, the traveler survives by deceit; one must "beleeve nothing, trust no man; yet seeme thou as thou swallowedst al, suspectedst none, but wert easie to be gulled by everie one" (298). Such deviousness was in fact common in an age when travelers gave odds against their safe return as a form of insurance (C. Howard, 90–95). These practices are not, however, natural for plain-dealing Englishmen. "Rats and mice ingender by licking one another; he must licke, he must croutch, he must cog, lye, and prate, that either in the Court or a forren Countrey will ingender and come to preferment" (299). The earl's mention of the court shows that travel is a metaphor for a way of living as well as an actual undertaking.

The banished earl's account of himself extends the symbolic implications of travel to include humanity's double alienation from the world and from God. "I am a banisht exile from my country, though nere linkt in consanguinitie to the best: an Earle borne by birth, but a begger now as thou seest. These manie yeres in Italy have I lived an outlaw" (302). In urging Jack to return home he compares his own state to the estrangment of Satan: "Get thee home, my yong lad, laye thy bones peaceably in the sepulcher of thy fathers, waxe olde in overlooking thy grounds, be at hand to close the eyes of thy kinred. The divel and I am desperate, he of being restored to heaven, I of being recalled home" (303). As might be expected, Jack scorns this "grave fatherly" advice, but the advice itself is not undercut. In attacking travel, the earl is attacking the wanderlust that motivates journeying to foreign lands without a specific goal. Travel is contrasted with staying at home, which stands synecdochically for loyalty to the land of one's birth and one's kin. Travelers become so corrupt that they abandon their families, disown their country, and lose their faith. Conversely, travel can be a symptom rather than a cause, as in the despair of Pierce Penniless, whose loss of faith in his country precedes his desire to travel and his resolution to sell his soul to the devil.

Travel easily acquired such symbolic overtones because of the pervasive analogy of the pilgrimage of life, a popular trope derived from classical and biblical sources (Chew; Hahn, 114–73). Nashe applied the *peregrinatio vitae* image to his own life in *The Terrors of the Night*, as we have seen: "He that writes this can tell, for he hath never had good voyage in his life but one, & that was to a fortunate blessed Iland" (1:374)—the Isle of Man, where Sir George Carey's patronage saved Nashe from being a "wretched banished exile," like his fictional earl. In literature the *peregrinatio vitae* has taken many forms, often being implicit in the voyage of a hero or quest of a knight. The series of obstacles confronting the hero—dangers to pass or temptations to resist—tests his mettle and, through the symbolic implications of the adventure, educates the reader in virtue. Such works often embody an opposition between the will of the hero and the hostility of fate, either in the form of the wrath of the gods or the indifference of fortune. Shipwrecks, the will of despots, or the power of enchantment might be evidence of the dominance of fortune or fate. This conception of a symbolic journey that tested the character of a hero even influenced the accounts of actual voyages in Hakluyt (Jewkes).

Jack's metaphoric travels are unfortunate not because he encounters ill luck but because he travels into the uncertain realm of fortune. Jack says that he will "beare halfe stakes with" Surrey "in the lotterie of travell" (2:243). As we have seen, Sidney saw life in history as subject to fortune; in the Christian framework we are all exiles destined to wander in a hostile world. In this sense there is no return home possible for Jack. His unfortunate travels are all the life that he has; it was the mortal threat of the sweating sickness in England that forced him back to the Continent. Unlike the hero of an epic, he neither desires to return home (or to create a new home) nor does he have a quest to fulfill. Much is made of Dr. Faustus, but Jack is the more archetypal modern man. He is a wanderer without destination, transported from place to place by chance, fear, and his own curiosity. He is indifferent to which side wins in the battle he witnesses, and he has no desire to earn glory as a military hero. His travels can be criticized as self-indulgent, but he is not vicious: ambition, avarice, and malice are sins too mortal for venial Jack. By the end of the book he has survived encounters with death, crime, and human suffering that show life to be in essence unfortunate. But the ethical implications are muted by the absence of any clearly defined alternative. The banished earl's advice is sound, but we are never told that Jack has any ancestral lands or kindred to return to in England.

In Christian terms the lives of Jack Wilton and of people like him are bound to be unfortunate, since life in this world should be a pilgrimage towards a better life, not an end in itself like the wanderings of a tourist. This religious perspective is implied in the banished earl's admonition, but it is not insisted on in the work; Nashe's cynical view of this world outweighs any vision he has to offer of the next. Even the overtly religious *Christ's Tears over Jerusalem* is more successful at depicting the sins and suffering of the old Jerusalem and of London than it is at pointing the way to the New Jerusalem. Still, like all Elizabethan literature, *The Unfortunate Traveler* was first read in a Christian context, even if that context remains external during most of the text. Jack's travels are in a Christian universe, however distorted and absurd that universe is at times. The very distortions and absurdities define themselves in Christian terms: the Anabaptists are guilty of pride; Surrey's obsessive love is idolatrous; Zachery, the Jewish anatomist, has an Old Testament fixation on the flesh and revenge. Nashe probably had no conscious religious intentions; if he had, he would have made a claim for them in the dedication or in the epistles to *Christ's Tears*. *The Unfortunate Traveler* is not an allegorical or consistently symbolic work, but it reflects Elizabethan religious attitudes towards the world.

The sublunary world was believed to be the realm of fortune, although a providential design underlay what often seemed chance to human intelligence (Chew, 35–45). To limit one's scope to the world was to subject oneself to the caprices of fortune—a fatal misdirection of one's desires, since the pleasures and goods of the world are transitory. The Elizabethans had a vivid sense of the instability of fortune because of the insecure conditions of life in sixteenth-century England, as well as because of Christian doctrine. Calvin's pessimistic view of reason and the human will found receptive ground in a society where economic deprivations and sudden death were common. Calvin stressed that life was a matter of endurance rather than the achievement of salvation through good works. Since the *peregrinatio vitae* was an obstacle course, not a vale of soul-making, one should remain detached (Hahn, 155–58).

There was an abundance of literature, epitomized by the popular *Mirror for Magistrates*, that depicted the interplay between fallible human wills and the arbitrary turns of fortune's wheel. The underlying design of providence was often not stressed, since much of this literature was intended more to promote a stoic detachment from the things of this world than to inculcate faith, which was assumed. When the alternative religious perspective is left implicit, such works can seem skeptical and fatalistic to the modern reader, and indeed, many writers and readers in the sixteenth century may have had little faith in providence, to judge from the criticisms of secular literature by the Puritans and others. Jack Wilton's adventures are often like those in literature written as a remedy against fortune, but the vivid depiction of suffering and the ugliness of the providential design that is adumbrated do not inspire confidence or hope.

Jack's initial attitude towards fortune is optimistic, both because he can master events through the exercise of wit and because he experiences a string of luck. Jack is a gambler who wins with his dice and his verbal skills. His success is set in a context of misfortune: the sweating sickness, the battle between the French and the Swiss, the massacre of the Anabaptists. Until he arrives in Italy, Jack's luck holds, so he is not deeply affected by what he sees, in part because his wit transforms ugliness and horror into whimsey. When he arrives at the battle of Marignano too late to choose sides, he comments, "It was my good lucke or my ill (I know not which)" (2:231). His ambivalence reflects the unpredictability of fortune: he might have prospered in the battle or ended up one of those wallowing in gore. In spite of the sufferings he witnesses, Jack's personal luck continues, as when he accidentally meets up with the generous Surrey: "Good Lord, see the changing chances of us knights arrant infants" (241). Throughout his northern European adventures, except for minor setbacks, Jack is a most fortunate traveler.

As soon as he and Surrey arrive in Italy, however, their mastery of fate is threatened by the supersubtle practices of Tabitha the Temptress and her pimp: "So it fortuned (fie uppon that unfortunate worde of Fortune) that this whoore, this queane . . . had given me a great deal of counterfeit gold" (2:258). After he is freed from jail, Jack prospers for a while because of Diamante's wealth, but in Rome misfortunes exceed his ingenuity. He begins to see fortune in providential terms when he is almost hanged on the false charge of raping Heraclide: he refers to his imprisonment as the beginning of his purgatory and to his subsequent capture by Zadoch as punishment for failing to heed the banished earl's advice: "God plagud me for deriding such a grave fatherly advertiser. List the worst throw of ill luckes" (303). His loss of control over his own fate is also evident in his comment on Juliana's lustful and potentially fatal designs on him: "Little did I surmise that fortune reserved me to so faire a death" (308). Perhaps Jack regains confidence in his control over fortune when Diamante saves him from Juliana and they flee to Bologna, but the fates of Esdras and Cutwolfe remind him of the limitations of the human will and the awfulness of providential design.

But Jack's fortunes, good and bad, are only one strand in the narrative; most of the characters he encounters are trying to master fortune by one stratagem or another. The solutions of the various individuals and groups are partial, as they must be, since their remedies against fortune all involve substituting a worldly end for a transcendent goal. Some involvements in the world are harmless enough, like Surrey's idolatrous love for Geraldine; others are vicious, like Cultwolfe's code of revenge. The Anabaptists are made arrogant by their willful and egalitarian heresy; the academic humanists lose themselves in the gestures and forms of their discipline.

The work is not schematic; any attempt to delineate its themes or make articulate its structure contradicts the random effect of the actual narration, which is as capricious as fortune. Nashe did not have firm intentions or a clear design. Nevertheless there is a pattern in the episodes: set against misfortune are various forms of pride, since pride is a cause and effect of people subjecting themselves to the world. The pride in question is the basic sin that was thought to underlie vanity and arrogance, the pride that causes people to forget their place in the social and cosmic hierarchies (Tuve, 119–25). The best gloss on Nashe's understanding of pride is his discussion of the "frontiers of sin" in *Christ's Tears over Jerusalem,* the work he presumably wrote immediately after the *The Unfortunate Traveler.* There, he saw the new sins of urban society as forms of pride and hoped that the plague would remind London of human mortality: "Why doe wee raigne as Gods on the earth, that are to bee eaten with wormes?" (2:90). In *The Unfortunate Traveler* the characters' attempts to circumvent fortune are manifestations of pride, while the grotesque depictions of human suffering and mortality expose the vanity of such aspirations.

The code of personal honor is one form of pride and one way of subjecting the self to the powers of fortune. As we have seen, Jack exploits the code in his duping of the Baron of Double Beer and Captain Gogs-wounds. His cynicism about honor is also reflected in the mock heroic style common in the work. The code of honor itself was no joking matter in Elizabethan England: the Tudors had attempted to moralize and control a system of values that, by focusing on the will of the individual knight, had traditionally given potentially seditious autonomy to knights and aristocrats (James). The code valued "steadfastness" and loyalty over Christian charity, and its rewards were in this world rather than in the next, although a knight might also be a good man who merited salvation. A knight could be shamed by apparent abjectness, even though his actions were virtuous in the eyes of God. As contentious and violent as it was, the honor code existed in uneasy truce with Christian values. It persisted into the sixteenth century, if anything, further secularized by the revival of classical texts, but it was under continual pressure from church and state (Watson, 102–35). A distinction was made between the personal ambition for honor that was a form of pride and the true honor that showed itself as duty to the state, and the conflict between these different conceptions of honor was a common theme in literature— Sidney's *Arcadia* and Shakespeare's history plays come to mind. As we have seen, Nashe himself subscribed to a version of the code of honor in many of his works.

The Florentine tourney is a travesty of the honor code from beginning to end. Besotted with love, Surrey's loyalty is not to his country or king but to Geraldine. Jack comments, "Onely the Earle of Surrie, my master, observed the true measures of honour, and made all his encounterers new scoure their armor in the dust: so great was his glory that day as Geraldine was therby eternally glorifid" (2:278). The Florentines are even more impressed than Jack: "Everie one strived to magnifie him more than other." Surrey planned more feats "worthie the Annals of posteritie," but because of the king's command, "his fame was quit cut off by the shins" (279). The code is also mocked in Jack's excuse for impersonating Surrey after they have parted: he had a large sum of money "which I knew not how better to imploy for the honor of my country, than by spending it munificently under your name. No English-man would I have renowned for bountie, magnificence, and curtesie but you; under your colours all my meritorious workes I was desirous to shroud" (268). Surrey is mollified by this implausible story, since Jack "clipte not the wings of his honour, but rather increast them with additions of expence" (269).

The code of honor is also satirized in the passing ritual Jack introduces among the pages at Windsor and in the puns on the granting of arms in his account of the carnage at Marignano. Honor in the form of glory and reputation is stressed in Jack's account of Rome. After viewing the monuments, he comments, "Tyll this daie not a Romane (if he be a right Romane indeed) will kill a rat, but he will have some registred remembraunce of it" (279). Rome is very much the city of man, an apt setting for the final misadventures of Jack: "Let me be a historiographer of my owne misfortunes, and not meddle with the continued Trophees of so olde a triumphing Citie" (281). This ironic treatment of the code of honor with its trappings and memorials illustrates how foolish pride is in a context of relentless misfortune.

The criticism of the religious pride of the Anabaptists is more scornful and incredulous: "Verie devout Asses they were, for all they were so dunstically set forth, and such as thought they knew as much of Gods minde as richer men: why, inspiration was their ordinarie familiar, and buzd in their eares like a Bee in a boxe everie hower what newes from heaven, hell, and the land of whipperginnie" (233). Although Jack later expresses compassion for the Anabaptists when they are massacred by the emperor's soldiers, their fanaticism is the occasion for an uncharacteristic digression on religious sects that recapitulates Nashe's long-standing opposition to Puritanism: "Let me dilate a litle more gravely than the nature of this historie requires, or wilbe expected of so yong a practitioner in divinity" (234). The diatribe is an explicit excursus on the dangers of religious pride. The humbly born Anabaptists violate the social hierarchy in their desire for power, and they are guilty of presuming on God's grace.

As so often in Nashe, pride in the form of singularity is set in opposition to humility and obedience. Nashe takes for granted the "lawfulness of the authority" that sects like the Anabaptists and the Puritans oppose. Their arrogant effort to assail heaven without regard for received tradition is doomed to fail. Christ demands the suppression of personal desires, but "these Anabaptists had not yet forsooke all and followed Christ, they had not forsooke their owne desires of revenge and innovation, they had not abandoned their expectation of the spoile of their enimies, they regarded their lives, they lookt after their wives and children, they tooke not up their Crosses of humilitie and followed him, but would crosse him, upbraid him, and set him at nought, if he assured not by some signe their prayers and supplications" (239). The sign they received is misleading, they are slaughtered, and their leader, John of Leyden, is hanged. "Heare what it is to be Anabaptists, to be Puritans, to be villaines; you may bee counted illuminate botchers for a while, but your end will bee, Good people, pray for us" (241). Because Nashe's dislike of Puritanism is so strong, Jack's ironic detachment is not maintained, and the contemporary application is pointed in a way not characteristic of the work. In part, this was because Puritans were a safe target, requiring no circumspection on the part of the writer.

Nashe was apparently not circumspect enough in his description of the academic pride of Wittenberg, which was read as a satire on Cambridge. Compared to the Anabaptists the academic humanists are harmless enough in their vanities and pretensions. That "bursten belly inkhorne orator called Vanderhulke" is both pompous and fawning in his bombastic Ciceronian oration to the emperor, but he is a comic butt, not a danger to anyone. Readers have suspected that he is a satiric portrait of Gabriel Harvey, an inference Nashe himself reinforced when he used Vanderhulke as one of the comic names for Harvey in *Have with You to Saffron Walden* (3:31; Stern, 121–22). Vanderhulke is the epitome of a pendantic humanism that lacks any connection with the world of events: his oration is mere rhetoric in the way that the academic play performed for the emperor is mere gesture.

Form without substance is also characteristic of the "solempne disputations, where Luther and Carolostadius scolded levell coyle" (2:250). This suggestion that religious controversy is mere rhetoric is discreetly kept within the context of Jack's unregenerate perspective: "A masse of wordes I wote well they heapte up agaynst the masse and the Pope, but farther particulars of their disputations I remember not. I thought verily they woulde have worried one another with wordes, they were so earnest and vehement. Luther had the louder voyce, Carolostadius went beyond him in beating and bounsing with his fists. *Quae supra nos, nihil ad nos*: they uttered nothing to make a man laugh, therefore I will leave them" (250). This and the subsequent description of the exaggerated mannerisms and gestures of the other disputants can be read as evidence that Jack is incapable of understanding theological issues, but the cumulative effect is that all the activities at Wittenberg are vanities. Agrippa, the skeptical ironist, contributes to this effect with his conjuring tricks.

The pride of the northern Europeans is self-centered folly: the singularity of the Anabaptists and the pomposities of the academic humanists are similar to Surrey's obsession with Geraldine or Jack's own pride in his knavery. Like Jack's victims in the opening joke-book section, all are wrapped up in their own delusions. In this sense all of them, except perhaps for Jack, are fools. But in Italy pride takes the form of villainy, and innocent victims are made to suffer. A contemporary pamphlet characterizes Italians as "verie wittie & subtill headed, all cunning slightes, craftie conveyances, and deceitfull cozinages." Italy is a country where external appearances outweigh inner values; the pamphleteer imagines Italians saying "we must have a religion which will helpe to augment our dignities and earthly riches, that we may live here in all voluptousness and securitie" (G.B.A.T., *A Discovery*, sigs. B1r, D1r). Another pamphlet says that Italians "are caryed away with a vision of vanity, with an externall shew of glory" (Rankins, sig. B1r). Thus the good works of Nashe's Roman matrons are more than counterbalanced by the "bad works" of villains like Esdras, whose crimes are, after all, sanctioned by the pope. It is also appropriate that Rome should be the home of a pair of archetypically villainous Jews, since the Jews were seen as being like the Catholics in their dedication to the Old Law of retribution and the flesh. Zachary and Juliana are two of a kind, although their designs on Jack's flesh differ in nature.

Although Jack's initial Italian adventure—his encounter with Tabitha the Temptress and her pimp—is comic, it introduces the theme of Italianate pride and defiance of fortune. An unprincipled whore, Tabitha could "set as civill a face on it as chastities first martyr Lucrecia. What will you conceit to be in any saints house that was there to seeke? Bookes, pictures, beades, crucifixes, why, there was a haberdashers shop of them in everie chamber" (255). This discrepancy between external show and internal worth, evident in the tournament in

Florence, becomes the dominant note when Jack arrives in Rome. He appears to be wandering, but his travels are centripetal: there is a narrative inevitability in his arrival in the city that symbolized pride and intrigue to the Elizabethans. Nowhere is fortune more capricious, and nowhere do men and women intrigue more outrageously to circumvent its power. As Jack moves towards the core of Italianate pride in "so old a triumphing city," the characters become more vicious and the events more grotesque until they begin to threaten first the reader's and then Jack's sense of a normal order in the world. As Jack's processing of events into wit and the reader's disgusted reaction diverge, the narration itself becomes grotesque and disorienting along with the events described (Larson; Millard). Readers have been disturbed, for example, by the account of the rape of Heraclide, which is vicious but also comic, since the participants are caricatured. Heraclide remonstrates at excessive length with her ravisher Esdras, attempting to dissuade him with the traditional argument that he has the free will to choose good over evil: "If thou be a man, thou wilt succour mee, but if thou be a dog and a brute beast, thou wilt spoile mee, defile mee, and teare me: either renounce Gods image, or renounce the wicked mind thou bearest" (290). The plague should remind him of God's power and his own mortality; she herself may well be infected and become the instrument of God's vengeance. He scorns her pleas on two counts. First, he has been lucky like Jack; he cites as an example his repeated good fortune in a fiendish dice game where the winner receives a pot of money and the loser is condemned to the galleys: "Thou telst me (quoth he) of the plague, & the heavie hand of God, and thy hundred infected breaths in one: I tel thee I have cast the dice an hundred times for the gallies in Spaine, and yet still mist the ill chance" (290). Secondly, his apparent control of fortune and his pride have made him resolute: "My owne mother gave I a boxe of the eare too, and brake her necke downe a paire of staires, because she would not goe in to a Gentleman when I bad her: my sister I sold to an old Leno, to make his best of her: anie kinswoman that I have, knew I she were not a whore, my selfe would make her one: thou art a whore, thou shalt be a whore, in spite of religion or precise ceremonies" (291). Esdras's exaggerated dedication to evil is comic, but his defiance of religion would not be, even to the backsliders in Nashe's audience. Nashe is serious about the rape of Heraclide, but the seriousness is found in the implications of the event, not in its mimetic representation.

Esdras's words and behavior underline the wide gulf between the Christian virtues Heraclide appeals to and the bestiality of unregenerate humanity; the lack of any natural virtue in Esdras is perhaps evidence of a calvinistic pessimism in Nashe. Some of the sliminess of human passions unconstrained by grace (or authority) oozes into Nashe's description of the rape itself, as he realizes: "Conjecture the rest, my words sticke fast in the myre and are cleane tyred; would I had never undertooke this tragicall tale" (292). Nashe's rhetorical device of asking us to picture further details of the rape, after starting us off with a few voyeuristic hints, may be a subtle way of appealing to our common fallen nature. Jack is merely an unwilling witness to Esdras's crime, but his own unsanctioned relationship with Diamante stands somewhere between Esdras's contemptuous violation of women and Surrey's idealism. There is thus a crude justice operating when Jack is wrongfully accused of the crime and sentenced to the gallows: he is no innocent even if the banished earl does establish that Jack is innocent of this particular crime.

Nashe's depiction of the criminal pride of the Romans is continued in the account of Jack's adventures with Zadoch, Zachary, and Juliana. All three are comic stereotypes, but also examples of pride of the flesh carried to extremes. The two Jews are like Shylock or Marlowe's Barabas in their apotheosis of their worldly wealth and in their preoccupation with revenge. Jack's fear of his impending dissection is a comic but vivid image of the precariousness of human life. Zadoch's passion to revenge himself on Juliana is a ludicrous portrayal of insane villainy, but again, the vivid details suggest the ugly physical reality that lies behind the fiction: "Ile goe to a house that is infected, where catching the plague, and having got a running sore upon me, Ile come and deliver her a supplication, and breath upon her. I knowe my breath stinkes so alreadie, that it is within halfe a degree of poison" (312). A similar use of details makes Zadoch's cruel execution a grotesque symbol of the vulnerability of human flesh. Throughout the book Jack's accounts of physical suffering and death are powerful reminders of human mortality, although the ugliness is distanced by the operation of wit. The macabre becomes the dominant effect in Rome, while Jack's efforts to transform it into comedy become increasingly strained.

Juliana is a female equivalent of Esdras: she recognizes no morality beyond her own passions and desires. The linking of eroticism and death, jokingly played with in Surrey's sonnet, becomes a threat to Jack's string of luck. Juliana's preferred medium of expression seems to be poison in various forms; thus it is fitting that she is finally brought low by an accidental dram. Her insatiable sexual appetite, which she indulges on the captive Jack, is a pornographic fantasy, but the suggestion that she infects him with syphilis adds an ugly touch. His physical debilitation—"I was clean spent and done, there was no hope of me" (316)—shows the mortal folly of making carnal pleasure the center of one's life. Juliana plans to kill him after she has used him up: "When I was consumed and worne to the bones through her abuse, she wold give me but a dram too much, and pop mee into a privie" (314). Although she is a melodramatic villainess without any real character, Juliana does acquire symbolic overtones, as in the description of how she dressed herself like an angel to attend the celebration of St. Peter's Day with her secret lover the pope. Like Spencer's Duessa, she is a type of the whore of Babylon.

Jack escapes Juliana only to experience in Bologna the ultimate example of Italianate pride and villainy. Cutwolfe is tiny, ugly, and of base origins, "a wearish dwarfish writhen facde cobler," whose "impiety" is presented as an example of personal pride gone insane in the name of honor and as evidence of a providential design underlying the apparently arbitrary turns of fortune's wheel. "Strange and wonderfull are Gods judgements, here shine they in their glory" (320). Nashe stresses that the episode has a significance that transcends a naturalistic conception of life: "Guiltlesse soules that live every houre subject to violence, and with your dispairing feares doe much empaire Gods providence, fasten your eies on this spectacle that will adde to your faith" (320). Such a providential emphasis answers Esdras's blasphemous rejection of Heraclide's plea that he fear God's power, and it also calls into question the criminality of Juliana, Zadoch, and Zachery, the empty humanism of Wittenberg, Surrey's idolatrous love for Geraldine, and Jack's own knavery and wanderlust. Cutwolfe's proud defiance of the Christian framework, his savage revenge on Esdras, and his own horrible fate join forces as a powerful demonstration of what human life is like without God. But as Nashe says of his own comments on the story, "This is but a glose upon the text" (320).

Cutwolfe remains defiant in his final oration of self-justification, although it was the custom for Elizabethan criminals to repent on the scaffold: "Expect not of me a whining penitent slave." His arrogance is underlined by the contrast between his size and his pride: "My bodie is little, but my minde is as great as a gyants: the soule which is in mee is the verie soule of Julius Caesar by reversion. My name is Cutwolfe, neither better nor worse by occupation than a poore Cobler of Verona; Coblers are men, and kings are no more" (320). He relates how he learned of his brother's death and pursued Esdras for twenty months throughout Italy, catching up with him in Bologna. Cutwolfe is so obsessed with revenge that he reacts like an excited child when he finally sees Esdras: "My hart hopt and danst, my elbowes itcht, my fingers friskt, I wist not what should become of my feete, not knewe what I did for joy" (321). He is hardly a heroic revenger. When confronted, Esdras begs not for his life but for time to repent; he claims that the murder of Cutwolfe's brother has activated "the guiltie gnawing worme of conscience" (322). Esdras also sees Cutwolfe's errand as punishment for his rape of Heraclide: "In revenge of thee, God hardens this mans heart against mee" (323).

The fear of hell may be upon Esdras, but Cutwolfe is not moved. He replies: "Though I knew God would never have mercy upon me except I had mercie on thee, yet of thee no mercy would I have. Revenge in our tragedies is continually raised from hell: of hell doe I esteeme better than heaven, if it afford me revenge. There is no heaven but revenge" (324).

Thus, Cutwolfe does not deny the Christian frame of values: he defies it in the name of his obsession, an obsession fueled by his own pride more than by his grief over his brother's death.

Cutwolfe has subsumed himself in the role of revenger, playacting and distorting his physical appearance: "My eyes have broken their strings with staring and looking ghastly, as I stood devising how to frame or set my countenance when I met thee. I have neere spent my strength in imaginarie acting on stone wals, what I determined to execute on thee" (324). Cutwolfe's acting is not merely practice; like Surrey's imaginary courting of Diamante as if she were Geraldine, his behavior shows that his obsession has taken on a life of its own, separate from any external reality (Davis, 227–29).

Cutwolfe's decision to concern himself with the damnation as well as the execution of his victim is blasphemous, like Hamlet's related excuse for not killing Claudius at prayer. He forces Esdras to curse God, grant his soul to the devil, and pray never to receive mercy, then shoots him in the throat so that he cannot repent before death. Cutwolfe's pride in this "notable newe Italionisme" is the climax of the book: "This is the falt that hath called me hether; no true Italian but will honor me for it. Revenge is the glorie of armes, & the highest performance of valure: revenge is whatsoever we call law or justice. The farther we wade in revenge, the neerer come we to the throne of the almightie. To his scepter it is properly ascribed; his scepter he lends unto man, when he lets one man scourge an other. All true Italians imitate me in revenging constantly and dying valiantly" (326). This creed is what results when one carries the code of honor to extremes, making justice an individual matter. Understandably enough in Nashe's Italy, Cutwolfe has no expectation that the state will bring Esdras to justice.

Cutwolfe's pride is an extreme example of the self-centeredness and obsession that show themselves more comically in other characters like Vanderhulke, Surrey, or Jack himself. His singularity shows itself as a defiance of everyone, including God; his wit, as an insane plot to circumvent God's providence. He appalls even his like-minded compatriots, but their reaction is ironic confirmation of his view that he lives in an anarchic society where vengeance is the rule of law: "Herewith all the people (outragiously incensed) with one conjoyned outcrie yelled mainely, Awaie with him, away with him. Executioner, torture him, teare him, or we will teare thee in peeces if thou spare him" (327). The ensuing professional dismemberment of Cutwolfe is described in detail, with grotesque imagery that both distances and makes vivid the cruelty of the event.

Jack's reaction to Cutwolfe's story and his execution mirrors the reaction of the reader. Although Jack's personal luck has never completely failed him, his faith in his ability to master fate crumbles in the face of this "truculent tragedy of Cutwolfe and Esdras." He concludes, "Unsearchable is the booke of our destinies," but he also sees that providence governs events, although it is a providence that is ugly and cruel: "One murder begetteth another: was never yet bloud-shed barren from the beginning of the world to this daie" (327). These two reactions are not contradictory, since the general pattern does not allow the individual to know his particular fate. When unregenerate humanity functions without legal or ethical restraints, society becomes savage and destructive in the way Jack has witnessed. It is appropriate that he is "mortifiedly abjected and danted," since he was excessively self-confident before he witnessed how human folly shades into vice and vice into a form of defiant insanity. Given the emphasis on the importance of the social order, it is also appropriate that Jack flees back to his king and that he arrives when the court is celebrating a peaceful alliance.

Jack returns to the king and not to England: the emphasis is not on nations, for all of Nashe's slurs on the Italians, but on the contrast between proper civil and religious order, as symbolized by Henry VIII, and the anarchy of self-centered individualism, as symbolized by the Rome of the pope. Nashe's "fantastical treatise" is fantastical because he gives his imagination free rein, expressing opinions he would have had to censor in a nonfictional work, and a treatise in the modern sense of the word in that it treats a variety of the ways in which humanity loses itself in the world. Nashe's more serious concerns are displaced into a Europe that is a creation of his imagination and reflects the Elizabethan England that so frustrated his hopes and betrayed his idealism. Nashe anticipates the belief of the Jacobean dramatists that "Italy was an awful warning about the state of Hobbesian individualism into which England seemed to be moving" (Hunter, "English Folly"). His Italy is a nightmare vision of what England might become if Jack Wiltons did not return to the fold and submit themselves to authority. Nashe himself was a Jack Wilton, eager to conform but not wanted by those in power. Not all masterless men choose their renegade status; some have it thrust upon them.

CHAPTER
6

Quarreling in Print: The Harvey-Nashe Controversy

NASHE'S flexible wit and skill at ironic impersonation are a link between his creation of Jack Wilton and his part in the pamphlet quarrel with Gabriel Harvey. He was able to keep shifting his stance, mocking himself and his opponent, while making Harvey appear a "grosse painted image of pride, who would faine counterfeite a good witte, but scornfull pittie, his best patron, knows it becomes him as ill, as an unweldy Elephant to imitate a whelpe in his wantonnes" (1:282). Harvey committed himself to a serious tone and integrity of person that made him a convenient target for Nashe's ridicule. His own life and works suggest, however, that he was also a "rhetorical man" whose inner integrity remains illusive because the variety of roles he assumed imperfectly cohere into a central personality (Lanham, *Motives*, 1–35). He and Nashe were much alike, although their attempts to cope with their singularity led them in different directions.

Their quarrel was never resolved; we still cannot decide which image of Harvey or Nashe reflects the real person. Was Harvey a neglected mastermind or a pedantic buffoon? Was Nashe an original talent or an irresponsible hack? Each man tried to define himself for posterity and denigrate his opponent. Their famous controversy has confused more readers than it has entertained or informed; indeed, many readers of the invective they exchanged have despaired of finding a pattern in what seems mere rhetorical exercise. A reader must search through McKerrow's notes to understand the topical references in Nashe, while Harvey's opaque style and the lack of any modern annotated edition of his works make it difficult to understand his side of the argument. Like the Marprelate controversy, the Harvey-Nashe quarrel is a literary landmark seldom viewed close up; even scholars of Elizabethan literature often content themselves with snippets of Nashe's wit and the odd quote from Harvey.

Much of the controversy is an exchange of insults, but Harvey and Nashe do argue from opposing positions that they developed in response to the transition from a traditional society. Three related issues give coherence to the quarrel. First, two divergent conceptions of literature are set against each other: both men pay obeisance to Sidney and Spenser, but the "golden" synthesis these two figures embody was splitting into a utilitarian conception of literature, which became in Harvey a secular version of the Puritan position, and the alienated, satiric view which Nashe helped popularize. Second, these different conceptions of literature are linked to the different rhetorical strategies of the two men: Harvey tries to create an effect of personal integrity and high-minded social concern, while Nashe plays the clown, deflating pretensions and turning decorum topsy-turvy. Third, these strategies reflect different beliefs about how individuals relate to society: Harvey advances the modern conception that a talented person creates his or her own role in society and that society is thus changed and renewed; Nashe, as we have seen, espouses the traditionalist view that one's character is less essential than one's social role and that the change caused by ambitious individuals is likely to be detrimental. These three differences between Harvey and Nashe become more explicit as the quarrel progresses, but they are obscured by a number of tangential issues and much irrelevant invective.

A short summary of the quarrel will help keep the chronology clear. Richard Harvey's 1590 criticism of Nashe in *The Lamb of God* was answered by Robert Greene in the summer of 1592, but Greene had misgivings, so he canceled the satiric passage shortly after the book was published. In September 1592 Nashe attacked Richard Harvey in *Pierce Penniless*, even as Gabriel Harvey was composing a response to Greene in his

Four Letters. As soon as Harvey saw the attack on his brother, he included criticisms of Nashe in his defense of his family's honor. Nashe responded in December with his *Strange News of Intercepting Certain Letters,* which defended *Pierce Penniless* and attacked Gabriel Harvey's pomposity. In terms of prestige the twenty-six-year-old satirist was outranked by the forty-three-year-old scholar and doctor of laws, but Nashe's agile wit gave him an edge over Harvey, who was too academic in his approach to vernacular pamphleteering.

Stung by Nashe's caricature of him, Harvey began *Pierce's Supererogation,* working through the spring of 1593 as a part-time employee and house guest of the printer John Wolfe, even though the plague made it dangerous to remain in London. After the work was finished in June, and perhaps even as it was being printed in September, Nashe apologized and sought reconciliation in the epistle to *Christ's Tears.* Harvey rejected the offer in *A New Letter of Notable Content,* dated September 16 and apparently published simultaneously with *Pierce's Supererogation.* In a revised epistle to *Christ's Tears* published early in 1594, Nashe reacted angrily to Harvey's rejection of his offer of peace, but he delayed the publication of his full response, *Have with You to Saffron Walden,* until 1597. Both men planned further pamphlets and new editions, but on June 1, 1599, an extraordinary order against satiric and contentious publications, issued by Archbishop Whitgift and Richard Bancroft, now bishop of London, banned all works by Harvey or Nashe. The bishops disapproved of what was essentially a private quarrel because it was a model of singularity and contention. Indeed, censure of the unwarranted advancement of the private self began the quarrel as well as ending it.

THE ORIGINS OF THE QUARREL

Behind Richard Harvey's criticism of the arrogance of "The Preface to *Menaphon"* lay a long-standing personal and ideological conflict. Nashe was probably singled out for criticism because of his association as an anti-Martinist with John Lyly, who had insulted Gabriel Harvey in *Pap with an Hatchet.* Lyly disliked Harvey because of what he perceived as an insult to his patron, the earl of Oxford, in Harvey's *Three Proper and Witty Familiar Letters*, published in 1580. Harvey denied that his satiric portrait of an Italianate Englishman referred to Oxford, but the passage in one of the letters was insulting to the earl in any case, since it scorned his lifestyle. Through his friendship with Spenser, Harvey had become acquainted with Sir Philip Sidney, Oxford's adversary in the famous tennis court quarrel of 1579, which dramatized the difference between the self-indulgent, traditionalist earl and the militant reformist Sidney (M. Wallace, 213–16). Although not a Puritan himself, Harvey shared with Sidney and his uncle, the earl of Leicester (Harvey's sometime patron), a Puritan enthusiasm for Ramus and a belief that literature should be useful. By 1590 Sidney and Leicester were dead, so the lingering hopes of their faction were focused on the earl of Essex, to whom Richard Harvey dedicated *The Lamb of God*. Since Whitgift was now the most powerful defender of the status quo, the Harveys were hostile to his protégés Nashe and Lyly (cf. Hibbard, 180–232; Sanders; Stern, 80–129).

Robert Greene answered Richard Harvey after an unaccountable two-year delay in an interpolated passage in *A Quip for an Upstart Courtier* that ridiculed a ropemaker and the three sons he maintained at the university. The reference was obviously to the ropemaker John Harvey of Saffron Walden and his three academic sons, Richard, John, and Gabriel. Greene's role and motives are unclear. Nashe said in *Strange News* that he was angered at Richard's general criticisms of playwrights and pamphleteers, (1:271) but it would not have been in Nashe's interest to admit that Greene was defending him, given Greene's notoriety. Whatever Greene's reasons, he canceled the passage in a second issue of the pamphlet. In *Four Letters* Gabriel Harvey said he did so because he feared a lawsuit; Nashe answered that it was because the change was urged on him by his doctor, who resented the criticism of John Harvey, a fellow physician (1:279–80). More recently it has been suggested that Greene canceled the passage when he heard of John Harvey's death in June 1592 (Hibbard, 184–85). The printer of *A Quip*, John Wolfe, may have also had a hand in the cancellation, since he was already friendly with Gabriel

Harvey, to judge from a book he gave him in August, shortly after *A Quip* was published (Stern, 223).

Inspired by Greene's example or disappointed by his retraction, Nashe attacked Richard Harvey in *Pierce Penniless*, as we have seen. He ridicules Richard for "abusing of Aristotle," a reference to the Ramist beliefs Richard shared with his brother. He reminds his readers of Richard's controversial *Astrological Discourse* of 1583, which had prophesied catastrophic events that never occurred. "The whole Universitie hyst at him, Tarlton at the Theator made jests of him, and Elderton consumd his ale-crammed nose to nothing, in bearbayting him with whole bundles of ballets. Would you, in likely reason, gesse it were possible for any shame-swolne toad to have the spet-proofe face to out live this disgrace?" (1:197). There are also slighting references to the ropemaking trade of John Harvey, Sr., and the almanacs of John, Jr., but Gabriel Harvey, whom Nashe had praised in "The Preface to *Menaphon*," is not mentioned.

While the controversy began as a feud between factions, it soon resolved itself into a personal quarrel between Nashe and Gabriel Harvey. John Harvey, Jr., died in June 1592, and Robert Greene, in September of that year. Richard Harvey withdrew from active participation, perhaps because as a clergyman he feared for his reputation. After his initial foray, Lyly kept aloof, although Nashe tried to draw him into the quarrel on his side. The shifting ideological differences of the feud became a simpler clash of personalities, but the conflict continued to reflect the different beliefs of the two men.

It is difficult to distinguish between their beliefs because the two men were alike in many ways. Educated at Cambridge and loyal to the Anglican church and the queen, both sought to identify themselves with the humanist tradition, but their attitudes towards change were different. To put it simplistically, Nashe was a traditionalist, while Harvey was a modernist. Nashe aligned himself with the court humanism of Archbishop Whitgift, with its emphasis on preserving the imperfect order that existed rather than risking innovation or further reform. Harvey, receptive to new political and intellectual ideas and eager for social change, was a leader in popularizing the

Ramist recasting of rhetoric, an innovation Nashe deplored. Harvey and his brothers were students of astrology and other pseudo and proto sciences, while Nashe followed Agrippa, Scot, and Henry Howard in his skepticisms about such studies. Harvey had cosmopolitan interests, following Continental politics with enthusiasm; Nashe was ethnocentric and xenophobic. Through his readings and his friends, Harvey maintained an interest in technological developments and trade; Nashe cared little about economic matters, beyond face-to-face transactions.

These differing attitudes reflect radically different views of the individual's role in society. Nashe had absorbed from his study of Ascham, Cheke, and other humanists of the mid-century an idealized conception of society and the role he himself should play as a university graduate and poet. His taste for skeptical authors and his own unfortunate experience as a writer made him bitter towards those social forces that seemed to corrupt the ideal and thwart his own ambitions. His conception of society was not worked out with any philosophical rigor nor was it subject to revision, since it was a myth of what should be, not a theory. If Elizabethan society fell short of the myth, that shortfall impelled him toward satiric bitterness rather than toward rethinking the ideal.

Harvey, on the other hand, has been singled out as the best example of new Renaissance ideals in Elizabethan England, a native-bred *homo universalis,* although at times he appears a parody of the ideal (Moore Smith, ed., in Harvey, *Marginalia,* 54–56). A formidable scholar and true polymath, he was not afraid to question received truth or explore the most advanced areas of thought. Ironically, his most original ideas were crowded into the margins of the books he owned rather than published to the world. His heterodox ideas, pompous manner, and lack of humor earned him a reputation for being arrogant and unsociable, slowing his advancement at Cambridge and probably blocking the preferment he sought at court. By the 1590s Harvey's prospects were blighted and his eminence as a scholar faded, but to judge from the margins of his books, he retained his enthusiastic belief in the value of the changes society was undergoing. His conception of society was more dynamic than Nashe's, in part because his individualistic conception of the self allowed for more ambition and initiative. Harvey saw the private person as self-creating, society as fluid, and history as a process of change (cf. Perkins; H. Wilson).

This basic difference between Harvey and Nashe is explicit in the last of Harvey's *Four Letters* of 1592, in which he tries to rise above the escalating quarrel. Print should not be wasted on private arguments, nor his own time spent, nor Nashe's talents squandered. In his opaque prose Harvey offers an optimistic view of the striving for excellence that should prevail. His stress is on pragmatic empiricism rather than traditional theorizing: "Pregnant Rules avail much: but visible Examples amount incredibly: Experience, the onely life of perfection, & onely perfection of life" (sig. G4r). Theory finds its fulfillment in practice; arts achieve their end in exercise. With his adversaries and himself in mind, he adds, "They that understand little, write much: and they that know much write little." He calls for an experimental approach in the natural sciences in particular, but suggests that in humane subjects as well there are too many words without the substance of experience behind them. Nashe and other popular vernacular writers produce a shallow art that is all manner. He cautions them, "Good sweete Autors infourme your selves, before you undertake to instruct other" (sig. H1r).

Like the Puritans, but from a secular perspective, Harvey objects to popular pamphlets: "The Print is abused, that abuseth: and earnestly beseecheth flourishing writers, not to trouble the Presse, but in case of urgent occasion, or important use" (sig. H1r). Such presumption by uninformed writers sets a bad example. "God helpe, when Ignorance, and want of Experience, usurping the chayre of scrupulous, and rigorous Judgement, will in a fantasticall Imagination, or percase in a melancholy moode, presume farther, by infinite degrees, then the learnedest men in a civill Common-wealth, or the sagest counsellours in a Princes Court" (sigs. H1v–H2r). His objection to Greene and Nashe is utilitarian: their pamphlets serve no purpose. Nashe also believed vernacular literature should be socially useful, but for him popular writing should buttress traditional values, in part through satire on departures from the norm. Harvey, however, wanted to adapt Sidney's idealistic conception of literature to the pragmatic needs of an expanding economy. Even Sidney's *Arcadia* is seen by Harvey as a repository of useful maxims (*Pierces Supererogation*, sigs. G3r-G4r). Satire and invective had little place in Harvey's enthusiastic vision of a positive, innovative, and expansive literature.

The Harvey-Nashe controversy was in many ways a fabrication, although the anger that both express and the damage that both suffered show the quarrel was not a mere flyting. While the animus and the differences between the two men were real, the controversy also sold books, at least at first. The role of the printer John Wolfe is evidence that the quarrel had its economic motivations. Although he was Harvey's friend and publisher, and apparently for a time his employer, he published Greene's *A Quip for an Upstart Courtier* with its passage on the Harvey family in the summer of 1592. In September he published *Four Letters*, with its attack on Greene and Nashe. In 1593, when the quarrel was at its height, he entered Nashe's *The Unfortunate Traveler* in the Stationers' Register, even as he was publishing Harvey's *Pierce's Supererogation*. Nashe's work was actually published by someone else, but this may be because Wolfe's appointment as printer to the City of London caused him to cut back on his publishing ventures in 1593 (Hoppe, "John Wolfe," 266-67). Wolfe was a shrewd and at times Machiavellian printer—he had printed surreptitious editions of Machiavelli and Aretino in Italian—who was no doubt more interested in selling books than in Harvey's reputation or in threats to the commonwealth from the publishing of pamphlets.

During the first round in 1592 and early 1593 the two adversaries hoped to profit in other ways from the controversy as well. Both were ambitious men who thought of themselves as skilled rhetoricians with unemployed talents. Harvey still hoped for a call into government service and the kind of success that had been achieved by his deceased patron, Sir Thomas Smith. Nashe's ambitions were less exalted, but he still hoped for a regular patron who would reward him for writing the satiric defenses of orthodox values that were his specialty. Thus, both offered their pamphlets as yet another sample of their quality and versatility. Both promoted themselves under cover of defending their reputations. It was a risky but not unheralded route to preferment: there were precedents in the medieval flytings, the mock academic debates, and in several notorious quarrels in print on the Continent, such as the one involving Poggius and Valla.

In such polemical debates, it was a regular strategy to attack the ethos and the character of one's antagonist, often by suggesting that the ethos was a fabrication masking the author's true intentions. In *Four Letters* Harvey directed his strongest attack at the dead Greene, who was already notorious; his attitude towards Nashe is more cautious. He even praises Nashe and hopes for his reformation. In *Strange News* Nashe raised the ante by ridiculing Harvey at length, probably because his own reputation was too fragile to withstand Harvey's patronizing criticisms. In trying to save himself, he needed to discredit Harvey; he did this so effectively that Harvey had to counterattack in *Pierce's Supererogation*. Nashe saw that the quarrel had become self-sustaining: "All the controversie is no more but this, he began with mee, and cannot tell how to make an end; and I would faine end or rid my hands of him, if he had not first begun" (3:19). Nashe makes it explicit in *Have with You to Saffron Walden* that he continues the quarrel more to salvage his own reputation than because of any hate for Harvey.

Each man tried to escape the escalating conflict: Harvey ended the *Four Letters* by promising to praise Nashe if he reforms his writing; Nashe offered submission in the epistle to *Christ's Tears*. But neither could afford to let the other have the last word, even though the quarrel became increasingly destructive. In *Pierce's Supererogation* Harvey worries that the continuation of the quarrel is damaging his career. Nashe delayed finishing *Have with You to Saffron Walden* because he saw that he and Harvey were destroying each other merely to amuse their readers. Bitterness and anger show through in both, although each tries to set another tone. In short, the quarrel took on a life of its own, dashing their prospects and damaging their reputations even before the bishops banned their works. Indeed, the damage they did has lasted to this day in the stereotypes of Harvey the vain pedant and Nashe the irresponsible malcontent.

RHETORICAL STRATEGIES IN THE FIRST EXCHANGE

The quarrel was not a game with agreed-upon rules; each of the participants invented his own strategy as he went along, redefining both his own and his opponent's position. Neither simply tells us what he thinks in a straightforward fashion. The resort to indirection and downright fabrication is in part a response to the fear of libel, in part an effort to fire shots without exposing oneself. Previous controversies provided only general guidelines, since most were debates about issues that dragged in personalities; this was a quarrel between persons that dragged in issues. The Harvey-Nashe quarrel was a new form of public interchange, requiring new rhetorical strategies and great agility at advancing oneself without appearing arrogant and undercutting one's opponent without seeming uncharitable and vindictive.

The necessity for artifice reflects a central discrepancy in the Elizabethan conception of acceptable behavior. Church and state inculcated humility and submission, yet the Elizabethans were often in fact a proud and cantankerous people. Duels were fought and private revenges exacted in spite of the religious exhortations and strict laws. Honor and reputation were sacred in practice even though they were seen as profane concerns by the church (James, 8–15). In social interchanges decorum protected not only class structure and the relation between the sexes; it also formed a shell around each Elizabethan's personal integrity. To judge from the drama, sensitivity to insults permeated all classes, the bellicose rustic being a frequent comic butt. Both Harvey in his somewhat pompous fashion and Nashe in his usual ironic and self-mocking manner are concerned to defend their honor. At the same time each works hard at appearing the victim of his opponent's aggression; Harvey in disdainful anguish and Nashe in aggrieved bewilderment protest that they neither began nor wished to continue the quarrel.

From the start of the controversy Harvey was self-conscious about his own and his opponents' use of strategies and contrivances. His long study of rhetoric and political behavior had convinced him that social interactions were artificial performances (Stern, 150–64). The hostility he had experienced because of his own unorthodox ideas had encouraged him to be circumspect and disingenuous. His attempts at imposition are evident in his own struggle for advancement. The margins of his books include many exhortations to himself which entail imposture and outright Machiavellian deceit, although he was adept at concealing his private concerns behind a public facade (H. Wilson, 720). This penchant for duplicity and indirection helps explain the labyrinthine obscurity of the pamphlets he contributed to the quarrel.

A manuscript notebook written a decade earlier, the so-called *Letter-Book*, shows that Harvey thought of a printed book as a public performance, not to be judged by a canon of sincerity. The *Letter-Book* also suggests why Harvey resorted to contrivance: his lack of a social role commensurate with his talents and the heterodoxy of his beliefs forced subterfuge on him. This emerges in his account of the difficulties he had in getting his M.A. degree in 1573. In a letter to John Young, the master of his college, he describes the criticisms of him that were circulating throughout the university: "Matters ar made wurs and wurs in the telling: and now forsooth mi not being sociable, arguith great arroganci; mi reprehending of others, arguith great arroganci; mi defending of paradoxis, arguith great arroganci; and, to be short, everi thing, mi going, mi speaking, mi reading, mi behaviur arguith great and intollerable arroganci" (18). Such difficulties dogged his subsequent career.

Thus, he was cautious when he decided in the late 1570s to use vernacular literature as an avenue to preferment, in imitation of George Gascoigne and Spenser. Gascoigne was a man of action who used his literary skills as an advertisement for his talents. He practiced subterfuges to conceal his self-promotion, publishing the first version of his works, *The Hundred Sundrie Flowers* (1573), as a collection of pieces by various hands presented by a fictional compiler. In the second version,

The Poesies (1575), he admitted authorship but added three long letters designed to defuse criticism. Spenser's *Shepheardes Calender* (1579), which was dedicated to Harvey and called upon him to publish his own vernacular works, was presented by the well-meaning friend E. K., who may have been to some degree a contrivance, while the author's name was modestly concealed by the pseudonym "Immerito," although the work was actually a bold undertaking and the author's identity an open secret (D. Miller).

Gascoigne's partial success and the apparent total success of Spenser at promoting themselves through vernacular literature inspired Harvey to attract attention to his talents by publishing his English works. His uncertain position at Cambridge at the time must have contributed to this resolve, and the flattering advance notice in Spenser's popular work made his own success seem all the more likely. Harvey's plans for his collected English works survive as the central section of the *Letter-Book*. In order not to appear arrogant, as he had at Cambridge, he followed Gascoigne and Spenser's examples and fabricated elaborate framing devices to make it appear that publication was thrust upon him. Such a fiction was common in Elizabethan publishing, although we seldom see behind the scenes as we can in Harvey's case. He pretends the introductions he wrote to his own works were by Spenser or some other friend. For example, an elegy on Gascoigne was to be introduced as "A neue Pamflett conteininge a fewe delicate poeticall devices of Mr. G. H., extemporally written by him in Essex, at the ernest request of a certain gentleman a worshipfull frende of his . . . immediatly uppon the reporte of the deathe of M. Georg Gascoigne Esquier, and since not perusid by the autor. Published by a familiar frende of his" (*Letter-Book*, 55). Like Nashe, Harvey wanted to emphasize that his works were extemporaneous so that he would appear a ready wit, fit for employment in matters of the world.

Harvey was also proud of the singularity of his works, which he praised through his fictional friend: "I am . . . loth, my good masters, to depryve you of any thinge that I can possibely communicate with you of this autors dooinge in whom nothinge is vulgar but ether in respecte of the manner or matter to my seeming very singular" (ibid., 95). The ruse of the fictional friend allows him to praise himself covertly. In a letter to the "friend" Harvey good-humoredly objects to the "unauthorized" publication of his works: "And canst thou tell me nowe, or doist thou at the last begin to imagin with thy selfe what a wonderfull and exceeding displeasure thou and thy prynter have wroughte me, and how peremptorily ye have prejudishd my good name for ever in thrustinge me thus on the stage to make tryall of my extemporall faculty, and to play Wylsons or Tarletons parte" (67). Harvey never actually published his English works, perhaps because they are in fact doggerel, or perhaps because the publication of *Three Proper and Witty Familiar Letters* (1580) caused him so many difficulties that he abandoned plans for vernacular publication altogether.

In his counterattack on *Four Letters*, Nashe makes much of Harvey's contrivances, which were transparent to him since he was a professional writer himself. He argued that Harvey had sought the publication of the *Three Letters* of 1580, despite his claim in *Four Letters* that the earlier work had been published against his wishes. Although Nashe could not have known of the letter book I have quoted, he accused Harvey of writing the epistle to the *Three Letters* headed "a well wisher to both the writers." Nashe comments, "Gabriell, thou canst play at fast and loose as well as anie man in England" (1:296). On the basis of the style, Nashe also accuses Harvey of having written the first of the *Four Letters* and its accompanying sonnet, and then having Christopher Bird, a prosperous friend in Saffron Walden, affix his name so that Harvey could praise himself without appearing arrogant. This sonnet is of a piece with those Harvey wrote himself, but Nashe is excessively suspicious in doubting the authenticity of Spenser's fine sonnet to Harvey, printed at the end of the collection. Nashe also believed that Harvey's professed reluctance to quarrel was a ruse and that he had actually seized on Greene's short attack on his family as an excuse to aggrandize himself in print and profit from the news value of Greene's death.

If Nashe saw through Harvey's fabrications, Harvey understood equally well Nashe's contrivances as a writer and even admired Nashe in a begrudging way. Nashe's program as a writer was, after all, similar to that attempted by Harvey a decade earlier. Both men tried to apply their humanistic training to contemporary society by writing vernacular works that would also draw attention to their talents. Both prized the extemporaneous style and singular wit, although both tried to soften the implicit arrogance of their singularity with avowals of personal humility. Harvey's praise of Nashe in *Four Letters* is part of his pose as the superior intelligence drawn reluctantly into a petty quarrel, but it probably also reflects a perception of Nashe as a younger and wilder version of himself. When he calls Nashe "a proper yong man, if advised in time," and when he praises him for his talents as a writer, he is probably responding to Nashe's ability to write the sort of popular vernacular work he could not write himself.

Both men set up Aretino as a special model of the kind of writer they wished they could be, although Harvey was cautious about praising Aretino in public because of his notoriety as an atheist and pornographer. In his marginalia, Harvey was more frank: "Aretines glory, to be himself: to speake, & write like himself: to imitate none, but him selfe & ever to maintaine his owne singularity. Yet ever with commendation, or compassion of other" (*Marginalia*, 156). He had wanted the aborted edition of his English poetry "sett in as witty and fine order as may be, Aretinelyke" (*Letter-Book*, 143). In *Four Letters* and *Pierce's Supererogation*, on the other hand, he uses Aretino's notoriety as a means of criticizing Nashe. Since he was still praising Aretino in a marginal comment that must have been written in the 1590s, it was not that Harvey had changed his view of the Italian satirist, but that his private opinion was different from his public position.[1] Nashe could not have seen the manuscript notes, but he detected the discrepancy between Harvey's use of Aretino to criticize him and the praise of Aretino in the 1580 *Three Letters* (1:283–84).

Nashe is right that the *Four Letters* is a remarkably contrived

---

1. Unpublished Harvey marginalia in Folger MS. H. a 2, (a double volume); Lodovico Domenichi, *La Faceitie Motti et Burle de Diversi Signori et Persone Private* [1571], sig. 2D8r; and Guicciardini, *Detti, et Fatti Piacevole et Grave* (Vinegia, 1581), sigs. I8v, K2r.

publication, although it was written piecemeal in response to events as they occurred (Johnson, "The First Edition" and "Gabriel Harvey's *Three Letters*"). The core of the pamphlet is the second letter, dated September 5, 1592, which includes a highly topical account of Greene's death on September 3. It purports to be a private letter to Christopher Bird, but it was rapidly published by itself shortly after it was written. It was then reissued as *Three Letters* along with a dedicatory epistle, dated September 16, the first letter, from Mr. Bird to Mr. Demetrius, praising Harvey, and a long third letter continuing the attack on Greene and beginning the quarrel with Nashe. The edition concludes with a set of sonnets on Greene's death, about which it is charitable to say little. Harvey's work was then issued again with a new title and the addition of the general fourth letter, written on September 11 and 12; finally the whole was reprinted, with the verses put after the fourth letter in a second edition. This extraordinary publishing history reflects the news value of Greene's death and the interest generated by the publication of *Pierce Penniless*.

The second letter, which is the genesis of the whole pamphlet, is only peripherally concerned with Nashe; Harvey's main business is a description of the shabby life and pitiful death of Robert Greene. As we have seen, Greene had become a controversial personality, anathema to the Puritans and to serious-minded writers like Harvey in part because a folk hero to his readers. He was a bohemian who attracted attention to himself and shocked the prudent with his extravagant appearance and his irreverent words. Harvey reports that he had ruffianly hair and that he had a reputation as an inventor of new, often blasphemous oaths. Harvey writes to the solid citizen Mr. Bird about his investigations into the circumstances of Greene's death, who was sick, not from the plague, but from a surfeit of pickled herring and Rhenish wine. Harvey pities his plight: "I would not wish a sworne enimie to bee more basely valued, or more vilely reputed, then the common voice of the cittie esteemeth him, that sought Fame by diffamation of other, but hath utterly discredited himselfe: and is notoriously grown a very proverbe of Infamy, and contempt" (sig. A4r). Greene is linked with the ballad writer Elderton as "two notorious mates, & the very ringleaders of the riming, and scribbling crew." Elderton's ballads were the epitome of vulgar hack writing, so the coupling of Greene with him is an insult to Greene's pretensions to write for a more educated public.

Harvey sees Greene's works as symptomatic of the debasement of written discourse. In particular he deplores Greene's resort to invective: "Invectives by favour have bene too bolde: and Satyres by usurpation too-presumptuous" (sig. A4v). Attacks on reputation and personal honor are particularly damaging to the commonwealth. The insults to himself he could endure, but he feels compelled to defend the honor of his father and brothers. His resolve to seek legal redress is thwarted by the news of Greene's death: "Whiles I was thus, or to like effecte, resolving with my selfe, and discoursing with some speciall frendes: not onely writing unto you: I was suddainely certified, that the king of the paper stage (so the Gentleman tearmed Greene) had played his last part, & was gone to Tarleton" (sig. B2r). Harvey muses on the opportunity a "conceited witt" might have to write an account of Greene's life and appropriate end. In conjecturing what someone else might publish, he rolls all the scandal he can about Greene into one long sentence, then asserts that there are worse reports he refrains from writing. He visits the house where Greene died to collect pathetic details. "Oh what notable matter were here for a greene head, or Lucianicall conceit: that would take pleasure in the paine of such sorry distressed creatures?" (sig. B3v). Harvey himself has small leisure for such sordid business, wrapped up as he is in matters of fine wit and humanity, so he trusts his reputation to the judgment of his friends and the wiser sort. "And as for Envy or hatred to any party: I did ever abhorre them both" (sig. B4r). He promises Bird that his next letter will treat serious matters.

One can suspect with Nashe that this second letter was less innocent than it pretends. It seems unlikely that a letter sent to Saffron Walden on September 5 was returned to the printer in time for its separate publication a few days later unless the printer's copy was provided by Harvey. In the letter Harvey remarks casually that the criticisms it contains would stir up a controversy "if this poore Letter should fortune to come in print" (sig. A4v), but it is difficult to imagine that publication was not anticipated even as he wrote. The letter is also contrived in the way it attacks the dead Greene while disdaining such an attack as the sort of thing a conceited wit like Greene would have undertaken. Harvey manages to defame the dead while protesting that libel is distasteful. In its contrivances the letter is very much the product of a "Lucianicall conceit."

The third letter is more straightforward, addressed as it is to "every reader, favorably or indifferently affected." Although it criticizes Greene and Nashe, it is cast as a dispassionate consideration of the contemporary literary scene. Harvey has trouble maintaining his Olympian tone: his contempt for Greene is devoid of charity, and his admonishing of Nashe is patronizing rather than friendly. He claims to have written the letter only because of the importuning of friends and concern for his family's reputation, since he believes nothing should "be committed to a publike view, that is not exactly laboured both for matter and maner: and that importeth not some notable use" (sig. C1r). He disapproves of petty quarrels, although he confesses he had been tempted into invective in the 1580 letters by anger at his failure to obtain the oratorship at Cambridge. When the letters were published against his will, he endured, he says, the ensuing controversy with patience and made amends without suffering the indignity of being imprisoned in the Fleet, as Greene had charged. Although he refrained from publishing a defense he wrote at the time, the new controversy may impel him to publish it and a number of other discourses he has at hand.

After this self-serving preamble, which also includes a defense of his advocacy of English hexameters and an account of his brother John's pathetic death, he resumes his attack on Greene. Rather than mixing profit with delight, Greene's works promote vanity: "Peruse his famous bookes: and in steede of *Omne tulit punctum, qui miscuit utile dulci* (that forsooth was his professed Poesie) Loe a wilde head, ful of mad braine and a thousande crochets: a Scholler, a Discourser, a Courtier, a ruffian, a Gamester, a Lover, a Souldier, a Travailer, a Merchaunt, a Broker, and Artificer, a Botcher, a Pettifogger, a Player, a Coosener, a Rayler, a beggar, an Omnigatherum, a Gay nothing" (sig. D2r). Harvey's point is that Greene was all things to all people but nothing essential in himself, "an Epitome of fantasticalitie." He has never read Greene's works, although he has glanced at them in stationers' shops and at friends' houses. "I pray God, they have not done more harme by corruption of manners, then good by quickening of witte" (sig. D2v). It offends Harvey that such works are sought after while more substantial works are neglected: "The Countesse of Pembrookes Arcadia is not greene inough for queasie stomackes, but they must have Greenes Arcadia: and I beleeve, most eagerlie longed for Greenes Faerie Queene. O straunge fancies: o monstrous newfanglednesse" (sig. D2v). Like Greene's Puritan critics and other popular pamphlet writers, Harvey is suggesting that such works are models of presumption that promote discord in the commonwealth.

Harvey's high-minded defense of literary quality has been accepted at face value by a number of modern commentators on the quarrel, including Nashe's editor, McKerrow, who was offended by nineteenth-century biases against Harvey (McKerrow, 5:65–67; cf. Perkins). His suggestion that Harvey's criticisms of Nashe were mild compared to the attack on Greene is true but misleading. The initial references to Nashe in the second letter are kindly enough, but they were written before Harvey had seen *Pierce Penniless*. It is also true that in attacking that work in the third letter he distinguished between the paltry pamphlet and the ill-advised young man that wrote it, conceding talent to Nashe and lecturing him on the useful literature he should write. If Nashe will reform, Harvey will be the foremost in praising Nashe and advancing his career.

Summarized in this way Harvey's position sounds more temperate and generous than it is. In fact, his attack on Nashe was potentially damaging. He discredits Nashe as a person by associating him with Greene and by identifying him with his persona Pierce Penniless without acknowledging the ironic exaggeration of the work. His transition to Nashe in the third letter—"what dowty yoonker may next gnash with his teeth"— includes the suggestion that followers of Greene are like the traitor Babington, a suggestion that much offended Nashe. Harvey can be conciliatory: "I protest, it was not thy person, that I any-way disliked: but thy rash, and desperate proceeding against thy well-willers: which in some had bene unsufferable: in an youth, was more excusable: in a reformed youth is pardonable" (sig. G1r). But the reform Harvey sought from Nashe amounted to a complete repudiation of his career. The praise has to be balanced against those passages that conflate Nashe with his works and link him with Greene: "No man loather then my selfe, to contend with desperate Malecontentes: or to overthwart obstinate Humoristes: or to encounter Incke-horne Adventures: nor to quarrell with any sorte of wrangling Companions" (sigs. F3r–F3v). When Harvey sees Aretino and the devil's orator as venomous writers who can be well spared in a Christian commonwealth, he is not distinguishing between Nashe and his persona nor merely requesting amendment.

Harvey is also calculatingly literal in his reading of *Pierce Penniless*, as we have seen. Although his own attempts at irony are clumsy, his wide knowledge of the classics of humanism must have made him aware of Nashe's ironic intent. Harvey ignores those passages in which Nashe argues for a humanistic literature, although the ideas expressed are similar to his own. He will not even acknowledge that *Pierce Penniless* is original in conception and inventive in style; instead he criticizes it as derivative from Tarlton's play *The Seven Deadly Sins*, "now pleasantlie interlaced with divers new-founde phrases of the Taverne: and patheticallie intermixt with sundry dolefull pageantes of his own ruinous, & beggerlie experience" (sig. D4r). Harvey's outrage at profane pamphlets like Nashe's deliberately echoes the objections of the Puritans and the civic authorities, whom he calls on to enforce good order, but his marginalia, which continue in the 1590s to praise Aretino and even Greene, suggest that the cosmopolitan scholar was merely pretending to be scandalized (see n. 1, above, and H. Wilson, 719–20).

In the fourth letter, Harvey tries to rise above the obvious charge that he had put considerable effort into a petty quarrel. After all, the passage in *A Quip for an Upstart Courtier* was only some twenty lines long, while Nashe's attack on Richard Harvey was a matter of a few pages. Harvey protests that he would rather spend his time at serious study. His zealous desire is "to see Learning flourish: Vertue prosper: the good proceede from better to better: the bad amend" (sig. H1v). Print should be devoted to such ends, not wasted in the corrupt arts of contention and self-advancement. Such works, like the pamphlets of Martin Junior or Puny Pierce, promote disorder; give these authors a pen "and God-night all distinction of persons, and all difference of estates." Although the fourth letter is general, it completes the theme of the work as a whole: as Greene's heir, Nashe is representative of the sort of presumptuous bad art that is supplanting and undermining the useful art that Harvey supports.

Nashe could hardly tolerate such a characterization of his work. His intentions were, in fact, quite similar to those Harvey urged on him. If Harvey favored literature that presented positive images of virtue and heroic action, so did Nashe. If Harvey scorned the presumption of Martin Marprelate and the pretensions of unlettered popular writers, why so did Nashe. Both men favored works that reflected sound classical learning and were useful to the commonwealth. Nashe admitted that Greene "made no account of winning credite by his workes . . . : his only care was to have a spel in his purse to conjure up a good cuppe of wine with at all times" (1:287), but he thought his own works served useful ends. It must have galled him to see his first popular success dismissed as presumptuous hackwork. Pious hopes for his amendment were little compensation.

As we have seen, printed defamation was especially threatening to Elizabethans, who were sensitive about their honor and reputation. Libel was a new phenomenon, worse than slander because print reached a wide audience and become a matter of public record. The press conferred a new kind of immortality, pleasing perhaps to the recipients of sonnets and to public heroes, but very disturbing to the victims of satire and calumny. If the Elizabethans seem unduly sensitive to published slights, it is because the printed word seemed more enduring than it does in our age of mass communications.

Moreover, print still had the magical power attributed to it in traditional societies. In a dialogue published in 1578 (and, incidentally, known to Nashe) a character asserts, "Well, sir, our Johns booke shall confounde your talke, for I did see it in writyng; and that whiche is written I will beleve, and follow by Gods grace, and no more" (Bullein, 61). Such attitudes towards the printed word contributed to the seriousness of libel.

Nashe also had particular reasons for refuting Harvey's criticisms of *Pierce Penniless*; he was still receiving some form of patronage from Archbishop Whitgift and was seeking aristocratic support like that he shortly received from the Carey family. He does not feel free to name Whitgift, but he refers to him in answering Harvey's accusations: "If I had committed *such abhominable villanies, or were a base shifting companion*, it stoode not with my Lords honour to keepe me" (1:329). Such a defense was double-edged, however: if Harvey's accusations were credible, then such patrons might stop supporting Nashe. Whitgift's eventual participation in the order banning Nashe's works suggest that Harvey was successful in discrediting him, perhaps more so than he wished, since his own works were banned as well.

Given these pressures, it was courageous of Nashe to answer Harvey defiantly rather than submissively, as he later did in *Christ's Tears*. Not only did he refute the criticisms of *Pierce Penniless*; he attacked the *Four Letters* as a self-serving contrivance, written to advance Harvey's own career. Harvey's reluctance to quarrel is pretense, his humility a sham, his dedication to higher forms of literature rank hypocrisy. Nashe is as bold in the ethos he adopts for himself. He speaks straightforwardly in his own person, rather than hiding behind a persona, and pretends to no virtues he lacks and affects no false humility. He scorns Harvey's characterization of him by assuming an extreme stance that mocks Harvey's charges. The outrageous title, *Strange News of the Intercepting Certain Letters, and a Convoy of Verses, as They Were Going Privily to Victual the Low Countries*, parodies the popular news pamphlets of the period and mocks Harvey's solemnity and elitist literary attitudes, in part by punning on "privy" and "low countries."

The dedicatory epistle is to a Master Apis lapis, a pun on the name Beeston, but nothing is known of the person intended except that he must have been a real person capable of taking offense, because an insulting passage was softened apologetically in a later issue of the pamphlet. As in his other burlesque dedications, Nashe mocks the conventions of appealing for protection and support. Mr. Apis lapis is obviously the sort of *bon vivant* one might have found in the company of the dead Greene, the antithesis of Master Christopher Bird. In *Four Letters* Harvey maintains a pose of dignity; Nashe responds in *Strange News* with mocks and mows, the same tactic Martin Marprelate used against the bishops. The "Epistle to the Reader" accuses Harvey in mock legal form of being a charlatan:

> Hold up thy hand, G. H., thou art heere indited for an incrocher upon the fee-simple of the Latin, an enemie to Carriers, as one that takes their occupation out of their hands, and dost nothing but transport letters up and downe in thy owne commendation, a conspiratour and practiser to make Printers rich, by making thy selfe ridiculous, a manifest briber of Bookesellers and Stationers, to helpe thee to sell away thy bookes (whose impression thou paidst for) that thou mayst have money to goe home to Trinitie Hall to discharge thy commons. (1:261)

The fiction that Harvey is on trial is maintained throughout the pamphlet; he is addressed directly and his text questioned as if it were being cross-examined. The charge that Harvey paid for the publication of his books may or may not be true, but it reflects Nashe's nascent pride in his own professionalism (Friedenreich).

By playing the clown himself and treating Harvey as a buffoon, Nashe trivializes the serious issues Harvey raises. Harvey says Nashe is a desperate malcontent; well then, "Sweet Gentlemen, be but indifferent, and you shal see mee desperate. Heere lies my hatte, and there my cloake, to which I resemble my two Epistles, being the upper garments of my booke, as the other of my body: Saint Fame for mee, and thus I runne upon him" (1:263). The passage is too impudent to be taken seriously, although Harvey later charged that the invocation to Saint Fame was vainglorious. Perhaps Nashe did desire publicity, but he is capable of laughing at himself, a talent lacking in Harvey. Like Dick Tarlton or Martin Marprelate, Nashe can divide himself among several exaggerated comic roles, which he is the first to laugh at, whereas Harvey is committed to creating in his published works (but not in his private marginalia) a single, coherent, and highly serious self.

Nashe uses his training as an anti-Martinist to elevate the *reductio ad absurdum* to a fine art. Parodying Elizabethan typographical conventions, he calls attention to the fact that printed discourse is artificial and that Harvey's serious ethos is a contrivance. His technique—quoting passages from Harvey's text in italic, then offering comments—is the one used in serious controversies of the period, but sober refutation, like Whitgift's of Cartwright, was primarily concerned with exposing weaknesses in an opponent's argument, while Nashe is more interested in attacking Harvey's motivation and character. He has no compunctions about quoting Harvey out of context, the more shamefully the better. Nashe's sheer foolery is part of a calculated plan to reduce the controversy to such conceits as clownage keeps in pay. He is more serious about defending the propriety of *Pierce Penniless* and his own reputation, but most of the pamphlet is made up of an irreverent attack on Harvey's pretensions.

An example of Nashe's strategy is the opening of his discussion of Harvey's third letter. Passages in italic are quoted from Harvey's text:

<blockquote>
The Arrainment and Execution of the third letter.
To everie Reader favourably or indifferently affected.
</blockquote>

TEXT, stand to the Barre. Peace there belowe.
Albeit for these twelve or thirteene yeares no man hath beene more loath, or more scrupulous than my selfe, &c.

The body of mee, hee begins like a proclamation: sufficeth it wee knowe you your minde though you say no more.

Is not this your drift? you would have the worlde suppose you were urgde to do that which proceeded of your owne good nature: like some that will seeme to bee intreated to take a high place of preferment uppon them, which privilie before they have prayde and payde for, and put all their strength to clymbe up to. (1:293)

Nashe is particularly acute on Harvey's self-serving statements; his more moderate reflections on literature and society are ignored.

Nashe's defense of Greene is equivocal, as Harvey later pointed out. Greene had been at least intermittently Nashe's friend and had helped him start his career; however, Greene was dissolute and an atheist by his own printed admission. Harvey's attack on Greene was severe, given that he had died, but his main criticisms were not easily refuted. By linking Nashe with Greene, Harvey jeopardized Nashe's career, particularly since *Pierce Penniless* was seen as a scandalous work. Nashe had even been suspected of writing Greene's putative last work, *Greene's Groats-Worth of Wit*, which was notorious because of its libelous attack on Marlowe and Shakespeare. The printer, Henry Chettle, contributed to Nashe's dilemma in *Kind-Heart's Dream*, published in the late fall of 1592. Because he had prepared the manuscript of *Greene's Groats-Worth of Wit* for the press, he was able to exonerate Nashe from having a hand in its composition, but one segment of *Kind-Heart's Dream* is a vision of the ghost of Robert Greene, who bears a message to Pierce Penniless to revenge the wrongs done to both of them. The ghost is ambivalent about invectives and revenge: "And albeit I would disswade thee from more invectives against such thy adversaries (for peace is nowe all my plea) yet I know thou wilt returne answere, that since thou receivedst the first wrong, thou wilt not endure the last" (36). In other words, Nashe should revenge himself to avoid ignominy, although personal invective is a breach of the peace. Chettle's harmless fiction may have built anticipation for Nashe's reply, but it also served to link him closer to a man who had come to represent the antithesis of the socially useful author Nashe aspired to be.

Nashe's defense of Greene is both cautious and charitable:

"Debt and deadly sinne, who is not subject to? with any notorious crime I never knew him tainted" (1:287). Greene's expansive spirit is contrasted with Harvey's austerity: "In one yeare hee pist as much against the walls, as thou and thy two brothers spent in three" (287). He wrote rapidly but well, and his works were eagerly sought by printers, although he set no value on them himself. Nashe denies the more scandalous details Harvey reports of Greene's poverty in his last days; he was with Greene "a month before he died, at that fatall banquet of Rhenish wine and pickled hearing (if thou wilt needs have it so)" and noted that Greene owned some very expensive clothing. He advises Harvey of "a very faire Cloake with sleeves, of a grave goose turd greene; it would serve you as fine as may bee," and would cost him ten shillings less used than it had cost Greene new (287–88). But Nashe also dissociates himself from Greene's lifestyle, denying that they were particularly close friends. He limits his praise of Greene to what he knows directly: "I had no tuition over him; he might have writ another Galataeo of manners, for his manners everie time I came in his companie: I saw no such base shifting or abhominable villanie by him" (330). He admits, however, that he has heard gossip of bad behavior on Greene's part. Nashe's account may well have been the simple truth as he knew it, but he was not going to let himself be tarred with Greene's bad reputation.

Nashe's defense of himself is the most serious portion of *Strange News*, since *Four Letters* threatened his career, however much Harvey pretended to goodwill towards his person. His justification of *Pierce Penniless* has been discussed in Chapter 3. He also answers indignantly the charge that his style is derivative, denying that he was influenced by Tarlton, Greene, or Lyly. His art is not all railing, although he can rail, as Harvey is finding out: "I have written in all sorts of humors privately, I am perswaded, more than any yoong man of my age in England" (320). Harvey's criticisms move him to defiance: "Gabriell, if there bee anie witte or industrie in thee, now I will dare it to the uttermost: write of what thou wilt, in what language thou wilt, and I will confute it and answere it. Take truths part, and I wil prove truth to be no truth, marching out of thy dung-voiding mouth" (305). In his response Harvey was to make much of the boldness of this challenge.

Aspersions on Nashe's character are refuted and defied. He cites the support of his patron, Whitgift, as evidence that his life "is as civil as a civil orenge; I lurke in no corners, but converse in a house of credit" (329). At the same time he plays with Harvey's imputation that he is a "pot-poet" like Greene. "Heigh, drawer, fil us a fresh quart *of new-found phrases*, since Gabriell saies we borrow all our eloquence from Taverns" (305). Although he jokes about drinking, he denies that he was ever as poor and desperate as his character Pierce Penniless. He had experienced debtor's prison, but his stay there was educational: "Come, come; if you will goe to the sound truth of it, there is no place of the earth like it, to make a man wise." Cambridge and Oxford cannot compare to it; he vows, "If I had a sonne, I would sooner send him to one of the Counters to learne lawe, than to the Innes of Court or Chauncery" (310). This is the sort of brazen defiance of an apparent disadvantage that Nashe claimed should have been Harvey's response to criticisms of his father's mundane occupation.

Behind the bickering over the details of each man's life lies a more essential conflict about the credibility of the ethos each develops in his pamphlets. Harvey presents himself as a man of integrity while deliberately conflating Nashe with the inconsistent Greene and with the malcontented persona Pierce Penniless, even though he also expresses solicitude for the proper young man who has been misled. These distinctions are disingenuous and unacceptable to Nashe; the relationship between public ethos and private character is too intimate. Moreover, Harvey's own integrity seems to Nashe an unconvincing fabrication and the sincerity of his ethos a subterfuge. He tells Harvey, "Squeise thy heart into thy inkehorne, and it shall but congeal into clodderd garbage of confutation, thy soule hath no effects of a soule, thou canst not sprinkle it into a sentence, & make everie line leape like a cup of neat wine new powred out, as an Orator must doe that lies aright in wait for mens affections" (307). As this sentence itself shows, Nashe had evolved a style that bears the stamp of a credible personality, even if that personality is mercurial and given to playing ironic roles. Harvey's prose, in comparison, seems a performance, for all that he protests sincerity.

In charging that "thy soule hath no effects of a soule" Nashe is criticizing Harvey's failure to create a rhetorically effective ethos, but more is at issue than Harvey's writing skills. To use a modern term, bad faith is the underlying charge; Harvey's posturing is depicted as a basic character flaw, not just a faulty rhetorical strategy. Nashe questions Harvey as a man as well as a writer: "All the world knowes him better than he knowes himselfe, & though he play the Pharisie never so, in justifiyng his owne innocence, theres none will beleeve him" (268). The repeated accusation that Harvey praises himself under cover of a well-wisher is evidence for Nashe that Harvey has a pathetic need for praise and self-justification that overrules integrity. "Ah neighbourhood, neighbourhood, dead and buried art thou with Robinhood: a poore creature here is faine to commend himselfe, for want of friendes to speake for him" (293–94).

Nashe's characterization of Harvey is summed up in a devastating sentence: "Gentlemen, by that which hath been already laid open, I doe not doubt but you are unwaveringly resolved, this indigested Chaos of Doctourship, and greedy pothunter after applause, is an apparant Publican and sinner, a selfe-love surfetted sot, a broken-winded galdbacke Jade, that hath borne up his head in his time, but now is quite foundred & tired, a scholer in nothing but the scum of schollership, a stale soker at Tullies *Offices,* the droane of droanes, and maister drumble-bee of non proficients" (301–2). Harvey had used his prestige as a scholar to attack Nashe's writings as pernicious; Nashe's defense is to portray Harvey as an hypocrite, pretending to high ideals but actually more self-centered than Greene or himself. It could be said that Nashe drags the pretentious Harvey down to his own level, but Nashe himself sees his strategy as being more one of exposing Harvey's selfish motives and devious methods. He makes few claims for Greene or himself, since we are all apparent publicans and sinners like Harvey; only some of us have the good grace to be tolerant and charitable rather than self-righteous. Nashe's own tolerance and charity are vulnerable to criticism, but Harvey emerges from the first interchange discredited and looking rather foolish.

THE SECOND EXCHANGE: FROM FLYTING TO CALUMNY

Nashe's offer of peace in the epistle to *Christ's Tears over Jerusalem* put Harvey in an awkward position: his long pamphlet counterattacking *Strange News* was already at the press and a truce at this point would leave Nashe with the last, rather damning word. In *A New Letter of Notable Contents*, dated September 16, 1593, Harvey tries to justify his rejection of the proffered truce. The brief pamphlet is difficult because of its elliptical style and obscure allusions, but its basic contention is that in a public quarrel, as in international diplomacy, an offer of truce must be looked into carefully, since everyone wants peace when it is to his or her advantage. If Nashe's self-proclaimed repentance in *Christ's Tears* should turn out to be a strategy, then Harvey would be exposing himself to further ridicule if he suppressed *Pierce's Supererogation* and came to terms. Accordingly he will consider peace only after he has answered the libels of *Strange News*.

The reasons for Harvey's demur are clear enough without speculating about the role of the intermediaries that passed between him and Nashe nor postulating betrayal by the printer Wolfe (McKerrow, 5:104; Hibbard, 214–15). Harvey will remain skeptical until "*a publique injurie* be publiquely confessed, and *Print* confuted in Print" (*New Letter*, sig. C4r). Although he would like to believe in Nashe's repentance, he suspects his adversary of expediency, particularly since report has it that Nashe's lifestyle is not reformed at all. Given the religious hypocrisy of Nashe's model, Aretino, and the Lucianism of Marlowe and Greene, Harvey suspects the lamentations of *Christ's Tears* are a performance, an attempt at the pathetical vein to suit the times. While ready to be proven wrong, Harvey suspects Nashe of a vicious exploitation of religion, beginning with the cynical stratagem of a fake apology to Harvey. *A New Letter* concludes with a fresh attack on Nashe occasioned by the sudden death of Marlowe: in a series of poems Harvey sees Marlowe's death as punishment for his arrogance and blasphemy, then cautions that Nashe's turn is next. Throughout the letter Harvey's resentment outweighs any generous impulse he has to accept Nashe's retraction and terminate the quarrel.

Nashe was understandably outraged, all the more so, one imagines, because Harvey's doubts about his reform were justified by events. In a revised epistle to *Christ's Tears* he violates his new humble tone by defying Harvey and promising vengeance. Nashe has been made a fool by having his submission answered by a thick pamphlet of abuse. "Impious Gabriell Harvey, the vowed enemie to all vowes and protestations, plucking on with a slavish privat submission a generall publike reconciliation, hath with a cunning ambuscado of confiscated idle othes, welneare betrayed me to infamie eternall, (his owne proper chaire of torment in hell)" (2:179-80). Nashe's account of the aborted reconciliation differs from Harvey's; probably the suspicion and hostility on both sides was too deep to be bridged. *Strange News* is too powerful an indictment of Harvey's character to be mitigated by Nashe's rather general apology in *Christ's Tears*, but, conversely, *Pierce's Supererogation* and *A New Letter* are too vehement in their condemnation of Nashe to be acceptable as a fair balancing of the account.

Pierce's Supererogation angrily repeats the accusations made against Nashe in *Four Letters*. Its prose is even more convoluted than that of the earlier pamphlet because Harvey is attempting a high style that will overwhelm Nashe with its *copia* and magisterial sentences. He makes frequent use of innuendo and obscure allusions: doubtful phrases and ambiguous giving-outs that may or may not refer to actual secrets. The overall structure is loose and confusing, since Harvey is seeking the striking phrase or rhetorically mounting passage more than a logically presented case. The title seizes on Nashe's claim that he is expected to do "workes of supererrogation in answering the Doctor" as evidence of insufferable arrogance. All the worst social and literary tendencies of the age have culminated in Nashe, the ultimate embodiment of the egocentric sins that threaten Christian humility and the civic order. Nashe's claim to be a humanistic poet is belied by the actual nature of his works. We cannot assess Harvey's criticisms of Nashe's private life, but his attack on the discrepancy between Nashe's goals as a writer and his actual performance is obviously true. Of course Harvey failed to appreciate what Nashe did accomplish, and his dismissal of Nashe's originality is unfair, but he was right that Nashe never wrote the kind of socially useful literature both men prized.

Harvey was not a pedant who admired only the classics nor was he adverse to popular vernacular works. His list of English works useful to the commonwealth is extensive: "In Grafton, Holinshed, and Stowe; in Heywood, Tusser, and Gowge; in Gascoigne, Churchyarde, and Floide; in Ritch, Whetstone, and Munday; in Stanyhurst, Fraunce, and Watson; in Kiffin, Warner, and Daniell; in an hundred such vulgar writers, many things are commendable, divers things notable, somethings excellent" (*Pierce's Supererogation*, sigs. 2A4v–2B1r). The best literature inspires, but all literature should be useful in its kind. Nor is Harvey a Puritan objecting to pleasurable literature; he opposes only works that are useless or actually damaging to the commonwealth. One such trend is the rise of the outspoken, contentious pamphlet caused by the success of Lyly, Greene, and Martin Marprelate. In an effort to establish Nashe's pedigree Harvey prints as the central section of *Pierce's Supererogation* a tract written but not published in 1589, titled "An Advertisement for Pap-hatchet and Martin Marprelate" (discussed above in Chap. 2). Harvey includes it in the present work because "Ink is so like Ink, spite so like spite, impudencie so like impudencie, brocage so like brocage, and Tom-Penniles now, so like Papp-hatchet, when the time was; that I neede but overrun an old censure of the One, by way of a new application to the Other" (sig. I3r). He again sees Greene as another source of Nashe's arrogance: "Nash, the Ape of Greene, Greene the Ape of Euphues, Euphues the Ape of Envie, the three famous mammets of the presse, and my three notorious feudists, drawe all in a yoke" (sig. S4r). If anything, Nashe has managed to surpass his masters.

Strange News has removed any hope that Nashe was better than his persona. "Though Pierce Penniles, for a spurt were a ranke rider, and like an arrant knight overran nations with a carreer; yet Thomas Nashe might have beene advised, and in pollicy have spared them, that in compassion favoured him; and were unfaynedlye sory, to finde his miserable estate, aswell in his style, as in his purse, and in his wit, as in his fortune. Some complexions have much adooe to alter their nature: & Nashe wil carrie a tache of Pierce to his grave" (*Pierce's Supererogation*, sig. E4r). In *Four Letters*, Harvey distinguished between Nashe and Pierce; now he conflates them, using the names interchangeably, as in Tom Penniless. The arrogant ethos of *Strange News* is the character of Nashe the man and the culmination of a succession of literary personas, including Pierce Penniless and Robert Greene (sig. C1r).

At greater length than in *Four Letters*, Harvey compares Nashe with Aretino, neglecting again to mention the admiration for the Italian expressed in his marginalia. Like Aretino, Nashe has written (but not printed) a "packet of bawdye, and filthy Rymes, in the nastiest kind" (sig. F4r), a reference to the pornographic "Choice of Valentines." Harvey had probably already alluded to the poem in *Four Letters* when he called Nashe "the devil's orator and his dam's poet," a reiterated phrase Nashe professes not to understand, since he had not published any poetry. But "The Choice of Valentines" circulated widely in manuscript, to judge from the number of surviving copies and allusions to it. We are less likely to be shocked by the sexual frankness of the poem than Nashe's late Victorian editor, but the poem, like much pornography, mechanizes sex and demeans women. Directly accused of its authorship, Nashe prevaricates: "Well, it may be so that it is not so; or if it be, men in their youth (as in their sleep) manie times doo something that might have been better done, & they do not wel remember" (3:129).

More damaging is the exaggerated accusation that Nashe was seditious in *Pierce Penniless*: "Be it nothing to have railed upon Doctours of the Universitie, or upon Lords of the Court, (whom he abuseth most-infamously, & abjecteth as contemptuously, as me) but what other desperate varlet of the world, durst so villanously have diffamed London, & the Court, as he notoriously hath done?" (*Pierce's Supererogation*, sig. Y4r).

Since Nashe neither understands himself or others, Harvey reports to him on his reputation: "He hath little witt: lesse learning: lest judgement: no discretion: Vanity enough: stomacke at will: superabundance of selfe-conceit: outward liking to fewe, inward affection to none: (his defence of Greene, a more biting condemnation, then my reproofe): no reverence to patrons: no respect to his superiors: no regard to any, but in contemptuous, or censorius sort: hatred, or disdaine to the rest: continuall quarrels with one, or other" (sig. Z1r). This characterization of Nashe easily leads to the further charge that he is an atheist, like Aretino: "Aretine, and the Divels Oratour, would be ashamed to be convicted, or endighted of the least respective, or ceremonious phrase, but in mockage or coosenage. They neither feare Goodman Sathan, nor master Beelzebub, nor sir Reverence, nor milord Governement himselfe: o wretched Atheisme, Hell but a scarecrow, and Heaven but a woonderclout in their doctrine" (sig. Z1v).

The accusations that Nashe is seditious and an atheist are unfair to his manifest orthodoxy, but Harvey's indictment had substance from an Elizabethan perspective. Nashe did entertain controversial ideas and promote his own views without any authority in highly singular pamphlets. Harvey complains that Nashe "neither knoweth himselfe, nor other: yet presumeth he knoweth all things, with an overplus of somewhat more, in knowing his Railing Grammar, his Raving Poetry, his Roisting Rhetorique, and his Chopping Logique" (sig. V3v). Nashe "can phansy no Autor, but his owne phansy" (sig. B4r). Others study authorities or draw on experience; Nashe spins out words from his own conceit: "Wordes amount, like Castels of vapours, or pillars of smoke, that make a mighty showe in the Aier, and straight Vanish-away" (sig. V1r). Harvey began reading *Strange News* with trepidation, only to find it had no substance; in publishing it Nashe immortalized "himselfe the prowdest Vaine sott": "For the end is like the beginning; the midst like both; and every part like the whole. Railing, railing, railing: bragging, bragging, bragging: and nothing else, but fowle railing upon railing, and vayne bragging upon bragging; as rudely, grosely, odiously, filthily, beastly, as ever shamed Print" (sig. I1v).

In this way, Harvey links Nashe's bad character and his pernicious ideas to his writing style: "his Life daily feedeth his Stile; & his Stile notoriously bewraieth his Life" (sig. F2v). Nashe may believe himself "a speciall penman; as he were the headman of the Pamfletting crew, next, and immediatly after Greene" (sig. Z3v), but Harvey has "seldome read a more garish, and pibald stile in any scribling Inkhornist; or tasted a more unsavory slaumpaump of wordes, and sentences in any sluttish Pamfletter" (sig. Z4r). Desolate Eloquence and forlorn Poetry "cladd in mournefull and dreery weedes, as becommeth their lamentable case, lye prostrate at thy dainty foote, and adore the Idoll-excellency of thy monstrous Singularity" (sig. Z4v). Such singularity is a dangerous model for the young men of the city. "If Wisedome say not, Phie for shame; & Autoritie take not other order in convenient time: who can tell, what generall plague may ensue of a speciall infection?" (sig. H2v). Nashe is "a bratt of Arrogancy, a gosling of the Printinghouse, that can teach your braggardes to play their partes in the Printe of woonder, & to exploit redowtable workes of Supererogation" (sig. D2v). Harvey continues to be troubled that the quarrel was lowering him to Nashe's level; he fears he will win at best a Pyrrhic victory.

Nashe accuses him of pride, which is in fact Nashe's "owne deerest hart-root," but Harvey protests before man and God that his soul abhors pride: "It is not excesse, but defecte of pride that hath broken the head of some mens preferment" (sig. E4v). In his marginalia Harvey recorded his belief that he needed to be more resolute, but, of course, personal insecurity can exist with pride. He is indignant at Nashe's accusations: "He upbraideth me with his own good nature: but where such an insolent braggard, or such a puffing thing, as himselfe?" (sig. E4v). He asserts, "The truth is, I stande as little upon others commendations, or mine owne titles, as any man in England whosoever," yet he must defend his reputation: "by the leave of God, I will proove miselfe no Asse" (sig. F1r). To accomplish this, he includes a long list of the distinguished people who have commended him.

Proving himself not an ass is a thankless project that forces Harvey into subterfuges, like those of *Four Letters*, which allow him to include praise of himself in a modest fashion. For example, there is poetry in support of Harvey from the minor writer John Thorius that, according to Thorius's own testimony in a letter to Nashe, was doctored by Harvey (3:135). In other places Harvey's style does betray him, as Nashe claimed: there is a highly critical account of Nashe attributed to a friend that was at the least redacted, if not composed, by Harvey (sigs. D1v–D2r). Harvey denies Nashe's charge that he fakes praise of himself: "As for his lewd supposals, & imputations of counterfait praises, without anye probability of circumstance, or the least suspition, but in his owne vengeable malitious head . . . they . . . doe but intimate his owne skill in falsifying of evidence, and suborning of witnesses to his purpose." Nashe "hath not studied his fellowes Arte of Cunnycatching for nothinge" (sig. F2v). This argument cuts both ways: neither man's books are as simple and straightforward as they pretend to be. Printing requires a certain amount of contrivance.

The praise of indirection in Harvey's marginalia make his protestations of simplicity hard to believe. In his imagination the world was divided into asses and foxes, his version of fools and knaves. *Pierce's Supererogation,* which is subtitled *A New Praise of the Old Asse,* includes a long mock encomium on the ass, which sees the animal's nature as a universal principle in human society. Nashe believes Harvey and everyone else are asses, but Nashe is an ass himself ("an ass" could be punned with "Nashe" in Elizabethan pronunciation). Most people are stupid in the passive, indifferent fashion of the ass, but the most stupid are those who glorify their own wit like Nashe.

Harvey's perfect example of a fox is his old adversary Andrew Perne, who blocked his advancement at Cambridge. Perne was notorious for the chameleon-like adaptability that allowed him to survive two changes of religion in the midcentury. Harvey claims to have learned the art of the fox from Perne: "Of him I learned to know him, to know my enemies, to know my frends, to know miselfe, to know the world, to know fortune, to know the mutability of times, and slipperinesse of occasions" (*Pierce's Supererogation,* sig. 2B2v). With a touch of admiration he describes the "omnidexterity" of the "great Temporiser," the masterful "Doctor of Hypocrisy." "I have seen spannels, mungrels, libbards, antelops; scorpions, snakes, cockatrices, vipers, and many other Serpents in sugar-worke: but to this day never sawe such a standing dish of Sugar-worke, as that sweet-tounged Doctor" (sig. 2B4v). He tells of one encounter with Perne that suggests he chose to emulate his enemy: "He once in a scoldes pollicy, called me Foxe betweene jest, and earnest: (it was at the funerall of the honorable Sir Thomas Smith, where he preached, and where it pleased my Lady Smith, and the coexecutours to bestowe certaine rare manuscript bookes upon me, which he desired): I aunswered him betweene earnest, & jest, I might haply be a Cubb, as I might be used: but was over-young to be a Fox, especially in his presence" (sig. 2D1r). Harvey never says he wants to be a fox himself—that would not be a very foxlike admission to make—but he is equally adamant that he will prove himself no ass.

In *Pierce's Supererogation*, then, Harvey focuses his argument more sharply on Nashe's character as revealed in his works, while defending his own integrity. The only charge of Nashe's that Harvey concedes is that he has affected taste in footware, "pumps and pantofles." Harvey returns frequently to the argument that Nashe's criticisms of him lack substance, but his own account of Nashe is general except for obscure allusions to Nashe's disreputable lifestyle. In *Four Letters*, he confined his criticism to the persona Pierce Penniless; now he attacks Nashe's ethos and argues that the ethos reflects the character of the man. Harvey continues to be a literary critic, since his case against Nashe is based on comparing Nashe's works with works by Aretino, Lyly, Greene, and others. He sees Nashe as a new kind of writer who arrogantly expresses his own views and prejudices while projecting his own corrupt values onto others; in such a case literary criticism becomes personal and social criticism as well.

Harvey's criticisms were too damaging to go unanswered, although it was three years before Nashe published *Have with You to Saffron Walden*. In the interim Nashe had published *The Terrors of the Night* and *The Unfortunate Traveler*, neither of which was the sort of substantial work that would have disproved Harvey's assertion that Nashe was a trivial writer. Nashe had not escaped chronic poverty; he did indeed still carry the taint of Pierce Penniless, as can be seen in his one surviving letter, written in August or early September 1596. He concludes a mocking report of gossip about town with a tacit appeal for money: "I am merry when I have nere a penny in my purse. God may move you though I say nothing" (5:196). In *Have with You,* Nashe is honest about his "decayed fortunes," which have contributed to the delay in his answer to Harvey. He had tried hackwriting for private gentlemen, only to be fobbed of his pay. By 1596 the young man who had tried to take literary London by storm was at a low ebb, too poor to make much use of the talents he had and too controversial to find regular employment.

A masterpiece of invective, *Have with You to Saffron Walden; or, Gabriel Harvey's Hunt Is Up* is cast in the form of a dialogue between Nashe and a group of friends who are concerned about his delay in defending his damaged reputation. He reads them the manuscript of his answer to Harvey, which consists of a short introduction ridiculing the bulk of *Pierce's Supererogation,* a pompous oration parodying Harvey's style, and an extended life of Harvey exposing his contrivances. After the manuscript has been read, Nashe and his friends pick over Harvey's text, answering some of his charges. By framing his answer in this way, Nashe subdivides his argument in an entertaining fashion and draws the reader into what was becoming a confusing quarrel. The dialogue format, which Nashe asserts is based on actual conversations with his friends, also allows him to diffuse the aggressiveness of his attack and affect some modesty. Those Elizabethan friends of the author who urge publication, so often alluded to in other works, are incorporated into the text of *Have with You.*

Nashe has no illusions about the value of continuing the quarrel when he should be concerned with his economic future. There is no profit in it, except "some foolish praise perhaps we may meete with, such as is affoorded to ordinarie Jesters that make sport" (3:18). The dearth of good books in Paul's churchyard has caused some people with "dull frozen and halfe dead" wits to encourage the quarrel, "so, to recreate and enkindle their decayed spirites, they care not how they set Harvey and mee on fire one against another, or whet us on to consume our selves" (30). Harvey and he are a "couple of beggars" that bandy factions and "spend as much time in arguing *pro & contra*, as a man might have found out the quadrature of the Circle in" (19). Because his reputation is at issue, he reluctantly turns to the task of refuting Harvey; afterwards he vows "to turne a new leave" and devote himself to repairing his fortunes.

Nashe was not willing to make peace, however; some six months before the completion of *Have with You*, he and Harvey had by chance lodged at the same Cambridge inn:

> Everie circumstance I cannot stand to reckon up, as how wee came to take knowledge of one anothers being there, or what a stomacke I had to have scratcht with him, but that the nature of the place hindred mee, where it is as ill as pettie treason to look but awry on the sacred person of a Doctour, and I had plotted my revenge otherwise; as also of a meeting or conference on his part desired, wherein all quarrells might be discust and drawne to an attonement, but *non vult fac,* I had no fancie to it, for once before I had bin so cousend by his colloging, though personally we never met face to face, yet by trouchmen and vant-curriers betwixt us: nor could it settle in my conscience to loose so much paines I had tooke in new arraying & furbushing him, or that a publique wrong in Print was to be so sleightly slubberd over in private, with Come, come, give me your hand, let us bee frends, and thereupon I drinke to you. (3:92–93)

Nashe goes on to joke that he feared Harvey would poison him, but his real reasons are like those that motivated Harvey's rejection of peace in 1593: a truce now would mean that the work Nashe had put into *Have with You* was wasted, and it would leave Harvey with the last word in print.

Through fictional exchanges with his friends, Nashe expresses his belief that his reputation as a writer is closely bound with the outcome of his quarrel with Harvey. Senior Importuno warns that Nashe's failure to answer Harvey will be a blot of ignominy while he lives and become even more damaging after his death: "There is an age to come, which, knowing neither thee nor him, but by your severall workes judging of either, will authorise all hee hath belched forth in thy reproach for sound Gospell, since . . . thou holding thy peace, and not confuting him, seemes to confesse and confirme all whereof hee hath accused thee" (3:27). S. Importuno's fear that "while Printing lasts, thy disgrace may last," may seem excessive with the hindsight of some four hundred more years of printing, but, as we have seen, Elizabethans endowed print with more permanency than we do.

Accused of ranting and spinning out words in *Strange News*, Nashe retaliates by making *Have with You* an unusually factual work, although he also mocks his own factuality. He claims that he has delayed publication because he needed "further time to get perfect intelligence of his life and conversation, one true point whereof, well set downe, wil more excruciate & commacerate him, than knocking him about the eares with his owne stile in a hundred sheets of paper" (29). Nashe has gone to some effort to gather his facts and in some cases offers them with an attribution. He heard details of Harvey's life in London from the printer John Wolfe, who had fallen out with Harvey. He backs up his accusation that Harvey wrote the anonymous complimentary letter of a well-wisher that was prefixed to *Three Proper and Witty Letters* by saying that "the Compositor that set it swore to mee it came under his owne hand to bee printed" (127). He prints a letter from Henry Chettle that refutes the charge that Nashe betrays his friends. A piece of gossip about Richard Harvey arrives even as Nashe is writing (the "information piping hot in the midst of this line was but brought to mee"); the story is that Richard Harvey spied on his wench "footing it aloft on the Greene" and secretly paid the fiddlers after preaching a sermon against dancing as a sin. Nashe comments, "Let it sink into ye, for it is true & will be verefide. Let Gabriel verefie anie one thing so against mee, and not thinke to carrie it away with hys *generall extenuatings, ironicall amplifications,* and *declamatorie exclamations*" (122). Nashe claims not to have enough space to report all the derogatory information he has gathered on Harvey.

The charge that *Strange News* is mere rhetoric is thus turned back onto Harvey's mode of argument in *Pierce's Supererogation*. By referring to Nashe as "young Apuleius," Harvey can deny he meant specific accusations if he is challenged. Such subterfuges are pernicious: "Rhetoricians, though they lye never so grosely, are but said to have a luxurious phrase, to bee eloquent amplifiers, to bee full of their pleasant Hyperboles, or speake by Ironies; and if they raise a slaunder upon a man of a thing done at home, when hee is a 1000. mile off, it is but *Prosopopeya, personae fictio*, the supposing or faining of a person" (120). Harvey is the one who rails; Nashe even suspects him of digging up an old invective against some traitor and substituting Nashe or Pierce Penniless for the original name. "No villaine, no Atheist, no murdrer, no traitor, no Sodomite hee ever read of but he hath likend mee too, or in a superlative degree made me a monster beyond him" (123). Such mere rhetoric is to be answered with facts.

Of course, Nashe's scorn for contrivance is itself a pose, as the slyness of the passages quoted shows. He is quite willing to mix fiction with his facts, playing with the boundaries between them. The epistle to the readers offers a "caveat to observe in reading my Booke, which Aristotle prescribes to them that read Histories, namely, that they bee not *nimis credulos aut incredulos*, too rash or too slow of beleefe" (23). Later he mocks his new dedication to the truth in his introduction to a ludicrous oration he has compiled from bits and pieces from Harvey: "Auditors, awake your attention, and here expect the cleare repurified soule of truth, without the least shadow of fiction" (42). He is also solicitous in his biography of Harvey to sort the true miracles from the fabulous, like a hagiographer. "Whether it be verifiable, or onely probably surmised, I am uncertaine, but constantly up and downe it is bruted, how he pist incke as soone as ever hee was borne" (62). Before including a number of other tall tales about Harvey's birth, he worries, "Should I reckon up but one halfe of the miracles of his conception, that verie substantially have been affirmed unto mee, one or other like Bodine wold start up and taxe mee for a miracle-monger, as hee taxt Livy" (62). Jean Bodin's *Method for the Easy Comprehension of History* is a source for Nashe's ironic interest in the veracity of history.

For the most part the tongue-in-cheek avowals of truth are transparent games, as in the introduction of a comic letter from Harvey's tutor: "In truth (as truth is truth, and will out at one time or other, and shame the divell) the coppie of this Tutors Letter to his father I will shew you, about his carriage and demeanour; and yet I will not positively affirme it his Tutors Letter neither, and yet you maye gather more than I am willing to utter, and what you list not beleeve referre to after Ages" (64). This playful attitude towards the truth continues when one of the fictional listeners comments that he will let the letter pass because it is "no indecorum at all to the Comedie we have in hand to admit Piers himselfe for his Tutor" (69). Nashe also exaggerates true incidents to make Harvey look ridiculous, as in his account of Harvey's attempt to impress the queen at Audley End, near Cambridge, "to which place Gabriell (to doo his countrey more worship & glory) came ruffling it out, huffty tuffty, in his suite of velvet" (73).

Nashe's comic concern to distinguish truth from fiction is related to his contention that Harvey is an outright liar himself. He answers Harvey's claim that he was unwilling to enter into the quarrel, "You ly, you ly, Gabriell" (118). Nashe uses his new-found devotion to the truth as a way of attacking Harvey's contrivances. Harvey's countercharges are dismissed as fabrications: Nashe has never betrayed his patrons or his friends, nor has he taken the seditious positions attributed to him. He denies an anecdote that he once made a glutton of himself by eating eight or nine eggs and a pound of butter for breakfast. He admits that he earns his living in part from the printing house, but he is not ashamed of it. If he did write an obscene poem, it was a youthful peccadillo. Harvey's attack is almost entirely lies in the form of rhetorical trickery, factual inaccuracies, and unsupported innuendo.

Nashe and the friends speculate about the reality of an unnamed gentlewoman who is said to be writing on Harvey's behalf. They conclude she is another contrivance, created by Harvey so that he can praise himself and criticize Nashe without taking responsibility for his words. One friend explains: "I have found him, I have the tract of him: he thinkes in his owne person if he should raile grosely, it will bee a discredit to him, and therefore hereafter hee would thrust foorth all his writings under the name of a Gentlewoman; who, howsoever shee scolds and playes the vixen never so, wilbe borne with" (111). Nashe answers that she might exist but then, on the basis of her style, decides she is "onely a Fiction of his." He quotes some phrases attributed to her that sound like Harvey: "Yea, Madam Gabriela, are you such an old jerker? then Hey ding a ding, up with your petticoate, have at your plum-tree: but the style bewraies it, that no other is this goodwife Megara but Gabriel himself" (113). If Nashe has guessed wrong and the gentlewoman did exist, he still has discredited and insulted her.

Harvey's contrivances and pretensions are the underlying theme of the mock biography in which Nashe emphasizes Harvey's efforts to achieve, or at least worm his way into, greatness. Much of the comedy comes from the contrast drawn between Harvey's "discontented poverty" and his high opinion of himself. This is dramatized in vignettes, such as his effort to curry favor at Audley End or his disbelief at finding himself in debtor's prison. Nashe depicts the young Harvey as a fop whose tutor complains:

> He is, beyond all reason or Gods forbod, distractedly enamourd of his own beautie, spending a whole forenoone everie day in spunging and licking himselfe by the glasse; and useth everie night after supper to walke on the market hill to shew himselfe, holding his gown up to his middle, that the wenches may see what a fine leg and a dainty foote he hath in pumpes and pantoffles, and, if they give him never so little an amorous regard, he presently boords them with a set speach of the first gathering together of societies, and the distinction of *amor* and *amicitia* out of Tullies *Offices*. (68)

This caricature of the young Harvey, who Nashe says was always in love, contrasts pathetically with the older Harvey of the mid 1590s: "A smudge peice of a handsome fellow it hath beene in his dayes, but now he is olde and past his best, and fit for nothing but to be a Noble mans porter, or a Knight of Windsor, cares have so crazed him, and disgraces to the verie bones consumed him" (94). But any compassion Nashe has for his target is soon dissipated.

Nashe is particularly interested in the life of contrivance Harvey's aspirations forced on him, which he sees as a kind of bad faith permeating Harvey's life and works. Nashe claims that he would never have ridiculed Harvey's father for being a ropemaker, except that it is Harvey's "fault to beare himselfe too arrogantly above his birth, and to contemne and forget the house from whence he came" (56). He also finds it ironic that Harvey mocks Nashe's poverty while being poor himself. Harvey's career is seen as a vain search for sustaining employment commensurate with his ambitions. Although Harvey scorns professional writing, he has done hack work under pseudonyms to earn a living. His more serious works, written to draw attention to himself, are tissues of contrived self-aggrandizing that he has had to pay to see in print. For a while he attracted the attention of the earl of Leicester, but Leicester soon saw through his pretentiousness and sent him back to Cambridge. The pamphlets written against Nashe are a last effort to salvage his reputation and call attention to his abilities.

In short, Nashe saw Harvey as another variety of Pierce Penniless, desperately pretending to be a man of affairs so that the appearance of importance would lead to the actuality. Just as Pierce was driven to trafficking with the devil, so is Harvey driven to the everyday equivalent, an Iago-like resort to strategems and role playing. Unlike Iago, Harvey is comically inept at his impositions. Nashe describes how a gentleman friend of his visited Harvey and was made to wait: "Two howres good by the clocke he attended his pleasure, whiles he (as some of his fellow In-mates have since related unto mee) stood acting by the glasse all his gestures he was to use all the day after, and currying & smudging and pranking himselfe unmeasurably" (91). Harvey finally greets the gentleman with the fulsomeness of Osric, so belaboring courtesy that "the Gentleman swore to mee that upon his first apparition (till he disclosed himselfe) he tooke him for an Usher of a dancing Schoole, neither doth he greatly differ from it, for no Usher of a dauncing Schoole was ever such a *Bassia Dona* or *Bassia de umbra de umbra des los pedes*, a kisser of the shadow of your feetes shadow, as he is" (92). Through the comic exaggeration emerges a picture of a man whose insecurities confounded his talents.

Nashe may well be right that *Pierce's Supererogation* is the product of angry frustration. With all of his previous schemes in shambles and his law practice unprofitable, Harvey lodged at John Wolfe's house for thirty-seven weeks, unwilling to venture out until he had answered Nashe; Nashe claims: "After I had plaid the spirit in hanting him in my 4. Letters confuted, he could by no means endure the light, nor durst venter himself abroad in the open aire for many months after, for feare he should be fresh blasted by all mens scorne and derision" (95). Harvey risked the plague, then at its height, in his desire to be revenged on Nashe. "The argument (to my great rejoycing & solace) from hence I have gathered was that my lines were of more smarting efficacie than I thought, & had that steele and mettall in them which pierst & stung him to the quick" (87). If Nashe is right, the anger that often prevails over the tone of disdain in *Pierce's Supererogation* is the desperation of a man whose personal credibility is in question.

We know from Harvey's marginalia that the Gabriel Harvey who aspired to a role on the stage of history was an elaborate fabrication, constructed in part from his detailed study of the hundreds of books he owned and annotated. Nashe saw this and presents a compelling portrait of Harvey as a quixotic figure trying to impose a vision of himself on a dubious public. His Gorboduc Huddleduddle may or may not correspond to the historical Harvey, but even as caricature it does reflect a self-conscious and willful fashioning of the self that contrasts with the obedient, subordinate self of Elizabethan orthodoxy. Harvey's exhortations to himself are a departure from the official humility of his time: "A man must take a delicate delight, and pryde in every thing, that concernith himself. A soverain conceyt in his own affayres" (Harvey, *Marginalia*, 194). His effort to will himself into action is both comic and pathetic:

"Lyttle or no writing will now serve, but only upon praesent necessary occasions, otherwise not dispatchable. All writing layd abedd, as taedious, & needles. All is now, in bowld Courtly speaking, and bowld Industrious dooing. Activity, praesent bowld Activity" (144–45).

Harvey's self-fashioning was unconvincing because the contrivance was too blatant, the impositions he attempted too transparent. Nashe himself was more honest because he did not pretend to be consistent or a man of integrity in the pamphlets he wrote against Harvey; he accepted the contradictions forced on him by his alienated status as Harvey would not. Between them, Nashe and Harvey—the man of contradictions and the man of false integrity—represent alternate modes of survival outside a framework of social roles and traditional values. They were kindred spirits for all that the paths they traveled diverged. Understanding Harvey as he did, Nashe might have shown more compassion, but Harvey's self-righteousness was intolerable, nor had he been generous in his treatment of Nashe. Nashe jokes that his delay in answering Harvey was an act of charity: he kept *Pierce's Supererogation* "idle by me in a by settle out of sight amongst old shooes and bootes almost this two yere, and in meere pitie of him would never looke upon it but in some calme pleasing humor, for feare least in my melancholy too cruelly I should have martyrd him" (3:19). But Nashe's compunctions do not last long: "You shall see me, in two or three leaves hence, crie Heigh for our towne greene, and powre hot boyling inke on this contemptible Heggledepegs barrain scalp" (20). Harvey was an irresistible target even if Nashe had not feared for his own reputation.

The Harvey-Nashe quarrel may have begun as a flyting, or staged literary quarrel, but by the second round each man's honor was at stake. On the Elizabethan streets, verbal defamation could easily lead to blows. Harvey is blustering but not merely joking when he threatens to fight Nashe: "I will batter thy carrion to dirt, whence thou camst; & squise thy braine to snivell, whereof it was curdled: na, before I leave poudring thee, I will make thee sweare, thy father was a Ropemaker; and proclaime thiselfe, the basest drudge of the Presse"

(*Pierce's Supererogation*, sig. V1v). Nashe mocks this threat and Harvey's claim that he learned fencing from a master of the art, but his counterthreat also has a note of violence behind its comic phrasing: "Not all the fence he learnd of Tom Burwell shall keepe mee from cramming a turd in his jawes (and no other bloud will I draw of him): I have bespoken a boy and a napkin already to carry it in" (3:134). The aggressiveness of the honor code is here displaced into words, but the words have a violence of their own.

RAILING LIBELS AND SLANDEROUS PAMPHLETS: THE BISHOPS TERMINATE THE QUARREL

The Harvey-Nashe quarrel drew much attention in the relatively small circle of London intellectuals, to judge from the number of allusions that have survived, but it was probably too arcane to attract popular interest. Harvey's *Four Letters* was the only work in the controversy to achieve a second edition, probably because of its colorful account of Greene's death. Nashe complained that there was no profit to be made from the quarrel and claimed that Harvey had to pay for the publication of his pamphlets. Much of the attention the controversy did attract was critical: Harvey and Nashe's verbal duel became a scandal. One of the first references to it was a complaint by Phillip Stubbes published late in 1593 in *A Motive to Good Works*. Stubbes had been criticized in *The Anatomy of Absurdity* and personally attacked in *An Almond for a Parrot*, but his criticism is general, in accord with his argument that Christians should not resort to invective:

> I cannot a lyttle mervayle, that our grave and reverend Bishops, and other inferiour magistrates and officers, to whom the oversight and charge of such thinges are committed, will either lisense, (which I trust they do not, for I wyll hope better of them) or in anie sorte tollerate such railing libels & slanderous pamphlets, as have beene of late published in print one man against another, to the greate dishonour of God, corruption of good manners,

breach of charitie, and in a worde, to the just offence & scandall of al good christians. (McKerrow, "Supplement," 5:77–78)

Stubbes's denunciation is further evidence that the quarrel ran afoul of the Elizabethan distrust of singularity; again Nashe is criticized for the personal element in his writing.

The quarrel also threatened the Elizabethan sense of hierarchical decorum, since Harvey was, after all, a doctor of laws. Harvey's own sense that he had more to lose because of his eminence was shared by Sir John Harington, who wrote an epigram:

> To Doctor Harvey of Cambridge.
> The proverbe sayes, Who fights with durty foes,
> Must needs be soyld, admit they winne or lose.
> Then think it doth a Doctors credit dash,
> To make himselfe Antagonist to Nash?
> (McKerrow, 5:146)

In 1595 William Covell wrote that it was a shame for Harvey to indulge in such a quarrel and that Nashe should find it revenge enough that Harvey "lives unregarded" (5:10). There was no agreement about who had won the quarrel: Harington's antagonism towards Nashe was shared by John Davies of Hereford, but others, such as Francis Meres and Thomas Middleton, were more critical of Harvey (5:150–53).

The quarrel also proved influential on the development of English verse satire and satiric drama. Hall and Marston both allude to it and borrow phrases from it and other writings of Nashe for their own satiric purposes. The satiric Parnassus plays, written and performed at Cambridge, where interest in the quarrel of two alumni would have been strong, also borrow from the pamphlets. Nashe himself is the model for the impecunious writer Ingenioso, who comments on his prototype, "I, heer's a fellow, Judicio, that carryed the deadly Stockado in his pen, whose muse was armed with a gagtooth, and his pen possest with Hercules furies." The character Judicio answers with an eloquent epitaph on the recently dead Nashe:

> Let all his faultes sleepe with his mournfull chest,
> And there for ever with his ashes rest.
> His stile was wittie, though it had some gal[l],
> Some thing[s] he might have mended, so may all.
> Yet this I say, that for a mother witt,
> Fewe men have ever seene the like of it.
> (*Three Parnassus Plays*, 245)

It has also been conjectured that Shakespeare alludes to the quarrel in *Love's Labor's Lost*, with Moth representing Nashe and Holofernes Gabriel Harvey, but the parallels are too general to be conclusive, and the borrowing of phrases proves an influence but not topical allusions. Alfred Harbage noted of the allegorizers of *Love's Labor's Lost*, "The method is not that of beginning with a mystery and finding a clue, but of beginning with a clue and finding a mystery" (22). Moth is probably merely Moth, but Shakespeare's general debt to Nashe and particularly to the Harvey-Nashe controversy has at least been demonstrated in this quixotic enterprise.

Richard Lichfield's *The Trimming of Thomas Nashe* illustrates the bad effect that critics of the quarrel feared and is evidence of the reputation Nashe had late in his career. A minor work of little intrinsic value, it is symptomatic of the contentiousness encouraged by Nashe and Harvey. Since it is an answer to *Have with You to Saffron Walden*, it has sometimes been assumed to be a pseudonymous work by Harvey, but it does not sound like him or concern itself with his reputation. Nashe's own comments in *Nashe's Lenten Stuff* suggest that he thought it was by Lichfield. It answers only the dedication to *Have with You*, which was addressed to Richard Lichfield, a barber at Trinity College, Cambridge. That dedication is another parody like those in *An Almond for a Parrot* and *Strange News*; Nashe was to use the device again in *Nashe's Lenten Stuff*. Lichfield, who was apparently a self-taught man of strong opinions, elected to take the dedication as an insult, so answers in kind. If the pamphlet is a hoax, it is very successful at representing itself as the extravagant invective of a witty barber.

In the dedication of *Have with You*, Nashe uses both the barber's humble trade and his colorful personality to mock Harvey's pretensions. As a barber, Lichfield was in the business of practicing minor surgery, trimming hair, and otherwise attending to the superficial good order of his customers' persons. Nashe uses this to undercut Harvey's pose as a social and literary critic. Thus, the dedication is titled "To the most Orthodoxall and reverent Corrector of staring haires, the sincere & finigraphicall rarifier of prolixious rough barbarisme, the thrice egregious and censoriall animadvertiser of vagrant moustachios" (3:5). Nashe plays at length with the analogy between the high endeavors of the Harvey brothers and Lichfield's mundane trade. But he also uses the barber's notorious character to satirize Harvey: "It is given out amongst Schollers that thou hast a passing singular good wit: now to trie whither thou hast so or no, let me heare what change of phrases thou hast to describe a good wit in, or how, in Pedagogue Tragotanto Doctors english, thou canst florish upon it" (16). If Lichfield wants to impress his customers, he will learn to talk like Harvey writes. Later in the pamphlet Nashe describes Lichfield as "a rare ingenuous odde merry Greeke, who (as I have heard) hath translated my *Piers Pennilesse* into the Macaronicall tongue" (33). McKerrow notes that nothing is known of this translation, but Nashe is probably mocking the barber's untutored Latin, using his pretensions to ridicule Harvey.

Lichfield does not seem to have known Nashe except by general reputation and through his printed works, so *The Trimming* has little value as a biographical source. Some information about Nashe's student days is included, but it is based on gossip and distorted to put Nashe in a bad light. Was Nashe for a time so poor that he had to share a single pair of breeches with a roommate, each venturing out on alternate days, or is this a conventional joke applied to Nashe? The pamphlet also claims Nashe is in prison, even printing a woodcut of a figure purporting to be Nashe in chains, but no details are given, so the charge may be slander. Lichfield is delighted that Nashe is a fugitive because of the *The Isle of Dogs*, hopes that he will be a prisoner, and looks forward to his suffering at the hands of the public executioner.

Lichfield's view of Nashe's public personality is similar to Harvey's but is expressed in a more scurrilous fashion. Nashe seems to him egocentric: "If you will understand any thing a right, you must ever apply it to your selfe" (Lichfield, sig. D3v). Such a person deserves punishment because "every booke which yet thou hast written is a libell, and whomsoever thou namest in thy booke hath a libell made of him, thou purposing to speake well of him: such is the malice of thy cankerd tongue" (sigs. G1r–G1v). Hearing of Nashe's flight to Yarmouth, Lichfield jeers: "What, a fugitive? how comes that to passe, that thou a man of so good an education, & so wel backt by the Muses, shuldst proove a fugitive? But alas, thy Muses brought thee to this miserie: you and your Muses maye even goe hang your selves: now you may wish, that he that first put the Muses into your head, had knockt out your hornes" (sig. F1r). It seems appropriate to Lichfield that such an irresponsible writer should end up fleeing the authorities.

Nashe is transformed into a caricature of the disreputable masterless man and malcontent. This is the sort of reputation the would-be humanist had achieved, at least among his critics, by the end of his career. Fairly or unfairly, he had become a model of antisocial behavior, like Greene before him. *The Trimming of Thomas Nashe* can also be seen as an example of the bad influence Nashe was accused of having on literature and the character of his readers. The pamphlet itself was too minor a work to attract anyone's ire, but the graceless fulminations of a barber who fancied himself a humorist are an example of the kind of trivial literature that serious-minded Elizabethans, including Nashe himself, thought was a waste of ink and paper. If Harvey in fact dirtied his name and lost credit by quarreling with Nashe, Nashe was being dragged even further down the social scale by becoming involved in a quarrel with Lichfield. The flyting threatened to turn into a brawl.

Nashe projected an answer to Lichfield, "I having a pamphlet hot a brooding that shall be called the *Barbers warming panne*" (3:153), but it was apparently forestalled by the order of the bishops against satiric literature. He had also planned a second edition of *Strange News*, just as Harvey had planned a third edition of *Four Letters*, a substantial refution titled *Nashe's*

St. Fame, and a gathering together of writings against Nashe by his redoubtable gentlewoman. All of these works may have been pipedreams or, in Harvey's case, part of a calculated strategy to overwhelm Nashe. But Whitgift and Bancroft took no chances; when they promulgated their order against satires on June 1, 1599, they specifically banned all of Harvey's and Nashe's works: "That all Nasshes bookes and Doctor Harvyes bookes be taken wheresoever they maye be found and that none of theire bookes bee ever printed hereafter" (McKerrow, 5:110). Nashe and Harvey are the only authors whose total corpus is banned; the rest of the order lists specific works or genres of literature that are to be scrutinized.

The bishops did not explain the reasons for their unusual order, although their motivation can be surmised from the group of works banned. They wished to cut off the publishing of satire and contentious works, which was expanding at an exponential rate in the late 1590s, and they also took the occasion to discourage a number of other potentially seditious works. Obscenity does not appear to have been a major concern: Marlowe's frank translation of Ovid's *Elegies* was probably included because it was published in the same volume with Davies' *Epigrams* (D. Thomas, 16). Historical works were included because they were long suspected of having seditious implications; this is clear from the nature of the censorship imposed. "That noe Englishe historyes be printed excepte they bee allowed by some of her majesties privie Counsell." The printing of plays was also restricted for similar political reasons.

The order must have been primarily political, like the 1586 act that had given the bishops power over the press; Whitgift and Bancroft were much more likely to be concerned with the preservation of the civic order than with the ethical improprieties in popular literature that disturbed the Puritans (Lecocq, 134–47). Both veterans of the anti-Marprelate campaign, they must have decided that the publication of contentious pamphlets was getting out of hand. Most of the books banned seem not to have contained any dangerous political commentary or topical allegory, but all were models of presumption, encouraging discontent with the existing order while inspiring verbal aggressiveness and self-assertion. The satires in particular reflected a contentiousness in intellectual circles that could well manifest itself as riot among the common people. The intellectual malcontent who acknowledged no master was matched among the lower classes by the literally masterless men who disrupted London life. The satirists themselves might be politically harmless, their bitterness in part a conventional pose, but the bishops feared their readers would turn literary convention into the nightmare of insurrection.

The inclusion of Nashe and Harvey in the order may be somewhat of an afterthought, since the quarrel was relatively quiet by 1599, but their quarrel had helped to spark the growth of satire and their controversial pamphlets were primarily personal invective, with only a pretense of social usefulness. The satires of Hall, Marston, and their imitators claim to be correcting vices, although that claim was contested by those that saw satire as an excuse to release aggression and indulge in the description of sin. Nashe's writings against Harvey, on the other hand, make no claims to virtue except as demonstrations of wit. And while Harvey represents his attacks on Greene and Nashe as literary and social criticism, he frequently loses himself in invective. The spectacle of two university graduates flailing at each other in print could not be allowed in a time of social tensions. Harvey and Nashe would probably not have been singled out by themselves, but they could not escape being included in a general order suppressing satire and contention.

Both men had in their way invited the order banning their works. Like Stubbes, Harvey had urged that the authorities take action to discourage the publishing of contentious pamphlets. Nashe, at the end of *Have with You,* uses Harvey's attack on Perne, a friend of Whitgift, to construct a case that Harvey scorns the Church of England and undermines the office of bishop, like Marprelate but without the wit. The upshot of these charges and countercharges was that the bishops saw fit to ban the works of both. We do not know how much either man was affected by the ban. Harvey, now twice burned in his efforts to publish vernacular works, never published again, although he continued to boast of the value of his unpublished dialogues in a letter to Robert Cecil and in his marginalia (Stern, 124–25). Within a year or two after the order Nashe was dead of causes unknown to us, although it is possible that the order so aggravated his chronic poverty that it contributed to his death. The publication of the uncontroversial *Summer's Last Will and Testament* in 1600 is not evidence that Nashe was free to resume his career. The ban may or may not have actually terminated Nashe's literary career, but symbolically it marks its end. Even before the edict was issued, Nashe shows in *Nashe's Lenten Stuff* that he knew his project of establishing himself as a satiric defender of orthodoxy had failed.

CHAPTER
7

Nashe as Ironist:
Nashe's Lenten Stuff

THE disillusionment of Nashe's later works is transformed into playful irony in *Nashe's Lenten Stuff; or, The Praise of the Red Herring*, a mock encomium that mixes real praise of the piscatorial simplicity of Great Yarmouth with a paradoxical glorification of its main product, salt herring. Nashe was grateful to the citizens of the Norfolk fishing port for providing him with safe harbor in 1597 after the Privy Council's disapproval of the suppressed play *The Isle of Dogs* forced him to flee London. Nashe denied that he had written the portions of the play that were thought to be "seditious and slanderous," but he did not stay in the city to argue his innocence. He was in personal danger even if the objections to the play were a political move against the entrepreneur Francis Langley, who owned the Swan where it was performed, as has been conjectured (Ingram, 167–96). Nashe spent some six weeks in Yarmouth in the autumn of 1597 and wrote his appreciative account of the visit in 1598, publishing it in 1599 shortly before the June 1 order banning all his works.

Nashe's Lenten Stuff is surprisingly exuberant, given the circumstances of its composition, but the hostility that surrounded its publication and Nashe's dejection at the collapse of his career give its playfulness somber implications. The straightforward fisherfolk and their humble staple are used to parody the rhetoric and satirize the value of the London Nashe escaped. In the process the conventions of Elizabethan "golden" literature are collapsed in on themselves. Thus the pessimism implicit in Nashe's satire throughout his career finds its final expression in detached irony. Nashe's later works reflect an increasingly cynical attitude towards ennobling rhetoric and the orthodoxy he began his career defending.

In *The Unfortunate Traveler* Nashe's disenchantment was embodied in the point of view of a self-professed rogue, but in *Nashe's Lenten Stuff* the speaking voice is his own. The work completes the evolution into self expression begun in *Pierce Penniless* and carried forward in *Have with You*, where Harvey's efforts to cut a figure in the world are contrasted with Nashe's less exalted conception of himself. The "Pierce Penniless, Respondent" of *Have with You* accepts his poverty and alienation: both he and his works may be shabby, but he does not claim a spurious gentility like Harvey. This honest self-presentation continues in *Nashe's Lenten Stuff* as he draws back from the sophistication of London and aligns himself with the simple values of Yarmouth. He confesses that he is a fugitive, dependent on the hospitality of friends, and laments that his career has been damaged, but he still has projects afoot and is capable of forgetting his problems in his enthusiasm for Yarmouth and delight in his own style. His wit and ironic vision continue to prevail over adversity.

Nashe's Lenten Stuff is a self-conscious and difficult work. It has been seen as an example of "meaningless" literature, a purely verbal *jeu d'esprit*, but it is, rather, a work hemmed in by its ideological context (Hibbard, 233–49; Steane, 42). It is deliberately chary of meaning and inconsequential in response to the hostile interpretation of Nashe's texts that had nearly destroyed his career. All of his works had aroused suspicion; *The Isle of Dogs* placed him in actual jeopardy. *Nashe's Lenten Stuff* was published with unusual trepidation, including a special condition in the Stationers' Register that the printer "gett yt Laufully Aucthorised" (3:141). Under pressure, Nashe was cautious, but at the same time he plays with the concept of meaning in literature, inviting misinterpretation from his readers. The apparent lack of meaning is a strategy, and the ambiguous ironies are a puzzle, designed to confront readers with the process of interpretation.

YARMOUTH AND THE RED HERRING

Nashe's marginal status and his extension of the range of satire had finally left him outside the pale. Like the banished earl in *The Unfortunate Traveler* he was driven into exile, but he sought refuge in Yarmouth, near Lowestoft, where he was born. His personal unfortunate travels were not to an exotic foreign country, but to the traditional England of his childhood. He does not detail his own adventures, but the flight must have been dangerous: "Avoide or give grounde I did; *scriptum est,* I will not goe from it: and *post varios casus,* variable Knight arrant adventures and outroades and inroades, at greate Yarmouth in Norfolke I arived in the latter ende of Autumne" (3:154). The furor over the *Isle of Dogs* had laid "such a heavie crosse . . . upon me, as had well neare confounded mee," not only because of the loss of his livelihood and "the deepe pit of dispaire wherinto I was falne, beyond my greatest friendes reach to recover mee: but that, in my exile and irkesome discontented abandonment, the silliest millers thombe or contemptible stickle-banck of my enemies is as busie nibbling about my fame as if I were a deade man throwne amongest them to feede upon" (3:153). The reference is to Richard Lichfield's rejoicing over Nashe's misfortune in *The Trimming of Thomas Nashe.* Nashe's despair has not left him indifferent to his reputation.

A Yarmouth friend extolled to Nashe the virtues of the city and the fish that made it prosperous and urged him to write the present work. The words attributed to the friend are a fair sample of the work's bombastic style, both in their far-fetched diction and hyperbole:

> If there be in thee any whit of that unquenchable sacred fire of Appollo (as al men repute) and that Minerva amongest the number of her heires hath addopted thee, or thou wilt commend thy muse to sempiternity, and have images and statutes erected to her after her unstringed silent interment and obsequies, rouze thy spirites out of this drowsie lethargy of mellancholly they are drencht in, and wrest them up to the most outstretched ayry straine of elocution to chaunt and carroll forth the

Alteza and excelsitude of this monarchall fluddy *Induperator*. (3:175)

Nashe is mocking the high style appropriate to heroic encomiums, both in his praise of Yarmouth and in the paradoxical praise of the red herring that follows, but he is not mocking Yarmouth itself nor the real value of humble fish that was the source of its wealth. The mockery is more self-referential, directed at Nashe's pretensions as a poet and the excesses of epideistic rhetoric.

Yarmouth earned its living in a way that appealed to Nashe's unsophisticated sense of economic justice. It caught herring and processed them into kippers, a salted and smoked fish that was durable, nutritious, and plentiful. There was a Lockean simplicity to Yarmouth's prosperity: its fishermen harvested herring with skill and at some risk (Nashe insists), then converted them into a commodity that was valuable, not because of its rarity or luxury, but because it was an inexpensive food. Nashe pointedly contrasts the trips of the Yarmouth fishermen with the more speculative voyages after exotic wealth chronicled in Hakluyt. He also contrasts the sober personal style of the fishermen with the more flamboyant style of sailors in other ports. The utility of the red herring is contrasted with the more luxurious desires of urban civilization, and the practical life of the fishing port with the affected life style of London. The history of Yarmouth is a triumph of human planning against the continual encroachment of the sea. Its government is ideal: "Here I could breake out into a boundlesse race of oratory, in shrill trumpetting and concelebrating the royall magnificence of her governement, that for state and strict civill ordering scant admitteth any rivals: but I feare it would be a theame displeasant to the grave modesty of the discreet present magistrates" (158–59). Its civic order reflects the honesty of its economic underpinnings.

Pointed comparisons are avoided, but clearly Yarmouth is an ideal commonwealth. Its just distribution of wealth contrasts with that of most communities: "All Common wealths assume their prenominations of their common divided weale, as where one man hath not too much riches, and another man too much povertie." In these terms Yarmouth is ideal, "not that it is sibbe or cater-cousins to any mungrel *Democratia*, in which one is all, & all is one, but that in her, as they are not al one, so one or two there pockets not up all the peeces" (168). Yarmouth is also praised for its contribution to the national economy: "It were to be wished that other coasters were so industrious as the Yarmouth, in winning the treasure of fish out of those profundities, and then we should have twentie egges a pennie, and it would be as plentifull a world as when Abbies stoode; and now, if there be any plentifull world, it is in Yarmouth" (171). The touch of self-mockery in the playful diction and ironic reference to the proverbial happier days of the past does not undercut the praise of Yarmouth.

Nashe's sincere admiration for the town is evident in the straightforward conclusion to his account: "Farewell, flourishing Yarmouth, and be every day more flourishing then other untill the latter day; whiles I have my sence or existence, I will persist in loving thee." He has not traveled far, except in books, "yet for ought I have read, heard, or seene, Yarmouth, regall Yarmouth, of all maritimall townes that are no more but fisher townes, soly raigneth sance peere." This idealization of the simple values of the town has as its context Nashe's more usual satire on the complex values of urban life. London's frontiers of sin have not reached Yarmouth: "Not any where is the word severer practised, the preacher reverentlier observed and honoured, justice sounder ministred, and a warlike people peaceablier demeanourd, betwixte this and the Grand Cathay, and the strand of Prester John" (172). Nashe has found an ideal to set against his satiric vision in a fishing port, not in a humanistic tract. His utopia has a geographical location, flesh-and-blood inhabitants, and a prosperity based on the most mundane of foodstuffs.

The praise of the red herring is more ironic than the praise of Yarmouth, cast as it is in the traditional form of a mock encomium or paradox. Such a paradoxical praise of a humble or nonexistent topic was a popular rhetorical form in the Renaissance (Colie; Geraldine; Malloch; H. Miller). A paradox could be a simple extended irony, like *The Praise of Nothing*, published in 1585, but the form could become quite complex in a work like

Erasmus's *Praise of Folly*, which Nashe admired. In true paradoxes the reverberations of the irony confuse the reader's ordinary process of interpreting a text. In Erasmus, the praise of foolishness by the speaker Folly often reverses itself and becomes a form of wisdom. In some cases writers were no doubt ambivalent themselves about the ideas they advanced, but the paradoxical mode was also a protective strategy, a way of entertaining controversial ideas without risking commitment to them. The preface to *The Defense of Contraries* (1593), translated by Anthony Mundaye, cautions that the heterodox arguments presented are mere exercises in rhetoric, not to be construed as the opinions of the author.

In traditional fashion, Nashe begins his praise of the red herring by citing a long list of precedents for such a mock encomium, ranging from Virgil and Ovid to recent English examples such as Sir John Harington's *Metamorphosis of Ajax* (1596), which praises the water closet in good set terms. Some of the works listed are simple exercises and parodies, but others, like Harington's, include true praise for their apparently ludicrous topic. Nashe's account of the importance of herring in the national economy shows that his encomium falls into this category: it is comic to praise salt fish in heroic terms, but respect for the fishing port and its product is evident. The basic value of red herring as a product of human industry turns the irony of the prose back on itself and on those topics that are the usual recipients of inflated praise. The section on Yarmouth establishes that Nashe is not operating from some epicurean perspective that scorns kippers as a food beneath contempt. The pamphlet is more than a rhetorical showpiece that praises an unworthy topic; it is a complex ironic text that questions Elizabethan heroic values by contrasting them with the true value of a staple food. The red herring is a touchstone to expose the false values usually enfolded in the high style parodied with such gusto.

The extravagant rhetoric and comic neologisms suggest that the golden world delivered by the poet is merely a verbal construct, not a property of the topic being elevated. For example, the red herring surpasses Helen of Troy: "The Poets were triviall, that set up Helens face for such a top-gallant Summer

May-pole for men to gaze at, and strouted it out so in their buskind braves of her beautie, whereof the only Circes Heypasse and Repasse was that it drewe a thousand ships to Troy, to fetch her backe with a pestilence. Wise men in Greece in the meane while to swagger so aboute a whore" (184). The heroic legend of Troy is a verbal fraud. "As loude a ringing miracle as the attractive melting eye of that strumpet can we supply them with of our dappert Piemont Huldrick Herring, which draweth more barkes to Yarmouth bay, then her beautie did to Troy" (185). Nashe expands on this, extolling the fish in fantastic heroic language, but the object of the satire is the language, not the fish.

This parody of exaltation as a mode gives point to the best-known excerpt from *Nashe's Lenten Stuff*, the comic retelling of Hero and Leander. The heroic idealization of love was often presented ironically even by those now thought of as its advocates, such as Sidney or Marlowe himself, whose "Hero and Leander" uneasily mixes a tragic theme with an ironic tone and comic touches. Nashe had satirized heroic love in his depiction of Surrey's passion for Geraldine in *The Unfortunate Traveler*. By making the classical legend a mythological account of the origin of herring, Nashe further lampoons human passion by subordinating it to a mundane food. Puns, colloquial speech rhythms, and details from common life reduce the story to the quotidian, a commonplace example of bad luck rather than a heroic tragedy with larger-than-life proportions. The parody is not simplistic, however, since it does not deny the emotions of the original story—passion, love, and grief are given some due—although the heroic amplifications characteristic of love tragedy are turned topsy-turvy (Davis, 213).

The tale is set in its literal context—not a romanticized classical past but the stalls of profit-minded booksellers: "Twoo faithfull lovers they were, as everie apprentise in Paules churchyard will tell you for your love, and sel you for your mony: the one dwelt at Abidos in Asia, which was Leander; the other, which was Hero, his Mistris or Delia, at Sestos in Europe, and she was a pretty pinckany and Venus priest; and but an arme of the sea divided them: it divided them and it divided them not, for over that arme of the sea could be made a long arme" (195). The exaggerated informality of the syntax undercuts any sense that the lovers are heroic. The awesome theme of fortune's hostility, at the heart of many a Renaissance tragedy, is here reduced to a comic proverb: "Fate is a spaniel that you cannot beate from you; the more you thinke to crosse it, the more you blesse it and further it" (196). This striking metaphor suggests a truth: fate is often trivial rather than the working out of some grand design of the gods or an imaginative author. When the gods do appear "all on a rowe, bread and crow, from Ops to Pomona," they are comic rather than divine, suitable deities to hit upon the device of metamorphosing Hero and Leander into ling and Cadwallader herring.

At his best, as in this twice-told tale of Hero and Leander, Nashe achieves a studied logorrhea that overwhelms the reader with a deluge of words. The mixture of high and low styles and the puns, neologisms, and outlandish metaphors combine into a rich texture that challenges comprehension and defies rhetorical analysis. When a storm separates Leander from Hero, his passion leads him to brave the sea:

> Rayne, snowe, haile, or blowe it howe it could, into the pitchie Helespont he leapt, when the moone and all her torch-bearers were afraid to peepe out their heads; but he was peppered for it; hee hadde as good have tooke meate, drinke, and leisure, for the churlish frampold waves gave him his belly full of fishbroth, ere out of their laundry or washe-house they woulde graunt him his coquet or *transire,* and not onely that, but they sealde him his *quietus est* for curvetting any more to the mayden tower, and tossed his dead carcasse, well bathed or parboyled, to the sandy threshold of his leman or orenge, for a disjune or morning breakfast. (197)

The wonder is that such fantastical embellishments of sentences do not completely destroy the narrative, but the story is retold after a fashion. The details and shorter syntactical units fly off in all directions, but the overall sense remains clear. Unusual words are usually clear from the context, or they are explained ("disjune or morning breakfast"). The style is so "singular" that it demands as much attention as the story it another reader suspicious of Nashe's intentions: "*Nashes Lentenstuffe*: and why *Nashes Lentenstuffe*? some scabbed scald squire replies, because I had money lent me at Yarmouth, and I pay them againe in prayse of their towne and the redde herring: and if it were so, goodman Pig-wiggen, were not that honest dealing?" (151). The defiance of hostile readers culminates in an avowal of his admiration for the controversial Aretino and a defense of his flamboyant style: "Know it is my true vaine to be *tragicus Orator*, and of all stiles I most affect & strive to imitate Aretines, not caring for this demure soft *mediocre genus*, that is like water and wine mixt togither; but give me pure wine of it self, & that begets good bloud, and heates the brain thorowly: I had as lieve have no sunne, as have it shine faintly, no fire as a smothering fire of small coales, no cloathes, rather then weare linsey wolsey" (152). Harvey had referred scornfully to Nashe as a "brave Columbus of terms" (*Pierce's Supererogation*, sig. B3r); Nashe's unconstrained style in this work mocks the characterization. But the bombastic language of *Nashe's Lenten Stuff* is a parody of the high style, an ironic smokescreen that is not at all forthright in the manner of Aretino.

Throughout his career, Nashe was conscious of his readers, whom he pictures as an assembled audience listening to him or to his persona. He thought of his readership as a group made up of subgroups with special interests, not as a mass or as a single reader, although he does sometimes imagine himself as entering into a dialogue with a member of his audience, such as the "scabbed, scald squire" refuted above. His medium is the printed page, but he still conceives of his task in terms of oratory (Ong, "The Writer's Audience"). For example, Jack Wilton's readers are imagined to be an audience sympathetically interested in his exploits; he asks them to let him pause while he drinks. Nashe's readers ask him questions and raise objections like the readers of Martin Marprelate. This device is made central in *Have with You to Saffron Walden*, where a group of sympathetic listeners is described and made to speak at length in Nashe's support. Nashe's rhetorical training made him as conscious of the probable responses of his audience as he was of his own authorial presence. Of course, his practice of addressing his audience was artificial in a printed text, just as was his vaunted extemporaneous style.

In *Nashe's Lenten Stuff*, the audience is for a time pictured as a group of tourists being shown the sights of Yarmouth, somewhat against their wills, since the title page led them to expect a mock encomium:

> There be of you, it may be, that will account me a paltrer, for hanging out the signe of the redde Herring in my title page, and no such feast towards for ought you can see. Soft and faire, my maisters, you must walke and talke before dinner an houre or two, the better to whet your appetites to taste of such a dainty dish as the redde Herring; and that you may not thinke the time tedious, I care not if I beare you company, and leade you a sound walke round about Yarmouth, and shew you the length and bredth of it. (159)

This attractive device of presenting himself as an informal guide includes Nashe's sense that his readers are restive: "The length and bredth of Yarmouth I promised to shew you; have with you, have with you: but first looke wistly upon the walles, which, if you marke, make a stretcht out quadrangle with the haven" (166). Later he imagines some of his readers as becoming antagonistic when they are confronted with tales that might contain topical allusions. Throughout, there is a dynamic interaction between Nashe and his audience, less static and more two-directional than the usual mode of printed tracts.

Nashe is always aware that he is penning manuscripts that will be turned into printed texts. This awareness is incorporated into his works by references to the actual process of composition and by witty manipulation of typographical conventions. In *Terrors of the Night*, for example, he complains that his melancholic topic is making his ink congeal, while in *Christ's Tears* he asks his pen to pluck up good courage. He often pauses to comment on his improvisational style or on the circumstances of writing. In *Nashe's Lenten Stuff*, he says at one point, "I had a crotchet in my head, here to have given the raines to my pen" (3:167). In the same work, he offers an aside in a parentheses when a phrase makes a sentence too long,

". . . at length (o, that length of the full pointe spoiles me, all gentle readers, I beseech you pardon mee)" (174). Since Nashe for a time earned part of his living working for the printer John Danter, he is also conscious of his works as printed texts. In *The Unfortunate Traveler* he somehow contrived that a printed page should begin, "In a leafe or two before was I lockt up: here in this page . . ." (2:314). His contributions to the Harvey-Nashe controversy are especially self-conscious about printing conventions. In *Nashe's Lenten Stuff* he ends the Epistle to the Reader by excusing himself: "Apply it for me, for I am cald away to correct the faults of the presse, that escaped in my absence from the Printing-house" (3:152).

Nashe's Lenten Stuff is thus self-conscious about being a printed text based on a manuscript written extemporaneously by Thomas Nashe for an audience whose desire to be amused is mixed with suspicion and hostility. His wary and ironically arrogant stance contrasts sharply with the humble self-effacement characteristic of Elizabethan authorship. The unconstrained style scorns the expectations of decorum, but it is even more provocative in its subversion of its audience's expectations about meaning in literature. According to Elizabethan critical theory, meaning was conveyed in literature either through direct statement, mimetic examples of desirable and reprehensible behavior, or allegory. The Elizabethans also prized literature in more formal terms as a source of rhetoric and style, so that we find Nashe and others emphasizing how writers purify the English language. All of these expectations about the value of literature are deliberately mocked in *Nashe's Lenten Stuff*. The style is so idiosyncratic that it becomes almost solipsistic: Nashe invents words and strings together sentences with a cavalier disregard for the communicative functions of language. This outrageously puffed-up style is used to glorify prosaic salt fish in a parody of Renaissance literature of praise. At the same time the Elizabethan taste for allegory, particularly its propensity for topical allusions, is tempted with enigmatic passages.

Nashe is uncomfortable with his readers because some of them have caused his present difficulties by complaining to various authorities about topical allusions in his works. He protests that self-conceited misinterpreters, as he calls them, are always posed to misconstrue his off-hand comments. Perhaps remembering Robert Beale's complaint about the treatment of the Danish in *Pierce Penniless*, he imagines or alludes to some young lawyer seeking to establish his reputation at Nashe's expense:

> For if but carelesly betwixt sleeping and waking I write I knowe not what against plebeian Publicans and sinners (no better than the sworne brothers of candlesticke turners and tinkers) and leave some termes in suspence that my post-haste want of argent will not give mee elbowe roome enough to explane or examine as I would, out steps me an infant squib of the Innes of Court, that hath not halfe greased his dining cappe, or scarce warmed his Lawyers cushion, and he, to approve hymselfe an extravagant statesman, catcheth hold of a rush, and absolutely concludeth, it is meant of the Emperour of Ruscia, and that it will utterly marre the traffike into that country if all the Pamphlets bee not called in and suppressed, wherein that libelling word is mentioned. (3:213)

Similarly, any reference to an animal will raise the charge that he is referring to some nobleman's heraldic device, as happened with the tale of the Bear and the Fox in *Pierce Penniless*.

In addressing the question of topical allusions, Nashe faces directly an issue that had bedeviled his career and often elicited disclaimers from him. The topic itself is potentially controversial, since he is criticizing the motivation of informers and the gullibility of those who listen to their contrived charges. The issue is further complicated by the high probability that his indignant innocency is a pose: both in his general comments and in veiled allusions he had ventured into controversial areas. Even if he was misinterpreted, it was often because he had invited it. The digression on topical allusions is introduced by an account of human gullibility: "That greedy seagull ignorance is apt to devoure any thing" (212). He warns that he is not to be trusted: "Let them looke to themselves as they will, for I am theirs to gull them better than ever I have done; and this I am sure, I have destributed gudgeon dole amongst them, as Gods plenty as any stripling of my slender portion of witte, farre or neere" (213). In short, Nashe boasts that it is his practice to bait his readers, often with obscure allusions and vague allegories that invite misinterpretation.

Nashe's confrontation with his critics is an ironic mixture of courage and caution:

> I will deale more boldly, & yet it shall be securelie and in the way of honestie, to a number of Gods fooles, that for their wealth might be deep wise men, and so foorth, (as now a daies in the opinion of the best lawyers of England there is no wisedome without wealth, alleadge what you can to the contrarie of all the beggarly sages of greece,) these, I say, out of some discourses of mine, which were a mingle mangle cum purre, and I knew not what to make of my selfe, have fisht out such a deepe politique state meaning as if I had al the secrets of court or commonwealth at my fingers endes. (213–14)

He complains that "the great potentate," believing such charges and not looking himself at the text, "showres downe the whole tempest of his indignation upon me." The matter is referred to lawyers who twist his text to make a case for his guilt. Nashe's account is detailed enough to suggest that he is alluding to some specific event or series of events in which his works were called into legal question. If he had a specific great potentate in mind, perhaps Burghley or Whitgift, then he is rather audaciously criticizing that person's care in the exercise of his office. But his deepest scorn is reserved for the lawyers who were more concerned to win their case than arrive at a just verdict.

The attack on lawyers is imprudent for a man under threat of indictment. He uses the phrase "learned counsel" sarcastically: "God forgive me if I slander them with that title of learned, for generally they are not" (214). Rather, he complains, lawyers "being compounded of nothing but vociferation and clamour, rage & fly out they care not howe against a mans life, his person, his parentage, twoo houres before they come to the poynt, little remembring their owne privy scapes." Quoting out of context, they "disjoynt and teare every sillable betwixt their teeth severally; and if by no meanes they can make it odious, they wil be sure to bring it in disgrace by ilfavoured mouthing and missounding it" (214–15). Realizing he has gone too far, he immediately qualifies his criticism—"I speake of the worser sort, not of the best, whom I holde in high admiration"—but this qualification notwithstanding, Nashe's tactic is to defy rather than to submit himself to criticisms of his works.

Nashe concludes by deliberately baiting "these lawyers and selfe-conceited misinterpreters" with a beast fable about the red herring that invites topical application: "Have with them for a riddle or two, onely to set their wittes a nibbling." Although the tale, Nashe says, contains neither rhyme nor reason, "they, according to their accustomed gentle favors, whether I wil or no, shall supply it with either, and runne over al the peeres of the land in peevish moralizing and anatomizing it" (216). The tale itself is a preposterous account of a "cropshin," or inferior herring, bristling with possible topical allusions. Presumably Nashe intended nothing specific, or if he did, he prides himself on having concealed it beyond the powers of his critics: "O, for a Legion of mice-eyed decipherers and calculaters uppon characters, now to augurate what I meane by this: the divell, if it stood upon his salvation, cannot do it" (218). Nashe's defiance has not stopped a modern critic from arguing that *Nashe's Lenten Stuff* contains topical allusions to Henry Brooke, Lord Cobham (Scoufos). The case is hardly conclusive, but it is a tantalizing possibility that Nashe's challenge to misinterpreters masks an attack on a powerful Elizabethan courtier. Although the use of the term "red herring" to mean a diversionary tactic dates from the nineteenth century, Nashe knew the practice that is the source of the expression: "to draw on hounds to a sent, to a redde herring skinne there is nothing comparable" (221).

The digression on misinterpreters concludes with further playful interaction with the readers as Nashe extends his self-conscious questioning of what constitutes his text. He confesses that he has wandered from his ostensible topic, the praise of the red herring: "Stay, let me looke about, where am I? in my text, or out of it? not out, for a groate: out, for an angell: nay, I'le lay no wagers, for nowe I perponder more sadlie uppon it, I thinke I am out indeede" (219). But *Nashe's Lenten Stuff* is not really a text about red herring so much as it is about Nashe's attitudes towards the good commonwealth of Yarmouth and the artificial urban society he has fled. In these terms the open defiance of the digression on misinterpreters is part of his text, not a departure. This is clearer if we remember that literature is at the center of culture for Nashe, since it shapes and embodies a society's values. *Nashe's Lenten Stuff* rejects both the utilitarian and aristocratic conceptions of literature by treating a "useless" topic in a parody of the high style. Nashe's deliberate meaninglessness serves as a denial of Elizabethan norms: the work lacks a serious topic, a formal structure, and a perspicuous style. The digression taunts the reader's suspicion that the work must at least contain topical allusions and makes light of Nashe's apparent loss of direction.

This toying with the reader is purposeful in that it mocks purposeful composition. In his digression Nashe promised two fantastical legends of the red herring; now he reneges: "Will you have the other riddle of the cropshin to make uppe the payre that I promised you? you shall, you shall (not have it, I meane) but beare with mee, for I cannot spare it, and I perswade my selfe you wil be well contented to spare it, except it were better then the former; and yet I pray you what fault can you finde with the former? hath it any more sence in it then it should have?" (219–20). The abrupt syntactical changes of direction in this sentence epitomize his disregard for ordinary intentional structures. He waxes proud that he can write a meaningless tale so well: "I will speake a proude word (though it may bee counted arrogancy in me to prayse mine owne stuffe)"; the tale is "more absurde then *Philips his Venus, the white Tragedie, or the greene Knight*" (220). In boasting of the absurdity of his own creation Nashe violates the common assumption that literature should be useful or ennobling, beliefs he had advanced himself. Thus he suggests that his work not only lacks topical meaning, but that it has no meaning at all. Not that this will stop those who seek to discredit him: "My readers peradventure may see more into it then I can; for, in comparison of them, in whatsoever I set forth, I am *Bernardus non vidit omnia*, as blinde as blinde Bayard, and have the eyes of a beetle: nothing from them is obscure, they being quicker sighted then the sunne" (220). Nashe entertains the idea that meaning is in the eye of the beholder rather than in the intentions of an author or the text itself.

Nashe hopes that his praise of Yarmouth will save his work as a whole from the charge of being as insignificant as the tale of the cropshin. The fishermen among his readers should defend him because he is "the first that ever sette quill to paper in prayse of any fish or fisherman" (224). He anticipates that they will hear him "mangled and torne in mennes mouthes about this playing with a shettlecocke, or tossing empty bladders in the ayre." Nashe commiserates with his muse about the reception of his work in London: "Alas, poore hungerstarved Muse, wee shall have some spawne of a goose-quill or over worne pander quirking and girding, was it so hard driven that it had nothing to feede upon but a redde herring? another drudge of the pudding house (all whose lawfull meanes to live by throughout the whole yeare will scarce purchase him a redde herring) sayes I might as well have writte of a dogges turde (in his teeth surreverence)." He defies such critics: "But let none of these scumme of the suburbs be too vineger tarte with mee" (225).

In his conclusion Nashe again attributes heroic status to his mundane subject, mocking the high style of the literature of praise: "The puissant red herring, the golden Hesperides red herring, the Meonian red herring, the red herring of red Herrings Hal, every pregnant peculiar of whose resplendent laude and honour to delineate and adumbrate to the ample life were a woorke that would drinke drie fourescore and eighteene Castalian fountaines of eloquence, consume another Athens of facunditie, and abate the haughtiest poeticall fury twixt this and the burning Zone and the tropike of Cancer" (225–26). One is reminded of Hamlet's "Nay, an thou'lt mouth, I'll rant as well as thou." Like Shakespeare's character or his own Jack

Wilton, Nashe finds refuge in words and the comfortable distancing of irony. The humanistic aspirations of a decade earlier terminate in a work that pretends to no noble or useful purpose at all. Irony turns inward on the text itself, canceling the ordinary processes of communication.

In *Nashe's Lenten Stuff* irony, instead of being a rhetorical strategy with a clear purpose, is an ambivalent attitude toward accepted verities, particularly those concerning the nature of literature itself. Humanistic irony, like that of Erasmus or More, has an elegant consistency: there may be some ambiguity, but there is no confusion, and the overall direction is clear. The later neoclassic ironists also controlled their ironic effects to serve their satiric or pathetic purposes. But Elizabethan irony, like Elizabethan satire, is often rough-hewn and confusing. Skepticism undermines the idealism in Nashe, and bitterness makes the wit seem flippant and iconoclastic. Nashe cannot attain the equanimity of an Erasmus. In this last work, as in *The Unfortunate Traveler* and *Have with You to Saffron Walden*, there is no classical sense of an achieved form that reflects an ordered universe; rather, an erratic art barely copes with chaos.

Nashe's increasing estrangement from his own society finds expression in this confused and willfully confusing final utterance. It is the logical conclusion both to his interest in the transforming powers of rhetoric and his growing skepticism about the humanistic conception of literature and the values it promoted. By 1599, when *Nashe's Lenten Stuff* was published and his career was suspended by order of the bishops, the idealized cultural synthesis of the Elizabethan "golden age" was coming apart and the literature that celebrated it was losing its conviction. Without being as cynical as Marston or as critical as Jonson, Nashe in his more playful fashion contributed to the disenchantment that characterized the next reign. He anticipates the bitterness of the Jacobeans, but through irony distances himself from the personal and political implications of his skepticism. Through irony he could advance Elizabethan ideals while implicitly criticizing them and entertain unorthodox ideas without committing himself. The ironic complexity of his later works cannot be resolved into a sustained critical understanding of the malfunctions of society, but the contradictions and ambiguities that complicate the reading of Nashe reflect the devolution of Elizabethan idealism more effectively than its outright rejection by later writers.

Works Cited

Agrippa, Henry Cornelius. *Of the Vanitie and Uncertaintie of Artes and Sciences*. Ed. Catherine M. Dunn. Northridge, Calif.: California State University, 1974.

Allen, Don Cameron. "*The Anatomie of Absurditie*: A Study in Literary Apprenticeship." *Studies in Philology* 32 (1935): 170–76.

———. *The Star-Crossed Renaissance: The Quarrel about Astrology and Its Influence in England*. Durham: Duke University Press, 1941.

Allen, J. W. *A History of Political Thought in the Sixteenth Century*. London: Methuen, 1928; reprinted with revised notes, 1957.

Almasy, R. "The Purpose of Richard Hooker's Polemic." *Journal of the History of Ideas* 39 (1978): 251–70.

Amis, George T. "The Meter and Meaning of Nashe's 'Adieu, Farewell Earth's Blisse.' " *English Literary Renaissance* 9 (1979): 78–85.

Anglo, Sydney. "Reginald Scot's *Discoverie of Witchcraft*: Scepticism and Sadduceeism." In *The Damned Art: Essays in the Literature of Witchcraft*, ed. Sydney Anglo. London: Routledge & Kegan Paul, 1977.

Anselment, Raymond A. *"Betwixt Jest and Earnest": Marprelate, Milton, Marvell, Swift, and the Decorum of Religious Ridicule*. Toronto: University of Toronto Press, 1979.

Arnold, Aerol. "Thomas Nashe's Criticism of the State of Learning in England." A private edition of part of a dissertation submitted at the University of Chicago. Chicago: University of Chicago Libraries, 1937.

Ascham, Roger. *The Schoolmaster (1570)*. Ed. Lawrence V. Ryan. Folger Documents of Tudor and Stuart Civilization. Ithaca: Cornell University Press, 1967.

Works Cited

Bacon, Francis. *The Works.* Ed. James Spedding et al. Vol. 8, *The Letters and the Life.* London: Longman, Green, Longman, and Roberts, 1861.

Baldwin, Frances Elizabeth. *Sumptuary Legislation and Personal Regulation in England.* Johns Hopkins University Studies on History and Political Science, series 44, no. 1. Baltimore: Johns Hopkins Press, 1926.

Barber, C. L. *Shakespeare's Festive Comedy: A Study of Dramatic Form and Its Relation to Social Custom.* Princeton: Princeton University Press, 1959.

Beier, A. L. "Social Problems in Elizabethan London." *Journal of Interdisciplinary History* 9 (1978): 203–21.

Bennett, H. S. *English Books and Readers, 1558–1603.* Cambridge: Cambridge University Press, 1965.

Bercovitch, Sacvan. *The Puritan Origins of the American Self.* New Haven: Yale University Press, 1975.

Best, Michael R. "Nashe, Lyly, and *Summer's Last Will and Testament.*" *Philological Quarterly* 48 (1969): 1–11.

Blench, J. W. *Preaching in England in the Late Fifteenth and Sixteenth Centuries.* New York: Barnes & Noble, 1964.

Bowers, Fredson T. "Nashe and the Picaresque Novel." In *Humanistic Studies in Honor of John Calvin Metcalf.* Charlottesville: University of Virginia Studies, 1941.

Boyce, Benjamin. *The Theophrastan Character in England to 1642.* Cambridge: Harvard University Press, 1947.

Bradbrook, M. C. *The Rise of the Common Player: A Study of Actor and Society in Shakespeare's England.* Cambridge: Harvard University Press, 1962.

Brissenden, Alan. "Shakespeare and the Morris." *Review of English Studies,* n.s. 30 (1979): 1–11.

Brown, Lewis. "*The Unfortunate Traveller* by Thomas Nashe (XVI Century)." *Journal of Jewish Lore and Philosophy* 1 (1919): 241–53.

Browne, Thomas. *Religio Medici and Other Works.* Ed. L. C. Martin. Oxford: Clarendon Press, 1964.

Buckley, George. *Atheism in the English Renaissance.* Chicago: University of Chicago Press, 1932.

Bullein, William. *A Dialogue against the Fever Pestilence.* From the edition of 1578 collated with the earlier editions of 1564 and 1573. Ed. Mark W. Bullen and A. H. Bullen. London: Early English Text Society, 1888.

Carlson, Leland H. *Martin Marprelate, Gentlemen: Master Job Throkmorton Laid Open in His Colors.* San Marino: Huntington Library, 1981.

Caspari, Fritz. *Humanism and the Social Order in Tudor England*. Chicago: University of Chicago Press, 1954.
Chambers, E. K. *The Elizabethan Stage*. 4 vols. Oxford: Clarendon Press, 1923.
Chettle, Henrie. *Kind-Hartes Dreame—1592*. And William Kemp. *Nine Daies Wonder—1600*. Bodley Head Quarto. Ed. G. B. Harrison. New York: E. P. Dutton, 1923.
Chew, Samuel C. *The Pilgrimage of Life*. New Haven: Yale University Press, 1962.
Colie, Rosalie L. *Paradoxia Epidemica: The Renaissance Tradition of Paradox*. Princeton: Princeton University Press, 1966.
Collinson, Patrick. *The Elizabethan Puritan Movement*. Berkeley and Los Angeles: University of California Press, 1967.
Coolidge, John S. "Martin Marprelate, Marvell, and *Decorum Personae* as a Satirical Theme." *PMLA* 74 (1959): 526–32.
Cooper, Thomas. *An Admonition to the People of England*. . . . London, 1589.
Crewe, Jonathan V. *Unredeemed Rhetoric: Thomas Nashe and the Scandal of Authorship*. Baltimore: Johns Hopkins University Press, 1982.
Croll, Morris W. "The Sources of the Euphuistic Rhetoric." In his *Style, Rhetoric, and Rhythm*, ed. J. Max Patrick et al. Princeton: Princeton University Press, 1966.
Croston, A. K. "The Use of Imagery in *The Unfortunate Traveller*." *Review of English Studies* 24 (1948): 90–101.
Cupper, William. *Certaine Sermons concerning Gods Late Visitation in the Citie of London*. London, 1592.
Curtis, Mark H. "The Alienated Intellectuals of Early Stuart England." *Past and Present* 23 (1962): 25–41.
———. *Oxford and Cambridge in Transition, 1558–1642*. Oxford: Clarendon Press, 1959.
Davies, Horton. *Worship and Theology in England: From Cranmer to Hooker, 1534–1603*. Princeton: Princeton University Press, 1970.
Davis, Walter R. *Idea and Act in Elizabethan Fiction*. Princeton: Princeton University Press, 1969.
Dawley, Powel Mills. *John Whitgift and the English Reformation*. New York: Scribner's, 1954.
Duncan-Jones, Katherine. "Nashe and Sidney: The Tournament in *The Unfortunate Traveller*." *Modern Language Review* 63 (1968): 3–6.
Ebel, Julia G. "Translation and Cultural Nationalism in the Reign of Elizabeth." *Journal of the History of Ideas* 30 (1969): 593–602.
Ehrenpreis, Irvin. "Personae." In *Restoration and Eighteenth-Century Literature: Essays in Honor of Alan Dugald McKillop*, ed. Carroll Cam-

den. Chicago: University of Chicago Press, for William Marsh Rice University, 1963.

Einstein, Lewis. *The Italian Renaissance in England.* New York: Columbia University Press, 1902.

Eisenstein, Elizabeth L. *The Printing Press as an Agent of Change: Communication and Cultural Transformation in Early-Modern Europe.* 2 vols. Cambridge: Cambridge University Press, 1979.

Elliott, Robert C. *The Power of Satire: Magic, Ritual, Art.* Princeton: Princeton University Press, 1960.

Esler, Anthony. *The Aspiring Mind of the Elizabethan Younger Generation.* Durham: Duke University Press, 1966.

Ferguson, Margaret. "Nashe's *The Unfortunate Traveller*: The 'Newes of the Maker' Game." *English Literary Renaissance* 11 (1981), 165–82.

Fink, Zera S. "Jaques and the Malcontented Traveler." *Philological Quarterly* 14 (1935): 237–52.

Foster, Frank Freeman. *The Politics of Stability: A Portrait of the Rulers of Elizabethan London.* London: Royal Historical Society, 1977.

Fraser, Russell. *The War against Poetry.* Princeton: Princeton University Press, 1970.

Freeman, Arthur. *Thomas Kyd: Facts and Problems.* Oxford: Clarendon Press, 1967.

Friedenreich, Kenneth. "Nashe's *Strange News* and the Case for Professional Writers." *Studies in Philology* 71 (1974): 451–72.

Friederich, Reinhard H. "Verbal Tensions in Thomas Nashe's *The Unfortunate Traveller.*" *Language and Style* 8 (1975): 211–19.

G.B.A.T. *A Discovery of the Great Subtiltie and Wonderful Wisedom of the Italians.* London, 1591.

Geraldine, Sister M. "Erasmus and the Tradition of Paradox." *Studies in Philology* 61 (1964): 41–63.

Gerrard, Ernest A. *Elizabethan Drama and Dramatists, 1583–1603.* Oxford: Oxford University Press, 1928.

Gibbons, Sister Marina. "Polemic, the Rhetorical Tradition, and *The Unfortunate Traveller.*" *Journal of English and Germanic Philology* 63 (1964): 408–21.

Gill, R. B. "A Purchase of Glory: The Persona of Late Elizabethan Satire." *Studies in Philology* 72 (1975): 408–18.

Giovio, Paolo. *The Worthy Tract of Paulus Iovius.* Trans. Samuel Daniel. Intro. Norman K. Farmer, Jr. Delmar, N.Y.: Scolar's Facsimiles & Reprints, 1976.

Gohlke, Madelon S. "Wit's Wantonness: *The Unfortunate Traveller* as

Picaresque." *Studies in Philology* 73 (1976): 397–413.

Greene, Thomas. "The Flexibility of Self in Renaissance Literature." In *The Disciplines of Criticism*, ed. Peter Demetz, Thomas Greene, and Lowry Nelson. New Haven: Yale University Press, 1968.

Hahn, Juergen. *The Origins of the Baroque Concept of Peregrinatio.* Chapel Hill: University of North Carolina Press, 1973.

Harbage, Alfred. "*Love's Labour's Lost* and the Early Shakespeare." *Philological Quarterly* 41 (1962): 18–36.

Harlow, C. G. "Nashe, Robert Cotton the Antiquary, and *The Terrors of the Night*." *Review of English Studies*, n.s. 12 (1961): 7–23.

———. "A Source for Nashe's *Terrors of the Night* and the Authorship of *1 Henry IV.*" *Studies in English Literature* 5 (1965): 31–47, 269–81.

Harvey, Gabriel. *Foure Letters, and certaine Sonnets: Especially touching Robert Greene, and other parties, by him abused. . . .* London: John Wolfe, 1592.

———. *Letter-Book . . . A.D. 1573–1580.* Ed. Edward John Long Scott. Camden Society, n.s. 33. London: Camden Society, 1884.

———. *Marginalia.* Ed. G. C. Moore Smith. Stratford-upon-Avon: Shakespeare Head, 1913.

———. *A New Letter of Notable Contents.* London, 1593. Facsimile rpt. Menston: Scolar Press, 1970.

———. *Pierces Supererogation; or, A New Prayse of the Old Asse.* London, 1593. Facsimile rpt. Menston: Scolar Press, 1970.

———. Unpublished Marginalia. Folger ms. H. a 2 (a double volume). Lodovico Domenichi. *La Facietie Motti et Burle de Diversi Signori et Persone Private* [1571]. Guicciardini. *Detti, et Fatti Piacevole et Grave.* Vinegia, 1581.

Harvey, Richard. *A Theologicall Discourse of the Lamb of God and His Enemies.* London, 1590.

Helgerson, Richard. *The Elizabethan Prodigals.* Berkeley and Los Angeles: University of California, 1977.

Hibbard, G. R. *Thomas Nashe: A Critical Introduction.* Cambridge: Harvard University Press, 1962.

Hill, Christopher. *Society and Puritanism in Pre-Revolutionary England.* 2d ed. New York: Schocken, 1967.

Holdsworth, W. S. *A History of English Law.* Vols. 1 and 5. Boston: Little, Brown, 1922, 1924.

Hooper, Wilfrid. "The Tudor Sumptuary Laws." *English Historical Review* 30 (1915): 433–49.

Hoppe, Harry Reno. *The Bad Quarto of Romeo and Juliet.* Ithaca: Cornell University Press, 1949.

———. "John Wolfe, Printer and Publisher, 1579–1601." *The Library*, 4th ser. 14 (1933): 241–88.

Howard, Clare. *English Travellers of the Renaissance*. London: John Lane, The Bodley Head, 1914.

Howard, Henry, Earl of Northampton. *A Defensative against the Poyson of Supposed Prophesies*. London, 1583.

Hunter, G. K. "Elizabethans and Foreigners." *Shakespeare Survey* 17 (1964): 37–52.

———. "English Folly and Italian Vice: The Moral Landscape of John Marston." In *Jacobean Theatre*, ed. John Russell Brown and Bernard Harris, 85–110. Stratford-upon-Avon Studies 1. New York: St. Martins, 1960.

———. *John Lyly: The Humanist as Courtier*. Cambridge: Harvard University Press, 1962.

Hurstfield, Joel. *Freedom, Corruption, and Government in Elizabethan England*. London: Jonathan Cape, 1973.

Ingram, William. *A London Life in the Brazen Age: Francis Langley, 1548–1602*. Cambridge: Harvard University Press, 1978.

James, Mervyn. *English Politics and the Concept of Honour, 1585–1642*. Past and Present Supplement 3. Oxford: Past and Present Society, 1978.

Jewkes, W. T. "The Literature of Travel and the Mode of Romance in the Renaissance." *Bulletin of the New York Public Library* 67 (1963): 219–36.

Johnson, Francis R. "The First Edition of Gabriel Harvey's *Four Letters*." *The Library*, 4th ser. 15 (1935): 212–23.

———. "Gabriel Harvey's *Three Letters*: A First Issue of His *Foure Letters*." *The Library*, 5th ser. 1 (1946): 134–36.

Jones, Ann Rosalind. "Inside the Outsider: Nashe's *Unfortunate Traveller* and Bakhtin's Polyphonic Novel." *English Literary History* 50 (1983): 61–81.

Jones, Dorothy. "An Example of Anti-Petrarchan Satire in Nashe's *Unfortunate Traveller*." *Yearbook of English Studies* 1 (1971): 48–54.

Jones, Richard Foster. *The Triumph of the English Language: A Survey of Opinions concerning the Vernacular from the Introduction of Printing to the Restoration*. Stanford: Stanford University Press, 1953.

Jusserand, J. J. *The English Novel in the Time of Shakespeare*. Trans. Elizabeth Lee. New edition, 1890; rpt. London: Ernest Benn, 1966.

Kaula, David. "The Low Style in Nashe's *The Unfortunate Traveller*." *Studies in English Literature* 6 (1966): 43–57.

Kearney, Hugh. *Scholars and Gentlemen: Universities and Society in Pre-*

Industrial Britain, 1500–1700. Ithaca: Cornell University Press, 1970.
Kennedy, William John. *Rhetorical Norms in Renaissance Literature*. New Haven: Yale University Press, 1978.
Kernan, Alvin. *The Cankered Muse: Satire of the English Renaissance*. New Haven: Yale University Press, 1959.
Knappen, M. M., *Tudor Puritanism: A Chapter in the History of Idealism*. 1939; rpt. Chicago: University of Chicago Press, 1965.
Knights, L. C. "Elizabethan Prose." In *Drama and Society in the Age of Jonson*, 301–14. 1937; rpt. New York: Norton, 1968.
Kocher, Paul H. *Christopher Marlowe: A Study of His Thought, Learning, and Character*. 1946; rpt. New York: Russell & Russell, 1962.
Koppenfels, Werner Von. "Two Notes on *Imprese* in Elizabethan Literature: Sidney's *Arcadia* and the Tournament Scene in *The Unfortunate Traveller*." *Renaissance Quarterly* 24 (1971): 13–25.
Lanham, Richard A. *The Motives of Eloquence: Literary Rhetoric in the Renaissance*. New Haven: Yale University Press, 1976.
———. "Tom Nashe and Jack Wilton: Personality as Structure in *The Unfortunate Traveller*." *Studies in Short Fiction* 4 (1967): 201–16.
La Primaudaye, Peter de. *The Second Part of the French Academie*. Trans. Thomas Bowes. London, 1594.
Larson, Charles. "The Comedy of Violence in Nashe's *The Unfortunate Traveller*." *Cahiers E* 8 (1975): 15–29.
Latham, Agnes M. C. "Satire on Literary Themes and Modes in Nashe's 'Unfortunate Traveller'" *English Studies*, n.s. 1 (1948): 85–100.
Lecocq, Louis. *La Satire en Angleterre de 1588 à 1603*. Paris: Didier, 1969.
Leggatt, Alexander. "Artistic Coherence in *The Unfortunate Traveller*." *Studies in English Literature* 14 (1974): 31–46.
Lichfield, Richard. *The Trimming of Thomas Nashe, 1597*. Fac. rpt. Menston: Scolar Press, 1973.
Little, David. *Religion, Order, and Law: A Study in Pre-Revolutionary England*. Oxford: Basil Blackwell, 1970.
Lodge, Thomas. *Wits Miserie and the Worlds Madnesse: Discovering the Devils Incarnat of this Age*. London, 1596.
Loiseau, Jean. "Deux Attitudes Elisabéthaines devant le Voyage: Lyly (Euphues) et Nashe (Jack Wilton)." In *Le Voyage dans la Littérature Anglo-Saxonne*, 13–19. Paris: Société des Anglicistes de l'Enseignement Supérieur, 1972.
Lyly, John. *The Complete Works*. 3 vols. Ed. John Warwick Bond. Oxford: Clarendon Press, 1902.

Lyons, Bridget Gellert. *Voices of Melancholy: Studies in Literary Treatments of Melancholy in Renaissance England*. 1971; rpt. New York: Norton, 1975.
McGinn, Donald J. "The Allegory of the Beare and the Foxe in *Pierce Penniless*." *PMLA* 61 (1946): 431–53.
———. "Nashe's Share in the Marprelate Controversy." *PMLA* 59 (1944): 952–84.
Mack, Maynard. "The Muse of Satire." *Yale Review* 41 (1951): 80–92.
Mackerness, E. D. "*Christ's Teares* and the Literature of Warning." *English Studies* 33 (1952): 251–54.
McKerrow, Ronald B., ed. *The Works of Thomas Nashe*. 5 vols. 1904–10; rpt. with correction and a separately paged "Supplement," ed. F. P. Wilson. Oxford: Basil Blackwell, 1958.
McPherson, David C. "Aretino and the Harvey-Nashe Quarrel." *PMLA* 84 (1969): 1551–58.
Malloch, A. E. "The Techniques and Function of the Renaissance Paradox." *Studies in Philology* 53 (1956): 191–203.
Manley, Lawrence. *Convention, 1500–1750*. Cambridge: Harvard University Press, 1980.
Marprelate, Martin [pseud.]. *The Marprelate Tracts, 1588, 1589*. Ed. William Pierce. London: James Clarke, 1911.
Marphoreus [pseud.] *Martin's Month's Mind*. London, 1589.
Millard, Barbara C. "Thomas Nashe and the Functional Grotesque in Elizabethan Prose Fiction." *Studies in Short Fiction* 15 (1978): 39–48.
Miller, David L. "Authorship, Anonymity, and *The Shepheardes Calendar*." *Modern Language Quarterly* 40 (1979): 219–36.
Miller, Edwin Haviland. *The Professional Writer in Elizabethan England*. Cambridge: Harvard University Press, 1959.
———. "The Relationship of Robert Greene and Nashe, 1588–92." *Philological Quarterly* 33 (1954): 353–67.
Miller, Henry Knight. "The Paradoxical Encomium with Special Reference to Its Vogue in England, 1600–1800." *Modern Philology* 53 (1956): 145–78.
Miller, Stuart. *The Picaresque Novel*. Cleveland: Case Western Reserve University Press, 1967.
Morris, Christopher. *Political Thought in England: Tyndale to Hooker*. London: Oxford University Press, 1953.
Mullett, Charles F. *The Bubonic Plague and England: An Essay on the History of Preventive Medicine*. Lexington: University of Kentucky Press, 1956.
Mundaye, Anthony, trans. *The Defense of Contraries*. London, 1593.

Nashe, Thomas. *The Works*. Ed. Ronald B. McKerrow. 5 vols. 1904–10; reprinted with corrections and a separately paged "Supplement", ed. F. P. Wilson. Oxford: Basil Blackwell, 1958.

Neale, J. E. *Elizabeth I and Her Parliaments, 1559–1581*. 1958; rpt. New York: Norton, 1966.

———. *Elizabeth I and Her Parliaments, 1584–1601*. 1958; rpt. New York: Norton, 1966.

Nicholl, Charles. *A Cup of News: The Life of Thomas Nashe*. London: Routledge & Kegan Paul, 1984.

Ong, Walter J., S. J. *Rhetoric, Romance, and Technology: Studies in the Interaction of Expression and Culture*. Ithaca: Cornell University Press, 1971.

———. "The Writer's Audience Is Always a Fiction." In *Interfaces of the Word: Studies in the Evolution of Consciousness and Culture*, 53–81. Ithaca: Cornell University Press, 1977.

Paule, George. *The Life of the Most Reverend and Religious Prelate John Whitgift*. London, 1612.

Pearson, Terry P. "The Composition and Development of Philip Stubbes's *Anatomy of Abuses*." *Modern Language Review* 56 (1961): 321–32.

Perkins, David. "Issues and Motivations in the Nashe-Harvey Quarrel." *Philological Quarterly* 39 (1960): 224–33.

Peter, John. *Complaint and Satire in Early English Literature*. Oxford: Clarendon Press, 1956.

Petti, Anthony G. "Beasts and Politics in Elizabethan Literature." *Essays and Studies*, n.s. 16 (1963): 68–90.

———. "Political Satire in *Pierce Penniless His Svpplication to the Divill*." *Neophilologus* 45 (1961): 139–50.

Pierce, William. *An Historical Introduction to the Marprelate Tracts: A Chapter in the Evolution of Religious and Civil Liberty in England*. London: Archibald Constable, 1908.

Pratt, S. M. "Antwerp and the Elizabethan Mind." *Modern Language Quarterly* 24 (1963): 53–60.

Pruvost, Rene. *Robert Greene et Ses Romans (1558–1592): Contribution à l'Histoire de la Renaissance en Angleterre*. Paris: Société d'Edition "Les Belles Lettres," 1938.

Quintilian. *Institutio Oratoria*. Trans. H. E. Butler. Loeb Classical Library. Cambridge: Harvard University Press, 1922.

Rankins, William. *The English Ape, The Italian Imitation, The Footesteppes of Fraunce*. London, 1588.

Read, Conyers. *Lord Burghley and Queen Elizabeth*. New York: Knopf, 1960.

Rhodes, Neil. *Elizabethan Grotesque.* London: Routledge & Kegan Paul, 1980.
Rich, Barnaby. *Allarme to England.* London, 1578.
Richmond, Hugh. "Personal Identity and Literary Personae." *PMLA* 90 (1975): 209–21.
Rosenberg, Eleanor. *Leicester: Patron of Letters.* New York: Columbia University Press, 1955.
Sanders, Chauncey. *Robert Greene and the Harveys.* Bloomington: Indiana University Studies, 1931.
Sasek, Lawrence A. *The Literary Temper of the English Puritans.* Louisiana State University Studies, Humanity Series IX. Baton Rouge: Louisiana State University Press, 1961.
Scoufos, Alice Lyle. "Nashe, Jonson, and the Oldcastle Problem." *Modern Philology* 65 (1968): 307–24.
Sidney, Sir Philip. *An Apology for Poetry; or, The Defense of Poesy.* Ed. Geoffrey Shepherd. London: Nelson, 1965.
Siebert, Frederick Seaton. *Freedom of the Press in England, 1476–1776: The Rise and Decline of Government Controls.* Urbana: University of Illinois Press, 1952.
Sisson, C. J. *Lost Plays of Shakespeare's Age.* Cambridge: Cambridge University Press, 1936.
Smith, Edward O., Jr. *Crown and Commonwealth: A Study in the Official Elizabethan Doctrine of the Prince.* Transactions of the American Philosophical Society, n.s. 66, no. 8. Philadelphia: American Philosophical Society, 1976.
Sprott, S. E. "Ralegh's 'Sceptic' and the Elizabethan Translation of Sextus Empiricus." *Philological Quarterly* 42 (1963): 166–75.
Staton, Walter F., Jr. "The Characters of Style in Elizabethan Prose." *Journal of English and Germanic Philology* 57 (1958): 197–207.
Steane, J. B., ed. *The Unfortunate Traveller and Other Works.* By Thomas Nashe. Harmondsworth: Penguin, 1972.
Stephanson, Raymond. "The Epistemological Challenge of Nashe's *The Unfortunate Traveller.*" *Studies in English Literature* 23 (1983): 21–36.
Stern, Virginia F. *Gabriel Harvey: His Life, Marginalia, and Library.* Oxford: Clarendon Press, 1979.
Stockwood, John. *A Very Fruitfull and Necessarye Sermon of the Most Lamentable Destruction of Jerusalem.* . . . London, 1584.
Strathmann, Ernest A. "Robert Parsons' Essay on Atheism." In *Joseph Quincy Adams Memorial Studies,* ed. James G. McManaway et al., 665–81. Washington: Folger Shakespeare Library, 1948.

———. *Sir Walter Ralegh: A Study in Elizabethan Skepticism*. New York: Columbia University Press, 1951.
Strong, Roy. *The Cult of Elizabeth: Elizabethan Portraiture and Pageantry*. London: Thames and Hudson, 1977.
Strype, John. *The Life and Acts of John Whitgift*. 3 vols. Oxford: Clarendon Press, 1822.
Stubbes, Phillip. *The Anatomie of Abuses*. Rpt. of 1583 Edition. In *The English Stage: Attack and Defense, 1577–1730*. Ed. Arthur Freeman. New York: Garland, 1973.
———. *The Theater of the Popes Monarchie*. London, 1585.
Summersgill, T. L. "The Influence of the Marprelate Controversy upon the Style of Thomas Nashe." *Studies in Philology* 48 (1951): 145–60.
Talbert, Ernest William. *The Problem of Order: Elizabethan Political Commonplaces and an Example of Shakespeare's Art*. Chapel Hill: University of North Carolina Press, 1962.
Tenney, Edward Andrews. *Thomas Lodge*. Cornell Studies in English, 26. Ithaca: Cornell University Press, 1935.
Thomas, Donald. *A Long Time Burning: The History of Literary Censorship in England*. New York: Frederick A. Praeger, 1969.
Thomas, Keith. *Religion and the Decline of Magic*. New York: Scribners, 1971.
Thomas, P. W. "Two Cultures? Court and Country under Charles I." In *The Origins of the Civil War*. Ed. Conrad Russell. Problems in Focus Series. London: Macmillan, 1973.
The Three Parnassus Plays (1598–1601). Ed. J. B. Leishman. London: Nicholson & Watson, 1949.
Tuve, Rosemond. *Allegorical Imagery: Some Medieval Books and Their Posterity*. Princeton: Princeton University Press, 1966.
Vos, Alvin. " 'Good Matter and Good Utterance': The Character of English Ciceronianism." *Studies in English Literature* 19 (1979): 3–18.
Walker, Alice. "The Reading of an Elizabethan: Some Sources of the Prose Pamphlets of Thomas Lodge." *Review of English Studies* 8 (1932): 264–81.
Walker, D. P. "Ways of Dealing with Atheists: A Background to Pamela's Refutation of Cecropia." *Bibliothèque d'Humanisme et Renaissance* 17 (1955): 252–77.
Wallace, Dewey D., Jr. "George Giffard, Puritan Propaganda, and Popular Religion in Elizabethan England." *Sixteenth-Century Journal* 9 (1978): 27–50.

Works Cited

Wallace, Malcolm William. *The Life of Sir Philip Sidney.* Cambridge: Cambridge University Press, 1915.

Walzer, Michael. *The Revolution of the Saints: A Study in the Origins of Radical Politics.* 1965; rpt. New York: Atheneum, 1974.

Watson, Curtis Brown. *Shakespeare and the Renaissance Concept of Honour.* Princeton: Princeton University Press, 1960.

Weimann, Robert. "*Jest-book* und Ich-Erzahlung in *The Unfortunate Traveller*: Zum Problem des *point of view* in der Renaissance-Prosa." *Zeitschrift fur Anglistik und Amerkanistik* 18 (1970): 11–29.

———. *Shakespeare and the Popular Tradition in the Theater: Studies in the Social Dimension of Dramatic Form and Function.* Ed. Robert Schwartz. Baltimore: Johns Hopkins University Press, 1978.

West, Robert Hunter. *The Invisible World: A Study of Pneumatology in Elizabethan Drama.* Athens: University of Georgia Press, 1939.

White, Helen C. *Social Criticism in Popular Religious Literature of the Sixteenth Century.* New York: Macmillan, 1944.

Whitgift, John. *Works.* Ed. John Ayre. Parker Society. 3 vols. Cambridge: Cambridge University Press, 1851–53.

Wilson, F. P. *Elizabethan and Jacobean.* Oxford: Clarendon Press, 1945.

———. *The Plague in Shakespeare's London.* Oxford: Clarendon Press, 1927.

Wilson, Harold S. "The Humanism of Gabriel Harvey." In *Joseph Quincy Adams Memorial Studies,* ed. James G. McManaway et al., 707–21. Washington, Folger Shakespeare Library, 1948.

Wright, Leonard. *The Hunting of Antichrist with a Caveat to the Contentious.* London, 1589.

Wright, Louis B. *Middle-Class Culture in Elizabethan England.* 1935; rpt. Ithaca: Cornell University Press, 1958.

Yates, Frances A. "Elizabethan Chivalry: The Romance of the Accession Day Tilts." In *Astraea: The Imperial Theme in the Sixteenth Century,* 88–111. 1975; rpt. Harmondsworth: Penguin, 1977.

Index

Agrippa, Cornelius, 87–88, 92, 132–33
Alençon, Francis, duke of, 64
Amyntas (Fernando Stanley?), 8, 81–82, 97
Anabaptists, 159–60
Anti-Martinists, 41–48, 191
Anti-Semitism, 150
Archilochus, 80
Aretino, Pietro: Gabriel Harvey on, 81, 104, 182, 187, 196, 199–200; Nashe's admiration for, 74–75, 133–34, 145–46, 233
Ascham, Roger, 15, 22, 29, 30, 150–51
Atheism, 39, 107–9, 114, 199–200. *See also* Skepticism
Audience (readership), 9–10, 20–21, 233–34
Authorship, 65, 235
Aylmer, John, bishop of London, 47

Babington, Anthony, 89, 186–87
Bacon, Francis, 46–47
Bancroft, Richard, bishop of London, 34, 41, 50; order banning Nashe's works, 218–20
Barber, C. L., 49
Beale, Robert, 76–77, 236
Ben Gorion, Joseph (Youssipon), 109
Bird, Christopher, 181, 183, 190
Bodin, Jean, 207–8
Book of Common Prayer, 53, 54
Bowes, Thomas, 73, 78
Bridges, John, 37–38
Brooke, Henry, Lord Cobham, 238
Browne, Sir Thomas, 85
Bullein, William, 189
Burghley, William Cecil, Lord, 28–29, 77, 151, 237

Calvin, John, 155, 163
Cambridge, 28, 141, 160. *See also* St. John's College
Carey, Elizabeth, 100
Carey, George, 91, 97, 99–100, 153, 189
Cartwright, Thomas, 28, 45–46, 77–78
Catholicism, 25–26
Cecil, Robert, 220

Index

Cecil, William. *See* Burghley, William Cecil
Censorship, 11, 26, 218–20
Cheke, John, 15, 29, 30
Chettle, Henry, 72, 192, 206
Christmas, 56–58
Cicero, 132–33, 209
Ciceronianism, 18, 29, 90, 132
Cooper, Thomas, bishop of Winchester, 38–39, 41
Cotton, Robert, 98
Cotton, Thomas, 97–98
Court, the, 74–75
Covell, William, 214
Crewe, Jonathan V., 2, 17–18, 111, 122–23
Cupper, William, 103–4, 107
Curry-knave, Cutbert (pseud.). *See* Nashe, *An Almond for a Parrot*

Daniel, Samuel, 130
Danter, John, 6, 62, 235
Davies, Horton, 111
Davies, John, of Hereford, 214
Davis, Walter R., 132
Deloney, Thomas, 142
Denmark, 73, 76–77, 236
Dering, Edward, 103
Devils, 82–89, 95, 97
Donne, John, 123
Drama, Nashe on, 19, 51, 72–73
Drayton, Michael, 127
Dreams, 96–97, 101

Education, 16, 56
Elderton, 173, 183–84
Elizabeth I, queen of England, 26–27, 28–29, 42, 58–60, 64, 208
Erasmus, Desiderius, 133, 134, 226, 241

Essex, Robert Devereux, earl of, 172
Ethos, 17–18, 119–20, 189, 194–95, 222
Euphuism, 12–13. *See also* Lyly, John, *Euphues*

Fortune, 155–57
Foxe, John, 142–43

Gascoigne, George, 102, 179–80
Gerrard, Ernest A., 141
Giovio, Paolo, 130
Gohlke, Madelon S., 144
Golden Age aesthetic, 9, 123–26, 170, 221–22, 241–42
Golding, Arthur, 108
Gosson, Stephen, 12, 103
Greene, Robert, 14, 22, 67–68, 145; Gabriel Harvey criticizes, 68, 183–88, 201; Nashe defends, 188, 192–93; *The Black Book's Messenger,* 138; *Greene's Groats-worth of Wit,* 67–68, 76, 192; *Menaphon,* 18–19; *A Quip for an Upstart Courtier,* 170, 172–73, 176, 187–88
Greene, Thomas, 146
Grindal, Edmund, archbishop of Canterbury, 28
Grotesque, the, 3, 123

Hakluyt, Richard, 151, 153, 224
Hall, John, 123, 214
Harbage, Alfred, 215
Harington, John, 214, 226
Harvey, Gabriel: and Cambridge, 179–80, 202–3, 205; controversy with Nashe, 104–5, 106, 145–46, 169–220, 230–31, 233; criticism of

Greene, 68, 171–73, 183–88; criticism of Lyly, 44–45, 65, 198; criticism of Nashe's *Pierce Penniless,* 66, 68–69, 78, 80–81, 82–83, 131; satirized as Vanderhulke, 160; *Four Letters,* 172, 175–76, 177, 181–88, 213; *Letter-Book,* 179–80; *Marginalia,* 182, 211–12; *A New Letter,* 196–97; *Pierce's Supererogation,* 171, 196–203; 211–13; *Three Letters* (1580), 172, 181, 206
Harvey, John, Jr., 172, 173, 185
Harvey, John, Sr., 172, 173, 210
Harvey, Richard, 79–80, 83–84, 171–73, 206; *The Lamb of God,* 22–23, 170, 171–72
Hibbard, G. R., 12, 93
High Commission, 29, 35
Honor, code of, 157–59, 178, 212–13
Hooker, Richard, 29, 50, 54
Howard, Henry, earl of Northampton, 83–84, 92, 96, 98
Humanism: Cambridge, 15, 20, 29–30, 174; court, 10, 30, 173–74
Hunter, G. K., 168

Iceland, 95–96
Imprese, 130–31
Irony, 70, 241–42
Italy, 144, 151, 161, 166–68

James I, king of England, 85
Jerusalem, 102, 109–10, 111–12
Jest books, 137–40
Jones, Ann Rosalind, 123

King, Humfrey, 232

Kyd, Thomas, 19

Langley, Francis, 221
Lanham, Richard, 169
Latham, Agnes M. C., 140
Lawyers, 237–38
Lazarillo de Tormes, 122
Leicester, Robert Dudley, earl of, 78–79, 172, 210
Libel, 78–79, 188–89
Lichfield, Richard, 215–17, 223
Literature: social role of, 15, 26–27, 72, 235; of warning, 102–3
Lodge, Thomas, 75, 78, 86, 87
London, 111–19, 224–25
Lopez, Roderigo, 150
Lucian and Lucianism, 134, 184–85, 196
Lyly, John, 65, 145, 171–73, 198; *Euphues,* 12–13, 144–45, 229; *Pap with an Hatchet,* 43–45, 47, 171

McKerrow, R. B., 12, 14, 60, 83, 93n, 186, 199, 216
Malcontents, 33, 39, 88, 217
Marlowe, Christopher, 19, 31, 192, 196–97, 218; *Dido—Queen of Carthage,* 6; *Hero and Leander,* 227–29
Marphoreus (pseud.), 42–43
Marprelate, Martin (pseud.), 34–48, 141, 145, 188, 198; *Hay Any Worke for Cooper,* 39–40
Marprelate controversy, 18, 34–48, 75
Marston, John, 123, 214
Masterless men, 10–11, 33
Melbanke, Brian, 12
Menippean satire, 134

Index

Meres, Francis, 214
Middleton, Thomas, 214
Miller, Stuart, 147
Mirror for Magistrates, A, 155
Misrule, Lord of, 36, 44
Montaigne, Michel de, 101–2
Moore Smith, G. C., 174
More, Thomas, 133, 134, 241
Mornay, Philippe de, 108
Morvyn, Peter, 109
Mundaye, Anthony, 226

Nashe, Thomas: life, 5–7
  Almond for a Parrot, An (attributed work), 34, 45–46, 56, 213
  Anatomy of Absurdity, The, 12–17, 56, 57, 213
  "Choice of Valentines, A," 5–6, 97, 199
  Christ's Tears over Jerusalem, 52, 91–92, 102–20, 154–55, 157, 196–97, 234
  Have with You to Saffron Walden, 160, 177, 203–13, 215–16, 233
  Isle of Dogs, The (lost work), 6, 221, 222, 230, 231
  "Letter to William Cotton," 146, 204
  Nashe's Lenten Stuff, 215, 221–42
  Pierce Penniless, 62–89, 107, 187, 191, 199–200, 216, 236
  "Preface to *Astrophil and Stella,*" 23
  "Preface to *Menaphon,*" 18–24, 171
  Strange News, 83, 90, 189–96
  Summer's Last Will and Testament, 48–61, 220
  Terrors of the Night, The, 85, 91, 92–102, 111, 234
  Unfortunate Traveler, The, 121–68, 176, 222, 235
Nicholl, Charles, 1

Obedience, doctrine of, 30–33, 41–42
Ovid, 218, 226
Oxford, Edward de Vere, earl of, 172

Paradox, 225–26
Parsons, Robert, 108–9
Pasquil (pseud.), 42
Paul, Saint, 31
Paule, George, 50, 58
Peele, George, 19
Penry, John, 35, 45, 59
Perkins, William, 56
Perne, Andrew, 202–3, 219
Persona: Harvey's use of, 64; Marprelate as a, 35–36, 40; Nashe's use of, 63–70, 119–20, 198–99
Picaresque novel, 122
Pictorius, Georgius, 82, 84, 86
Pilgrimage of life as a theme, 153–55
Plague, the, 52–54, 119, 126, 211
Praise of Nothing, The, 225
Presbyterian movement, 28
Pride, 13, 111–15, 157, 201
Printing: criticism of, 13–16, 103–4, 175–76, 201; Nashe and, 190, 234–35; power of, 33–34, 188–89, 206
Privy council, 28–29, 221
Prodigality as a theme, 55, 62–63, 71–72, 86–87, 144
Puritanism, 13–15, 26–34, 51–52, 55–61, 71–72, 113–14, 134, 159–60

Index

Pyrrhonism, 88. *See also* Skepticism

Quintilian, 21–22

Ramus, Petrus, 16, 29–30, 54, 172, 173–74
Rhetoric, 17–24, 141–42, 207
Rhodes, Neil, 3
Rich, Barnaby, 87–88

St. John's College, Cambridge, 5, 12, 20, 27–28, 29, 231
Satire, 65–66, 102–4, 219; topical, 11, 49, 70–82, 116–18, 235–38
Scot, Reginald, 83–84, 85–86, 92, 98
Sextus Empiricus, 88
Shakespeare, William, 55, 158, 192; *As You Like It,* 70; *Hamlet,* 19, 240–41; *Henry IV,* 141–42; *Love's Labor's Lost,* 215; *Lucrece,* 141
Sidney, Sir Philip, 64–65, 131–32, 172; mentioned as literary model, 24, 80–81, 123, 170; *Arcadia,* 127, 129, 158, 176, 186; *Astrophil and Stella,* 23–24; *The Defense of Poetry,* 21–22, 124–25, 133
Singularity, 3, 22, 180–81, 182, 201
Skepticism, 87–88, 96–97
Smith, Henry, 72, 108
Smith, Thomas, 176, 203
Spenser, Edmund, 54, 77, 125, 127, 172, 179–80, 181; mentioned as literary model, 24, 80–81, 123, 131, 170
Stanley, Fernando, earl of Derby, 97. *See also* Amyntas

Star Chamber, 79
Steane, J. B., 140
Stockwood, John, 112
Stubbes, Phillip, 45, 145, 219; *The Anatomy of Abuses,* 13–14, 26, 51, 56, 103, 115; *A Motive to Good Works ,* 213–14; *Theatre of God's Judgement,* 36n
Summers, Will, 36, 67. *See also* Nashe, *Summer's Last Will and Testament*
Surrey, Henry Howard, earl of, 129. *See also* Nashe, *The Unfortunate Traveler*

Tarlton, Richard, 36, 66–67, 141, 187, 191
Theophrastan characters, 86–87
Thorius, John, 202
Three Parnassus Plays, The, 56, 62, 214–15
Throkmorton, Job, 35, 37
Topcliffe, Richard, 6
Travel, as a theme, 148–53

University wits, 68
Usury, 113–14

Virgil, 226

Waldegrave, Robert, 35
Whitgift, John, archbishop of Canterbury, 25, 28–29, 48, 49–52, 58, 59, 172, 191, 237; as Nashe's patron, 29, 50–51, 60–61, 76, 91, 189, 194; order banning Nashe's works, 218–20; sermon on obedience, 31–33
Wilson, F. P., 9
Wit, 70, 147–48

Wolfe, John, 171, 172–73, 176, 196, 206, 211
Wright, Leonard, 41–42

Yarmouth, Great, 221, 223–25, 230
Young, John, 179
Youssipon, (Joseph Ben Gorion), 109

Northern Michigan University

3 1854 003 740 308

EZNO
PR2326 N3 H55 1986
The singularity of Thomas Nashe

Rossof, Dovid
Land of our heritage

Land of our Heritage

Land of our Heritage

Dovid Rossoff

Targum Press / Feldheim

First Published 1987
ISBN 0-944070-00-0

Copyright © 1987 by Dovid Rossoff and Targum Press

All rights reserved

No part of this publication may be translated, reproduced, stored in a retrieval system or transmitted, in any form or by any means, electronic, mechanical, photocopying, recording or otherwise, without the prior permission in writing from the copyright holders.

Edited by E. Schneider

Graphics by D. Hirsch

Photo credits:
The Jewish National Library, Jerusalem—
pp. 45, 69, 79, 82, 133;
Dave Dombey, Southfield, Michigan—pp. 110, 112;
The Jerusalem Map House—pp. 179, 183.

Phototypeset at Targum Press

Published by:
Targum Press Inc.
22700 W. Eleven Mile Rd.
Southfield, Mich. 48034

Distributed by:
Philipp Feldheim Inc.
200 Airport Executive Park
Spring Valley, N.Y. 10977

Distributed in Israel by:
Nof Books Ltd.
POB 23646
Jerusalem 91235

Printed in Israel

Contents

	Haskamoth	vii
	Preface	ix
	Introduction	xi

Part 1. A Terrestrial Abode

1	Pilgrimage to the Holy Land	19
2	The Measure of Holiness	25
3	The Corresponding Powers	31
	Creation of Utopia	32
4	A Treasure-Chest of Names	43

Part 2. The Treasured Island

1	An Island in the Image of Man	53
2	The Patriarchal Borders: *G'vuloth HaAvoth*	59
3	The First Influx: *Olei Mitzrayim*	65
	A Land of Precedence and Miracles	71
	Jericho: Key to the Future	83
4	The Conquest of Suria: *Kibush Yochid*	89
	Oversight or Overview	94
5	The Second Influx: *Olei Bavel*	97
	The Principle of Sanctification	104
	Laws of Tithes	111
	Era of the Diaspora	116
6	The Messianic *Eretz Yisrael*	123

Part 3. Beneath the Holy Altar

1	Altar of Atonement	131
	The Process of Resurrection	141

2	Between Man and G-d	143
	Lips of the Righteous	148

Part 4. *Yishuv Ha'Aretz:* Commandment to Settle in Israel

1	Longing for the Land	155
2	The Commandment of *Yishuv HaAretz*	161
	A Four-sided Coin	163
3	Prerequisites for Immigration	169
	Why Torah Leaders Did Not Come	174
	"Immigration" of the Spirit	178
	Suffering for *Eretz Yisrael*	182
4	Departure Visa	187

Notes	197
Glossary	217
Bibliography	219

THE TORAH CENTRE

P.O. BOX 3131
JOHANNESBURG 2000
REP. OF SOUTH AFRICA.
TELEPHONE
(011) 648-5374

RAV & DIRECTOR
RABBI MOISHE STERNBUCH

Rabbi Rossoff has shown me his book about *Eretz Yisrael*, where he explains the holiness of the Land, and the duties it imposes on all those who live there.

I have not read through all the book, but the parts I did read show the author can be admired for his determination to explain the holiness of the Land, and to impress upon those living there the duties it involves.

Today many are trying to sway those living in the Holy Land away from Torah life, and it is important to explain the holiness of the Land, and as this book impresses this point and explains that love of *Aretz* is interwoven with observing *mitzvos*, I feel sure it will be serving a great purpose.

I end blessing the author that his book will bring a *kiddush HaShem*, and the Almighty should help him to continue explaining *Daas-Torah*, and we will all be *zocheh* soon to complete redemption.

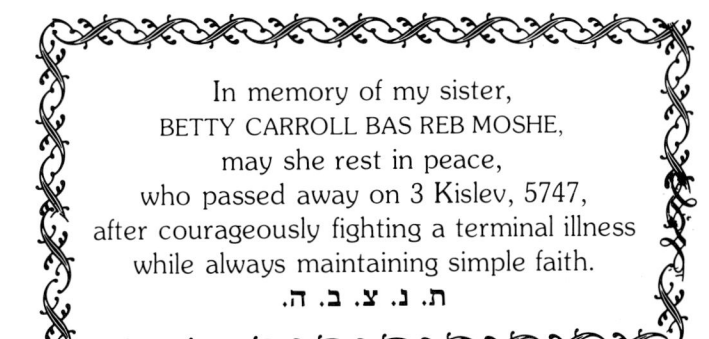

In memory of my sister,
BETTY CARROLL BAS REB MOSHE,
may she rest in peace,
who passed away on 3 Kislev, 5747,
after courageously fighting a terminal illness
while always maintaining simple faith.
ת. נ. צ. ב. ה.

Preface

There is an ancient custom that the title of a book should hint at the author's name. In Hebrew each letter has a numerical value and quite easily the *gematria*, as it is called, of the title can equal the numerical value of the author's name. In English this method does not work out. Therefore, in keeping with tradition, I have subtitled this book *Pardess Chayim, The Orchard of Life*, which is the *gematria* of *Dovid ben Moshe*.

A number of *rebbeim* were extremely helpful in various aspects of this book. Special mention is extended to Rabbi Moshe Sternbuch and Rabbi Y.M. Zacharish, *shelita*, for giving their time to read through various parts of the manuscript and answering an array of questions. Editorial suggestions by Rav Uri Kaploun, Rav Shlomo Fox and Rabbi Noach Orlowek, *shelita*, gave the manuscript direction and format; and the editor, Eidit Schneider, applied her talents and skills to develop and clarify the readability of every passage. Special thanks are expressed to Reb Kalman Samuels for supervising a number of the technical stages. Recognition is made to my father-in-law, Mr. Sherman Shapiro, for his patient encouragement.

Most of all I'm indebted to my wife, Devorah, whose constant support and self-sacrifice allowed me the time to complete this volume. It is our prayer that we will be worthy in *HaShem Yisborach*'s eyes to continue our work in *Eretz Yisrael*, and that our children will grow to constantly feel that they are in the courtyard of the King of Kings.

The sections on *halacha* are not definitive. They are presented to stimulate the reader's awareness of the subject and encourage him to delve into the *halacha* more thoroughly. Likewise the maps are presented as an aid to help the reader understand the intricacies of the various historical boundaries and are not authoritative. In fact, the more one investigates the x / *Preface*

sources to clarify the 'true' cartographic representation of any of these historical maps, the more one becomes aware of their speculative nature.

May this book be an aid and resource for every traveler in the Holy Land. Any comments and suggestions by the reader are welcome (P.O. Box 5437, Jerusalem).

Introduction

The Land of Israel captivates both visitors and residents alike. Embedded in her historical sites is the spark of a potential flame that could ignite the heart of every Jew. Its power is in part its nostalgia, and yet it goes much deeper than that. The Western Wall is more than an engineering wonder whereby an ancient civilization managed to stack two-ton stones into an eighty-foot high wall. It is the place on earth where G-d's Presence is most revealed. Massada is not just the last stronghold of the Jewish peoples' rebellion against the Roman Empire. It is the heroic emblem of their devotion to their ideals even unto martyrdom. Safed is not just a picturesque art colony situated along cobblestone lanes mingled with sixteenth century synagogues. It is a place to renew spiritual energies by praying at the gravesites of the greatest Torah leaders in history. Jerusalem is not just an eclectic potpourri of churches, mosques, synagogues, Jewish shops and Arab markets. It is the center of the universe!

The purpose of this book is to rediscover Eretz Yisrael, excavating the sparks that lie hidden in the holy sites and monuments which chronicle the odyssey of our people. The intention is to resurrect history, bringing new life to old tales. The words and deeds of righteous men and women throughout the generations form a link through time which connects our lives with theirs. Their stories, prayers, and acts of self-sacrifice are indelibly imprinted upon the collective soul of Israel. We today are the custodians of that legacy.

Those sparks, now hidden and dormant, may yet be kindled into flames which, if enough are touched, could ignite into a consuming fire that might even draw *Mashiach* into our midst.

Tradition teaches that Eretz Yisrael is a microcosm of all creation, and so reflects the "image" or totality of G-d in a way that other lands do not. Thus love of G-d must include love of Eretz Yisrael, which is His reflection below in the world of inanimate matter. Today we lack the spiritual sensitivity to understand the significance of all this—to verify it experientially in our lives. One eighteenth century commentator writes: "When the Torah describes the Holy Land with such synonyms as 'good and spacious,' it is not referring to the square miles of land mass included within its boundaries. One who questions the validity of the Torah's claims, because he sees with his physical senses that Israel is small and not 'spacious,' is making a grave error. Rather he must accept that such statements apply to a level that is not immediately perceptible to him. He must trust that dwelling in Eretz Yisrael is good for him in the same way that laying *tefillin* or sitting in a *succah* provides positive benefit, although why and how and even what these effects may be is not clear.

"How can one begin to develop his love and appreciation for Eretz Yisrael? The Talmud addresses this question. Rabbi Yehoshua ben Levi said that G-d spoke the following words to the children of Israel: 'You caused Me to destroy My house and to send My children into exile. For this I am very dismayed at you. But, if you will show that you long for the Land by asking how it is doing and praying for its peace, then I will forgive you.' While the Jewish people remain in exile, this advice still applies. It means that we must stay informed about the current events of Eretz Yisrael, inquiring after the well-being of the people there, praying for peace and the ingathering of Jews, yearning to touch her dust and stones...."

Rabbi Yoel Shwartz explains why Jews today feel such apathy towards Eretz Yisrael and offers some solutions. First, the pervasive and invasive materialism of the modern world has dulled people's spiritual sensitivities, twisted their values, and lured them away from the religious life. The material comforts and glamour of *chutz l'aretz* (any land other than Israel) have become more attractive than the spiritual and more intangible benefits of living in Israel. This distortion of values creates a lack of appreciation for the Land, and people are no longer motivated to make the material sacrifices required to live there.

Another deterrent is people's over-reaction to the Zionist claim that Israel is a *secular* homeland. The orthodox Jew's attachment to Israel is religious — based on Torah, rather than nationalistic — based on race, culture and history. Therefore a number of observant Jews are anti-Zionist. Consequently, in their zeal to reject secular nationalism, they reject the Land of Israel as well, and end up endorsing a policy of non-settlement and even refuse to acknowledge its precious holiness.

A third cause for this apathy applies particularly to those who are already residents of Israel. They begin to take the privilege of living in Eretz Yisrael for granted, and her holy sites and monuments no longer excite them. Slowly, as time passes, they are dulled into apathy. To a certain extent this is human nature. The Sages anticipate this problem and aptly point out that it is our responsibility to maintain a fresh and vital appreciation of the preciousness of living in Eretz Yisrael. They bring a verse from Scripture to support this advice. "When the L–rd shall bring you into the land of Canaan, as He swore to you and to your forefathers, and shall give it to you..." (Exodus 13:11). The Sages explain that when the Torah says, "And shall give it to you" — it is telling us that we should not relate to the Land of Israel as though it were a paternal inheritance — rather it should be in your eyes as if *today* He gave it to you. One way of fulfilling this advice of the Sages is to imagine the ecstasy and exhilaration that Joshua and the Jewish people must have felt when they crossed the Jordan River and first set foot on the Holy Land! To hold this image fresh in one's mind is a certain antidote to apathy.

The first step toward engendering a love and appreciation for Israel is to reaffirm one's primary commitment to spirituality and relegate material comfort to a secondary status. Next, one should read what the Sages say about Eretz Yisrael, and study the laws and commandments which apply to one who is living in the Land. Third, one should meditate on the prayers, blessings, and psalms which express a deep yearning for the Jewish people to return to Zion and Jerusalem. In this way he will come to recite them with sincerity and deep emotion and his heart will open in love and attachment to the Land. Finally, Rabbi Shwartz recommends that one travel around the country. Seeing is believing! The views, the air, the holy sites cannot help but touch one's soul and arouse a deep love of the Land. One should remember that even commonplace acts such as business transactions, bureaucratic encounters, and agricultural field work are all part of the commandment of *yishuv ha'aretz*, settling the Holy

Land. In this way even mundane acts become sanctified and take on the status of *mitzvoth*.

On the precautionary side, one must be careful not to say anything disparaging about the land, the climate or the people, even if it is true. The Land is holy. It is a microcosm of G-d's entire universe, and He gave it to the Jewish people as an inheritance. To express ingratitude, by complaining or speaking negatively, is a serious offence. However, one may offer constructive criticism when his sole intention is to bring about positive changes.

Chofetz Chaim also offers a word of caution. One's love of Eretz Yisrael should not overbalance one's basic commitment to religious obligations, especially the study of Torah. In fact, when there exists a conflict of interest (as will be discussed in Part IV) the *mitzvah* of Torah study may supersede the commandment of *yishuv ha'aretz*. It unfortunately happens that an overzealous love of the Land sometimes unbalances a person's Torah perspective such that the relative value of things becomes distorted. As in all areas of Torah life, halachic and spiritual advisors must be consulted for proper guidance.

During the last half a century the influx of Jews into Eretz Yisrael had reached phenomenal proportions. There have not been so many Jews living in Israel in over 2,000 years! Furthermore, the growth and development of religious Jewry, institutions, and *yeshivoth* have been disproportionately greater than one would imagine. Today one can find the populace of a whole city keeping the Sabbath holy in a place where only fifty years ago lay stretches of sand dunes. More and more farmers and *kibbutzim* are diligently keeping the laws pertaining to the Land, including the *shemitah* laws, which forbid working the Land for a whole year (the Sabbatical year). Surely these events are dramatic in the history of our people. Rabbi Dessler saw this growth as a Divine act of benevolence after the tragic loss of six million Jews. The glorious crown of Torah was utterly erased from Europe by the Holocaust. Its revival in Eretz Yisrael is an undeniable sign of G-d's loving kindness to the remnant of His people. Not since the time of Rabbi Joseph Karo and the *Ari Zal* nearly five hundred years ago has Israel been the focal point of Torah dissemination to the world.

The events in recent years, which have led to more soil coming under Jewish sovereignty, have been publicly acclaimed as beyond the traditional know-how of tactical warfare. The reuniting of Jerusalem in 1967, the bringing of vast areas of Judea, Samaria, Sinai, and the Golan under Jewish authority, and the Almighty's miraculous intervention on our behalf during the Yom Kippur war in 1973 have verified that *this* Land and *this* people are under G-d's personal supervision. Chazon Ish said that the events of this generation cannot be called the beginning of the Redemption—rather, they may be viewed as the end of *galuth*.

The privilege to live in Eretz Yisrael is indeed great, and so, too, are the responsibilities profound and immense.

May this book help awaken us to the wealth of natural and spiritual resources that permeate our Holy Land. May we be worthy to join together soon with *Mashiach* and parade triumphantly through the streets of Jerusalem. Amen.

Jerusalem
Shevat, 5747

Part 1

A Terrestrial Abode

Rabbi Yossi ben Chalafta commented to his son, "You seek to perceive the Shechinah in this world— then go study Torah in Eretz Yisrael."

Midrash Shachar Tov 105

1

Pilgrimage to the Holy Land

A Seventeenth Century Pilgrim

In the year 1622 the Chief Rabbi of Prague and renowned Torah authority, *Shelah HaKodesh*, Rabbi Isaiah Horowitz, embarked on his arduous and historic journey to the Holy Land. Leaving the security of home, career, wealth and community, he determined to reach Eretz Yisrael. His journey by land and sea took many months and entailed great dangers for himself, his wife and their personal attendant. His ship was fired upon as it approached the Tripoli harbor in northwest Lebanon, and when the captain succeeded in steering the vessel out into deeper waters, warships approached to attack them. "The L-rd saved us," testified Rabbi Horowitz, "for He sent a strong wind from the south and we were able to sail speedily along while their ships lingered behind."

Coastal wars forced them to anchor in northern Syria and travel by caravan a hundred miles inland to the city of Aleppo near the Turkish border. From there they headed south to Hamath and then continued down to Damascus — a long journey under the torrid summer sun. The Jewish communities in each city honored him in a manner befitting an important rabbi and beseeched him to remain, but he was single-mindedly determined to reach the Holy Land. Depleted of finances, weary from hardships, nevertheless his love of Eretz

20 / A TERRESTRIAL ABODE

Acco was one of the ancient seaport cities on the Mediterranean Sea. It is situated ten miles north of Haifa.

Yisrael and his dream of settling there compelled him onward.

When at last he crossed into the northern Galilee, and came to the city of Safed, he fell on the ground and kissed the stones and earth in fulfillment of the verse (Psalms 102:15), "For Your servants hold her stones dear, and cherish her very dust." "How deeply I thanked G-d for His abundant miracles which enabled us to reach our blessed homeland."

The Stakes Involved

What made *Shelah HaKodesh* leave the place of his birth, separate from his children, renounce his position as leader of European Jewry, and even jeopardize his life to live in the Holy Land? What did he see in the land of our forefathers that outweighed the majesty, wealth and material comforts of Prague? How did he make his decision? On what did he base his calculations? The cities of Israel were impoverished, and the Jewish communities small and leaderless, while Europe was the fountain of wealth and the center of Torah, flourishing with *yeshivoth* and Torah personalities. The question reduces to, "What makes Eretz Yisrael different from all other lands?"

Finding a Key

The answer is "holiness." In the same way that gravity operates according to certain laws which, though invisible to the naked eye, can, with proper instruments, be detected; so it is with holiness. Just as there are physical laws, so are there spiritual ones that are no less real and verifiable. Holiness is an actual, measurable quality that expresses the extent to which G-d is revealed through a person or thing. That Eretz Yisrael is called the *Holy* Land, means that of all places on the planet, G-d's sovereignty is most apparent in the Land of Israel.

Israel is not an arbitrarily designated area of the earth's crust. Rather it is intrinsically unique and inherently different from all other places. Furthermore it, and no other place, was designated the homeland of the Jewish people. They are wedded to each other and G-d was their matchmaker.

Parable: The King's Only Daughter

The Maggid of Dubno illustrates the relationship between G-d, the Jewish people and Eretz Yisrael with a parable. There was a wealthy man who had an only daughter. She was cultured and beautiful. Naturally, her father wanted the perfect groom and waited until the right match appeared. In the meantime, the girl watched her peers marrying and raising families. She became jealous of their good fortune and beseeched G-d to help her. "Please, O L-rd, remove this disgrace from me and let me marry." The L-rd heard her prayer, and caused a handsome and talented young man to be chosen for her mate. He was a distinguished craftsman and his workmanship, which brought him a good living, was coveted throughout the world.

The marriage was a success and her love for him grew boundlessly. Yet shortly after their wedding, false and disparaging claims threatened to endanger the groom's security, forcing him to flee for his life. His new bride pleaded to him not to go. "How I longed for you before I met you and how short has been our wonderful marriage. Even if you say that separations like this have occurred to other women, their suffering does not compare to mine. They were separated after years of marriage and were barely able to withstand the loss and loneliness, while I have just begun to realize the deep love I have for you and am afraid that a long separation will cause forgetfulness. Perhaps, also, you will not return. Oh, how will I be comforted?"

a human life is born. Similarly, in this analogy, the Torah is the soul, the spiritual element, and it cannot act in the world without its body which is Eretz Yisrael. The Land is necessary if the Torah is to fully express itself through Jews fulfilling its truths and wisdoms in this world.

The ultimate expression of Judaism is in the unification of these two aspects — the study and practice of Torah within the setting of Eretz Yisrael, especially since many of the Torah's commandments cannot be performed except in the Holy Land. Likewise, Eretz Yisrael is an empty husk without Jews fulfilling the Torah within her boundaries. Thus each needs the other to realize its highest expression in this world.

The Land of Perfection

A person might wonder what makes the particular area of land called Eretz Yisrael so special? What distinguishes it from other countries, such that it was chosen as the Jewish homeland? The Midrash interprets the verse, "He stands and measures the earth" (Habakkuk 3:6), to indicate that the Almighty surveyed the entire planet and found Eretz Yisrael the only place suitable for the Jewish people.

Once *HaShem* (lit. "the Name," another way of saying G-d) designated Israel as His Land and infused it with holiness, the Jewish people were able to reach their highest potential there. The *Zohar* teaches that Eretz Yisrael is the only place where Jews can achieve their perfection, for there is a chemistry between the nation and the Land that enables this to happen on the highest possible level.

2

The Measure of Holiness

... In time

Jewish cosmology recognizes three dimensions of reality: time, space and soul. In each of these realms there is a central radiating point of holiness where the Divine Presence is most revealed.

Since holiness is measured by the extent to which G-dliness is manifest in an object or moment, various points in history are "holier" than others. A Midrash discusses this. The Divine Presence dwelt in totality on earth until the sin of Adam, when it departed to the first heaven. With the crime of Cain, it ascended to the second heaven. When the generation of Enosh began to practice polytheism, it again ascended. At the time of the flood it removed itself to the fourth heaven, and with the sin of the Tower of Babel it went still further away. Because of the sins of Sodom the Divine Presence went into the sixth heaven and with the immorality of Egypt it ascended to the seventh and highest heaven. On the merit of seven righteous men, this Divine Presence, the *Shechinah*, returned and descended stage by stage. Abraham sanctified sexuality through the commandment of circumcision and so negated the immorality of Egypt. Isaac's holiness counteracted the sins of Sodom, Jacob's the tower, Levi's the flood, Kohath's the generation of Enosh, Amram's the crime of Cain, and

Moses' corrected the sin of Adam. Thus when Israel received the Torah at Sinai, the Divine Presence dwelt below with the same intensity as in Eden before the sin of Adam and Eve. The sin of the golden calf once again caused the *Shechinah* to withdraw from the world.

At the time of the revelation of Torah, Israel was compared to the moon at its zenith. The next full moon was in the time of King Solomon at the inauguration of the First Temple. But once again her holiness began to wane. Indications of this were the cessation of prophesy during the time of the Second Temple, and the fact that its most sacred objects, such as the Ark, *cherubim*, and the *urim* and *tumim* (the breastpiece and oracle worn by the High Priest), were hidden away.

. . . In Space and Soul

In the dimensions of space and soul, Eretz Yisrael and the Jewish people were infused with special sanctity. The Midrash mentions that when G-d created all the lands, He separated Eretz Yisrael as a tithe. Jerusalem was set apart as the choicest part of Eretz Yisrael, and the place of the Temple was separated as the tithe of Jerusalem. So it was also with the nations. G-d created all people in His image, yet He separated Israel as a tithe. And from the Jewish people He set aside the tribe of Levi, and from them, in turn, He separated the priestly families and granted them special sanctity.

Thus there is a correspondence between the gradations of holiness in the people, *Israel*, and in the Land, *Israel*. G-d gave the Jewish people Eretz Yisrael—and so the tithe of the nations was paired with

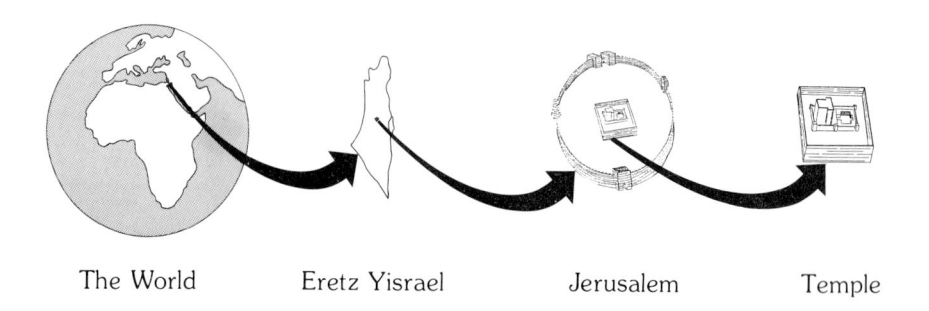

The World   Eretz Yisrael   Jerusalem   Temple

Tithes of the World

the tithe of the lands. The tribe of Levi was brought to Jerusalem, and the children of Aaron were assigned responsibility for the Temple.

The One Temple

HaShem designated a particular place for the Temple and no other place would do. The Hebrew word for Temple is *mikdash*, meaning holy place (from the root *kadosh*, holy). A full size replica was built in Alexandria by the son of Simeon the Righteous during the time of the Second Temple and it stood for over two hundred years. Nevertheless, it was never sanctioned by the Sages, and the priestly services performed there were considered a desecration. For there is only one place for the *mikdash*, the Land of Israel, and one nation who can perform its service, the Jewish people.

The Western Wall is the outer wall of the Temple Mount. It is also called the Wailing Wall because it is the last place where the Divine Presence dwells on the earth, and here the prayers and tears are most poignantly felt and heard.

Ten Levels of Holiness

In the dimension of space, "there are ten levels of holiness...." The Mishna (*Kellim* 1:6-9) enumerates them in ascending order: walled cities in general, the area within the walls of Jerusalem, the Temple Mount, the enclosure, the women's section, the men's section, the priests' section, the area between the altar and the sanctuary, the Holies, and finally the Holy of Holies, "which is the most holy of all since only the High Priest may enter there after extensive purification on Yom Kippur while performing the sacred service of atonement."

28 / A TERRESTRIAL ABODE

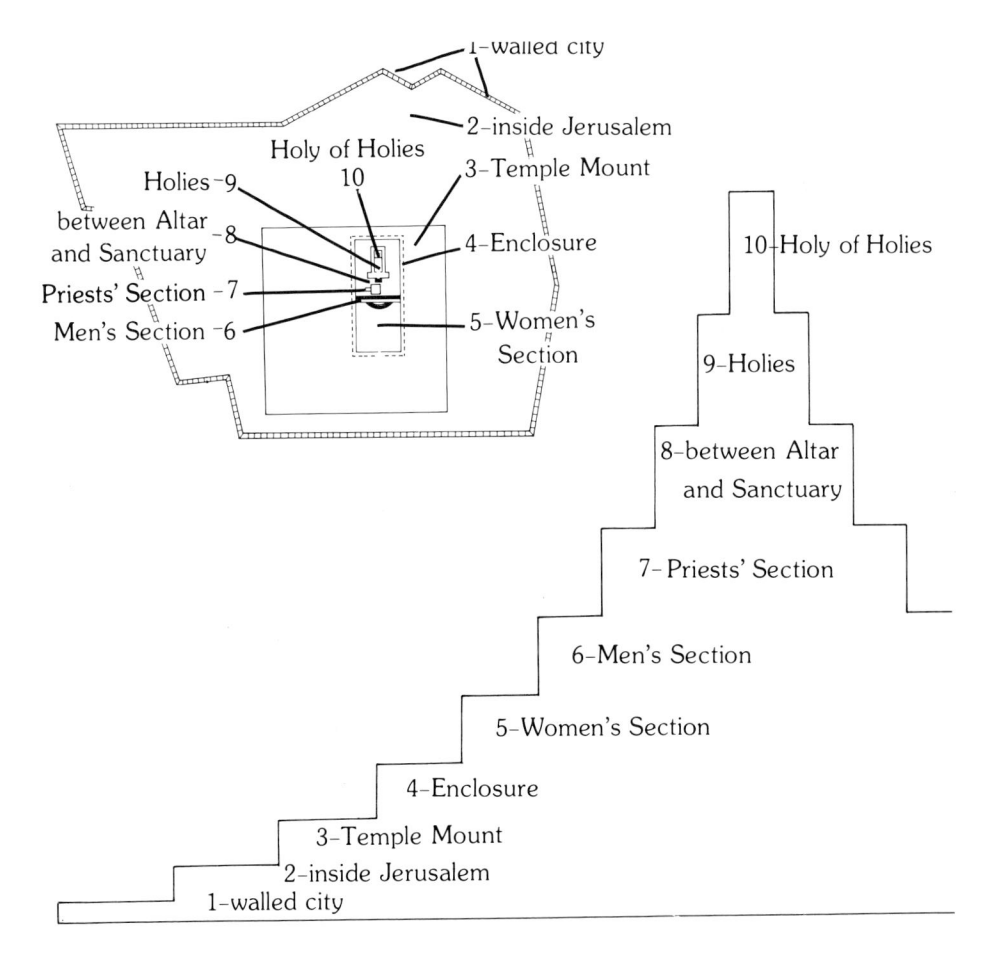

Ten Levels of Holiness

The quality of holiness which expresses itself in varying degrees through inanimate objects has implications for the human being. Each successive level of holiness in the physical world can be accessed only by people who have attained an equivalent degree of sanctification within themselves. Thus Eretz Yisrael itself is not included in the ten degrees of holiness mentioned previously because anyone may enter the land. There are no preliminary purifications required or restrictions imposed, at least by religious law.

On the other hand, men who have had seminal emissions, or women in their menstrual cycle are forbidden entrance to the Temple

Mount (3—the third degree of holiness as outlined by the Mishna). Non-Jews, and those who have come in contact with a dead body cannot proceed beyond the enclosure (4). A man who is pure by all external standards, must still immerse himself in a *mikveh*, (a ritual bath which confers spiritual purity upon a person) before entering the men's section (6).

The Western Direction

Another quality of holiness is that it has direction—it orients toward the west. The Sages allude to this in a story from the *Gemora*, where the Roman Emperor Antoninus engaged the venerable Judah the Prince in a speculative dialogue. "Why does the sun rise in the east and set in the west?" he asked.

"And if it was the other way around," retorted the Prince, "would you not still ask the same question?"

"This is what I meant to ask. What is it about the direction 'west' that the sun chooses to set there?"

Rabbi Judah the Prince answered, "In order to give *shalom* to his Maker, for we know that the *Shechinah* dwells in the west as the verse in Nehemiah proclaims, 'The heavenly host bows down to You' (implying that their 'setting' is their bowing, and for this reason the sun, moon and stars all set in the west)."

"In that case," probed Antoninus, "the sun needs only to reach its zenith point in the sky, give *shalom*, and immediately set."

"The reason the sun continues on its course, and only very slowly approaches its horizon to set in the West," admitted the Prince, "is to give workers and travelers a warning that nightfall is approaching. This grace period enables them to reach their homes before dark."

But G-d is Everywhere!

Yet the notion that holiness has direction, and that G-d's Presence (*Shechinah*) dwells in the west seems to contradict a basic principle of Jewish monotheism, for *oneness* implies that G-d is present throughout creation, equally. This idea is supported by many Scriptural passages, most notably, "The *whole* earth is filled with His glory" (Isaiah 6:3).

The paradox is resolved quite simply. True it is that G-d is present equally in every point of time and space, yet the extent to which He and His perfection are revealed to a creature, thing or moment varies according to many factors. A classic metaphor will help to illustrate this point. The soul is the vital force of the body, enlivening every cell, organ and limb. Yet while the life force is equally distributed throughout the entire organism, its potential for consciousness is most revealed through the brain, and its potential for emotion through the heart. So it is with *HaShem*. His Presence, which contains the potentiality for ultimate holiness and ultimate consciousness, is distributed equally throughout creation. Yet certain times, things, people, and directions express and reveal these potentialities more than others. Certainly, everyone has felt the "G-dliness" that emanates from a holy man. In fact, this *potential* exists in all of us, but is only *actualized* by the saint.

One 19th century commentator, after grappling with the question of why holiness inheres in one direction more than others, concludes that the talmudic axiom, "The *Shechinah* dwells in the west," describes a level of truth that is beyond the capacity of a human being to apprehend.

The Land is Like a House

Eretz Yisrael is holier than any other land and the Jewish people are infinitely more elevated still. The earth, with all its sanctity, is still physical matter...lifeless...while the Jewish people are human beings with souls that derive from the very Throne of Glory, enabling them to experience and express the most exalted levels of G-dliness. Israel's relationship to the Land is thus like a person and his home. The house is secondary yet absolutely essential and even more, it reflects the character of its owner. A person should treat it with respect, keeping it clean and creating a healthy, growth-promoting environment, which bespeaks the holiness of those who dwell within.

This also parallels the relationship between soul and body. The Jewish people are the spiritual principle and life force of Eretz Yisrael. The soil itself welcomes their presence by supplying their physical needs so long as they live up to the moral and spiritual standards demanded of them by G-d and His Torah.

3

The Corresponding Powers

An Eye-Witness Report

In exact proportion to the Land's potential for holiness, as expressed through the abundance of produce with which it supports its inhabitants when their lives are devoted to G-d, so is its potential for barrenness. Ramban, on his journey to the Holy Land in the 13th century, wrote to his family: "What can I tell you about the Land? — how forsaken it is and how extensive the desolation. The principle that the holier the place the greater the destruction is clearly so. Jerusalem (the place of the Temple) is more ravaged than anywhere else, and the territory of Judah (wherein lies the cave of Machpelah) is more desolate than the Galilee...."

The prize trophy of monarchs was to conquer this land and its capital city, Jerusalem. Whether for strategic positioning, pure despotism, or religious crusade, the Land of Israel and its citizens were constantly ravaged, devastated and trampled upon.

Scriptural Warning Against Imitating the Seven Nations

Torah teaches that the Canaanite nations originally dwelling on the Land were the most morally and spiritually depraved people in the history of mankind. For this reason *HaShem* is emphatic when warning the Jews not to follow after their ways. "You shall not learn to do after the abominations of those nations. There must not be found among you anyone that makes his son or his daughter pass through the fire. Neither shall you use divination. Nor shall you engage a soothsayer, enchanter, witch, charmer, medium, wizard, or necromancer. For all who do these things are an abomination to the L-rd. *Because of these abominations* the L-rd, your G-d, drives them out from before you" (Deut. 18:9-13). "The people dwelling in the land committed despicable acts...and polluted it. Let not the land vomit you out because of your desecrations as it vomited out the nation which preceded you" (Lev. 18:27-28).

Rashi compares the emetic reactions of the Land to a king's son who ate a loathsome thing and immediately vomited. Likewise Eretz Yisrael is repulsed by transgression. Malbim develops this idea. Israel, as the Holy Land, is sensitive to the sins and abominations committed on its soil. This is not the case with other lands, for they themselves are impure. Thus the expression "vomiting out transgressors" does not apply to them. A person's stomach only reacts to that which is foreign and offensive to his nature. Since Eretz Yisrael is holy, it only tolerates those whose behavior is compatible with its sanctity. Everyone else, it vigorously expels.

Creation of Utopia

A Question of Ends, Not Means

Why did G-d give to the Jewish people the territory of the seven nations instead of creating a new and unblemished land for them? History proved that the imprint of Canaanite sins remained in the Land long after they were expelled, and actually exerted a negative influence on the Jewish people, inducing them to sin and idolatry. Why did the L-rd give them a "second-hand" land, stained and ragged, instead of a new territory, never inhabited, free of the stumbling blocks of other peoples' sins? Why didn't G-d perform a miracle, manipulate the laws of nature, and cause a new land mass to form where before there was none? This virgin country could have been the Holy Land, the homeland of His favored people.

He who performed miracles in Egypt, parted the Red Sea, sustained His beloved nation with manna, could certainly have wrought a new continent for them, if He desired them to start with a clean slate, unsullied by previous use. Wouldn't this have been a more appropriate environment to plant His "nation of priests, His holy nation"?

Answer I: The Yoke of Torah

Yet, had G-d created an entirely new land for the Jewish People, He could not have insisted that they fulfill the commandments as a condition for possessing it. When tiring of the "yoke of Torah" they could complain that all the other nations have their homeland without the obligation of 613 *mitzvoth*...why should they be different? A verse in Psalms (105:44) alludes to this. "He gave them the lands of the nations (the Land of Eretz Yisrael and not a newly created land)...so that they would observe His statutes and keep His Torah." Since the Land was taken from others because of their sins, and given to them only on the condition that they observe the Torah and *mitzvoth* with ultimate devotion, their continued possession and enjoyment of the Land hinged upon their fulfillment of that stipulation. Otherwise, they would break the contract and forfeit their claim to the country. Thus the Israelites earned the gift of Eretz Yisrael at Mount Sinai when they accepted upon themselves the "yoke of Torah" and proclaimed (Ex. 24:7), "We will do (all that is commanded of us) and then we will understand (by devoting ourselves to the study of Torah)."

Answer II: Revealing G-d's Might

The Midrash presents an alternative answer. G-d admitted to Israel, "I can create for you a new land, but instead I choose to give you this one in order that you shall see My might as I destroy your enemies before you and cause this Land to be given into your hands as it is written: "He declares to His people the power of His works, that He may give them the heritage of the nations" (Psalms 111:6).

On a simple level, G-d's might is more apparent and meaningful when an Israelite soldier feels Divine aid in hand-to-hand combat, slaying many attackers in one bout, than an impersonal miracle no matter how dramatic. He feels *HaShem*'s presence actually with him, guarding him and bestowing superhuman power to vanquish his opponents. This personal experience of G-d's might, and the opportunity to be an agency for His miracle has a whole different effect on a person than if he were a spectator. From a very inner place he acknowledges his debt to his Creator. A miraculous fashioning of a new land would excite the Israelites like some unbelievable dream, but since it was *outside* them it would not have the same deep impact as the other.

Furthermore, how could G-d promise the Land of Israel to the Patriarchs, who lived hundreds of years before the Exodus, if the actual territory did not yet exist? When Abraham walked the length and breadth of Eretz Yisrael, he was, in a real sense, taking possession of the Land. Their very commitment to live in the Land and to be buried there, was a crucial factor in the claim and ability of their descendants to inherit it.

Heavenly Powers

Another factor which confers upon Eretz Yisrael a special holiness is its status as "The Land which *HaShem* your G-d cares for. Always the eyes of G-d are upon it, from the beginning of the year to the end of the year" (Deut. 11:12). G-d created the world as a hierarchy, writes Ramban, and allocated certain powers to the higher levels in order that they could take responsibility for supervising the lower creatures. Thus the angels and heavenly hosts direct the constellations, planets, and astrological forces which in turn influence the various lands and nations. This is supported by a verse in the Torah which reads, "...the stars and even all the hosts of heaven...which the L-rd your G-d has allotted to all the peoples" (ibid. 4:19). Tradition holds that *HaShem* assigned to each nation a constellation and a guardian angel that would rule over it and mediate between it and G-d. Thus writes Daniel (10:13), "The guardian angel of the kingdom of Persia withstood me."

Guardian of Israel

In contrast, continues Ramban, the Master of the Universe did not place a supervising angel over either the Land or the people called Israel. Instead they receive His direct and unmitigated providence, free of intervening layers and intermediaries. Israel, the Land upon which the L-rd has placed His Name, was destined for the Jews, the people who unite His Name in the watchword of Jewish faith (the *Shema*, which reads, "Hear Israel, the L-rd our G-d, the L-rd is One"). Thus Scripture declares, "You shall be My own treasure from among all peoples, for all the earth is Mine" (Ex. 19:5). And again, "You shall inherit their land...I am the L-rd your G-d who has set you apart from the nations" (Lev. 20:24). When the Torah says that G-d separated us from the nations, it means that His relationship to us, which is direct and unmediated, is qualitatively different from His relationship to the

The Corresponding Powers / 35

A panoramic view of Eretz Yisrael. This remarkable photograph was taken by an American satellite more than a 100 miles above Lebanon. The Mediterranean coastline extends from north of Beirut in the foreground to the Delta in Egypt. The Sea of Galilee, the Dead Sea, and the Gulf of Eilat vividly stand out, and the Gulf of Suez sweeps across the top of the picture.

nations who are governed by guardian powers and receive Divine influence through intermediaries. Thus it is appropriate that the Land which receives the L-rd's constant attention, should become the homeland for Israel, the nation which G-d designated as His chosen people.

The Seventy Powers and The One

Tradition teaches that there are seventy guardian powers ruling the seventy nations of the world, and together with Israel they total seventy-one. These numbers are not arbitrary. When Jacob migrated to Egypt, his household numbered seventy, apart from himself which brought their count to seventy-one. Later, G-d said to Moses, "Gather for Me seventy men from the elders of Israel" (Num. 11:16), and together with Moses they, too, were seventy-one. The Sanhedrin, the High Court and governing body of Israel, comprised seventy members and a chief justice, thus also totaling seventy-one. There are seventy angels surrounding the heavenly Throne of Glory, and with the L-rd G-d of Israel, they, too, are seventy-one.

Is it arbitrary, or pure favoritism that *HaShem* gave Israel direct access to Him, while other nations must relate through angels and intermediaries? The Midrash explains that G-d assigned the seventy guardian angels to mediate between Himself and the nations as a punishment for their insubordination in constructing the Tower of Babel. Abraham, then forty-eight years of age, was the only person in that generation to oppose the project, and for this he was rewarded with the privilege of remaining under the Almighty's direct and personal supervision. This honor was extended irrevocably to his descendants forever more.

These intermediaries were not invested with equal power, and some were more potent than others. Of the seventy supervising powers, the seven governing the Canaanite nations were the most fearful. This is learned by inference. Since the *physical* attributes of a nation mirror the *inner* character of its heavenly counterpart, that being its guardian angel, and since some of the Canaanite peoples were *physical* giants, it necessarily follows that their governing agents must also have been "giants," but in a *spiritual* sense.

Rain from Heaven

G-d's direct and sovereign rulership over Eretz Yisrael is the feature which most distinguishes it from *chutz l'aretz*. The Talmud is filled with statements and stories illustrating this point. For example, the second paragraph in the *Shema* reads, "I will give rain on your Land in its proper time" (Deut. 11:14). The Midrash explains that when G-d says, "*I* will give..." He means *Myself*, and not through an angel. And when He continues with "...rain on *your* Land," He is distinguishing it from other lands.

Another Midrash teaches that G-d first bestows rain upon Eretz Yisrael before giving it to the rest of the world. Today, any meteorologist will counter this apparently flippant assertion by pointing to a weather map. Certainly, the claim that Israel's rain comes first is not born out by cloud and precipitation patterns. Yet, one commentator explains that this Midrash refers to the decree issued every Rosh HaShannah whereby *HaShem* fixes the world's allotment of rain for the coming year, a decision based on His assessment of the entire generation's merits. In this regard, Israel is primary, meaning G-d judges and decrees for Israel first, and the world's prosperity depends upon them. Thus the actual rain which falls in each country—including Eretz Yisrael—is based on the results of this two-step process by which G-d makes His decision, and this is not discernible on a weather map.

Signs of G-d's Special Supervision

Historians document that the Holy Land produced fruit that was disproportionately large and sweet. A hundred years before the destruction of the Second Temple, the rains, which fell moderately but auspiciously on Wednesday and Friday nights, produced wheat grains the size of kidney beans and barley as big as olive pits. Samples were collected and preserved for future generations as a graphic reminder of how things could be if they would serve G-d with purity of heart. It is sin which diminishes the bounty of His blessings. The productivity of Israel is dependent upon G-d's will and nothing else. If He decrees that it shall be bountiful, then minimal efforts will bring forth lush harvests; and if He decrees scarcity, then even intensive labor and sophisticated technology will not bear fruit.

When Herod rebuilt the Second Temple, the rains fell at night and winds dispersed the clouds so that always there was sun the next morning. This confirmed that the Temple's rebuilding was a heavenly decree, and not simply Herod's desire for personal grandeur.

The fruits of Israel are remarkably sweet, particularly those from Gennosar, a town near Tiberias. Maharsha explains, however, that

On the road to Jerusalem

resolved to return to Europe. Yet how could they be wrong, he pondered? Perhaps the fault is mine. Perhaps I am not worthy of true vision because of my many sins. What can I do to be among those who are granted the privilege of witnessing His Holy Presence — whose belief in the sanctity of Eretz Yisrael is verified by their experience rather than shattered by it? He meditated on the problem and decided to fast and pray wholeheartedly that G-d grant him his wish. For forty days he fasted (eating only at night) and supplicated himself before the Almighty. Then, to his wonder, awe, and gratitude, his inner eyes were opened and he actually saw the holiness of Eretz Yisrael emanating from the rocks, the dust, and produce of the market place. Yes, the Sages were right. Israel *is* the Holy Land — but only one who recognizes holiness will appreciate her beauty.

Hidden Treasures

How is it possible that people visit Eretz Yisrael and see so many places without grasping the power and significance of what their eyes behold — without penetrating behind the surface, and affirming her holiness? The Gerrer *rebbe* answers that G-d reveals the hidden treasures of Eretz Yisrael only to those who fear Him.

Gold, silver, and precious stones are the buried treasures of other countries while holiness is the natural resource of Eretz Yisrael. This is the Land where the Divine Presence dwells—where G-d's influence is most revealed and tangible.

Israel is not distinguished by her physical assets for these foster jealousies, resentments, opportunism, and conflicts between people. If Israel were rich with material resources, she would be even more vulnerable to invasion, and the twelve tribes might (G-d forbid) have argued over land claims.

4

A Treasure-Chest of Names

The Holy Land, besides Eretz Yisrael, has a number of other Scriptural appellations: Land of the Gazelle, Land of Life, Land of Pleasantness, and Land of Canaan. Each title emphasizes a different facet of the country's holiness.

Land of the Gazelle

Eretz Yisrael is called the Land of the Gazelle, and the Talmud explains this as follows. Just as the hide of the gazelle will no longer cover all the flesh once it has been removed, so Eretz Yisrael can sustain its people with ample space and produce while they dwell therein, but once they leave, the land shrivels and dries up.

This, that the land swells and contracts, produces and grows barren, in response to the Jewish people's presence or absence, is proof that Eretz Yisrael was destined for them. Only the Jewish people can make her fertile, transforming her desert into forest, her wilderness into cultivated field. Obviously they belong together, a match that was made in heaven and decreed from the time of Creation.

The Land of Life

Eretz Yisrael is called *Eretz Chayim* (Land of Life) since it is the gateway through which souls descend and are born into the *temporary life* of this world and also the door of access to the *eternal life* of the world-to-come. The Land of Israel is a fitting place for this portal since it was from her soil that *HaShem* formed Adam and thus gave *life* to the progenitor of mankind.

Dual Nature of the Lands of the Living

Eretz Chayim appears once as *Lands of the Living*, conspicuous for its plural form. This refers to the dual quality of Eretz Yisrael—the converging point of the physical and spiritual worlds. On the one hand it abides by natural law, and sustains physical life with fruits, grains, vegetables, and fresh air. Even without mentioning the spiritual "vitamins" that distinguish her produce from those of other lands, Eretz Yisrael is truly a Land of Life, nurturing the health of her inhabitants.

Yet there is a spiritual sense in which the Land of Israel is also a "Land of the Living" and this is what the Patriarchs cherished most. Tradition teaches that Israel is the gateway to the world-to-come, the world where souls live after their bodies have passed away. What does it mean that Israel is the gateway to the spiritual realms? It means that Eretz Yisrael represents and enables the highest fulfillment of earthly life, whereby the physical is brought into perfect harmony with the soul. The aphorisms that "burial in Israel atones for sins," that "Israel has its own exclusive angel of death," that "the dead of Eretz Yisrael will be the first resurrected"; all allude to this quality of Israel as gateway to the spiritual realms.

Paralleling this terrestrial *Eretz Chayim* is a celestial counterpart where the soul resides after death and basks in the radiance of G-d's light and Presence. Yet this idea that a soul has a dwelling place after death should not be misinterpreted as a physical reality. The soul is not bound by time or space. The world-to-come is not a "world" as we understand the word, nor is paradise an actual place. Rather they are states of being, unconstricted by the limitations of a physical body. In the world after death when the righteous enter the spiritual counterpart of the original Garden of Eden, it means their souls realize their lifelong passion of cleaving to G-d. The parallel in the physical world is the Temple site, Mount Moriah, where *HaShem*'s Indwelling Presence is most palpable on the earthly plane. When the Temple stands and G-d's Presence is revealed on earth, all residents of the Holy Land bask in the glow of the *Shechinah* emanating from Zion.

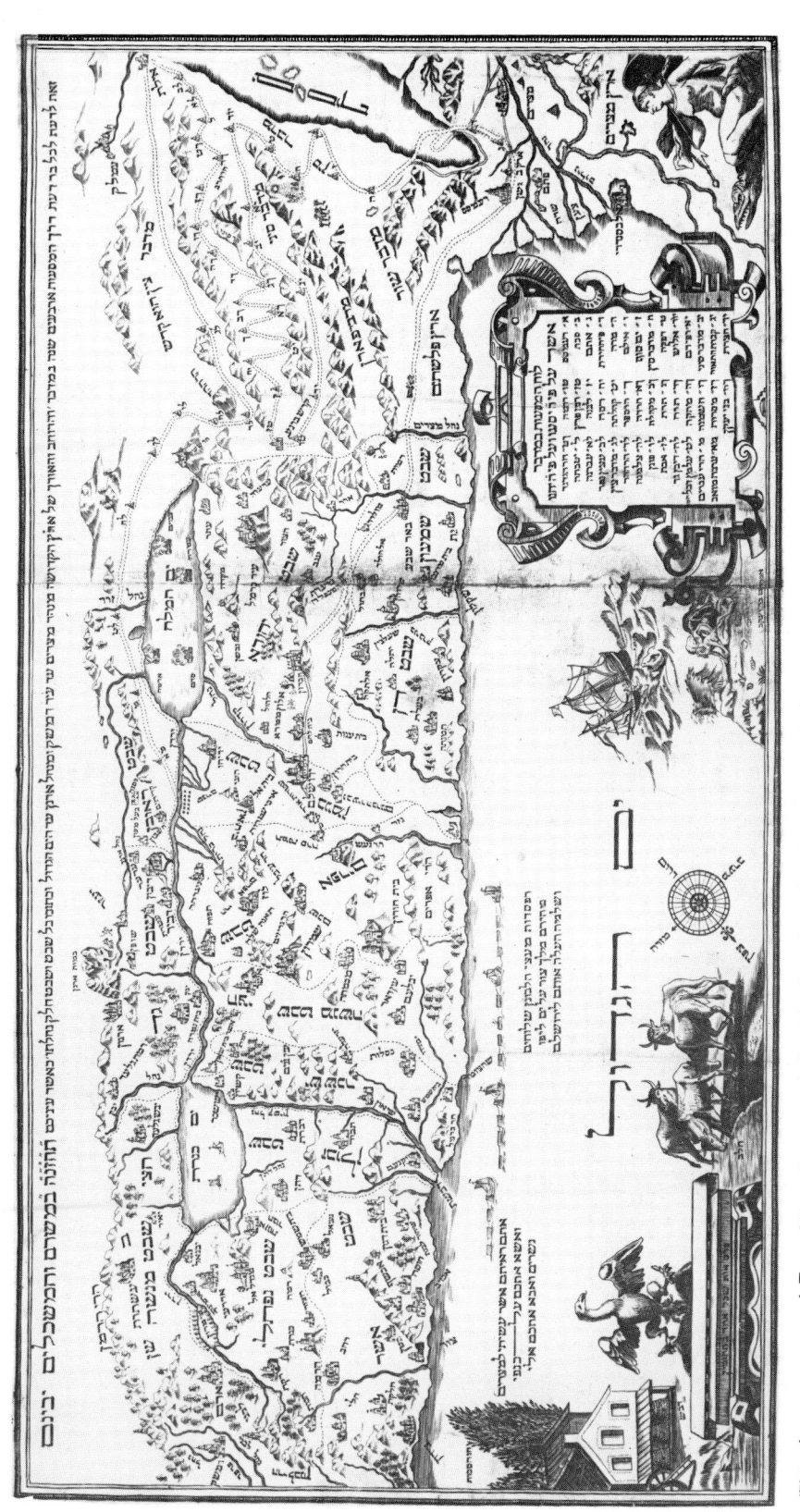

This famous map of Eretz Yisrael was made by Abraham ben Jacob and published in the Amsterdam Passover Haggadah in 1695. The Mediterranean Sea is in the foreground and the boundary of each tribe is marked with a dotted line. The double-dotted line on the right half of the map shows the route taken by Jacob into Egypt, the Exodus, and the forty year sojourn through the wilderness.

Land of Eternal Life

The "Land of Life" also refers to the time of the resurrection which will take place in Eretz Yisrael. Those buried there will be the first to arise, while the bones of those buried in *chutz l'aretz* will roll through underground caverns until they reach the Holy Land, there to be resuscitated. Thus this title, Land of Life, substantiates the principle of faith that there will be in the future a resurrection of the dead, a second "life" that will begin in the Holy Land.

In a world of externals, where death seems final, one must work to affirm this belief. Even King David was tested on this principle. "Do not deliver me over to the will of my enemies," he cried out in despair, "for false witnesses have risen up against me...(to whom I would succumb) were it not that I believed I should see the goodness of the L-rd in the Land of the Living" (Psalms 27:12-13). He was describing his struggle of faith. The "false witnesses" were feelings of skepticism born out of seeing the pious suffer and the wicked prosper—neither appearing to receive their just reward.

Only by drawing upon his deep-seated belief in the world-to-come was King David able to vanquish these heretical thoughts. "Were it not that I believed I should see the goodness of the L-rd in the *Land of the Living*, (in the future world of Truth and Final Judgment), how the false witnesses murmuring in my heart would have persuaded me, Heaven forbid, to deny G-d's supervision."

The Desirable Land

The Midrash presents three reasons why the Holy Land is called *Eretz Chemdah*, the Desirable Land. First is that the Patriarchs yearned (*chamad*) to settle there as recorded throughout the Book of Genesis. Second, Eretz Yisrael, as the central point of holiness on the planet and the place of the Temple, is the Land which the L-rd chose for His dwelling place as it says, "The mountain which G-d desired (*chamad*) for His abode" (Psalms 68:17). Finally, even gentile kings sought (*chamad*) to possess at least a foothold in the Holy Land. For instance, the distance between the cities of Jericho and Ai was three miles, yet each one had a gentile king. So Jeremiah verifies in his prophesy that "He (*HaShem*) will give you a pleasant land, the finest heritage of the *hosts of nations*."

Neither a country of abundant resources, nor strategically significant, yet the rulers of kingdoms and empires throughout history strove to possess her. Why? Of what value was it to them? It seems

Mount Tabor is located in the lower Galilee and like the other mountains in the Land it is full of a long, rich history.

that they were drawn, on some unconscious level, to her spiritual power and inner dignity. They even prided themselves on their possession as the Talmud teaches: "Why does the Torah refer to Mount Hermon by four different names? The Sidonians called Mount Hermon, Sirion, the Amorites called it Senir, and elsewhere it is called Mount Sion. Why does the Torah need to mention each one? It is to declare the praise of Eretz Yisrael. Each kingdom prided itself in that mountain and said, 'By my name let it be called.'"

Land of Canaan: An Apparent Contradiction of Terms

The title, Land of Canaan, appears to praise a cruel, pagan nation, in conspicuous contrast to the positive connotations of the other names. Furthermore, since Canaan was one of seven nations ruling within the territorial boundaries of Eretz Yisrael, why is Israel called by its name and not the others?

To answer that question, one must invoke the principle of correspondence, that "G-d made one parallel the other" — ten levels of holiness opposite ten levels of impurity (called *kelipoth*). Each of the pagan nations occupying Eretz Yisrael embodied one of these ten unclean qualities which oppose holiness. Seven were conquered by Joshua's armies and three will be defeated in the time of Messiah. Of these, Canaan was the strongest, both physically and spiritually, and so the Land is called in its name.

A Call for Humility

Surprisingly, Canaan (*kenan* as a noun) actually means submission and humility. Thus Eretz Yisrael was called *Eretz Kenan* to remind us that we can only claim our inheritance when we are humbled and submitted to G-d. Otherwise the land will simply spit us out. *Eretz Kenan* is the private garden of the L-rd, the grounds surrounding His Dwelling place, the Holy Temple. Because of their "proximity" to the King, its residents must be especially loyal and devoted to Him. Neuroses, lusts, and untamed character traits seduce a person to disobey His Law (the Torah), and precipitate their expulsion from the Land. Only through complete surrender of self-will to G-d's Will, can the Jewish nation claim Eretz Yisrael, dwell securely there, and expect the Land to give forth in abundance.

The Land of Israel

The name Eretz Yisrael, itself is an enigma. *Yisrael* (Jacob's assumed name) was the third Patriarch and father of the twelve tribes. Yet why was it more appropriate to name the Land after him, and not his father, Isaac, or his grandfather and progenitor of the Jewish people, Abraham? Isaac never left the land his entire life, and so on some level he is more identified with it than any of them. And were it not for the merit of Abraham, we would have no claim to the Land at all. He was the first to bring an awareness of G-d's purest level of unity into the world, and for this, he and his seed were promised Eretz Yisrael as a homeland.

The answer is very deep. The fact that Israel fathered the twelve tribes proves his perfection, *par excellence*. All his offspring were righteous, and all of them were Jews. There was no impurity within him that needed to be sloughed off. The patriarchal lineage reached its consummation with Jacob. This was not the case with Isaac who fathered Esau, and Abraham who fathered Ishmael.

The Torah describes Jacob as a "dweller in tents" (Gen. 25:27), indicating his devotion to Torah, which he pursued with awesome perseverance and self-sacrifice. His inner strength, which derived from his deeply internalized Torah, rendered him victorious in various spiritual tests, and for this he was given a second name, *Yisrael* (Israel). At the point that the L-rd's angel called him thus, he entered an entirely new level of spiritual perfection, and became, as it were, a new man.

Israel means literally "one who is straight and honest (*yashar*) with G-d (*E-l*)," and this is exactly the criterion his descendants must meet if they are to claim their inheritance of Eretz Yisrael. Otherwise, try as they might, the Land will expel them, vomit them out, if they are anything other than "straight with G-d."

In Waves of Holiness

Eretz Yisrael is a microcosm of the universe. From its center there radiate waves of holiness outward to the four directions. To a casual observer, this aura is invisible to the outer senses and conscious mind. Yet sometimes it still affects the person on a more subliminal level, awakening a sense of nostalgia and a vague longing for some higher good. To a serious seeker this holiness has a more tangible quality, and influences his life consciously and concretely. He behaves differently when he remembers that he is in the palace of the King of Kings. He guards his tongue and thinks twice before doing things which would be considered unbefitting to a King's loyal subject. Most of all, he loves his Land and feels a great debt of gratitude for the opportunity to draw especially close to his Creator that comes from living there.

Part 2

The Treasured Island

"You shall dwell in the Land which I gave to your forefathers. There you shall be My people and I shall be your G-d."

Ezek. 36:28

1

An Island in the Image of Man

The Power of Immersion

First, Eretz Yisrael is an island, of sorts, in that it is surrounded by water. On the east is the Jordan River, on the west is the Mediterranean Sea, on the south is the Egyptian Brook (Wadi El Arish), while the northern border is the Euphrates River. The saintly Rabbi Moses Cordovero, a 16th century Kabbalist in Safed, explained that these natural water boundaries allude to the initiatory leap one must make when immigrating to the Holy Land, for water is the element of purification. *Chutz l'aretz* is an impure environment, and this leaves its impression on the soul. Before a person can enter Eretz Yisrael, he must cleanse himself of these impurities, an act which is actually and symbolically accomplished by immersing in a *mikveh*, a natural body of water capable of conferring spiritual purity. The water boundaries of Eretz Yisrael act as natural *mikvoth* making one's immigration from *chutz l'aretz* to Eretz Yisrael also a transition from impurity to wholeness.

The Munkatsher Rebbe, Chaim Elazar Shapira, came to the Holy Land in 1930. The ship carrying the Rebbe's group landed in Egypt and from Cairo they journeyed by train to Jaffa. Before boarding the train the rebbe was careful to immerse in a *mikveh*, following the advice of the great Kabbalist, Rav Moshe Cordovero mentioned above.

Rabbi Zeira Crosses the Jordan River

Even if one does not actually immerse himself in one of these bodies of water, he must certainly cross over them in order to enter, and even that can be a purifying and exhilarating experience. For example, Rabbi Zeira, a leading Babylonian scholar, finally realized his goal of immigrating to Eretz Yisrael. As he approached the Jordan River he was informed that only a flimsy, narrow bridge with a rope railing was available, and was advised to wait for the ferry boat. Without a moment's hesitation, Rabbi Zeira dashed across to the Holy Land. A Sadducee (the heretical sect of Jews who opposed the established forms of religious practice) witnessed him scurrying across the bridge and called out sarcastically: "A rash people you were at Mount Sinai when you allowed your mouths to anticipate your ears and proclaimed, 'We will do (whatever Your Torah requires of us) even before we hear (what it is)' (Ex. 24:7). A rash people you remain. Here

This riverboat enabled travellers to safely cross the Jordan River. A pully system was used. Perhaps Rabbi Zeira was unwilling to wait for one similar to this one.

you go risking your life in your impatience to reach your homeland!" Yet what appeared as recklessness to the onlooker, was actually something quite different. Rabbi Zeira questioned whether he had sufficient merit to enter Eretz Yisrael. He reasoned that if Moses and Aaron, the holiest of saints, died before entering the Land, he should not delay an instant, even for a ferry boat. Perhaps he, too, might die (G-d forbid) or be permanently prevented from crossing. He replied to his taunter, "Who can say that in the place where Moses and Aaron did not merit to enter, I shall succeed in passing through!"

Prerequisites for Entry into the Holy Land

Ramban notes that upon entering Eretz Yisrael, Jacob specifically commands his household to "dispose of the strange gods that are among you. Purify yourselves and change your garments" (Gen. 35:2). Jacob is speaking both literally and metaphorically. The term "strange gods" includes any idolatrous paraphernalia they might be carrying with them, whether for real or sentimental reasons. Yet it also refers to any doubts they might harbor concerning *HaShem*'s perfect and beneficent providence. These, too, are "strange gods," for they imply that a force other than G-d is directing their lives. It is understandable that they might have seen the world in this way for they had been living in *chutz l'aretz*, where G-d's governing force was communicated through the agency of angelic intermediaries, and so His Unity was not always so apparent. But now that they were entering Israel, the Land which receives His direct and unmediated providence, there was no tolerance for even this slight hint of heretical thinking. Jacob insists that they shed all their old ways of thinking, speaking and behaving—ways that were conditioned by *chutz l'aretz*, and begin anew with an absolutely clean slate in the Holy Land. The first step in the purification process, that must precede their entry into Eretz Yisrael, is the removal of "strange gods," the elimination of gross and blatant impurities. Then comes the more subtle and delicate work of whitening the "garment" of the soul. All this is necessary before one can enter the Holy Land, both in body and in spirit.

This purification must be expressed on the physical level. Thus the Midrash elaborates on the verse, "This is why Joshua circumcised the men immediately upon entering Eretz Yisrael" (Josh. 5:4). Joshua, says the Midrash, berated the people: "Do you expect to enter the Land uncircumcised? Surely you recall what G-d said to Abraham. 'I have given you and your seed the Land' *on the condition* 'that you keep My covenant (of circumcision)'" (Gen. 17:8-9). Yet the concept of circumcision applies also to the the heart and refers to the removal of "callousness" which makes the heart insensitive to truth. One commentator explains the Midrash in these terms. He concludes that anyone settling in the Holy Land must first tear away the layers of armor that keep his heart from serving G-d. If this work is done it will be visibly expressed as deeds of kindness, devoted Torah study, and peaceful family life.

Eye of the World

Israel's claim as the center of the world sparks the imagination to conjure metaphors for this idea. The planet is an eye and Jerusalem its pupil, the tunnel which connects the outer to the inner. The oceans which encompass the continents are the white of the eye which surround its working parts. The iris represents the land masses other than Israel. The thin band of color which joins the pupil to the iris is Eretz Yisrael. Finally, the optic nerve, the navel of the eye, is the Holy of Holies and the pathway to higher worlds.

Maharal of Prague writes that this vision of the world as a series of concentric rings surrounding the central point of Eretz Yisrael is alluded to in the name *Eretz Chayim*. Since *chayim* is the opposite of death, it refers to all that is eternal, transcendent and immortal. The spark of *chayim* in all things is its center point of essence and soul.

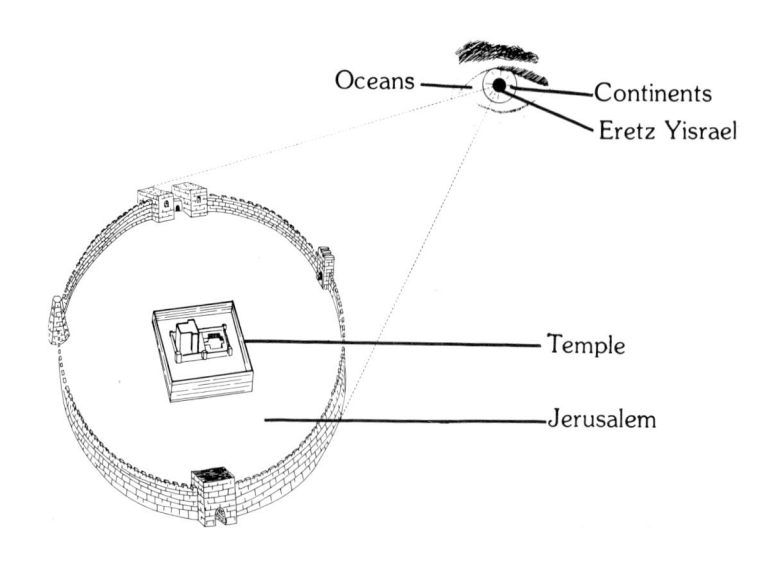

Eye of the World

Everything surrounding this nucleus is superficial and consequently impermanent. It will eventually fall away. Thus the nature of *chayim*, continues Maharal, is analogous to the hub of a wheel which, unlike the spokes, does not extend outward. Only pure spirit and absolute truth will endure, while anything material or relative will die. Thus Israel, as the Land of holiness and spirituality, represents this inner, central point of *chayim*.

The Heart of the World

Eretz Yisrael, as the spiritual plexus of the earth, resembles the focal organ of the human body, the heart. Just as the heart, which is the primary organ of circulation, allocates life-giving blood to all parts of the body, so Eretz Yisrael serves this function among the nations, by disseminating Torah's truths. This was particularly so in the time of the Temple when Israel's role among the nations was clear and uncontested. For example, on the festival of Succoth seventy oxen were offered, one for each of the seventy nations, and the intention was to elicit Divine sustenance and benevolence upon each of them. Also, the water libation on the Temple altar was meant to evoke a proper amount of rainfall for Eretz Yisrael as well as for the other lands.

This metaphoric relationship of Eretz Yisrael as the heart of the planet remained true until the destruction of the Temple. At that point, because of our sins, we forfeited the pleasure of G-d's dwelling among us and He, figuratively speaking, withdrew His revealed Presence from the Land. As a consequence, its holiness was no longer visible to the outer senses. The heart grew weak and the limbs became sickly. The primary source of nourishment was lost and everything turned upside down. The body assumed a fast-like status, where the heart draws its nutrients from the storage reservoirs of the limbs, and so it is with Eretz Yisrael. Now its resources must come from *chutz l'aretz*. The "body" is starving and displays the sluggishness characteristic of a fast. The limbs and organs recognize that their survival depends upon a vital heart and donate from their storehouses of blood and fat to insure its survival.

In the Image of Man

Tradition portrays Eretz Yisrael as a man reclining on the ground with his arms and legs outspread. Although the Land does not actually resemble the outline of a man, the parallel relates to the beginning of Creation.

Adam was a microcosm of the universe. His body was formed from "the dust of the earth" (Gen. 2:7), which tradition reckons to have come from the spot where the sacrificial altar of the Temple was later erected in Jerusalem. This is the place of atonement for transgression, where a person brought an animal sacrifice in exchange for the gift of his own life. When the Torah states that "His people will be atoned by His earth" (Deut. 32:43), it is referring to the dust which was taken from that site and formed into the progenitor of mankind. That dust which is, even today, necessarily part of every person by virtue of their common ancestry, still has an affinity with its point of origin, the Temple Mount, and consequently the doorway to atonement remains open to him and to his seed.

Eretz Yisrael, as mentioned earlier, is a microcosm of the universe, and its choicest earth was selected to form Adam's body. His physical body, together with the Divine soul breathed into him by his Creator, elevated man to a unique position among created beings, for he was fashioned in the very "image of G-dliness." G-d exalted man by delegating him as His representative below and designing him, too, as a microcosm of all creation. To communicate this unique relationship between Eretz Yisrael and Adam—that both are the perfect microcosm, on their respective levels—tradition teaches that the outline of the Land resembles a man.

2

The Patriarchal Borders: G'vuloth HaAvoth

Ancient Maps

The boundaries of Israel shifted at various points in history. First, there was the area promised to Abraham. This is the theoretical boundary of Israel. Next, there was the territory actually conquered by Joshua, and finally, there was the land redesignated Israel when Ezra and his followers returned after the Babylonian exile. Each of these territories has a different significance and a different status in Jewish law.

A Divine Promise

"On that day G-d made a covenant with Abram, saying, 'I shall give this Land to your seed, from the Egyptian Brook to the... Euphrates River'" (Gen. 15:18). Although only two demarcations are mentioned, these northern and southern boundaries are broader than any others specified for Israel in the Torah. They include the Gaza Strip and according to some, the Transjordan.

These same boundaries are restated in the Book of Exodus (23:31). "I will set your border from the Sea of Suf even unto the Sea of the Philistines, and from the Desert unto the River." The Sea of Suf is the northern shore of the Gulf of Eilat, and the Sea of the Philistines

60 / THE TREASURED ISLAND

is the Mediterranean, the River is the Euphrates, and the desert is the Sinai (see Map 1).

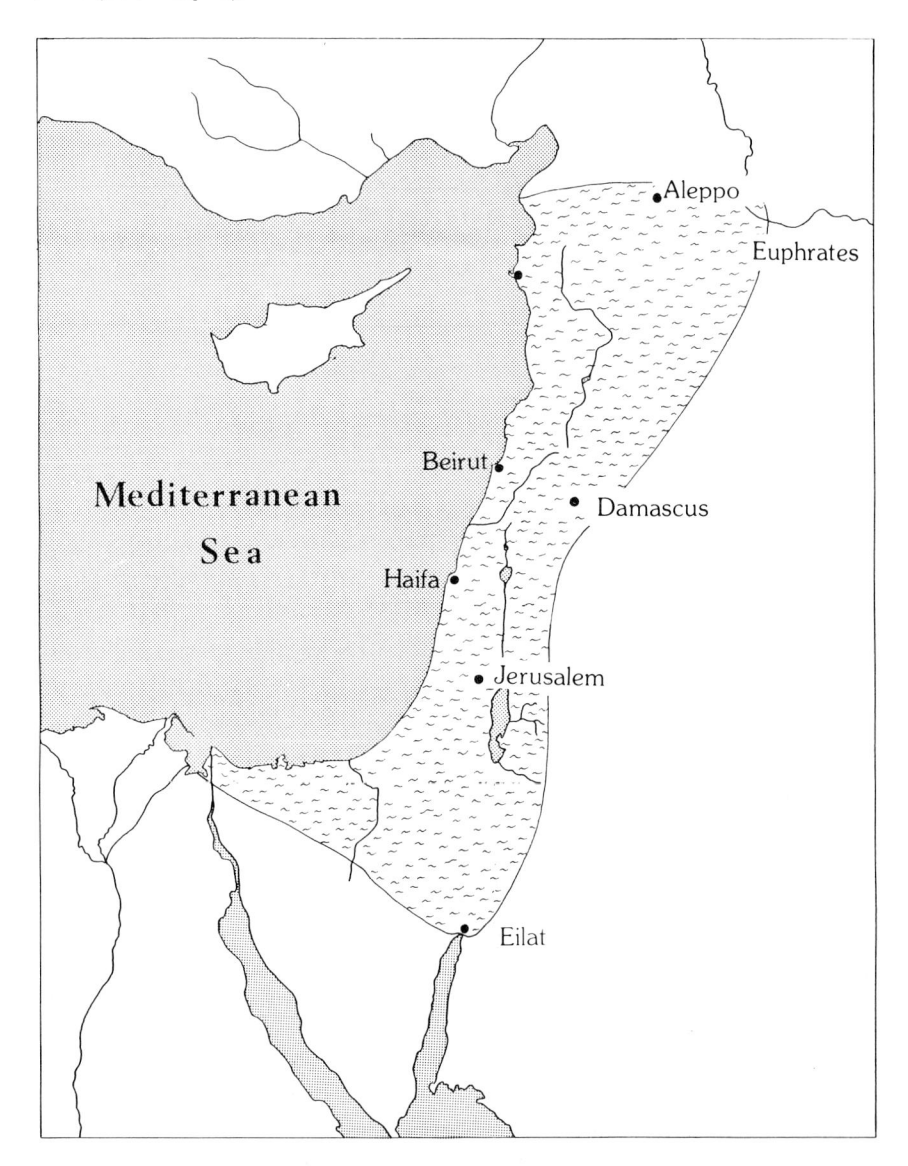

Map 1: *Patriarchal Boundaries.* These include the territories ruled by the Ten Nations. Today, their location is very speculative. Thus some authorities include the entire Sinai peninsula and others extend the eastern boundary all the way along the Euphrates River until to the Persian Gulf.

Abraham's Gift: Eretz Yisrael

Ramban notes that three times G-d reiterated the promise that He would give to Abraham a specific territory as a homeland for his descendants. The first time was when Abraham first arrived in Eretz Yisrael and G-d promised him, "unto your seed I will give this Land" (Gen. 12:7). At that point there was no mention of boundaries and by default it was limited to the land upon which he had actually walked, for this was one way of legally claiming possession of an area of land.

The second time was after Abraham had passed his many tests while living in the Land and *HaShem* desired to reward him. "Lift up your eyes and look from the place where you are, northward and southward, eastward and westward. All the Land which you see, I will give to you, and your seed forever" (ibid. 13:14). According to Malbim, He gave Abraham all the regions inside the absolute and objective boundaries of Eretz Yisrael. Abraham acquired them with his spiritual eyesight which could distinguish the exact point of transition from the holiness of Israel to the mundane of *chutz l'aretz*. From that time onward, the inherent sanctity of the earth of Eretz Yisrael began to emerge.

On the third occasion, G-d actually defined boundaries and identified the ten nations presently occupying that territory. He strengthened His covenant with Abraham by assuring him that sin would never extinguish their right to the Land. This promise was sealed by the covenant of circumcision. Eretz Yisrael would be "an eternal possession" to Abraham's descendants and even if exiled from the Land they would, in the future, return to inherit it.

At that time *HaShem*'s special supervision over both the Land and Abraham became effective, and G-d concluded His promise with these words, "I shall be your G-d" (ibid. 17:8). With this declaration He is saying that "I alone shall rule over you and this Land (when your descendants inherit it), and no intermediary—whether star, constellation, or any of the powers above—shall have dominion over you.

The Ten Nations Which Become Seven

Rashi, citing the Midrash, explains that although G-d promised that Abraham's descendants would inherit the territory of ten nations, only seven were actually occupied by the Jewish Commonwealth. The other three habitations of the Kenites, Kinizites, and Kadmonites will be inherited in the future when the Messiah ushers in a time of harmony between peoples — when boundaries will be uncontested and peace will prevail.

Thus, whenever Scripture mentions that "seven" nations occupied Eretz Yisrael, it refers to those that Joshua conquered, the seven with which Moses authorized him to do battle.

The Ten Nations Promised to Abraham	Conquered by Joshua	To be Conquered by *Mashiach*
1) Canaanite	Canaanite	————
2) Hittite	Hittite	————
3) Perizzite	Perizzite	————
4) Amorite	Amorite	————
5) Jebusite	Jebusite	————
6) Girgashite	Hivite	————
7) Raphaim	Raphaim	————
8) Kenite	————	Kenite
9) Kinizite	————	Kinizite
10) Kadmonite	————	Kadmonite

The Three Missing Nations

The original promise, that Eretz Yisrael would include all of the land then occupied by the ten nations and that this would require a military conquest, can only reach fruition in the Messianic era.

Each of the ten nations embodied the attributes of one of the ten supernal powers of unholiness. They can be arranged in a hierarchy. The six lowest, Joshua conquered by force and the seventh emigrated and assimilated. The last three are the highest and most insidious. The Jewish people were not yet on a level of spiritual purity where they could wrestle with these powers and prevail. The sin of the golden calf disabled them, and even today the damage lingers. Only in the era of the Messiah, when all people will have realized their highest spiritual potentials, can this final work be done. At that time, after four thousand years, G-d's promise to Abraham will finally be fulfilled.

The Mysterious Hivites

Interestingly, one of the six conquered nations was the Hivites, yet Abraham was never promised a nation by that name. This curious *nome de plume* hints to a very deep secret. *Hivi*, in Aramaic, means snake, alluding to the primordial serpent who tempted Adam and Eve. According to Jewish tradition, this creature was the archetypal embodiment of abomination and malevolence. Every possible expression of evil, subtle and gross, that ever was or will be, is an offspring of this infamous serpent. And since the Girgashites/Hivites were not actually conquered, but rather fled and assimilated into other nations, their contamination and corruption spread to those outlying countries as well.

As discussed previously, the ten wicked and pagan nations occupying Eretz Yisrael represent the ten aspects of evil, which can only be subdued by an equal and opposite strength of holiness, a spiritual purity that Israel will not attain until the era of *Mashiach*. The names of the nations themselves provide a clue to this future sequence of events that will annihilate wickedness from the planet. The serpentine powers of evil (*hivi* from Hivites) will be driven out (*girgash* from Girgashites) of existence. Following this will be an era of healing (*rephuah* from Rephaim) culminating in a revelation of G-d, the Ancient One (*Kadmoni* from Kadmonites, the tenth and final nation). This sequence of events will transform the world into a Garden of Eden but this time without the serpent (*hivi*).

Only by the Fullest Love of G-d

The L-rd states explicitly that an expansion of boundaries is conditional upon our devotion to Him, and our obedience to the Torah, as it says, "When the L-rd your G-d will expand your borders as He swore to your forefathers...you shall guard all of this commandment...to love the L-rd your G-d and to go in His ways..." (Deut. 19:8). G-d judged the people in Joshua's era worthy of inheriting the land of the seven nations. The additional territories occupied by the last three nations remained beyond their grasp, a reflection of their spiritual imperfections. In the future, G-d willing, we will circumcise our hearts and remove those impurities that prevent us from fulfilling *HaShem*'s demand. As a consequence, Eretz Yisrael will assume its true and ideal boundaries. This is what the L-rd promised to the Patriarchs, and in their merit, it will be so.

3

The First Influx: *Olei Mitzrayim*

The Second Ancient Map

In Numbers 34:3-12 Scripture outlines the boundaries of Eretz Yisrael with more than fifteen points of demarcation. Beginning with the Salt Sea on the eastern side, the border moves clockwise to the south (Ascent of Akrabbim) and westward (Kadesh Barnea) to the Egyptian Brook (Wadi El Arish) on the coast. It continues up the Mediterranean coastline to Mount Hor. From there the border proceeds inland until it reaches Hazar-enan and turns southward to the Sea of Galilee, following the Jordan River to where it enters the Salt Sea. This completes the map. There is, however, confusion as to where certain of the landmarks actually lie. Which peak is the Bible identifying as Mount Hor? There is disagreement among topographers, and opinions vary as much as 200 miles. The northeastern point (Hazar-enan) and the southern point (Ascent of Akrabbim) are also disputed. Some cartographers include the Sinai Desert until Eilat within these Torah-designated boundaries, while others fix the southern border just fifty miles south of Beer Sheva, a difference of more than 4,000 square miles (see Map 2).

Why is the Torah so careful to elaborate the boundaries precisely? Why should nine verses be devoted to this land survey of Eretz Yisrael? Why didn't it simply designate the general area and let history establish its borders according to need and military strength? Yet the boundaries of Israel are not arbitrary. There is a certain sanctity that

66 / THE TREASURED ISLAND

pervades that Land, and *only* that Land, and it demands special attention. Thus, there are certain *mitzvoth* (religious obligations) that apply only within the Land of Israel and not to its neighboring countries, or the rest of the world. The boundaries are critical, then, for they define the area within which these obligations are binding.

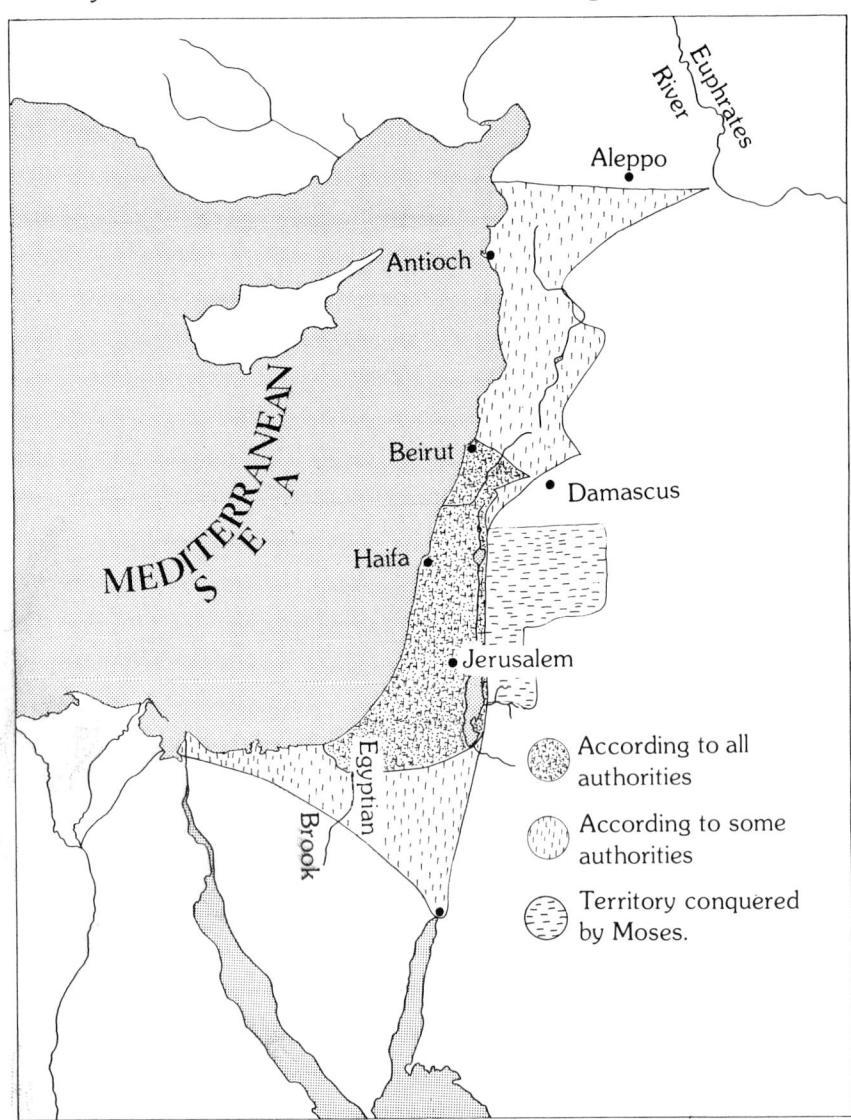

Map 2: First Influx — *Olei Mitzrayim* (c.1200 B.C.E.), as outlined in Numbers 34:3-12. The territory conquered by Moses in Transjordan was settled by the tribes of Reuben, Gad, and half of Manasseh.

The twelve tribes did not actually occupy this entire territory immediately upon entering Eretz Yisrael. Rather, they had to acclimate themselves to their inheritance as the L-rd explained to them, "Little by little I will drive them out from before you" (Ex. 23:30). Only some 400 years later, during the reign of King Solomon, did the nation's settlements extend into all these regions. Nevertheless, these borders are known as the borders of *Olei Mitzrayim*, the territory of those first Jews who fled Egypt.

Transition from Desert to Holy Land

The transition from desert to Holy Land was intrinsically a difficult one for the incipient nation, and it was further complicated by extenuating circumstances. For years to come they would be in a state of military siege. Their entry into Israel marked a coming of age, wherein they were now responsible for their own food and material needs. And finally, they lost Moses, their beloved shepherd and saint, upon whom they had relied for guidance of every sort. One can scarcely appreciate the psychological upset it must have created when everything familiar was wrenched from them, amidst pressure to assume life-supporting responsibilities immediately. Moses' death created a gnawing vacuum that would not be easily filled. So consuming was their sense of loss that they forgot thousands of laws, and many others became unclear. The Divine manna which had fallen in the merit of Moses ceased on that day, though through Divine grace whatever remained in their pots miraculously lasted until they crossed the border into Eretz Yisrael, over a month later. Their vitality and enthusiasm for the future collapsed into bewilderment and uncertainty.

Joshua as Leader

Moses, through prophesy, had appointed Joshua ben Nun as his successor. Moses groomed him for the position, and charged him to "be strong and courageous, for you shall bring these people into the Land which the L-rd has sworn to their fathers to give them" (Deut. 31:7). G-d also demonstrated his trust in Joshua as successor. At one point He gave Joshua the authority to act, even against the wishes of the Counsel of Seventy Elders when He said: "Bring them into the Land even against their will. If need be, take a rod and smite their heads!" Moreover, G-d promised him that his leadership would be secure, that no one would usurp him, that his gift of prophecy would not disappear, and that he would live to see the nation settled in the

Holy Land. The radiant sunlight of Moses was gone forever, but the lustrous moonlight of Joshua had begun to rise and lighten the night.

Even so, the nation did not accept him easily. True, he was a prophet, the holiest and most knowledgeable among them, yet he did not approach the stature of Moses. This was symbolized by the thousands of laws that were forgotten at Moses' death. This loss was so painful to the people that they reacted in pure frustration by threatening Joshua's life. G-d averted their anger by commanding them to prepare for war against Canaan. In the bustle of their preparations, as well as the miracles at the Jordan river, they soon forgot their anger and came to accept him as their rightful and beloved leader.

Joshua, commander-in-chief of the Israelite forces, was a paragon of Torah leadership. Not only was he a devoted disciple of Moses and his prize student in Torah, Joshua was also an expert military leader, a talent which he had perfected in the desert, during the miscellaneous battles the Jews encountered there.

Commandment to Destroy the Seven Nations

Immediately upon crossing the Jordan, certain commandments would become actualized. First and foremost was the positive obligation (no. 425) to destroy the seven Canaanite nations. This commandment was derived from Deuteronomy 7:1-2, "When the L-rd your G-d shall bring you to the Land...and shall cast out many nations before you...seven nations greater and mightier than you. The L-rd your G-d shall deliver them before you...and you shall utterly destroy them. You shall make no covenant with them nor show them any mercy." This was an obligatory war, commanded by the Torah, and binding upon every man of Israel. In this way it was different from subsequent wars which could not be initiated without prior approval from the Sanhedrin, the official governing and highest legislative body of the nation. Furthermore, one who evaded the issue and shunned an opportunity to comply with the command during a time of war, transgressed a negative commandment (no. 528) derived from the verse "You shall not save any soul" (ibid. 20:16).

The Jews were not murderers by nature. This commandment to annihilate an entire nation grated against their deep concern for the sanctity of life. Yet G-d had required this of them, and they could see that these nations were truly depraved. They had sunk to such depths of abomination and bestiality, that even their "image of G-dliness" was

The First Influx / 69

Jacob Auspitz's map of Eretz Yisrael (1818) includes a picture of the two leaders who led the Jewish nation into the Holy Land. Joshua is standing on the right side holding a flag with the names and emblems of the twelve tribes. Above his outstretched hand is the sun and the moon which miraculously stood still at Ajalon. Sitted on the left is Elazar the High Priest, the son of Aaron.

squelched within them. These, who had been charged with tending the King's garden, had abused their privilege, revolted, and reused to return it to the King's stewards. Now they were being punished for their insurrection.

Joshua's Three-fold Ultimatum

Before crossing the Jordan, Joshua sent a three-point ultimatum to the Canaanite people.
(1) Anyone choosing to flee Eretz Yisael may evacuate and be left unharmed.
(2) Anyone choosing to remain in the land must comply with the following terms:
   (a) They must obey the seven Noachide laws which apply to all mankind.
   (b) They must pay a special tax, and
   (c) They must accept a secondary status as only partially franchised citizens.

Anyone who agrees unconditionally to these stipulations may enjoy a secure existence as our neighbors in the Land of Israel.
(3) Finally, anyone deciding to resist our occupation of the land will be treated as enemies in war.

The Girgashites chose the first alternative and emigrated *en masse* to Africa. The citizens of the city of Gibeon chose the second alternative (see Josh. 9). Their decision came about after Joshua's conquest of Jericho and Ai. The Gibeonites were afraid that their option to remain in the land under the conditions set down by the second alternative were negated by the Israelites' triumph. Once one Canaanite nation went out to battle, they feared that all Canaanite peoples would automatically be declared enemies in war. In desperation they devised a plan. They disguised themselves as ambassadors from a foreign land. They dressed in worn-out garments to simulate road-weary travelers, who had just completed a long, overland journey. Their satchels contained dried crusts of mouldy bread and their water supplies were down to the last drop. They beseeched Joshua to accept them as loyal gentiles — to spare their lives and those of their people. Joshua accepted them after a routine investigation and made a peace pact with them without first seeking Divine counsel from the *urim* and *tumim*. Shortly thereafter the truth was discovered. It was concluded that the peace pact was invalid anyway since it made no mention of their obligation to pay taxes or that their citizenship was only partially franchised. Thus, at that moment, the Gibeonites had not fulfilled or even sought their freedom under the conditions of the second option. Therefore, by law they were subject to the death sentence as members of a Canaanite nation. Yet in order that Gentiles should not say that the Israelites transgressed their vow, they decided to honor the agreement and accept them under the second alternative of the three-point ultimatum and thereby avoid a desecration of G-d's name. The Gibeonites agreed and, as semi-franchised citizens, they would carry water for the Temple. They were circumcised but intermarriage with a Jew was forbidden. The other nations chose the third alternative and prepared themselves for war.

Commandment Not to make a Covenant with Them

A third commandment (no. 93) applying to the Israelites and their Canaanite enemies was "not to make a covenant with them or with their gods" (Ex. 23:32). Yet one is immediately struck by the contradiction: If they were obligated to "utterly destroy them," how could there then be any possibility of covenant? How can one negotiate with a non-existent people? Yet G-d anticipated Israel's resistance and laxity in obeying the commandment of annihilation, as it says, "These are the nations which G-d left to test the Israelites..." (Judges 3:1). Consequently they often did not destroy civilian populations and eventually formed bonds of friendship with them, until even the problem of intermarriage arose. This prohibition against covenants was a fence erected by G-d to cover all contingencies, and prevent the possibility of any camaraderie with the nations. Given that His Highest Will, that these pagan and utterly corrupted nations be completely eliminated from the Land, might not be fulfilled, He prepared for a second and less desirable option. Covenants implied a formal acknowledgement of their right to exist and this was the first of a domino effect that would end (G-d forbid) in intermarriage. Therefore Scripture likens one who makes a covenant with them to one who has given credulity to their gods.

A Land of Precedence and Miracles

A Miracle: Splitting the Jordan River

Twice in history G-d split bodies of water for the Jewish People. He split the Red Sea at the Exodus from Egypt and the Jordan River when Joshua led them into Eretz Yisrael. "The sea saw it and fled, the

Jordan was driven back" (Psalms 114:3). There was one notable difference between them. At the Red Sea they were wedged in and incapable of fleeing their pursuers. The Egyptian army was approaching from one side and the sea, deep and wide, blocked their escape on the other side. Their only hope lay in a miracle. Otherwise they were doomed to death. Miraculously the sea split and a means of escape appeared before them.

At the Jordan River, on the other hand, no hostile army was hot in pursuit. Rather they would be crossing *into* a territory controlled by enemy forces. The Jordan was less than a hundred feet wide and a bridge or ferryboat could have accomplished the task. Why, then, did G-d split the Jordan? The miracle had a dual objective. First, its similarity to Moses' splitting of the Red Sea would elevate Joshua in the eyes of the Israelites, and prove his true position as Moses' successor and undisputed leader of the Jewish nation. Second, it was designed to instill fear in the Canaanite nations and psychologically throw them off balance. Both were accomplished. The day was Tuesday, the 10th of Nisan, 1270 B.C.E. "On that day G-d magnified Joshua in the sight of all Israel; and they feared him as they feared Moses..." (Josh. 4:14). "It came to pass, when...all the kings of Canaan...heard that the L-rd had dried up the waters of the Jordan...that their hearts melted..." (ibid. 5:1).

The miracles that took place when crossing the Jordan River were a sign to the nation that G-d was indeed still with them even though Moses was not. Then they knew that they would successfully enter the Land and conquer it. In order to reinforce this with visible reminders, G-d communicated through prophesy a number of changes in the arrangement of the tribal procession. Throughout their sojourn in the wilderness the holy Ark, carried by the Levites, had followed the tribes of Judah and Reuben who led the entourage. Now, the Ark was to lead the procession, no longer supported by the Levites but now by the priests themselves. When the Ark-carriers entered the river, immediately the waters split. Miles away people witnessed these walls of water rising towards the heavens while the Jewish people triumphantly crossed into their homeland. Malbim compares this to a king assuming his place of honor and leadership before his troops as they prepare to conquer a foreign country. His gesture indicates that he is both commander of his army and master of his land. Just as the troops part to allow his passage, and gatekeepers open their doors to the approaching king, so the Jordan split enabling the King's emissaries to pass into their Holy Land.

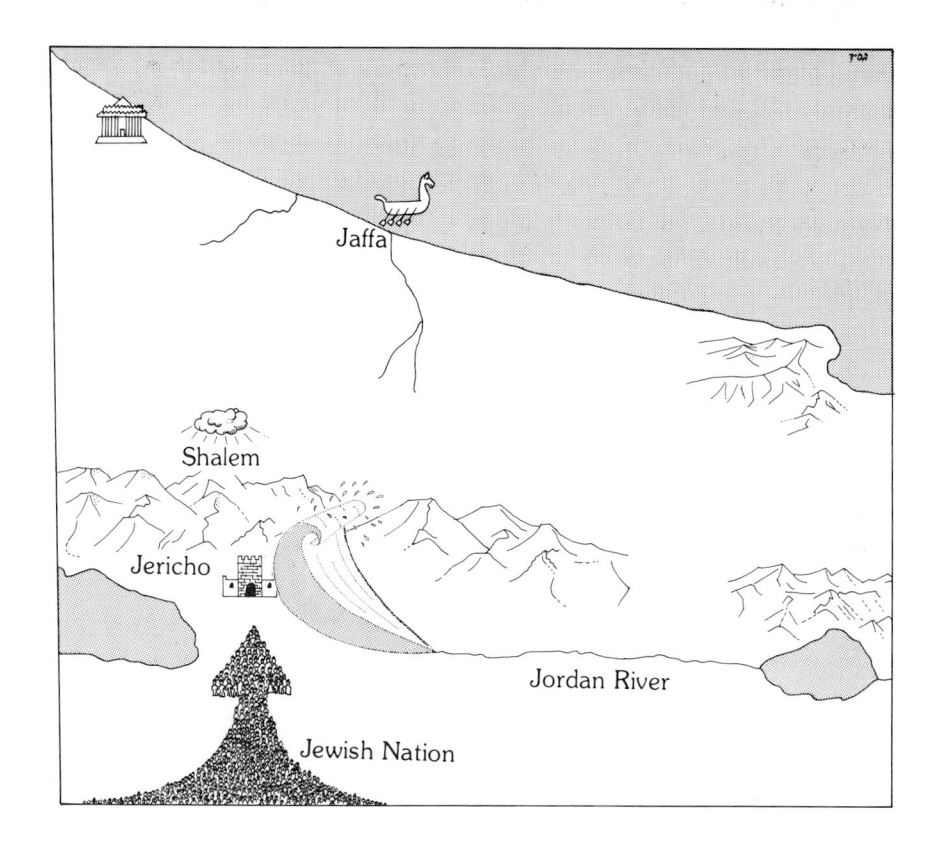

Crossing the Jordan River (1210 B.C.E.)

Above Nature

The splitting of the Jordan River was the first in a series of miracles which G-d performed for the nation in Eretz Yisrael. The sun and the moon stayed fixed in the sky over the Valley of Ajalon for twenty-four hours as Joshua's army finished defeating the Amorite enemy (Josh. 10:12-15). Boulders fell from heaven killing the enemy at Beth Horon (ibid. 10:11). In the time of King Hezekiah, Sennacherib's army of 185,000 men miraculously died in one night as they prepared to besiege Jerusalem (II Kings 19). The Book of the Prophets and the Oral Tradition are replete with stories of G-d's miraculous intervention on behalf of His people.

A miracle occurs when G-d chooses to alter the fixed and natural order of things. Whether to save an individual, or a people, or to show His might, a miracle always demonstrates G-d's complete dominion over man and nature. Although G-d is everywhere, He is felt more intensely when He makes His Presence known by performing the "impossible" such as parting a sea or freeing an entire people from the midst of a nation much stronger than they.

Eretz Yisrael is the place where His supervision is experienced most acutely. It is the Land where G-d directly interacts with man through the medium of natural phenomena, rather than indirectly so. "It is a Land which the L-rd your G-d cares for. Always the eyes of the L-rd your G-d are upon it" (Deut. 11:12). For this reason, it is appropriate to mention the laws commemorating miracles at this point.

Laws Concerning Visiting Places Where a Miracle Occurred

1. Upon visiting the site where a miracle was performed for Israel one is required to recite the following blessing: Blessed are You, L-rd our G-d, King of the universe, who has done miracles for our forefathers at this place.
2. The blessing is only recited if thirty days have passed since the previous visit (not including the present visiting day or the last one). Within that 30-day period it is forbidden to make that blessing. Even if one passed by the site and did not say a blessing, or did not even realize that he was at a holy site, nevertheless he may not make a blessing until another 30 days have passed.
3. Examples of the many historic sites in Israel related to Joshua's occupation of the land include: The place where the Jordan River split ("the people passed over *opposite* Jericho"—Josh. 3:16); where the boulders were cast down from heaven (near Beth Horon); and of course the remains of the ancient walls of Jericho which miraculously sunk into the ground. Yet when the *exact* spot of these places is unknown, no blessing is made. Instead, a song of praise may be said when seeing, for instance, a stretch of the Jordan river. For other reasons, no blessing is recited on Mount Carmel where Elijah built an altar (I Kings 18), or outside Jerusalem where Sennacherib's entire army miraculously died in one night (II Kings 19:35).
4. There is another blessing which one can say at the site of a miracle which was publicly performed for a great individual (as opposed to the entire nation). "Blessed are You, L-rd our G-d, King of the universe, who performed a miracle for the righteous at this spot." Examples would include: the lion's den into which Daniel was thrown (Dan. 6), and the burning furnace from which Hananiah, Mishael and Azariah were saved (ibid. 3:13-30). Today, the exact location of these sites is not known.

5. Scripture records that Lot's wife was turned into a pillar of salt (Gen. 19:26). At that site, it is appropriate to say two blessings: "Blessed...the true Judge," and "Blessed...who remembers the righteous."
6. Any person who himself was saved by a miracle recites the blessing *hagomel* in *shul*, at the Torah reading, within three days of the occurrence. "Blessed are You, L-rd our G-d, King of the universe, who bestows good things upon the undeserving and who has bestowed every goodness upon me." He says nothing at the time that the miracle actually took place. However, the next time that he passes the site of the miracle he recites a special blessing, "Blessed are You, the L-rd our G-d, King of the universe, who performed a miracle for me at this spot." He can say this prayer even when no visible mark of the miracle remains. He may continue to do so, after every 30-day period, for the rest of his life. Likewise, his descendants (even those born *before* the miracle took place) may also bless at this site. A son or daughter says, "Blessed...who performed a miracle for my father at this spot," and a grandchild blesses, "...who performed a miracle for my grandfather at this spot."

The Jordan River today

A Song to be Sung at the Jordan River

The renowned 14th century topographer of the Holy Land, Rabbi Ishtori Haparchi, composed a poem to be recited upon seeing the Jordan River.

> By the bank of the Jordan I will bless, praise,
>   exalt and acknowledge Your Name,
> For Your people You split it, like the Red Sea...
> And for Elijah, You divided (it...before he departed
>   heavenward in a chariot); and there, too, for Elisha
>   (his disciple) who was not hasty when the Jordan
>   split for him.
> Uncovered was Your holy arm (revealed was Your
>   dominion over the laws of nature), You who bring
>   salvation to a humble nation. Do as You see fit,
>   O redeemer of Zion.

Mass Circumcision at Gilgal

The day after crossing into the Land Joshua circumcised all the men, except for the Levites and the righteous ones who had observed the *mitzvah* throughout their forty years in the wilderness. The masses of people had justifiably refrained from performing this sacred rite because they feared endangering the infant's life. G-d directed their itinerary and no one knew from one day to the next what would be. If the pillar of cloud rested upon the Tabernacle, then they remained where they were. If it ascended, then they would pack up and move on, following the route marked by the Clouds of Glory. A newborn child, recently circumcised, was especially susceptible to illness and infection. The people feared that the hectic assembling and wearisome marching would endanger the child's life. The mild, northern breeze, known for its medicinal properties, never blew during their sojourn in the desert in order that the Clouds of Glory should not be displaced. This, too, the people argued was reason to postpone the *mitzvah* of circumcision until more favorable circumstances should arise. Since the Sanhedrin could not guarantee the safety of the children, they could not compel the people to observe the commandment. But now, encamped at Gilgal where they would remain for some time, and with the Canaanite nations paralyzed in awe, they finally felt secure enough to fulfill this precious commandment.

First Passover Seder in Forty Years

Joshua circumcised the people on the 11th of Nisan, and the normal three day recovery period ended on the eve of Passover in time for them to prepare the paschal lambs that were offered and consumed on that festive eve. Circumcision is one of the prerequisites for participating in the Passover ritual. Since this was their first time serving Passover since leaving Egypt forty years earlier (for observance of that commandment was bound up with first entering the Land), a few preliminary measures were required: circumcision and spiritual purification which involved immersion in a *mikveh* and sprinklings of specially prepared holy water. With bodies and souls sanctified to the Almighty, they could observe their first Passover with clean hands and an open heart, joyfully celebrating their Exodus from Egypt and its successful conclusion, their entry into the Holy Land.

Circumcision is an act which directs a person's sexuality into spiritually appropriate and sanctified channels. Thus, according to Ramban, they needed to perform this ritual immediately upon entering the Holy Land. The special sanctity of the Land lies dormant beneath the soil like an ungerminated seed. Once the Jewish nation crossed the threshold, the Land immediately began sprouting forth its intrinsic holiness. The seeds germinated and it was appropriate to call their homeland the *Holy* Land. Obviously, this unleashed a great force of energy which, if untamed, could be misused by the Jewish settlers. Thus they were circumcised to insure its proper and wholesome direction. The foreskin represents the *kelipoth*, the evil forces of impurity and separation from G-d which pollute man's relationship with his Creator. Its removal transforms him into a pure and unblemished "image of G-dliness," where his entire being, including his sexuality, is submitted to doing the will of the L-rd. Thus the Jewish people, upon entry into the Land, were warned: "Now that you are circumcised and are able to restrain your sensual desires, you may enter the Promised Land and it will sustain you. Beware, however, lest you fail to maintain this standard of purity and fall into acts of 'uncircumcised flesh,' for then the Land will spit you out as it is doing now to these perverse heathens."

The *Omer* Offering

The first, entirely new commandment the Jewish nation performed after entering Eretz Yisrael was the *Omer* offering. *Sefer HaChinuch* writes that this *mitzvah* brings blessing upon all the crops of the field, that they should be healthy and grow abundantly. Naturally, this inspires one to meditate on G-d's ways — how wonderful is the Creator to renew another year's cycle of crops, the physical key to continued life. The offering of flour ground from newly cut barley grains permitted farmers to harvest their crops. Just as a person must bless the L-rd before he eats, so must the *Omer* offering be brought at the Temple before he harvests.

For forty years the Jewish nation had been freed from the burden of producing their own succor. The manna was heaven-sent and so the nation was sustained like an infant nursing from his mother's breast. The weaning period ended after they crossed into Eretz Yisrael. The *matzah* they ate at the Seder table was the first "human food" they had put into their mouths. With the bringing of the *Omer* offering on the 16th of Nisan, all crops were now permitted for harvesting and could be prepared for human consumption. The Jewish People had matured and were capable of standing on their own feet — in their own homeland.

The Midrash in its enigmatic style states that Abraham was deemed worthy to inherit Eretz Yisrael because of the *Omer* offering. This is interpreted to mean that G-d's promise to Abraham, that his descendants should inherit the Land, only became a reality when the children of Israel, Abraham's representatives, proved their merit by bringing the *Omer* offering at its proper time. Although the commandment of circumcision was performed five days earlier, it was not a new *mitzvah* since they had fulfilled it, as a people, at the time of their Exodus from Egypt. Likewise, the Passover ritual which they performed on the 14th of Nisan commemorated the original Paschal sacrifice in Egypt and its first anniversary observance in the wilderness forty years earlier. With the *Omer* offering, they passed through into the expanses of Torah which only now opened before them as a result of their entering the Holy Land.

First 14 Years of Conquest and Settlement

During their first fourteen years of conquest and settlement, the nation was exempt from most commandments pertaining to the Land itself. When Scripture prefaces a command with "when you shall enter the land," it identifies that particular obligation as one which was not implemented until after the 14-year period of conquest was completed and daily life had returned to normal. There were, however, certain exceptions to that rule. For example the *mitzvah* to separate *challah* (a portion of one's dough) and give it as food for the Temple priests

This map was drawn by the famous topographer Rabbi Joseph Schwartz and printed in 1829. His book on Eretz Yisrael, *Tivuoth HaAretz*, was published in 1845, and included his own original drawings of the holy sites.

and their families applied immediately upon entering the Land. Also, the prohibition of *orlah*, which forbids one from enjoying the fruit of a newly planted tree for the first three years, became immediately binding.

The Earthly Garden of Eden

"When you shall enter the Land and plant all types of trees for food...for three years it shall be forbidden (*orlah*)to you" (Lev. 19:23). G-d instructed them to begin their settlement of the Land by doing agricultural work, specifically by planting fruit trees. The Midrash points out how tactfully the Almighty sought to implant within the Nation an important lesson. Before crossing the Jordan River Moses had told them to "follow after the L-rd your G-d...and cleave to Him" (Deut. 13:5). This seems to be asking the impossible. How can a human being go up to heaven and cleave to the *Shechinah*? And isn't "G-d a consuming fire" (ibid. 4:24)? Rather, by emulating G-d's ways one can succeed in following after and cleaving to Him. The *mitzvah* of planting trees was a perfect example. Just as *HaShem* had first occupied Himself with planting a garden in Paradise, so His children should begin their entry into the Holy Land by planting saplings. And would they continue to scrupulously follow in G-d's ways, this Land would surely become an earthly Garden of Eden.

Why the Manna ceased to Fall

Kabbalistic teachings emphasize that in those years that the Temple stood the fruit of Eretz Yisrael was as sweet and otherworldly as the manna. For that reason the manna never fell in Eretz Yisrael. Interestingly, the people never complained about its absence.

Joshua Institutes a Second Blessing in the Grace After Meals

Eating a wholesome meal is a good way of keeping body and soul together. Before leaving the table, G-d asks us to offer thanks to Him for sustaining us: "When you have eaten and are satisfied, bless the L-rd your G-d" (Deut. 8:10). The blessings comprising the Grace after Meals were instituted in stages. Moses initiated the first blessing commemorating the One who "sustains the entire world by His goodness."

Joshua instituted the second blessing as a thanksgiving to G-d for bringing them into the Holy Land. "We thank You, L-rd our G-d, for having given a desirable, lovely and spacious land to our fathers as a heritage..."—this precious Land where the Patriarchs and Matriarchs were buried, this holy Land that Moses longed to enter, this promised Land of milk and honey that generations of Jews from Abraham to Moses had patiently waited to inherit. And now he, Joshua, and his Jewish brethren had finally realized this age-old dream of entering the Garden of the L-rd. On this occasion he composed the second blessing of the Grace wherein we praise G-d for the gift of the Land every time "we eat and are satisfied."

The Sages say that two additional ideas must be enumerated in this blessing—the covenant of circumcision and the gift of Torah. "We thank You for the Land...and for the covenant which You have sealed in our flesh and for Your Torah which You have taught us." Both relate indirectly to the Land. In the merit of Abraham's acceptance of the obligation of circumcision, he was given the Land of Israel, as it says in Genesis (17:8-9), "I will give you and your seed after you the Land...therefore you shall keep My covenant." The Torah is the means by which they remain worthy of their inheritance, generation after generation, as it says, "He gave them the lands of the nations...so that they might observe His statutes and keep His laws" (Psalms 105:44-45).

Joshua mentioned inheriting the Land prior to circumcision and Torah, although chronologically it happened in the opposite order. First was the covenant of circumcision in the time of Abraham. Then was the Giving of the Torah in the time of Moses, and finally they inherited the Land in Joshua's time. However, it preceded them in that it was promised to Abraham even before the covenant and the Torah, and so became the sole and underlying purpose of everything that happened to the Jewish people from that point onward. The exile and Exodus of Egypt, and the revelation of the Torah all were preparations for their entry into the Land, as Scripture says, "I will bring you up out of the affliction of Egypt into the Land..."(Ex. 3:17). If this vision of the Holy Land had not preceded the unfolding of Jewish history then an Exodus would not have been necessary. G-d could have given them the Torah in Goshen, annihilated their oppressors, and established them as an independent Jewish republic in Egypt.

Jacob Paved the Way for Israel's Military Success

How could such a small, inexperienced, and nomadic nation be so successful at waging war against nations seemingly much mightier than themselves? They were assisted by a blessing which G-d had given Jacob hundreds of years earlier. One fateful night on the road,

82 / THE TREASURED ISLAND

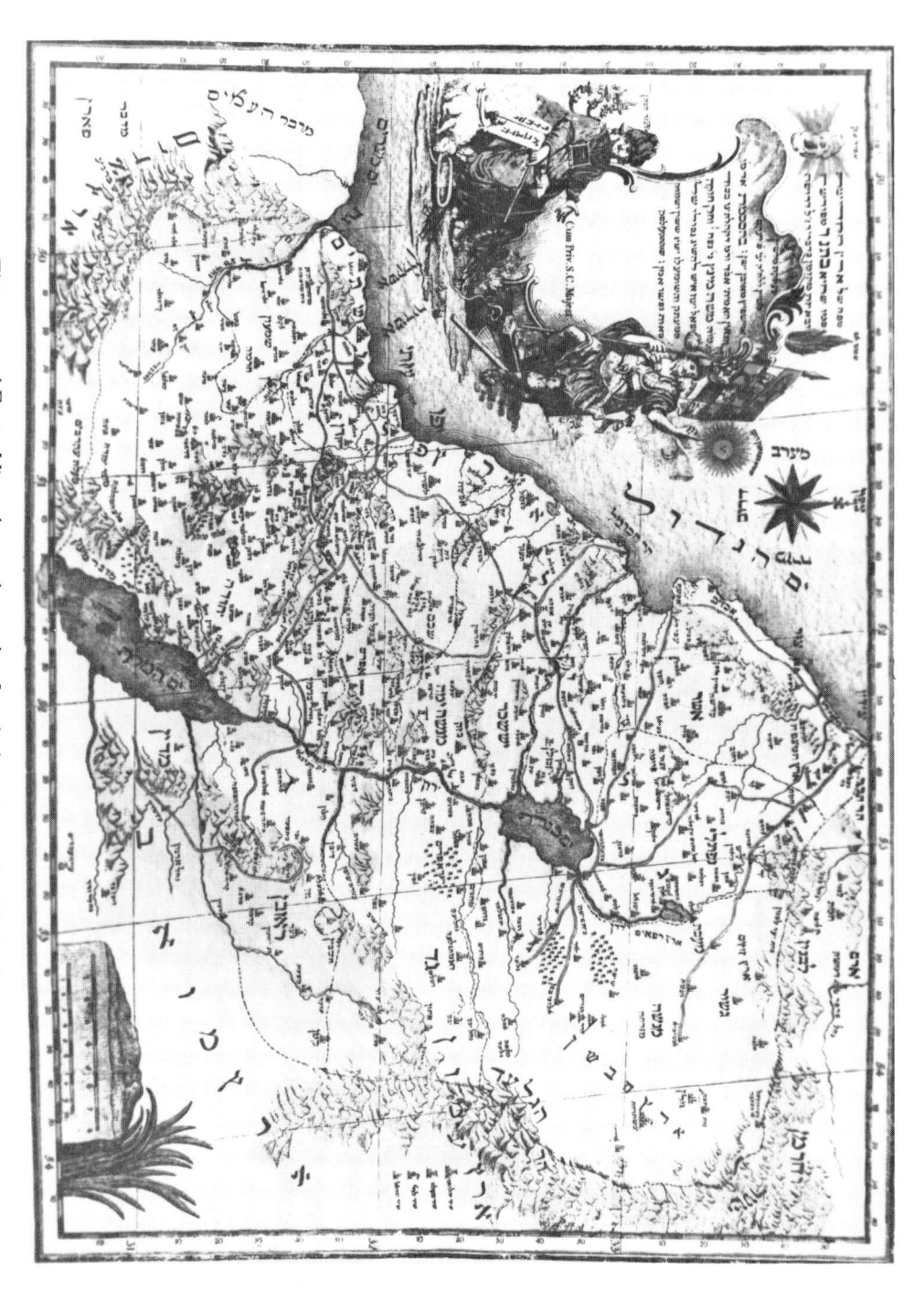

This map of Eretz Yisrael was drawn by Jacob Auspitz and published in 1818.

as Jacob travelled from Beer Sheva to Haran, he unknowingly slept at the future site of the Holy Temple and had a prophetic vision wherein G-d made the following vow. "The land upon which you lie, I shall give to you and to your seed" (Gen. 28:13). The Talmud explains that in that moment the Almighty, figuratively speaking, folded up the entirety of Eretz Yisrael and placed it under Jacob's sleeping body in order to include it in that vow, so that his descendants would conquer it easily. This blessing was an essential amendment to G-d's original promise to Abraham, for without G-d's active involvement, the conquest would have been prohibitively expensive in terms of time, lives and money.

Further proof of the L-rd's commitment to the process of inheritance and not just its fact, is a Midrashic interpretation of a verse in Numbers (34:2) which reads, "This is the Land that shall *fall* unto you for an inheritance." The Midrash explains this to mean that G-d caused the guardian angels of the seven nations to fall down from heaven and He bound them before Moses, proclaiming: "Behold, they are now completely powerless." Thus the spiritual lifeline of the nations was severed and they were doomed to defeat. Even so, their appearance was as frightful and threatening as ever.

Jericho: Key to the Future

Jericho was the city most entrenched in evil. Their ardent devotion to malevolence and abomination was unparalleled in Eretz Yisrael. Even the locks on the gates were fortified by means of sorcery. All the seven nations joined forces to defend their "un-holy" city. They stationed commando units along the perimeter of the city walls. Each nation conjured its demonic magic and besought its deities for assistance.

The Conquest of Jericho

The G-d of Israel, who had proven His dominion over water through the parting of the Jorden River, would now demonstrate His sovereignty over land through the triumphant victory of His people over Jericho. This battle was the decisive one in the Israelites' planned offensive to conquer the entire Land of Israel. For this reason it was the only Canaanite city obviously vanquished by the Hand of G-d. Each day, for seven days, the Israelite army circled the walled city led by battalions from the tribes of Reuben, Gad and half of Manasseh. Behind them came seven priests each holding a ram's horn, and they were closely followed by the holy Ark. Next marched full regiments from all the other tribes including the Levites, with the soldiers of Dan positioned last. On the seventh day, the Sabbath, again they circumscribed the city seven times, accompanied by shofar blasts. Then, amidst shouts of victory, the huge stone walls miraculously sunk into the ground, leaving no debris to hinder the soldiers' final conquest of the city. Jericho was utterly destroyed.

The Prayer of *Aleinu L'Shabeach*

It was a momentous occasion. Special prayers were composed to praise and to record this miraculous expression of G-d's loving assistance. The most noteworthy of these is the first paragraph of *Aleinu L'Shabeach* ("It is upon us to praise...."), which Joshua wrote and recited on this fateful seventh day. He actually composed it in anticipation of the miracle and tradition tells how he repeated it both forwards and backwards with each circling of the city, meditating on certain esoteric letter combinations. Later this prayer was fixed into the daily liturgy by Rabbi Yochanan ben Zakkai as a protective device for the Jewish people following the destruction of the Second Temple when the powers of evil and impurity were again in their strength. This prayer powerfully declared the sovereignty of G-d—His omnipotence and His absolute unity. Its truth stuns the forces of evil and paralyzes them. They can no longer feed off the higher energies generated in the prayer service. Rabbenu Hai Gaon writes, "There is no other praise to our Creator like this one. It towers over all other praises in the world." *Aleinu* should be recited with concentration and awe, for tradition teaches that the heavenly hosts are attentive to a person's prayer and G-d stands beside the angels as they respond in unison, "Happy the people who affirm the Oneness of the Heavenly Kingdom. Happy the people whose G-d is their L-rd" (Psalms 144:15).

Seven Years of Warfare

In spite of G-d's demonstrable assistance, the wars raged for seven years. They conquered thirty-one Canaanite kings and eliminated much of their foothold in the Land. Even so, only the tribes of Judah, Ephraim and the half of Manasseh successfully eliminated every trace of heathen impurity from within their midst.

Telescopic View of the Ten Victories

The phrase, "...when G-d will bring you into the Land," appears in two places (Exodus 13, verses 5 and 11). Yet there is one difference between them. In the first verse the word "will- bring-you" contains a silent *yud* which does not appear in the second citation. The Sages teach that this letter *yud*, whose numerical value is ten, alludes to the ten triumphant wars that Joshua's army fought in Jericho, Ai, Gibeon, Makkedah, Libnah, Lachish, Eglon, Hebron, Debir and Meron. The second verse, without the *yud* refers to the Messianic era, when wars will be abolished.

Song of Victory

After the victory over the Amorites, when the sun and the moon stood still, Joshua composed this song of praise to his Creator and Protector:

> How numerous are Your deeds, Oh L-rd! How great
> Your mighty acts. Who can be compared to You...?
> With thanksgiving to You I sing. You are my strength.
> All the kings of the earth bow to Your sovereignty...
> We trusted in You, our G-d and You sheltered us in a
> tower of strength, protecting us from our enemies...
> We called to You without shame. We trusted in You
> and You delivered us...
> The sun and moon stood still in the firmament while You
> stationed Yourself in fury over our enemies, casting
> Your judgements upon them...
> In rage You arose against them, destroying them with
> Your anger...
> You saved us, delivered us from our enemies, and
> destroyed them in our midst...
> Likewise, may all *Your* enemies be destroyed, the
> wicked fleeing like chaff in the wind....

Seven Years of Settlement

Following the seven years of conquest there began another seven year period of normalization. Each tribe settled into its allocated territory, each family had its own plot of land to homestead and from which to carve out a livelihood. So preoccupied were they with the task at hand that they did not mourn Joshua's death with due respect.

The remains of the oldest synagogue in the world are in the upper Galilee, probably built in the time of Joshua.

Moses designated the territory that would belong to Reuben, Gad and half the tribe of Manasseh, the tribes which chose to settle in Transjordan, while Joshua distributed land to Judah, Ephraim and the other half of Manasseh. Before Joshua's death he fixed the boundary lines of the remaining tribal territories, although their actual possession did not take place until afterwards. This insured against boundary disputes and eliminated the possibility of an "individual conquest." These borders were marked by a shrub called *chazuba* especially adapted to this purpose since its roots grew straight down deeply into the ground.

A Mystery of Creation

"The highest level of sanctity that any human being can attain is only possible in Eretz Yisrael, for there dwells the Holy Divine Presence." Thus writes an 18th century Kabbalist who continues, "and just as the individual's sanctification requires the *Shechinah*, so it is one of the greatest mysteries of Torah that the *Shechinah's* realization of Her perfection similarly depends upon the Jewish people. Since there was *never* a time when all Jewry lived in Eretz Yisrael, for even in the time of Joshua two and a half tribes settled in Transjordan, the perfection of the Jewish people, the Divine Presence, and the Land of

4

The Conquest of Suria:* *Kibush Yochid*

Joshua and the National Conquest

Joshua's campaign against the seven Canaanite nations falls into the category of *kibush rabim*, a national conquest, for which no formal authorization is necessary, whether from the Sanhedrin or from the *urim* and *tumim*. *HaShem*, via Moses, had commanded Joshua to conquer Eretz Yisrael through battling the nations and this was a Divine and irrevocable obligation.

Were Joshua to have successfully conquered the seven nations and occupied the entire territory designated as Eretz Yisrael, then he would have been Divinely empowered to broaden his military campaign as he deemed appropriate. The L-rd had permitted him to expand into "every place that the sole of (his) foot shall tread" (Josh. 1:3). However, he never actually completed the first phase of conquest, and so never invoked his authority to extend further.

King David: A Legend in His Time

King David, some four hundred years later, was the first to be in a position to extend the territory of Israel beyond the original

---

* The territory called Suria does not correspond completely with present day Syria.

boundaries of the seven nations. He was a military genius, a master of strategy, a courageous soul in the midst of combat, and a true lover of and believer in G-d. He inspired the affections of his soldiers and citizens, and wrought fear in the hearts of his enemies. Yet, always he praised *HaShem*—both in victory and defeat. The Book of Psalms, which is primarily his poetry, shows King David's unwavering trust in G-d as the real Director of the events in his life and his military conquests. "I trust not in my bow, nor shall my sword save me. You (L-rd) have saved us from our enemies and You have shamed those who hated us" (Psalms 44:7-8).

One could classify King David's eighteen military campaigns into two categories, with one exception. Most were defensive. The Jewish nation was attacked from without and he mobilized troops to meet the threat. An example would be the Ammonite offensive when they hired 30,000 Syrian soldiers and mobilized against Israel. King David successfully combatted their murderous ploy. Secondly, King David completed Joshua's work of conquering the land of the seven nations and thereby consolidating the original territory of Eretz Yisrael. The one exception to these two categories was his conquest of Aram, also known as Mesopotamia, a territory north of Eretz Yisrael.

Kibush Yochid: Prerequisites for Extending Territorial Boundaries

King David's annexation of territories beyond the pre-existing borders of Eretz Yisrael has the legal status of *kibush yochid*, the conquests of an individual monarch. This vast area extending north to the Euphrates River is called Suria (see Map 3). For certain matters it is treated as Eretz Yisrael while in other respects it is considered *chutz l'aretz*.

According to Torah law a Jewish king may only expand the boundaries of Eretz Yisrael under very restricted conditions. If these are met, then all acquired territory becomes an extension of Eretz Yisrael. It is subject to all the agricultural laws such as *shemitah*, tithes, etc., and assumes a sanctity indistinguishable from the originally occupied Land.

— Before a king can annex *new* territory, he must already have conquered the entirety of Eretz Yisrael according to the boundaries defined in Numbers, 34:3-12.
— A king cannot enter into battle without prior consent from the Great Sanhedrin, the legislative and judicial body composed of the seventy wisest men of the generation.

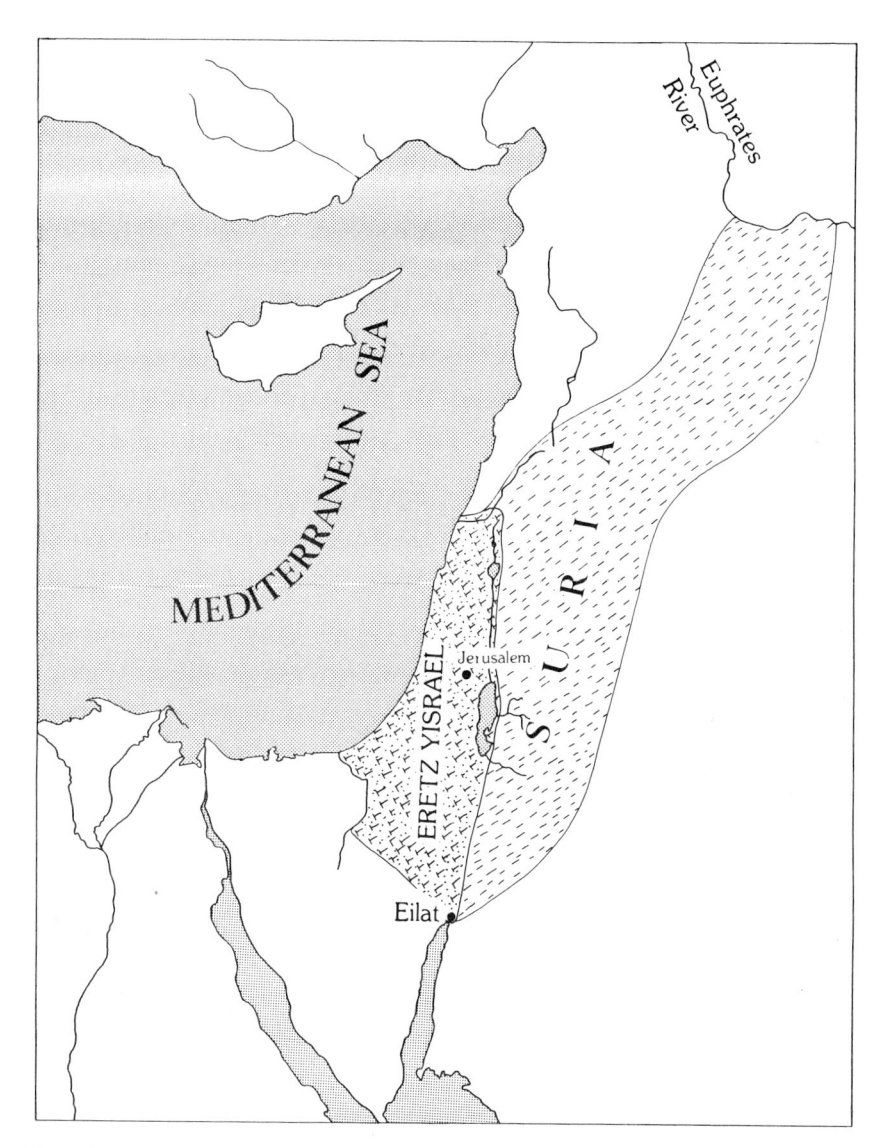

Map 3: *Kibush Yochid*—Conquest of Suria by King David (c. 850 B.C.E.). These are the largest boundaries ever under Jewish sovereignty.

—The *urim* and *tumim*, the mediators of Divine counsel, must indicate G-d's approval of the plan.

Only after meeting these stipulations, may the king mobilize his armies and begin his expansion.

Yoab Advances toward Aram

When Yoab, the commander-in-chief of the Israelite forces, began his advance toward Aram, their leaders cleverly tried to avert his attack by raising an halachic protest which they delivered to the front by messenger. "Are you not the descendants of Jacob? Did he not make a bilateral treaty with Laban from whom we trace our ancestry? At that conference of our forebears Laban said to Jacob: 'Come, let us make a covenant, I and you...Behold this pillar which I have set between me and you...shall be a witness that I will not pass over to you and you shall not pass over to me for harm...and Jacob swore...' (Gen. 31:44-54). Are you not going to abide by that treaty and remain true to the words of your own Scripture?"

Yoab saw that there was basis in their petition, halted his troops, and hurried to Jerusalem so as to discuss it with the king. David immediately convened the Sanhedrin to determine whether this ancient covenant was still binding. After careful deliberation the judges concurred that the treaty between Jacob and Laban would still be enforceable were it not for a previous breach of contract by Chushan Rishathaim, a former King of Aram, which had already voided the agreement. The treaty was no longer binding on either side. This decision freed the troops for battle. Yoab returned to the front, sent a one-word communique back to Aram, and began his campaign which Scripture records as a series of phenomenal victories. King David dedicated the spoils of this war to the building of the Holy Temple, the House of G-d in Jerusalem.

The Complexities of *Kibush Yochid*

This expansion into Suria seems to fulfill the requirements of *kibush yochid* and thus render the acquired land indistinguishable from Eretz Yisrael proper. Nevertheless, it never actually assumed this status. The Midrash explains that when King David conquered Aram the Yebusites still held their Mount Zion enclave. Thus, when David requested from G-d that Suria be annexed to Eretz Yisrael and granted full status as Holy Land, G-d retorted, "Why do you insist upon waging campaigns in Suria while your real enemy enjoys reprieve within your borders? It is a blemish on this holy city that the Yebusites thrive next to the palaces of Jerusalem!" Since, according to Jewish law, *kibush yochid* is only valid once the seven nations have been *completely* conquered and expelled, and since this was not the case when David took Aram, the newly occupied land did not assume the status of Eretz Yisrael.

Later, David did take the Jebusite stronghold and incorporated Mount Zion into the nation's capital. He designated it the monarchic sepulcher and as such its very earth became infused with the sanctity that emanates from even the corpse of a holy person.

The tomb of King David on Mount Zion

The same Midrash explains why complete elimination of the seven Canaanite peoples and Jewish sovereignty over the entirety of Eretz Yisrael must precede expansion into surrounding lands. When charging the Jews with their task of entering and conquering the Land, G-d stipulated as an essential prerequisite to success, their unwavering devotion and compliance with Torah. "If you diligently keep all these commandments...to love the L-rd your G-d, and walk in all His ways...then (and only then) will the L-rd drive out these nations from before you and you shall dispossess nations greater and mightier than yourselves" (Deut. 11:22-23). Only after this first phase is accomplished does the second promise that "every place where the sole of your foot shall tread, it will be yours," come into play.

The inner sanctum, the areas within the Biblically defined boundaries of Eretz Yisrael, must be cleared of all impurity, idolatry, and moral corruption before the power of holiness, inherent in the Land, can come forth in strength and purity. Even a single heathen stronghold threatens the wholesome expression of the Land's sanctity. An idolatrous sect might seduce the weaker members of the nation to idolatry and forbidden sexual practices, and their influence could then spread to an ever-widening segment of the population. This would damage the spiritual fabric of the entire nation, thus blocking and distorting the Land's holiness. For this reason the Israelites' successful occupation of the Land must include a total rejection of all forms of paganism and reflect the nation's sincere and uncompromising devotion to Torah and *mitzvoth*. Only once the holiness of the originally designated Land was free to blossom forth, could it then radiate into ever-widening circles of influence.

Oversight or Overview

Did King David Err?

Given the uncompromising nature of Torah, that its commands are not negotiable, how could David initiate his campaign against Suria before purging the land of every trace and stronghold of the seven nations? And how could the Sanhedrin, the seventy wisest and most knowledgeable scholars in Torah law, approve his plan? And even more perplexing, how could the channel of Divine counsel, the *urim* and *tumim* have given consent? And if David actually violated Torah law, why isn't it mentioned in the Talmud or Midrash?

A Possible Solution

One explanation is that both the Sanhedrin and the *urim* and *tumim* approved his plan to subjugate Suria, with no mention of annexation. The war was strategically critical to the security of the Commonwealth, and was permitted on those grounds. Never was there a stated intention of expanding boundaries. There was therefore no violation of Torah law involved, and the principle of "every place the sole of your foot shall tread" was not invoked. Only after the tumult of victory did David petition the Sanhedrin to annex Suria. Their response was of course negative. No outlying lands could amalgamate with Eretz Yisrael proper while even pockets of Canaanite autonomy still remained. Until the Land was fully sanctified, no further expansion was possible.

A Second Solution

Rabbi Yoel Teitelbaum, the late Satmar *rebbe*, gives an alternative solution. He writes that although King David customarily petitioned the Sanhedrin and *urim* and *tumim* before going to war as per Torah law, in this case he did not. Rather he had a prophetic vision and acted accordingly. In this prophesy G-d commanded him to subjugate Suria in what is legally termed "an emergency measure involving *temporary* suspension of Torah law" (*hora'ath sha'ah*). In such cases a proven and established prophet of Israel can require those around him to violate a Torah law for one time only, based on the authority of his prophesy. The law does not change, it is merely suspended in that particular moment. Thus Elijah sacrificed upon an altar he had built on Mount Carmel, even though the Torah only permits sacrificial offerings in the Temple itself. Yet, in prophesy, Elijah was told of the miracle that would take place through his act, and the sanctification of *HaShem* that would result when a fire from heaven consumed his offering while the sacrifices to Baal would not ignite, even with human intervention. Elijah relied on the principle of *hora'ath sha'ah* to perform this act. There are several incidents of this sort in Torah. So, according to Rav Teitelbaum, was David's decision to invade Aram. If this is true, then King David didn't need to consult the Sanhedrin, (whose function is to evaluate questions of law and forbid action which violates Torah), for this mission came from a higher place—from prophesy and *hora'ath sha'ah*.

Suria in Jewish Law

Whichever explanation is correct, the halachic outcome is clear. Suria was occupied but not annexed. It never assumed the status of Eretz Yisrael. Nevertheless, the Rabbis required Jewish residents of Suria to observe certain agricultural *mitzvoth* such as tithes and *shemitah*, even though they were not obligated to do so according to Torah law. This was primarily to discourage farmers from emigrating to Suria in the Sabbatical year.

In other areas of law Suria is assigned an intermediate status between Israel and *chutz l'aretz*. For example, based on the verse, "You shall make no covenant with them (the Canaanites), nor show them any mercy" (Deut. 7:2), a Jew in Israel may rent his house to an idolator but not sell to him; while land may not be rented to him at all. In Suria he may sell his house to a gentile *and* rent out land to him (but still not sell it). In *chutz l'aretz* sale of houses and land is permitted without restriction.

On the other hand, a divorce contract which is sent from Suria to Eretz Yisrael must be accompanied by witnesses as if it were sent from *chutz l'aretz*. On a spiritual level also, the land of Suria has no intrinsic sanctity, and is indistinguishable from the rest of the world.

From Solomon to Messiah

King Solomon and all succeeding monarchs waived their right to *kibush yochid*, and all their military engagements were strictly defensive. There will be no need for such laws until the era of the Messiah, at which time many changes concerning the boundaries of Eretz Yisrael will take place.

רפסדות מעצי הלבנן שלוחים
מחירם מלך צור עלים ליפו
ושלמה העלה אותם לירושלם

King Solomon ordered cedar wood for the Temple from King Hiram.

5

The Second Influx: *Olei Bavel*

The Babylonian Exile.

King Solomon expanded the boundaries of Israel to include a larger territory than ever before. His reign brought Israel to her glory. For the first time in history the *permanent* House of G-d was built in Jerusalem. So jubilant was the nation with its completion and dedication that the Rabbis, in an unprecedented move, annulled the Yom Kippur fast that fell at that time. It was an era of spiritual and material abundance, and the country was honored and respected by the nations of the world. People from neighboring and distant lands sought to convert to this religion whose principles were propounded by a wise and righteous King, and whose Law created an exceptionally just and humanitarian state.

No subsequent king could duplicate Solomon's achievements. As the crown passed along its lineage, the borders shrank in size and likewise the integrity of the state, the religious devotion of the people, and the status of Israel among the nations. The people strayed further and further from Torah until the L-rd decreed upon them the punishment of exile as the only way to eventually force them back onto the straight path. In 422 B.C.E., four hundred and ten years after its construction, the Temple was ravaged and the Jews were taken captive to Babylonia.

98 / THE TREASURED ISLAND

For seventy years the Land of Israel bore the indignity of foreign rule. The Temple lay ruined, the orchards neglected, and the memory of a once-glorious Jewish kingdom faded and threatened to disappear altogether. Only a handful of the conquered people were allowed to remain, yet through them was maintained an unbroken presence of Jews in the Land since Joshua's conquest. In this way they never relinquished their claim to the Land in spite of their bitter and humiliating defeat.

Even amidst this dark night of exile, a spark of hope flickered in the hearts of this indomitable people. The same prophet who had predicted their captivity also promised their redemption. "After a duration of seventy years, I shall take heed of you...and let you return" (Jer. 29:10). As truly as he had predicted their disgrace, so had he assured their restoration. And it was so.

In 352, King Cyrus, the Persian monarch, allowed Jews to return to Israel and authorized the Temple's reconstruction. Immediately, Zerubbabel set out with the first wave of "trailblazers" who laid the groundwork for the subsequent influx, led by Ezra, which was envisioned to be of major proportions.

Comparison Between the Two Influxes

The original entry of Jews into their promised Land, and this Second Influx, vary in several important respects. With Joshua, the Jews entered as a free and sovereign nation, and the entirety of the people participated in that event. In Ezra's time they were a minority group within the Persian Empire and their entry into the Land and the Temple's construction required the permission and supervision of a foreign ruler.

Additionally, only a small portion of the exiled Babylonian Jews chose to return to Israel when it finally became possible to do so. This disparity of participation indicates another distinction between the two ingatherings, there being a great difference between the bitter oppression of their slavery in Egypt versus their relatively comfortable sojourn in Babylonia. Eretz Yisrael was a wasteland, while Babylonia was a sophisticated urban center with all the material and cultural amenities attached to such a center. The Jews experienced complete religious freedom in their newly adopted homeland, and so felt less motivated to brave the discomforts, frustrations and back-breaking difficulties of starting a country virtually from scratch. Only those totally devoted to Israel as the true homeland of the Jewish people, actually roused themselves from their false but seductive complacency and set out for their holy destination. Furthermore, it took a person of hearty stock and pioneering spirit, for the conditions were primitive, the country poor, and the work was very demanding.

That only a portion of the Jews in Babylonia would respond to Ezra's urgings and return with him to their homeland was anticipated by Moses and hinted at in his "Song of the Sea." Praising G-d for His miraculous display of might and grace in parting the waters and redeeming the Israelites from their Egyptian pursuers, Moses sang the following words (Ex. 15:1-19): "By the greatness of Your arm...Your people pass over, O L-rd...they pass over—the people You have acquired." "*Your* people (shall) pass over" refers to Joshua's crossing of the Jordan River at the First Influx. Since the *Shechinah* was with them, as is by definition the case when the entire Jewish people are together and united, they were called "*Your* (*HaShem's*) people." "They pass over" refers to the Jews' return to Israel following the Babylonian exile. Since there was only partial participation, the *Shechinah* was not with them, and they are referred to as "the people" indicating that they are not, at this point, as obviously connected to G-d. Had the entire Jewish population returned with Ezra, the *Shechinah* would have accompanied them and their occupation would have included revealed miracles similar to those marking Joshua's conquest. Instead, Ezra led only a portion of the Jews back to their Homeland. G-d's participation was less apparent and so they needed to secure permission from an earthly king, the Persian monarch, before they could return and construct their Temple.

Both Joshua and Ezra, upon entering Eretz Yisrael, began counting the seven years of the Sabbatical cycle. Joshua waited until after his fourteen years of conquest and settlement before initiating the process, while Ezra began immediately upon arrival. The first of the fifty-year Jubilee cycle also began with Joshua's counting. Yet, since the Torah requires that all Jews be in the Land for its proclamation, its observation ceased when the Ten Tribes were captured and exiled.

Story of Resh Lakish and the Babylonian Scholar

Resh Lakish, a third century Torah scholar, was bathing in the Jordan when a Babylonian Jew extended a hand to help him from the water. Resh Lakish, recalling the refusal of Babylonian Jewry to leave their adopted homeland and return to Israel when it finally became possible to do so, waived the assistance and admonished his would-be helper. "Were it not for your ancestors in the time of Ezra, who would not immigrate *en masse* to Eretz Yisrael, the Divine Presence would have rested on the Second Temple as it did on the first. I say this based on a verse in Song of Songs (8:9)."

When Resh Lakish repeated his interpretation to Rabbi Yochanan, his mentor disagreed. "Even had all of Babylonian Jewry immigrated with Ezra, the Divine Presence still would not have dwelt in the Second Temple. I base this on the verse which reads, 'G-d will enlarge Japheth, and he shall dwell in the tents of Shem' (Gen. 9:27). Since the Persians, who are descendants of Japheth, built the Second Temple, the Divine Presence could not rest there. Rather, only in the First Temple built by King Solomon, a descendant of Shem, could the *Shechinah* dwell in all its glory."

A Setback: A Two-Edged Sword

This apparent setback, that only a portion of Babylonian Jews chose to return with Ezra to Eretz Yisrael, had its costs and its benefits. Their indifference, and indeed arrogance, toward the imperative of returning to Israel undoubtedly precipitated the harsh decrees that were later to fall upon many of them. One township, Vermizah, responded to an official dispatch from Jerusalem by boasting, "*You* may dwell in the *great* Jerusalem, *we* will remain here in the *little* Jerusalem!" The Jews of this community, at that time quite prosperous and prominent, slowly began to suffer from prejudicial legislation and eventually lost all wealth and status.

On the other hand, the *yeshivoth* in Babylonia prospered. They were spared the turmoil of foreign invasion which harassed the Jews of other countries, particularly Eretz Yisrael. Within their adopted Babylonian homeland, their religious pursuits were sanctioned by their national rulers and they were allowed to dedicate themselves to pure, uninterrupted Torah study.

Historical Synopsis of Ezra's Immigration

Ezra emigrated from Babylonia in 347 B.C.E., five years after a royal edict from the Persian Empire instructed Zerubbabel to rebuild the Holy Temple. Ezra had planned to come as soon as the decree was announced, but delayed his departure to remain under the tutelage of his teacher and mentor, Baruch ben Neriah, who was too old to make the journey. Shortly after Baruch's death, Ezra, then eighty years old, embarked on his five month journey to the Holy Land.

He set out with a relatively small group of men, women and children, armed with a letter from the Persian monarch authorizing him to appoint magistrates and judges to enforce Torah law in the Land, and to receive from the local governor large quantities of supplies for the Temple. Too embarrassed to request a royally appointed security guard because of a previous conversation with the king where he had said, "The hand of G-d is upon all who seek Him for good, and His strength and wrath are against all who forsake Him" (Ez. 8:22), Ezra had no choice but to trust in G-d's protection. After such an assertion of Divine Providence how could he have then contradicted himself, demonstrated mistrust in G-d's providence, and preferred instead to rely on the strengths of man? Rather, Ezra declared a fast day to endear themselves to *HaShem* and thus insure their safety. Not only was their personal security in question, but they were travelling with a large amount of money that had been placed into their charge by the royal treasury. Their five month journey suffered neither foreign attack nor misfortune.

Ezra descended from a priestly family and would logically have become the first High Priest of the Second Temple. Instead he appointed his nephew to fill that honored and coveted position, a title which remains with a person until his death. Ezra relinquished his rights to the High Priesthood for two reasons. First, he had decided to delay his departure and remain with his teacher until his death, while the position needed to be filled immediately. Second, he felt that since someone else could fill the post of High Priest, his own energy and talents were best used for leading the Great Assembly, and nursing the community of impoverished residents and displaced immigrants back to health.

The Impact of the Men of the Great Assembly

The work before him and the members of the Great Assembly was overwhelming. They were charged with developing a viable economic plan that would enable the long term survival of the new and fragile settlement. They organized and supervised both the architecting and the constructing of the Temple. They implemented a system for training the priests and Levites in their extremely complex and demanding responsibilities. Everything had to be done with utmost attention to detail. Since the specifications were G-d's, no amount of compromise was acceptable. The population, mostly agrarian, had to be instructed in the numerous laws pertaining to husbandry. They could not sow mixed seeds (*kelayim*) nor pick fruit from a tree less

The Principle of Sanctification

Process of Sanctification

To begin with, one must understand that sanctification is a spiritual transmutation whereby something is formally and legally separated for sacred use. It can be temporary, and apply only so long as the object is actually engaged in that purpose. Or it can permanently alter the status of a person or thing. An example of temporary sanctification is marriage (which is revoked upon divorce). Examples of permanent sanctification are a Torah scroll and a king ("Your throne shall be firm forever" — II Sam. 7:16). The Sages concluded that certain periods of occupation effected temporary sanctification of the Land and others, permanent.

In one sense, the two ingatherings (Joshua's and Ezra's) were similar in that both initiated profound changes in the actual dust of the earth whereby the mysterious process of sanctification was begun. Their mere presence in the Land awakened the spiritual potency of the earth which had lain dormant under foreign rule. Wherever Joshua conquered and trod, there holiness was awakened. Ezra, on the other hand, limited Jewish settlements to certain carefully selected areas, choosing to sanctify only a portion of the biblically defined boundaries of Eretz Yisrael. He tempered his occupation so as to reduce the area of land bound by the laws of *shemitah*. In this way settlers could farm these unsanctified areas in the seventh year since they were not halachically Eretz Yisrael, and thereby avoid the danger of food shortage.

Concerning the *mitzvoth* pertaining to the land, Joshua's sanctification was conditional upon all Jews living within the boundaries of Eretz Yisrael. Consequently, it ended with the destruction of the First Temple and the subsequent exile of Jews to Babylonia. Conversely, Ezra's sanctification was permanent and unconditional. It persisted after the Second Temple's ruin and continues today, even with a majority of Jews in exile.

The question of why Joshua's occupation only engendered a temporary sanctification while Ezra's was permanent, is a problem that has baffled commentators for centuries. One scholar suggests that the solution is in the extent to which each exile was prophesied and so formally authorized by G-d. Since Jeremiah brought *HaShem*'s personal warning that if the people did not repent of their wrongdoings and return to Torah, He would lay waste their Temple and spit them from the land, it is as though He had "signed His Name" to that event.

The Egyptain Brook. Wadi El Arish is accepted by most authorities as the Biblical southwestern border of Eretz Yisrael (see Map 2 and Map 4). Scripture calls it *nachal mitzrayim* (Gen. 16:18, Ex. 23:31, Josh. 1:4).

And just as G-d has exclusive power to sanctify, so has He exclusive power to revoke that sanctification. Therefore, the prophetically foretold destruction of the First Temple and the ensuing exile cleared the slate, and Eretz Yisrael reverted to her original, unsanctified condition.

Since no prophet specifically foretold the Second Temple's destruction, it had a different status in relation to G-d. It was not preordained and so was, in a sense, an unauthorized and unsanctioned event. Something stated explicitly by G-d (i.e., the sanctification of the Land resulting from Jewish occupation) cannot be cancelled by something unstated (i.e., the Second Temple's destruction), even though it, too, was ultimately His doing, since nothing happens without at least His tacit approval.

Another commentator distinguishes between the extent to which the command to inherit the land was conditional upon their fulfillment of Torah — a factor which varies between the two periods. Joshua was both commanded to conquer the Land and warned to adhere to the commandments (Psalms 105:44). When the people breached their responsibilities, they voided the contract and G-d annulled the sanctification, amounting to a virtual withdrawal of Divine protection, which then made possible the Babylonian invasion and victory.

Ezra and his followers, however, were never personally commanded to conquer the Land. Moses' prophecy that "they pass over" foretold only of Ezra's ingathering and construction of the Second Temple. The sanctification was not an obligation nor was it conditional upon their Torah observance. They made an oral declaration of formally claiming this land as Eretz Yisrael — affirming its sanctity (within newly designated boundaries) without stipulating any conditions. It is precisely because this new sanctification was inferior to the first that it *never* depended upon a Jewish presence in the Land nor upon their allegiance to the Torah. Therefore, generations later it was not annulled by foreign invasion nor by a yet more extensive exile from the homeland.

Rabbi Joseph Schwartz (1804-1860) was a famous topographer of Eretz Yisrael. Today rabbis use his findings to help determine the boundaries of *Olei Bavel.*

Importance of New Boundaries

The agrarian commandments apply only within the established boundaries of Eretz Yisrael. Yet a problem arises. Which set of boundaries to use? Those communicated to Abraham? The boundaries of Joshua? David? The Second Commonwealth?

In fact, each of the boundaries is relevant to the question which, though seemingly simple, is actually quite complicated. In general, however, the boundaries established by Ezra during the Second Influx are the most practically significant in determining the areas within which the land-related commandments are binding today. The previous Commonwealth had merely effected a temporary sanctification of the Land which applied only so long as it was occupied by Jews, Temple, and Sanhedrin.

The Great Assembly of Ezra announced through proclamation which territories should be sanctified. They carefully weighed the pros and cons of each sector of land in relation to the needs of the people. The areas chosen were orally declared to assume the status of sanctified Eretz Yisrael, and they immediately became so. All Torah obligations then applied there. This was fine except for the commandment of *shemitah*, the Sabbatical year, which obligated farmers to leave land fallow for an entire year, forfeiting most produce, which was their main source of income at that time. This posed a danger of starvation for many of the impoverished settlers who relied on *maaser oni* (tithe for the poor) as their sole means of support. The possibility arose that many settlers would desert the Land and emigrate in order to survive. Ezra thus officially left certain areas unsanctified. Jewish homesteaders could then farm these plots during *shemitah*, and the poor would receive their portion of *maaser oni* from these crops.

But G-d Provides for Those who Keep the *Shemitah*!

Ezra's plan was ingenious, yet it conspicuously ignored the blessing which G-d gave them. "If you shall say, 'What shall we eat in the seventh year?'...Then I will command My blessing upon you in the sixth year, and it shall bring forth produce for three years" (Lev. 25:20-21). Ezra could have relied upon this promise, sanctified all the Land without restriction, and watched the fulfillment of Divine blessing. Yet he did not choose to do so.

Ezra was a man of foresight. He understood what reciprocal conditions must be met by the settlers before the blessing would become effectual. The people had to be G-d fearing, of pure lineage, and scrupulous in keeping the Law. Not only had Ezra found a problem of intermarriage among some of the new settlers, but he had intentionally forced all Jews of dubious descent to emigrate from Babylonia along with him. He took this extraordinary measure to insure the high caliber of Babylonian Jewry which was left virtually leaderless with his departure. Therefore, Ezra's prudence in leaving areas unsanctified was a safeguard for that generation and set the standard for the generations to come.

The Borders of *Olei Bavel*

The general consensus as to the boundaries of Ezra's Commonwealth is as follows. The southern border extends eastward from the

108 / THE TREASURED ISLAND

Egyptian Brook to the southern tip of the Dead Sea. The northern border follows a line from Kaziv (ten miles north of Acco on the Mediterranean Sea) eastward to the Jordan River (see Map 4). Purposely he avoided Beth Shean, Ashkelon, and Caesaria. The borders of the Second Influx were smaller than the first and did not

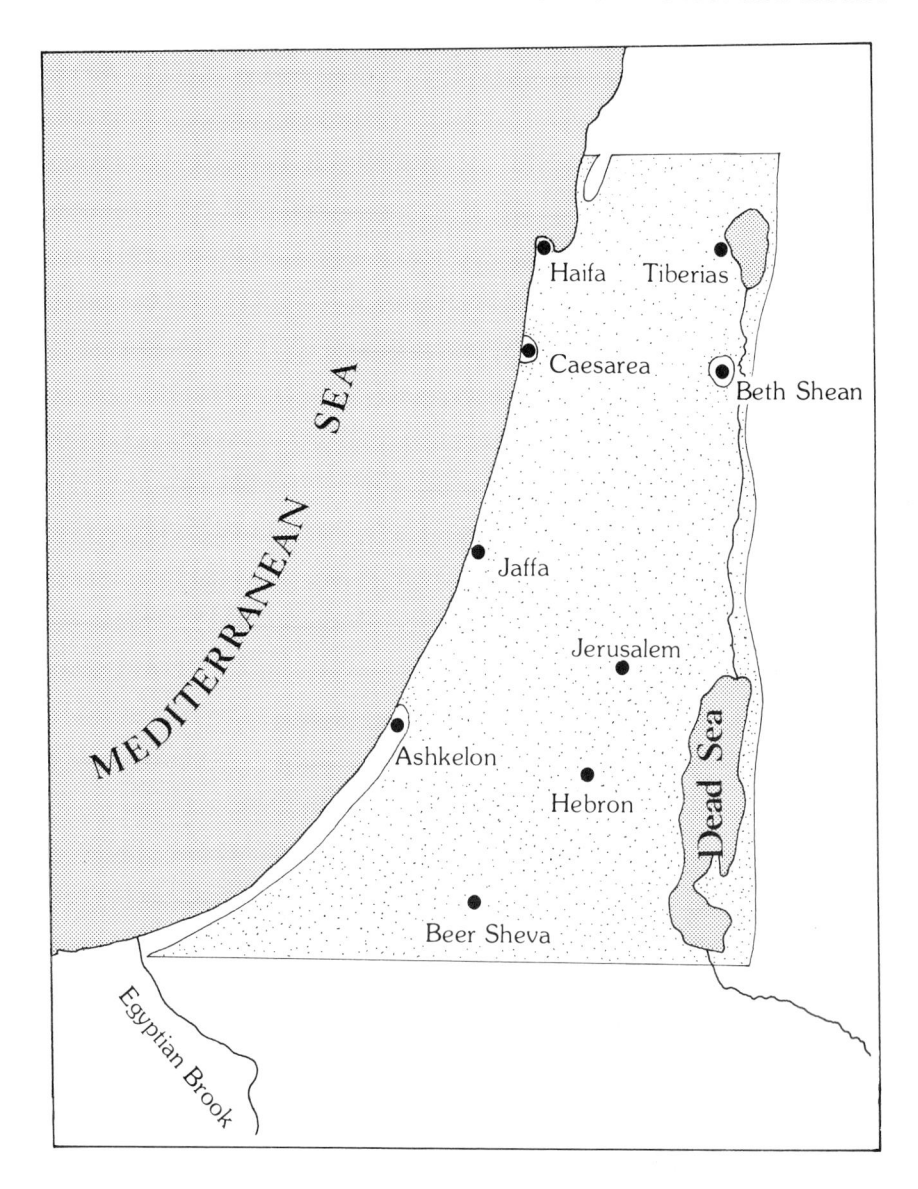

Map 4: Second Influx—*Olei Bavel* (c. 350 B.C.E.) Based on Rabbi N. Tukatzinsky's map.

encompass parts of the Upper Galilee, the Gaza Strip, and other Negev regions.

Ezra's Sanctification of Jerusalem

Whereas the previous Commonwealth had only effected temporary sanctification of the Land, King Solomon had, in fact, permanently consecrated the walled city of Jerusalem and the Temple Mount. Therefore Ezra's ceremony of sanctifying Jerusalem (Neh. 12:27-47), as dictated by law, was commemorative rather than actual. He paraded around the walls with two Thanksgiving loaves of bread, followed by the Sanhedrin and Levites joyfully singing Psalms. Two essential elements were conspicuously absent — the king and the *urim* and *tumim*. Without them the ceremony was legally invalid. Nevertheless, it honored the memory of King Solomon's first and permanent sanctification of Jerusalem.

Over the course of history the walls of Jerusalem were built and destroyed four times. This is a photograph of the present wall built 300 years ago by the Turks.

Ezra's sanctification of Jerusalem was only ceremonial. This photograph shows a section of the upper rampart along the outer wall of the Old City built by the Turks.

Rambam asks, "Why do we hold that the Temple and Jerusalem were sanctified for all time while the rest of Eretz Yisrael (in regards to the laws of tithes and so on) was not?" *HaShem* declares this Himself when He says, "For now I have chosen and sanctified this house, that My name may be there forever, and My eyes and My heart shall be there perpetually" (II Chron. 7:16). The holiness of the Temple and Jerusalem stems directly from the Divine Presence which, once attaching itself, never ceased to exist there. The verse, "...and I will bring your sanctuaries to desolation" (Lev. 26:31), hints to this. The Talmud explains that even while in desolation, they are still *sanctuaries* and their holiness remains with them.

Significance of Ezra's Occupation of the Land

As we have seen, the land of Eretz Yisrael was formally and legally sanctified twice in history. Through Joshua's conquest the seeds of holiness unique to the Land of Israel sprouted forth for the first time, but with the Babylonian exile they wilted and receded back to their original latency. The second sanctification was effected by Ezra. Once again the seeds germinated, this time with an indomitable spirit that would never again be cancelled, and the Land became unconditionally and eternally holy in a legally significant way. Thus the boundaries of *Olei Bavel* became effective then and remain so today even while we are exiled and only a small percentage of world Jewry actually dwells in the Land. Most agree, however, that this sanctity is Rabbinically derived and does not originate with the Torah itself.

Nevertheless, laws concerning the produce of the land apply unequivocally within the boundaries fixed by the Second Influx and are secondarily extended by Rabbinic decree to include the additional territories of the First Commonwealth, Suria and certain other areas.

Laws of Tithes

By way of introduction, Rabbi Samson Raphael Hirsch writes: "One portion should be taken from what the earth has yielded as commodities for use by human beings...You should not use that portion for personal purposes but dedicate it to G-d, declaring thereby that G-d is L-rd of the earth and that only through Him have you any right to the earth and to the fruit it yields....

"The purposes which are to be served by (the different types of tithes) correspond entirely to the purposes to which our material means altogether could be, and should be, directed. They are the care of the spirit, one's spiritual life—the tithe to be given to the Levite; the care of the body, one's material life—the tithe to be eaten by oneself in Jerusalem; the care of the well-being of one's fellowman—the tithe to be given to the poor...These three tithes are just to bring to our minds our duty to assign, dedicate and direct the whole of our fortune to these three purposes prescribed by G-d, as is expressed in the verse, 'so that you may learn to fear the L-rd your G-d at all times'" (Deut. 14:23).

1. All produce grown for human consumption in Eretz Yisrael must be tithed before being eaten. This means that a portion must be separated and dedicated for one of several holy purposes. Before tithe is taken the produce is considered *tevel* (*lo*=not, *tev*=good) and a Jew is forbidden both from eating and deriving benefit from it. He may not even sow the grains in his field. One who transgresses this obligation is punishable with premature death. All food grown in Israel and sold without rabbinical endorsement is considered *tevel*, and must be tithed.

2. The Torah only mentions (Deut. 18:4) seven types of produce—wheat, barley, rye, oats, spelt, olives and grapes (including their oils, juices and wines)—as being subject to the law of tithe. Today, since the Biblical command is contingent upon all Jewry living in Eretz Yisrael, tithing is generally considered a Rabbinic ordinance and *all* fruits and vegetables are equally subject to this obligation.
3. Four tithes are required by law. When the Temple stands there are eleven commandments regulating tithes and the farmer separates his crop according to the following percentages:

	NAME OF TITHE	PERCENT	RECIPIENT OF TITHE
1	*terumah gedolah* the priestly tithe	2%	any priest
2	*maaser rishon* the first Levite tithe	9.8%	any Levite
3	*terumath maaser* priestly portion of the Levite tithe		Levite separates 10% of his *maaser rishon* and gives it to any priest.
4	*maaser sheni* the second tithe or *maaser oni* the tenth to the poor	8.8%	The farmer himself eats his *maaser sheni*, but only in Jerusalem during Temple times. *Maaser sheni* applies in four of the seven years of any Sabbatical cycle. *Maaser oni* is separated in the third and sixth years.
		20.6%	This is the percentage of the harvest that is separated for tithe. (11.8% went to the priests and Levites; 8.8% was either eaten in Jerusalem or given to the needy.)

4. Today, since the Torah forbids us from wasting food, we separate a much smaller percentage (slightly over 1%) and dispose of it. We must throw it away rather than eat it because no one other than authorized priests are permitted to consume these tithes (no. 1 and 3), even today. And since all priests are halachically

impure — and purity is a necessary condition to eating their portion — no one can make use of it.

5. Therefore we separate one percent as *terumath maaser* (the priestly portion of the Levite tithe) and a fraction of a percent for *terumah gedolah*, the priestly tithe. (Since the Torah does not specify a minimum amount, even the smallest percent fulfills this obligation.) *Maaser rishon* (the first Levite tithe) is separated in name only. The value of *maaser sheni*, the portion previously eaten by the farmer himself in Jerusalem, is transferred to a coin, freeing the food of its sanctity, and allowing it to be eaten by anyone.

6. It is important that tithes be separated in the proper sequence: first the priestly tithe, then the Levite tithe, and finally the second tithe. If one separates the second tithe before the Levite tithe, or the Levite before the priestly tithe, he has violated a Rabbinic law. Nevertheless, he does not repeat the separation. The priestly portion of the Levite tithe may be separated either before or after the second tithe. The produce is considered *tevel*, untithed, and is forbidden for enjoyment until *all* separations have been completed.

7. Separate tithes must be taken from each type of fruit or vegetable purchased from the same place, *and* from identical types of produce purchased from different places. This insures against violating certain stipulations. For example, the tithe from fruit grown in a previous year cannot cover fruit grown in the current year, nor vice versa. It is possible that the same fruits from different stores actually grew in subsequent years, but were stored for different lengths of time. Additional restrictions include the following: separations from already tithed produce will not cover that which has never been tithed; tithes from imported fruits and vegetables which are exempt from the obligation altogether will not cover indigenously grown species which *must* be tithed; tithes from marketed produce will not cover that grown in one's private garden. Since the origin, history, and status of commercially marketed produce is not known, one should separate tithes as recommended above.

8. The official year for taking tithes begins on Rosh HaShannah for everything except fruits. Their new year begins on Tu b'Shevat. Therefore produce which has reached a certain point of maturity before the official New Year is considered produce of the previous year and tithed accordingly (particularly in regard to whether *maaser sheni* or *maaser oni* is required). Grains, beans, olives and grapes of one third maturity; fruits when recognizable; and vegetables from the time of harvesting, are all included with the previous year.

9. It is forbidden to tithe on the Sabbath or festivals. The tithe of a minor is not valid, and the food remains *tevel*. Food of the Sabbatical year is exempt from the obligation of tithes.
10. Today after separating slightly over 1% of the food(s) in question, we make an oral declaration and designate certain portions of both the separated and remaining food to fulfill each of the obligatory tithes. The tithe and its produce must remain stationary while reciting the statement. Liquids should be at rest. After completing the declaration, one wraps the separated portion in plastic or foil, etc., and discards it.
11. As mentioned previously, the value of *maaser sheni*, the second tithe, was transferred onto a coin, thus freeing the food for ordinary consumption. There are certain conditions for conducting this transfer.
    — The coin must be of local currency and worth at least a *perutah* (1/40 gram of pure silver), a value which fluctuates with the currency market.
    — Each time the declaration is made, whether for one or many types of foods, a single *perutah* is required. However many *perutoth* there are in the coin, that is the number of times it can be used. When it becomes "full" one must begin with another coin.
    — A coin which has been used for tithing must be handled in a special way. It cannot be used as pocket money. One should consult a rabbi for details.
    — The coins need not be in one's possession at the time of declaration. As long as they have been set apart and designated as *maaser sheni* coinage, it is sufficient.
12. It is forbidden to redeem *maaser sheni* in this way within the ancient walls of Jerusalem. Under such circumstances a rabbinic authority should be consulted.
13. As discussed previously, only certain years require separation of *maaser sheni* (the second, pilgrimage tithe), and the others require *maaser oni* (the tithe for the poor). Therefore every third and sixth year after *shemitah* (the Sabbatical year) *maaser oni* replaces *maaser sheni*. If it is certain that the food has not been tithed, the 9% *maaser oni* must be given to a needy person. However, a rabbinical authority should be consulted. If it is not clear whether the fruit needs separation of *maaser oni* or *maaser sheni*, both are removed and the latter is redeemed.
14. It is forbidden to eat fruit produced during the first three years of a tree's growth (known as *orlah*). In the fourth year the fruit is called *ravai* (a fourth-year tree), and is distinguished by the Torah with special holiness which exempts it from the laws of *terumah* and *maaser*. The sanctity of *ravai* is identical with that

The Second Influx / 115

Many fruit shops hang a sign similar to the one on the right showing the buyer that all necessary tithes have been taken by a representative of the rabbinical court. The sign on the left is a shemitah sign showing that there is no problem of forbidden Sabbatical fruit at this market.

of *maaser sheni* (to be eaten in holiness in Jerusalem, etc.), and is redeemable on the coins used to redeem *maaser sheni*.

15. In practice, one proceeds as follows when separating tithes.

a. He removes slightly over 1% of each type of produce and sets it aside. All the food should remain before him, both the tithe and the remainder. Everything should be stationary.

b. If the food is definitely *tevel* (untithed) he recites the following **two** sets of blessings and declarations. If one does not know for certain whether the food has been tithed (which is generally the case with commercial produce today), he omits the blessings and recites the declarations.

c. **Blessing I**: Blessed are You, *HaShem*, our G-d, King of the universe, who has sanctified us with His commandments and has commanded us to separate *terumoth* on tithes.

d. **Declaration I**: Whatever is more than 1% of all that I have set aside is hereby declared to be the priestly tithe and is the northerly side of the portion. The one percent remaining here together with nine similar portions on the upper side of this produce is declared to be the first Levite tithe. The one percent which I set aside as the first Levite tithe is hereby declared to be the priestly portion of the Levite tithe. Nine more equal portions on the southerly side of the produce are declared to be the second tithe, but if this produce must have the tithe of the poor separated from it — let the lower nine portions be the tithe of the poor.

e. If the second tithe had definitely not been separated as yet, the following blessing and declaration are recited. If there is doubt as to whether the second tithe has been redeemed (which is the usual case in commercial produce), the blessing is omitted, but the declaration is recited.

f. **Blessing II**: Blessed are You, *HaShem*, our G-d, King of the universe, who has sanctified us with His commandments and has commanded us to redeem the second tithe.

g. **Declaration II**: This second tithe — and its extra fifth — is redeemed by one *perutah* out of the coin which I have set aside for the redemption of the second tithe.

h. The separated tithes are now wrapped in plastic, etc., and discarded. Liquids may be poured down the drain.

Agrarian Laws: Division of the World into Three Sectors

The agricultural *mitzvoth* do not apply uniformly to all lands. Rather, in relation to these commandments the world divides into three areas: Eretz Yisrael as defined by Joshua and Ezra, Suria, and *chutz l'aretz*. The latter is subdivided into those countries which immediately surround Israel, and the rest of the world. Each of these territories is regulated, to a different degree, by the Torah's agricultural laws.

For example Israel's neighboring countries, Egypt, Moab and Amon are Rabbinically obligated in a number of agricultural laws, while the rest of *chutz l'aretz* is, with one or two exceptions, completely exempt. Suria, Israel's northern neighbor, possesses a certain degree of holiness which subjects it to a wider range of Rabbinical injunctions.

Era of the Diaspora

During the four hundred and twenty years that the Second Temple stood, four separate empires reigned over the Land of Israel. First was the Persian monarchy which ruled for only thirty-four years and then followed one hundred and eighty years of Greek influence. A small band of heroic Jewish patriots, successfully rebelled against the suppression of Torah and religious observance imposed by Greek reign and substituted a Torah government which ruled for one hundred and three years. (The miraculous success of the Hasmoneans, the family of Jews directing the revolt, is remembered and celebrated on the festival of Chanuka). The final one hundred and three years, Israel was governed by the corrupt Herodian dynasty, the ruling family of Judea at the time. The Roman Empire's invasion of the Land reached its climax with the destruction of the Holy Temple in 69 C.E.

The Temple in ruins, a foreign and oppressive government ruling the Land, their center of gravity was gone and the Jews drifted throughout the world, becoming more and more dispersed with each passing generation. Centuries later, Eretz Yisrael became a dream to the Jews in the Diaspora, Jerusalem a mythical legend, an impossible reality. The Temple Mount lay desolate for more than five hundred years until the Moslem authorities converted it into one of their sacred sites.

Only a Dream?

An independent Jewish nation on its own soil with its own king? A Holy Temple that all kingdoms considered the spiritual center of the world? Had this ever really been? And even more unbelievable, would these come to be again? A long, dark exile threatened to swallow the Jewish people. Yet the scattered nation survived and even prospered at times. It was their Torah and their devotion to G-d, which they carried with them throughout their wanderings, that sustained them both individually and collectively.

Jewish scholarship reached its pinnacle with the progressive codification of the Oral Law. First with the Mishna and Talmud, then Maimonides' encyclopedic masterpiece, the *Mishna Torah*. It was during this exile that Rashi wrote his now famous commentaries on *Chumash* and Talmud. The hidden, Kabbalistic dimensions of Torah began to be revealed and explicated. The *Shulchan Aruch* and other codes of Law were composed in these "dark ages."

With continents and centuries separating the Jew from his homeland, still the remembrance and the dream of Eretz Yisrael lived on in the hearts of her people. The Rabbis instituted yearly fast days to mourn the destruction of the Temple and the loss of the Land. In every wedding of every Jew throughout the world, the groom breaks a glass to remind all present that even in this most joyous of occasions, our rejoicing is incomplete as long as the Temple lies in ruins. Every Jewish home leaves a portion of the wall unpainted, for no house can be finished while the House of G-d is yet unbuilt. Daily the Jew prays for his return to Jerusalem, not as a secular city, but as the site of the Temple, the Sanhedrin, and center of the Messianic Commonwealth.

Reason for Second Day *Yom Tov* Today

After the destruction of the Second Temple, the Sages fixed a calendar based on astronomical calculations that would apply during exile, when it would no longer be possible to rely on the system of witnesses and couriers. Since no one anymore would be relying on messengers, the observance of two days became theoretically unnecessary. Nevertheless, the Sages decreed that all areas outside this ten-day radius of Jerusalem should continue to observe two days of *yom tov* in remembrance of two things. First, that they live in exile and must continue to follow the ancient custom of their forebears. Second, to constantly remind us that the original declaration of the months depends on Jews living in Eretz Yisrael. He, the Jew, is above time. He decrees the calendar, and his power and ability to do so originates in Jerusalem, the center of the world and dwelling place of the *Shechinah*.

Today, while Rambam rules that only those living within the boundaries sanctified by Ezra may observe one day of *yom tov*, all other authorities include the entire area occupied by Joshua in this category. This includes the present borders of Israel. Those areas of *chutz l'aretz* which are within this ten-day radius of Jerusalem generally keep two days *yom tov*.

The Laws of Festival Observance for a Temporary Visitor in Israel

1. A temporary visitor to Israel must still observe the second day of *yom tov* since his actual home is in *chutz l'aretz*.
2. When visiting Israel, second day *yom tov* prayers must generally be said privately unless there is a minyan of travellers who are able to pray together.
3. A visitor may be called to the Torah on his second day *yom tov*, which for the congregation is the first of their intermediate days, even though he needs to hear a different portion of the Torah read.
4. If the visitor decides to settle in Eretz Yisrael then he only observes one day of *yom tov*. A rabbinical authority should be consulted before changing one's own status in this way.

The True Freedom

Even throughout this long, dark night of exile the hope of return never perished from the Jewish heart. Their sense of nationhood remained with them in all their wanderings through foreign lands, marking history with expulsions, pogroms, and exterminations. Collectively the Jewish People retained their loyalty to G-d, Torah, and the obligations of their religious observance. Nevertheless, these tribulations have taken their toll. Weary of the strain of such unceasing and existential insecurity, many Jews have succumbed to the lure of materialism as a way of introducing comfort and stability into their lives. The dream of Israel, Jerusalem, the Holy Temple, and Messiah grows dim. The vision becomes interpreted as mirage. Yet still a spark remains. A deep inner sense of connectedness to one's legacy as a Jew, to one's noble history. And always, there burns the primal, subconscious longing for the era of perfection...peace...*Mashiach*, may he come soon.

6

The Messianic *Eretz Yisrael*

Futuristic Map Based on Ancient Sources

The boundaries of Eretz Yisrael, in the Messianic era, will change drastically. As the influence of Torah—its monotheism and morality—extends throughout the world, so will the real and metaphorical territories of Eretz Yisrael expand accordingly. The details of these changes and the final redrafting of the map of the Land are mentioned only cryptically in the Pentateuch, Prophets, and various talmudic sources.

Much discussion centers around this verse in Scripture which is understood to have foreshadowed all that was to come. "Behold, I set before you this Land. Go in and possess this Land which the L-rd swore to give to your forefathers...and to their seed after them" (Deut. 1:8). Breaking the verse down into pieces, it outlines the phases of history in relation to Eretz Yisrael. "Go in and possess the land" commands them to possess it without weapons and warfare. Had they been on a proper level of loving and trusting G-d, they would have entered and no one would have opposed them. With the sin of the spies they forfeited this option. The verse continues, "...to give it to them." This refers to those Jews of the First Influx. "And to their seed." These are the Jews of the Second Influx. Finally, "...after them." This is the Messianic era.

Ezekiel's Prophesy

The Messianic phase is described in the Book of Ezekiel, chapters 47-48. The prophet traces the boundaries and allocates to each of the twelve tribes an identical portion of land. Ezekiel divides the country into thirteen equal and parallel strips (approximately 53 miles wide) running east and west. The strip which includes Jerusalem lies between tribes seven and eight, and is given to the priests and Levites (see Map 6).

Beginning with Dan in the north and ending with Gad in the south, (a distance of over 600 miles), this apportionment is strikingly different in two ways from the original division of land. First, Joshua assigned the territories, not uniformly and arbitrarily, but by Divine lottery. Second, the size of each portion directly accommodated the tribe's population. Here, however, Ezekiel assigns specific land to each tribe, and size is not a consideration.

Decoding the Mysterious Maps

It is curious that Ezekiel's Messianic boundary lines duplicate those marked out by the Torah in Numbers 34:3-12, in the passage which designates the Land to be occupied by the First Influx. Yet the Third Messianic Commonwealth is to include the territory of *ten* nations (rather than seven) and so should cover a larger area of land. How is this future expansion represented in Ezekiel's prophesy? Also, why should a tribe with twice the population of another be confined to the same area of land? (Such a policy would seem to "punish" large tribes, for the plot of land inherited by individuals of the large tribe becomes half the size of homesteads in the less populated portion.) Finally, where are these Lost Tribes? How will we recognize them? How will they appear to claim their inheritance?

The Riddles Unraveled

Malbim, a nineteenth century Torah scholar and saint, solves these riddles by carefully scrutinizing the text. He derives from Ezekiel's words that Eretz Yisrael will, in fact, expand beyond its previous boundaries, stretching northward to include Mount Gilead and King David's acquisitions in Aram; east into the Transjordan and south into the wilderness of Sinai. This defines an area of land greatly excelling that occupied during either of the previous Commonwealths.

By studying carefully the exact language of Ezekiel's vision, Malbim concludes that the tribal allocations of land are flexible and

The Messianic Eretz Yisrael / 125

will vary according to population. He bases this on the phrase, "This is the eastern direction" (Ezek. 28:18). Malbim explains this to mean that although the width of each strip is equal for each tribe, its length is variable and could extend indefinitely beyond the Jordan and will do so in accordance with the multitude of each tribe. Furthermore,

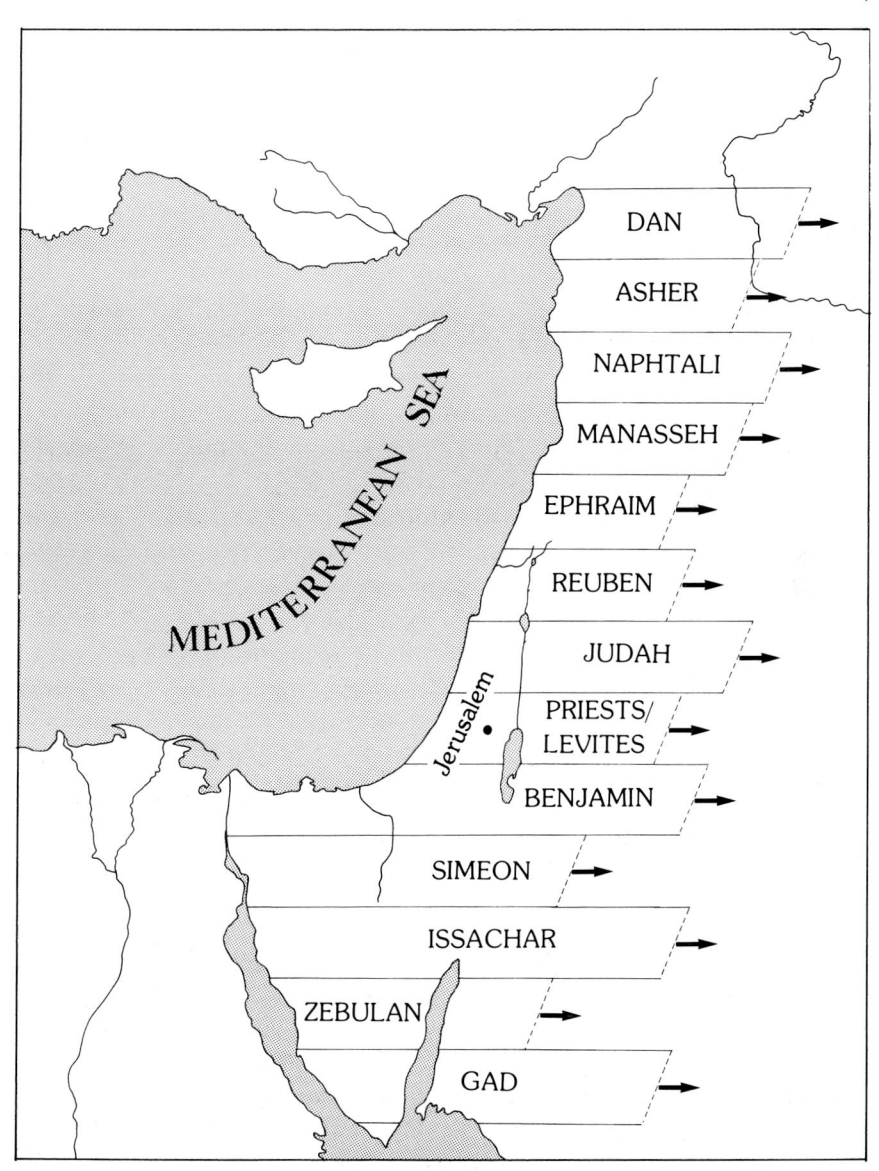

Map 6: *Boundaries of the Future* (Ezek. 48-49). This speculative map is based on the commentaries of Rashi and Malbim.

the vast Arabian Desert in the south and east will be transformed into lush and fertile farmland, as it says, "For the L-rd shall comfort Zion. He will comfort all her destroyed places. He will make her wilderness like Eden, and her desert like the garden of the L-rd..." (Isa. 51:3).

Finally, Malbim explains that the prophesy of Ezekiel is G-d's personal guarantee that the tribes will not atrophy into extinction during the long night of exile, and that in the Messianic era He will make their identity known, and He will bring them back to claim their inheritance. Malbim learns from the text that these ten Lost Tribes will actually be more populated than they were before their exile.

The Final Redemption

The Midrash asks, Why does Scripture refer to song in the feminine form (*shirah*, the "*-ah*" being a feminine ending) except for the "Song of the Future" (Psalms 96:1, and Isa. 26:1) where it uses the masculine case (*shir* without the feminine "*-ah*")? This is because the two types of song parallel the qualities of maleness and femaleness. A woman's nature is cyclical. Her rhythms follow the moon. When she becomes pregnant and bears her child, she may thus conceive again, and the spiral turns round. This simulates Israel's history — its cycles of redemption and exile. Yet its future deliverance, the Messianic salvation, will be final. Never again will the Jews be spit from their Land, and dispersed among the nations. This end to their cyclic history is expressed by the linguistic shift from feminine to masculine case.

Another Midrash cites Rabbi Levi's statement that "In the future Jerusalem will be like Eretz Yisrael and Eretz Yisrael like the entire world." This means that on some level, the actual land mass of those ten nations originally promised to Abraham will have expanded to include the whole world. This is most easily understood figuratively. It means that all peoples will recognize G-d's Oneness, and His sovereignty will extend throughout the planet. Since Israel's only purpose is to reveal this message of G-d's ultimate unity, then wherever they succeed, it is as though that "territory" were annexed. Since the Messianic era is, by definition, a time of *world* peace, harmony and awareness of G-d, then the "psychological state" of Israel will have expanded to include the entire planet. "G-d shall be King upon all the earth. In that day G-d shall be One and His Name One" (Zech. 14:9).

Yet if Israel's boundaries are to expand in this way, why doesn't the Torah say so explicitly? This is because the broader boundaries represent a further stage in the End of Days and the Torah only brings

The Messianic Eretz Yisrael / 127

This aerial photograph was taken by an American satellite and shows Eretz Yisrael from the beginning of the Sinai desert until Lebanon and eastwards into present-day Jordan. The Dead Sea and the Sea of Galilee are connected by the Jordan River.

us to the threshold of this entirely new chapter in human existence. It is well known that the Torah only alludes to the world-to-come, choosing not to discuss such things explicitly. Words cannot describe these realities, and the mind cannot comprehend that which is so totally beyond its experience. Imagery is easily misinterpreted and can even be dangerous. Therefore, the Torah refrains from mentioning such things altogether. This includes the latter stages of the Messianic era when the world will begin its transition into the world-to-come. First the Messiah will conquer the three remaining nations promised to Abraham. Later, the Lost Tribes will return and the borders traced by Ezekiel will be realized. Finally, and this is something we cannot imagine, evil will be utterly destroyed and only righteousness will have existence. This is what it means that the sovereignty of the Holy Land will spread out to engulf the planet, transforming the earth into a global *Eretz Chayim*.

Next Year in Jerusalem

It was a Passover Seder in Jerusalem, and someone asked the renowned Kabbalist, Rabbi Asher Zelig Margolyoth, why we still say "This year we are here, next year may we be in the Land of Israel" since we are already here. Perhaps we should leave out these lines of the Haggadah. The Kabbalist smiled and answered by explaining the esoteric meanings of these statements. "Though we live within the territory of Israel, still we are in exile. Redemption is not just a physical reality, it is a psychological and spiritual one as well. Furthermore, no single Jew can be redeemed until every one is freed from the bondage of exile. The Jerusalem of the Haggadah is not this teeming metropolis, nor is Eretz Yisrael this political state which actually breeds animosity between Jews. No, this is not redemption. True it is preferable to live here than in *chutz l'aretz*, but G-d willing, may we live in *Mashiach's* Jerusalem, and plow the land of *redeemed* Israel. May we celebrate the Passover Seder in spiritual freedom, when all Jews will have claimed their inheritance in the *eternal* Eretz Yisrael."

Part 3

Beneath the Holy Altar

Everyone who binds himself to the Holy Land while alive, will merit to bind himself with the heavenly Eretz Yisrael upon his death.

Zohar

1

Altar of Atonement

The Visible Side

The beauty of Israel — its landscapes, historical monuments, and holy sites — excites the senses and satisfies the soul. The Western Wall of the Great Temple where G-d's glory was most revealed; Machpelah, the burial place of Abraham and Sarah, Isaac and Rebecca, Jacob and Leah, the spiritual giants in Jewish history; Mount Zion, the site of David's palace; Massada, where a stronghold of Jews held out against the entire Roman army, strengthened by their faith in G-d and commitment to Torah — these are Israel's tourist attractions — these, which document her people's rich and glorious odyssey. No one can see them and remain unmoved. They touch the heart and inspire a pride in one's Jewish heritage. For residents Israel has even more to offer. The opportunity to fulfill *mitzvoth* specific to Eretz Yisrael, *mitzvoth* that one cannot perform elsewhere, enriches a person's life and deepens his relationship to G-d.

The Sages elaborate. As soon as a person walks four strides (*amoth*) in Eretz Yisrael, he is guaranteed a portion in the world-to-come, and all his sins are forgiven. One can even rely on the technicality and disembark from a ship or airplane, walk several strides, return to *chutz l'aretz*, and still merit this great reward. Rebbe Nachman of Breslov, reflecting on his visit to Eretz Yisrael in 1801,

132 / BENEATH THE HOLY ALTAR

The Western Wall of the Temple is the focal point of Jewish prayer. Here a group of 12-year old school children from Tel Aviv visit the Wall. They are all wearing paper yarmulkes provided to them by the gatekeeper.

recalled his sense of accomplishment upon fulfilling the Sages' dictum when he said, "I achieved my goal of coming to Israel the moment I walked four *amoth* in the Holy Land."

Why should the soil of Eretz Yisrael inspire such passion in its visitors? Maharal of Prague answers this question. Every Jew has a share in Eretz Yisrael, a four-*amoth* plot of land that is particularly his. His portion of Eretz Yisrael in this world secures him a share in the world-to-come, for that, too, is called land, as it says, "The righteous shall inherit the land" (Psalms 37:29), and the reward for righteousness is clearly in the world-to-come. Thus when a Jew takes four steps in Eretz Yisrael, he assumes ownership of his legal inheritance in this world, and thereby claims his portion in the world-to-come.

The venerable Rabbi Hamnuna immigrated to Eretz Yisrael from Babylonia with a dozen of his disciples. En route he revealed the purpose of his trip. "I am travelling to the Holy Land not for my sake and my pleasure, rather all these years I have held my soul as a security and now I must return it to its owner." That is to say, in coming to Israel, the Land of Jewish inheritance, his soul could assume its position and fulfill its responsibilities in the collective soul of Israel.

Four Expressions of Love of Eretz Yisrael

The Talmud relates, in its own cryptic style, four instances where Sages dramatically expressed their love of Eretz Yisrael. The stories are not easily decipherable and require explanation. Rabbi Abba kissed the stones when he landed at Acco. Rabbi Chanina was travelling on foot to the Holy Land from Babylonia and as he approached Eretz Yisrael, he began to stop every mile or so to weigh a fist-sized stone. When he noticed their weight increasing he knew he was in Israel. Rabbi Ami and Rabbi Asi would study under the shade of a tree. Hours would pass and when the sun began to invade their recluse, they would shift to another shady spot. In wintertime the opposite was so. They would move from shade to sun. This was their practice so as not to show disrespect for yishuv ha'aretz, the mitzvah of dwelling in Israel. Rabbi Chiya bar Gamda, expressed his love of the Land by rolling in its dust and so fulfilling the words of praise, "Your servants hold her stones dear. They cherish her very dust."

The Talmud did not choose to record these anecdotes arbitrarily. Rather each illustrates one of the four dimensions and elements of the Holy Land. The stones which Rabbi Abba kissed represent the wellsprings of "water" in Eretz Yisrael as it says, "A land of brooks, fountains, and depths" (Deut. 8:7), for throughout their journeying in the desert, it was stones that supplied their water. Rabbi Chanina's prediction that the rocks of Eretz Yisrael would be heavier than elsewhere was based on the wisdom he imagined infused within them. How did he know this would be so? Scripture describes Eretz Yisrael as "A land whose stones (abaneya) are steel" (Deut. 8:9). The Sages make a play on words and read builders (boneya) instead of stones (abaneya), referring to Torah scholars who are called *builders* because they *construct* the oral tradition, and whose study of Torah sharpens their minds like a steel blade. The anecdote of Rabbis Ami and Asi moving from sun to shade and shade to sun demonstrates how their love of the Land affected their studies. In those early generations almost *nothing* would interfere with a Sage's learning—neither cold nor heat, sun nor shade. Although totally immersed in Torah studies, these Sages never lost contact with their surroundings—the Holy Land. Therefore, in the summer they purposely interrupted their studies when the sunlight invaded their recluse and, like anybody else—except a Torah Sage—moved to another shady spot. This was their way of acknowledging the importance of yishuv ha'aretz. When Rabbi Chiya chose to roll in the dirt, he was dramatizing the fact that those buried in Eretz and accompanying it to the gravesite are considered expressions of *pure* giving, for one's generosity will not be reciprocated—the recipient, the dead person, is no longer in this world.

Burial allows the body to return to the dust from which it came. "The dust (of the body) returns to the earth as it was. The spirit returns to G-d who gave it" (Ecc. 12:7)—and thus a cycle of life is completed.

Interestingly, the Scriptural commandment to bury the departed is not only for the dead person himself but for the land as well, particularly Eretz Yisrael, as the verse continues, "You shall surely bury him...that you defile not your Land which the L-rd your G-d gave you for an inheritance." This is another piece of evidence that connects the Land of Israel with the soul's inheritance of the world-to-come. Unless the soul is free to claim her portion above (which can only happen once the body is buried below), then the earth cannot repossess the dust which is its rightful property and the Land is called defiled.

Under the Temple's Altar

Rabbi Enan, a Sage of the fourth century, taught concerning the desirability of burial in Eretz Yisrael. He compared it to having one's grave under the Temple's sacrificial altar, based on the verse, "An altar of earth you shall make for Me" (Ex. 20:21). Since Scripture also says, "His people will be atoned by His earth" (Deut. 32:43), Rabbi Enan proved that burial in Israel atones for transgression as if each body were on the very spot of the Holy Temple's altar, the one point on the entire planet's surface where sacrifices were offered in accordance with Torah as atonement and reparation for sin.

Similarly, Maharsha explains that just as the soul returns in purity to the place from whence it was taken, so does the body return in purity to its place of origin, the site of the altar, and source of the dust used to fashion Adam's body. Based on the sanctity of Eretz Yisrael and the inherent purity of the land itself, Scripture says, "His people are atoned by His Land." Tradition teaches that regardless of where in Eretz Yisrael one is buried, it is reckoned as if it were at the place of forgiveness, the site of the altar, the place where *HaShem* gathered the dust for His primordial man.

Abraham Secures a Burial Cave

Another seventeenth century writer comments, "So paramount is the importance of burial in Eretz Yisrael that it is beyond the power of speech to describe. Yet it is hinted to in the story of Abraham's extraordinary efforts to secure a burial plot for his wife Sarah in the cave of Machpelah. Scripture, which is maximally terse, devotes much time to explaining the details of this encounter. Obviously the Torah considers his efforts most significant, and we, as descendants of Abraham, must follow his precedent and seek energetically to be buried in the Holy Land."

Abraham's determination to secure an appropriate burial spot for his wife, writes Malbim, was a public demonstration of his belief in the basic tenet of faith that the soul lives beyond the body and there will be a resurrection of the dead. For these reasons we learn from Abraham that one should choose a respectable burial plot in a Jewish cemetery, and be careful not to place righteous persons next to sinful ones. The Hittites, the original owners of Machpelah, the cave which Abraham purchased as a burial site, were atheists. They viewed death as the end of existence on all levels. The soul did not live on without the body and did not have to clear its account with the Creator. There were no consequences for misdeeds and no future resurrection.

They buried their dead only to protect the living from having to be reminded of their loss, and to prevent diseases caused by a decomposing corpse. Whenever it became more trouble than it was worth, they would simply bury the body in an unmarked spot in a

Machpelah is located in Hebron. It is the burial site of Abraham and Sarah, Isaac and Rebecca, Jacob and Leah, Adam and Eve.

corner of a field or forest. Abraham, on the other hand, was willing to pay any price and make any effort to secure a proper burial place for his wife. He understood that the peace of her soul and the resurrection of her body depended upon this. The cave itself has two stories. The lower cave symbolizes this material world where man toils to perfect his life through good deeds and devotion to G-d. The second story is the celestial realm where a soul ascends after death, to bask in the spiritual radiance of its Creator.

"Immigration" After Death

Proof that the value and privilege of burial in Israel is part of our instinctive Jewishness is the number of people who, after living their entire lives in *chutz l'aretz*, nevertheless request burial in the Holy Land. They are following the precedent of their ancestors, Jacob and Joseph, who made their progeny swear to carry their remains to Israel for burial.

Recently, in the Spring of 1986, Rabbi Moshe Feinstein, *zatzal*, passed away in New York City. For nearly half a century he was the most prominent rabbinical authority in America. Yet he requested to be buried in Eretz Yisrael. It came to pass that on Purim-in-Jerusalem (*Shushan Purim*) a quarter of a million mourners escorted him to his last resting place.

Signs like this one announce the arrival of a coffin for burial in Eretz Yisrael. The words in bold letters read: His coffin has arrived.

Even when someone is buried in *chutz l'aretz*, a handful of soil from Eretz Yisrael is often placed in the coffin, since the soil itself is said to carry this power of atonement.

A story is told of two Sages walking through the streets of Tiberias who saw several coffins arriving from *chutz l'aretz* awaiting burial in Israel. One criticized the practice, wondering at the hypocrisy of these people who lived their entire lives in other lands, and only now came to Eretz Yisrael when it no longer involved any sacrifice of material comfort. "Are they not guilty of 'making (*HaShem*'s) heritage an abomination...' (Jer. 2:7) by abandoning Eretz Yisrael in their lives, and now '...defiling (His) land' by having their impure bodies brought here for burial?" His companion disagreed. "Once they reach Eretz Yisrael and a clod of earth is placed on their coffins, they are forgiven all their sins, including, obviously, their decision to live outside of Israel, as the verse says, 'His people are atoned by His soil'" (Deut. 32:43).

The soil of Eretz Yisrael has the power to atone for sins.

A commentator supports this idea with a verse from Psalms 146:4, which reads, "His breath (spirit, soul) leaves him and he returns to his earth." This passage may be read as follows: "His soul leaves him (in *chutz l'aretz*) causing his body to return to the primordial earth (which is Eretz Yisrael)." This is based on the promise that this will bring expiation for all his sins, as it says, "His people are atoned by His earth."

Rabbi Meir's Last Wish

Rabbi Meir passed away in Essa, a town in *chutz l'aretz* east of the Sea of Galilee. A distinguished Rabbi of Israel, he insisted that the people of Eretz Yisrael take responsibility for bringing his body to the

Rabbi Meir's tomb is located on the southeastern shore of the Sea of Galilee, just outside of Tiberias.

Holy Land for burial. Despite assurances that his wish would be fulfilled, he requested the local inhabitants to place his coffin on the seashore until it could actually be brought to the Holy Land. He based his unusual demand on a verse from Psalms which reads, "For He has founded it upon the sea, and established it (Eretz Yisrael) upon the rivers" (Psalms 24:2). Since Israel is in fact an island surrounded by seven bodies of water, every seashore has at least an indirect link with the Holy Land.

Ulah, a Sage of the fourth century, travelled back and forth from Eretz Yisrael to Babylonia. Much to his dismay, death threatened to overtake him in *chutz l'aretz*, and he was anguished by the fact that he was dying outside of the Holy Land. "Don't cry," comforted his Rabbis and companions, "we'll take you to Eretz Yisrael for burial." Ulah was not appeased. "What pleasure will that give me?" he sighed. "My jewel, my soul, will be lost in an impure land. One cannot compare a soul's departure while resting on the breast of his mother to its departure while supported by the arms of a strange woman."

Despite the benefits of burial in Eretz Yisrael— unconditional atonement, and being spared the anguish of tumbling through underground caverns at the resurrection of the dead—Ulah was still unhappy. Since his moment of death was to take place outside of Israel, his soul would ascend along the painful, circuitous route from *chutz l'aretz*, rather than following a direct path through the refined firmaments of Eretz Yisrael.

The Process of Resurrection

Physical and Spiritual Rejuvenation

In order to flourish, every plant needs soil, water, air and sunshine. Wherever these elements are found, the earth is fruitful and the cycles of life are strong. The soil nourishes, the water is catalyst, the air supplies gases which enable respiration and oxidation, and the sun, through photosynthesis, energizes the growth of plant life. A dormant seed is placed in the earth, and inspired to grow by the interaction of these four elements.

So is the process called resurrection. A body is placed in the soil and a certain bone in the spine (called *luz*) is like a dormant seed awaiting the time of the resuscitation of the dead. The heavenly dew (water) will catalyze the rejuvenation of a new and eternal body, qualitatively different from what we know as flesh and blood today. *HaShem* breathes into it a soul of eternal life and the Divine Presence, paralleling sunlight, warms it with light and joy and peace.

Dying in Eretz Yisrael

While the stages of resuscitation will be identical everywhere, Eretz Yisrael has certain properties which make it unique. Anyone buried in the Holy Land will be:
- (a) spared a punishment in the grave,
- (b) forgiven of sins,
- (c) among the first restored to life,
- (d) spared the suffering that comes from tumbling through underground caverns as one's bones migrate to the Holy Land.

The Talmud proves the resurrection of the dead with the following verse, "Your days, and the days of your children will be multiplied upon that earth which the L-rd swore to your fathers that He would give *to them*" (Deut. 11:21). Since "your fathers" refers to the Patriarchs who have long since passed away, and since Scripture clearly states that it is "to them (personally)" that the Land will be given, it must mean that they will return through resurrection to fulfill the verse and claim their inheritance. If this were not Scripture's intention, the verse would have ended, "...that he swore to your fathers that he would give *to you*" (who are alive now and are about to cross over into Eretz Yisrael).

The First to be Resurrected

Rabbi Shimon ben Lakish said in the name of Bar Kappora that those buried in Eretz Yisrael will be the only ones resurrected in the era of final redemption, and brought a verse to support his assertion. While it would seem that Jews in the Diaspora will lose out altogether, Rabbi Shimon explained that the Almighty will cut out underground channels and they will roll through them like leather sacks. Once they reach Eretz Yisrael their souls will return to them, as the prophet said, "I will open your graves, and bring you into the Land of Israel...(and there) I shall put My spirit in you and you shall live" (Ezek. 37:12-14).

Just as Eretz Yisrael is preeminent in holiness, and the Divine grace flows first through its borders from whence it radiates to the rest of the world, so at the unfolding of a new era in world history, the resurrection of the dead, it is fitting that it should commence in the Holy Land. The time lag between the resurrection of the dead in Eretz Yisrael and that of *chutz l'aretz* is forty years.

Just as a king gives precedence to his local citizens and only afterwards graces his distant subjects, so the sequence of resurrection will express these same priorities.

2

Between Man and G-d

View from Afar

The Mount of Olives is the most prestigious of Jewish cemeteries. It faces the Old City of Jerusalem, a stone's throw from the Temple Mount. It is common to see people congregated around a particular gravesite swaying back and forth in prayer, for Jewish people honor the anniversary of a person's death. In midwinter, on the 10th of Shevat, hundreds gather at the grave of the revered Sephardi Kabbalist, Rabbi Shalom Sharabi, and in summertime, on the 15th of Tamuz, thousands stream to the site of Rabbi Chaim ben Attar, the *Or HaChayim*, buried 250 years ago on that sacred spot. Candles are lit, prayers are whispered, all mixed with the cries of beseeching mothers echoing across the mountainside.

Questions for the Living and the Dead

Yet this custom raises a number of questions. To whom are these people praying—to the deceased, to G-d, to both? Can the dead hear their prayers? And even if so, can they really do anything to help the living? Aren't these people transgressing the prohibition against supplicating the dead (Deut. 18:11)? What is the purpose of praying at the grave of a *tzaddik*? Why should one invest time, energy, and money to do so? These questions are critical and only after resolving

144 / BENEATH THE HOLY ALTAR

On the *yartzeit* of Rabbi Chaim Attar, known as the *Or HaChayim*, thousands flock to his grave site on the slopes of Mount Olives. In recent years a huge canopy has been specially erected to shade the people. Below them is the solid stone tomb of Zechariah, who was the High Priest in the time of King Joash (c. 650 B.C.E.).

them can a Jewish pilgrim in the Holy Land visit its sacred sites with peace of mind and proper intentions, and derive the most from his experience.

Sources for Praying by a Grave

Over six hundred years ago, the first Jewish topographer of Eretz Yisrael, Rabbi Ishtori Haparki, wrote that "Just as Samuel the prophet visited the holy sites of Eretz Yisrael which existed in his time, so should we follow his example. The sanctity that infuses a particular spot does not diminish with time, and we can benefit from it even today."

"This applies also to the gravesites of *tzaddikim*," he continues. "The Talmud asks concerning the custom of visiting a cemetery on a fast day and praying for G-d's mercy particularly in that place. One Sage explains that they are invoking the dead to plead mercy for them. The custom derived from a Talmudic source about how Caleb saved himself from joining the conspiracy of the spies. The explanation is based on the Biblical verse which reads, 'They (the spies) came up from the Negev and came (singular) until Hebron' (Num. 13:22). Why the switch from plural to singular? It should have read, '...and *they* came until Hebron,' rather than 'he.' Rabba explains that the singular inflection teaches that Caleb left the group and travelled *alone* to the cave of Machpelah (the burial site of the Patriarchs and Matriarchs in Hebron), and prayed to his holy ancestors, 'Oh Patriarchs and Matriarchs! Plead mercy for me that I be saved from the treacherous advice of the spies.'"

There are other episodes of this sort recorded in the Talmud, Midrash, and *Zohar* as well as writings of the *Ari Zal*. For example, Rabbi Yehoshua went and prostrated himself on the grave of Beth Shamai and implored, "Answer me, O bones of Beth Shamai..." In another instance, cash belonging to orphans had been entrusted into the safekeeping of Shemuel's father. Unfortunately, his father passed away before Shemuel could reach him and elicit the whereabouts of their money. Therefore he went to the cemetery and spoke with his father's spirit directly, and so acquired the critical information. Similarly when the caravan carrying Joseph to Egypt passed by the grave of Rachel, he dashed over and fell upon it, crying out, "Mother, Mother, you bore me. Please awake, arise, and gaze upon your son who has been sold as a slave!" Finally the *Ari Zal* often sent disciples to prostrate themselves on the graves of the *Tannaim and Ammoraim*, requesting *HaShem*, in the merit of the dead, to reveal to them secrets of Torah.

The Prohibition of Necromancy

What distinguishes these acts from necromancy, the prohibition against supplicating the dead? The Torah's definition and criteria for necromancy are quite precise. It forbids one from fasting for a particular period of time and then sleeping in a cemetery for the express purpose of conjuring and communing with the dead. All these elements must be present before the act is considered a violation of Torah law. Here, however, in every case, the purpose was pure-minded and no method of conjuring was used. Moreover, each one approached the grave with a deep sense of repentance over his own lack of self-perfection, burdened by the weight of his sins. The *Zohar* summarizes with these words, "...but when Jews come to a cemetery, they approach it in a spirit of repentance, with a broken heart." They were appealing to G-d in the merit of the deceased for guidance. Some say that Caleb and the others went a step further and asked the deceased to "champion their cause" in heaven. Based on these distinctions, such instances do not violate the stricture against necromancy, nor do those who pray by the burial site of a *tzaddik*, or the grave of a parent, transgress that command.

The Approved Way of Praying by a Grave

There is a controversy among later authorities as to how one should relate to the dead. All agree that the living may stand by a grave and pray to G-d for their personal needs in the merit of the person buried there. For example, one might pray in the merit of Rambam that G-d help him reconcile within himself the seeming contradictions between Torah and the secular sciences and philosophies. Or one might ask in the name of Rabbi Shimon Bar Yochai that the spiritual and mystical dimensions of Torah open to him.

Many authorities go even further and permit one to enlist the dead person to "champion his cause" *before G-d*. They base their leniency on Caleb's daring and effective gesture of arousing the Patriarchs to invoke *HaShem*'s assistance to strengthen him against the evil influence of his compatriots, the spies. This is a very delicate matter. The very same act with one intention is permissible and even praiseworthy, while with another "motive" is considered idolatry and one of the most serious infractions of Torah law.

Thus one must be careful not to shift his frame of mind, and begin to beseech the buried one *himself*, imagining that the dead person's soul will save him from his dilemma. All assistance and redemption must originate with G-d if it is to be for one's ultimate good. The pleader must remember this at all times.

One's manner of approaching the grave of a saint should be similar to his asking advice and assistance from a living *tzaddik* or *rebbe*. Just as one is permitted to ask a person to pray for him—to enlist another's support in requesting Divine intervention for a speedy recovery, or the resolution of some other predicament—so one can engage the soul of a *tzaddik*, even after his death, to plead on one's behalf and to praise him to G-d, who is the source of all Providence.

A Golden Opportunity

The opportunity to pray at the site of a *tzaddik* is most efficacious. People pilgrimage across continents and oceans, at great expense and travail, to enlist the assistance of a particular *tzaddik* who, because of the experiences of his life, will be most sympathetic to his cause, and

Rachel's tomb is located on the Jerusalem-Hebron highway outside Bethlehem. The story of her passing is decribed in Genesis 35:16-20. This photograph was taken around the turn of the century.

most influential upon the L-rd. For example Rachel, who selflessly enabled her sister Leah to marry Jacob even before herself, who was barren for many years, and who died in childbirth, is a most powerful ally when seeking marriage or children. Rabbi Akiva, the classic *baal teshuva*, who only first began to study Torah at age forty and yet became a great Sage, is a valuable friend to those returning to Judaism later in life, and who despair of ever learning how to read Hebrew, or study Talmud.

Furthermore, the Talmud teaches, "Greater are the righteous in death than in life." Their assistance is even more potent in the nether realms for they are no longer bound by the limitations of a physical body in the physical world. Rabbi Abba said, "From where do we know that the prayers of the dead protect the living? From the verse reporting Caleb's secret stopover at the cave of Machpelah where he enlisted the prayers of the Patriarchs and Matriarchs to draw forth G-d's protection. Another example is when Barzillai, the Gileadite, requested that King David allow him "to die in (his) own city" (II Sam. 19:38). *Sefer Chassidim* explains that the dead take pleasure in their loved ones coming to their grave and seeking their assistance before G-d, for they *are* able to fulfill such requests and help their loved ones out. This is satisfying both for the dead, for they have an opportunity to give to those they love, and the living, who are aided in their cause.

148 / BENEATH THE HOLY ALTAR

Story of Opening the Grave of Rabbi Shimon ben Levi

On certain rare occasions, the graves of *tzaddikim* were opened, usually by gentile proclamation, affording the world a revealing glimpse into the effect of holiness on the body itself. One incident involved the grave of Rabbi Shimon ben Lavi, a holy saint, pillar of Torah, lover of humanity, and author of the song "Bar Yochai." He died in Tripoli, Libya, in 1585.

His tomb was a continual source of relief and salvation for all who prayed there. So famous and precious was his gravesite that the Arab population of Tripoli became jealous of its status and attention.

When the Italian army invaded Tripoli in 1911, and both Jewish and Arab residents temporarily fled the city, the Arabs took advantage of the confusion of foreign rulership, and claimed the tomb as their own, identifying it as the burial site of an Arab holy man. A dispute broke out between the two communities, news of which reached all the way to Rome. The Italian government decided to resolve the conflict by opening the sepulcher and examining the remains for any determining marks of identification. A special committee was dispatched from Rome to supervise the investigation. Everyone gasped when the diggers uncovered the body of Rabbi Shimon Lavi lying with a *talith* draped around him, appearing as if he was taking a nap, there being no trace of bodily decomposition. The Jewish origin of this saintly man was undeniable, and their cause was vindicated before the Italian government. Roman officials erected a plaque at the holy site and the renown of Rabbi Shimon Lavi spread far and wide.

Lips of the Righteous

More Jewish *tzaddikim* are buried in Eretz Yisrael than anywhere else in the world. Kings and prophets, Patriarchs and Matriarchs, Sages and scholars of every era—the tombs of our saints and leaders infuse the earth with their holiness.

Honoring the Dead

"If one, passing a gravesite, becomes aware that a righteous person is buried there, he should mention some deeds of kindness or words of wisdom associated with that *tzaddik*." The commentator of this Midrash, Rabbi David Luria, cites this as a source for the practice of reciting verses at the grave of *tzaddikim* and retelling the stories of their lives and their greatness. Rabbi Saloman Mutzafi (1900-1975) compiled a book of important burial places in Eretz Yisrael with prayers to say at each site, as well as the anecdotes and teachings of each *tzaddik*. The book, entitled *Sifthei Tzaddikim*, "The Lips of the Righteous," explains that the most propitious time to pray at the grave of a holy man is on the anniversary of his death, his *yartzeit*. This has been the custom since ancient times.

Lips Whispering in the Grave

We are taught that when repeating a statement in the name of its author, one should imagine the *tzaddik* actually standing before him. This has a dual effect. It brings redemption to the world, for the holiness of the *tzaddik* becomes a *present* reality in that moment, and it brings an elevation to the soul of the *tzaddik* as well. The former effect is traditionally described by the phrase, "his lips whisper in the grave," based on the verse in Song of Songs, "the lips of the sleepers murmur" (7:10). The word sleepers refers to those *tzaddikim* who are deceased.

Another example of a *tzaddik*'s "lips whispering in the grave" is found in a Midrash concerning King David. In one of his Psalms he beseeched mercy upon his soul with the following request, "May it be that I shall dwell in Your tent forever, that I shall be protected by the shelter of Your wings..." (Psalms 61:5). Did David really think he would live forever? Obviously not. Rather, his intent was as follows: "Master of the universe!" he implored, "If I be found worthy before You, please let it be that my words and my Psalms be remembered for all time. Let them be recited by Jews in synagogues, homes, and holy places; in times of joy and need, for evermore. In this way I shall live forever, for my 'lips will whisper (even) in the grave' through the prayerful utterances of the living."

Maharsha, anticipating the reader's skepticism, explained this idea in terms that even a rationalist would find satisfying. First he brings a basic religious principle. He writes that although the body decomposes in the grave, the soul, which was always a spiritual entity, continues its existence in the spiritual worlds. It simply sheds its "overcoat," the body, and continues on. When a human being speaks a word in *this* world, that speech is simply the physical expression of an inner power of soul, the power to think and articulate thought. Thus every verbal statement is an outer manifestation of a previous, inner spiritual state. When a person quotes the words of a *tzaddik*, he allows that original that they, too, wanted the merit of escorting him to his final resting place. The disciples were called back and the march continued without incident.

When the camel reached Tiberias he halted near the grave of Rabbi Yochanan ben Zakkai and refused to take another step. At last the disciples had found the place chosen by Heaven as the burial spot for Rambam.

> May the merits of Rambam and
> all the *tzaddikim* protect us,
> the living. Amen.

Part 4

Yishuv Ha'Aretz: The Commandment to Settle in Israel

> *"Of Zion it shall be said, 'This man and that man (were) born there...'" (Ps. 87:5). "This man" refers to a native born Israeli, and "that man" refers to one who yearns to see his holy homeland. He, too, receives a blessing as if he was born there.*
>
> Ketuboth 75a

1

Longing for the Land

Whether or not the Torah actually obligates a Jew to live in Eretz Yisrael, (a subject discussed further on), truly it is a blessing and a privilege to do so. Yet there are responsibilities involved and prices to pay. The holiness permeating the Land exerts an influence on people's lives, imbuing their every action with added significance. Thus even trivial, mundane activities assume a certain importance by virtue of this air of sanctity. And so, residents of the Holy Land are held to more exacting standards in every facet of their lives— both religious and secular. After all, Eretz Yisrael is *HaShem*'s private garden and Jerusalem, His castle. The King requires undeviating allegiance from those living on the palace grounds, and nothing short of this will do.

The commandment to live in Israel is unique, in that every aspect of a person participates in that *mitzvah*. When a Jew moves to Israel, his body, soul, possessions, secular involvements, religious practices, inner thoughts and outer expressions, dreams and waking moments are all suddenly happening as part of a *mitzvah*. When a person immerses in a *mikveh* the waters surround him and bring spiritual cleansing to his entire being. Thus is the power of dwelling in Eretz Yisrael. Yet even more, one's immersion in a *mikveh* is only momentary, while the influence of living in Israel is constant...even in sleep...and even in death.

A Chronicle From 250 Years Ago

One of the most insidious consequences of our two-thousand-year exile is that it has eroded our sense of connectedness with our homeland, and dulled our longing to return. Rabbi Jacob Emden wrote in the early 18th century:

"The Holy Land, once a source of hopefulness in our long and bitter exile full of trial and tribulations, has now been almost forgotten. The sufferings have taken their toll. So preoccupied are we with survival that we forget the importance of settling in Eretz Yisrael. Today, not one Jew in a thousand is motivated to move to the Holy Land; maybe one in a country, two in a generation. No one any more longs to see her soil. We create a niche of security in *chutz l'aretz* and forget that it is only a temporary dwelling. And even worse, we imagine we've discovered a second Eretz Yisrael, another Jerusalem. Indeed, this is why misfortune befell our people. We settle in foreign countries, at first under tranquil circumstances and grow complacent. We should be lovesick for Eretz Yisrael. Instead we forget her and at that point the political tide changes and again we are expelled and dispersed. This is what happens when we forget our call to return to the Land of our inheritance, the birthplace of our people, the resting place of our Patriarchs and Matriarchs."

A Travelog of Early Settlers

Yet throughout this long night of exile, individuals and small groups of faithful ones have immigrated to the Holy Land to fulfill the *mitzvah* of *yishuv ha'aretz*, and to observe the commandments exclusive to the Land of Israel. Rabbis and laymen alike, lovers of Torah throughout the world have felt the call, and endured the hardship of travel and resettling. Some of the more noted of these early settlers included:

— three hundred *Baalei Tosefoth* scholars led by Rabbi Jonathan HaKohen in 1210 C.E.,
— Rabbi Ishtori Haparchi (c. 1300), the first to publish the findings of his topographical examination of the Land, in the classic work, *Kaftor v'Ferach*,
— Rabbi Obadiah of Bartenora, author of the still current commentary on the Mishna,
— Rabbi Joseph Karo, compiler and codifier of the *Shulchan Aruch*, and various other halachic commentaries,
— Rabbi Isaac Luria, the holy Kabbalist and saint also called the *Ari Zal*,

Longing for the Land / 157

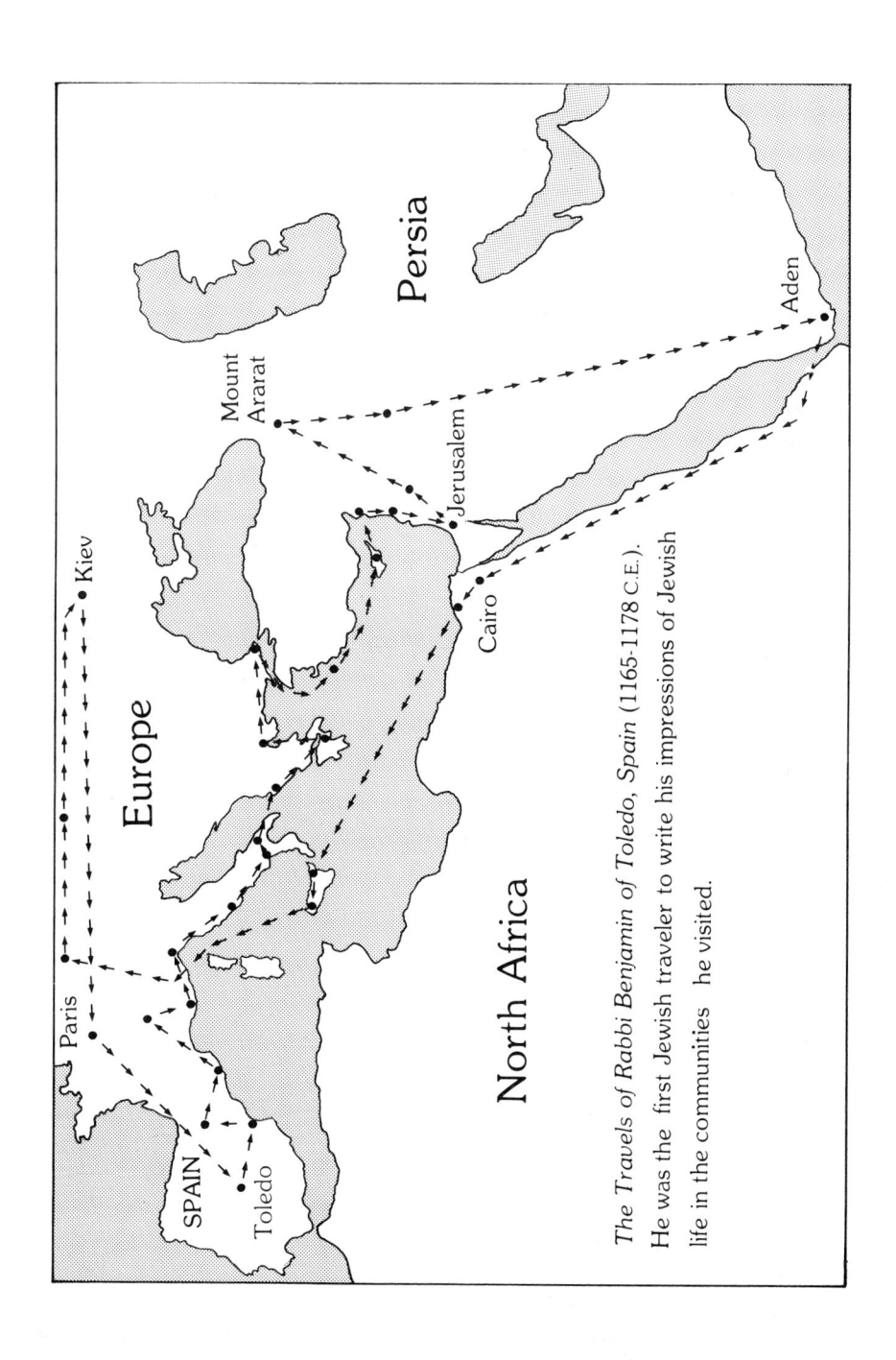

The Travels of Rabbi Benjamin of Toledo, Spain (1165-1178 C.E.). He was the first Jewish traveler to write his impressions of Jewish life in the communities he visited.

—Rav Moses Alshich,
—Rav Moses Chaim Luzzatto, author of the classics of Jewish philosophy, *Path of the Just* and *The Way of G-d.*

The eighteenth century brought *chassidim*, and many disciples of the Vilna Gaon, thus beginning the first ripples of a Jewish immigration which has continued up into this century.

Thanks to these brave, dedicated and self-sacrificing souls, there has always remained a continuous Jewish presence in Eretz Yisrael, a fact which is significant for a number of reasons. The Jewish claim to Israel as its legal homeland is in part based upon this piece of evidence — that the Jews have never surrendered their hold on the Land. Second, the calendar and certain other Rabbinical *mitzvoth* are binding upon Jews in *chutz l'aretz* only so long as there are actually Jews living in Israel. Finally, the greater Jewish community and the world at large are affected by the *mitzvoth* of religious Jews. And since certain *mitzvoth* are only performed in Israel, it is important that there remain at least a handful of Jews who are living there and doing them. If this were to cease, the world would be affected. It might not be obvious, but it would be true.

The Source For One's Yearning For Eretz Yisrael

The innate yearning of a Jew for Israel is part of our inheritance from Abraham. G-d commanded him to travel through Eretz Yisrael and then resettle in Mesopotamia until *HaShem* should again sanction his return. During those years of exile Abraham longed for the Land, and prayed that the L-rd should let him live there. "Oh that I had wings like a dove! For then I would fly away and be at rest" (Psalms 55:7). Finally, this long awaited moment arrived. "Abram departed as the L-rd had spoken to him" (Gen. 12:4). The Sages teach that he set forth on the very day that permission was given, wasting not a moment to fulfill this *mitzvah*, barely arranging provisions for the journey.

Isaac was a unique case. When a long drought made living conditions in Eretz Yisrael very difficult, he set out for Egypt. He thought to follow his father's example who, under similar circumstances, had sojourned there. But to his surprise G-d stopped him when he reached Gerrar. "Live in this Land," announced the Almighty, "and do not travel outside it. You were sanctified as a pure offering on Mount Moriah at the binding ceremony, and even that subtlest of impurity which comes from placing one's body outside the Land of Israel (even while one's soul remains bound to his Creator) — you must be free also from this." Thus Isaac remained in the Land all his days, loving it, and sanctifying his life to G-d.

Jacob carried on this tradition of longing for the Land of Israel. His return to Eretz Yisrael from Aram where he had fled from his brother Esau, initiated a new era in his life — an even closer and more intimate relationship with G-d. *HaShem* commanded and promised in one breath. "Return to the Land of your fathers, to your birthplace, and I will be with you" (Gen. 31:3). Jacob pondered the meaning of these words. What can be the reason I have been unworthy of perceiving the Divine Presence all these years in Aram Naharaim? It must be because I have been living in *chutz l'aretz*. Now that G-d tells me to return to Eretz Yisrael, emphasizing that *there* He will be with me, surely He will shine His radiance upon me in a new and more revealed way.

Now that Jacob realized the cause and effect relationship between living in Eretz Yisrael and G-d's closeness, he became frightened when Esau, who had sworn vengeance against him, approached with a multitude of men as he and his caravan of family and possessions prepared to cross into The Holy Land. Many commentators wonder whether this was not a flaw in Jacob's trust in G-d, that he should fear Esau, a mere mortal of flesh and blood. One explanation is that Jacob realized that Esau might have accumulated much merit from having lived all these years in the Holy Land of Eretz Yisrael, while he himself had not. On the basis of this, he feared that Esau's vengeance might have spiritual clout beyond his *physical* strength (which it did as expressed by the angelic emissary of Esau with whom Jacob wrestled that very night). For this reason, he feared his brother's threatening approach.

And no one's passion for Israel can compare to that of Moses, who pleaded with *HaShem* for permission to at least "pass over and see the land" (even if he did not have the merit to live there, Deut. 3:32). His longing was so poignant, the Midrash teaches, that he "was consumed away like a moth" (Psalms 39:12). Why was it so important for him to enter Israel? Moses understood that the L-rd's presence is more revealed and tangible there, and as a lover of G-d, he desired to experience that extra closeness. Also he longed to perform those commandments that can only be performed in Israel.

"One who dwells in Eretz Yisrael," the Talmud asserts, "is like one who has a G-d." It bases this seemingly rash statement on the verse in Leviticus which reads, "I shall give you the land of Canaan, to be your G-d" (25:38). The Sages derive from this the practical principle that it is preferable to dwell in Eretz Yisrael, even in a city populated with gentiles, than to live in *chutz l'aretz* surrounded by Jews.

2

The Commandment of *Yishuv HaAretz*

From Babylonia to Israel — With Love?

From Rabbi Zeira's classic story of *aliyah*, the Sages derive several conditions to the *mitzvah* of *yishuv ha'aretz*. Rabbi Zeira was a fourth century Torah scholar who grew up in Babylonia, at a time when its Torah academies were at the height of their grandeur and excellence. Yet, the more he learned, the more he thirsted for the Holy Land, and the opportunity to learn under such personalities as Rabbi Yochanan and Rabbi Abbahu. Yet his mentor and teacher, Rav Yehuda of Pumbeditha, dissuaded him from realizing his heart's desire, for he subscribed to the opinion that emigration from Babylonia to Eretz Yisrael transgressed the prophesy of Jeremiah (27:22). "Unto Babylonia they (the exiled Jews) shall be taken and there they shall remain until the day I take heed of them." Yet, Rabbi Zeira interpreted this verse differently from his teacher. He understood "they" to refer to the sacred vessels, the subject of the previous verse, in which case it said nothing about whether a Jew could return to Eretz Yisrael.

The rift between teacher and student widened, each bringing verses from Scripture to support his position, and refute his opponent. In particular they focused on a verse which appears three times in the Song of Songs. It reads, "I charge you (with an oath)...not to stir up or awake My love until it pleases Me" (2:7, 3:5, 8:4). Since the Torah is never redundant, each mention of the verse expresses something different, yet each is understood to establish a contractual obligation between G-d and the Jewish people. The point of controversy is the content of each of these vows.

The Talmud lists them as follows. Through these three verses G-d make the Jewish people swear:
1. not to return to Eretz Yisrael *as an entire people* before He brings the Messiah, and
2. not to rebel against the gentile ruling powers under whose governments they would live during their periods of exile.

The third was a reciprocal obligation that the gentile nations would have to make toward the Jews, namely, that they would not unduly oppress their Jewish subjects.

According to Rav Zeira, the first vow could remain intact, yet *aliyah* still be permitted if it was done on an individual basis or in small groups, for the contract only forbade *mass* immigration.

A Dreamer of Dreams

They debated back and forth in lively dialogue. Rabbi Zeira lingered in Babylonia but not because he accepted Rabbi Yehuda's doctrine. Rather, he questioned whether he merited to live in the Holy Land for the Talmud states quite explicitly that "Whoever lives in Eretz Yisrael dwells without sin." Rav Zeira interpreted this as a prerequisite to *aliyah* and since he had not attained a level of perfection whereby he was purged of sin, he remained in Pumbeditha, praying that one day if he worked hard enough he might reach such a state. One night he dreamt of barley grains, a vision known to indicate that one's sins have now been expurgated. He considered this a sign from heaven and prepared immediately to journey to the Holy Land.

Just before leaving Rabbi Zeira stopped one last time to hear some words of Torah from his master, Rav Yehuda. He had not announced his exit plans for he feared that Rav Yehuda might take legal measures to ban his departure. He found his teacher in the bathhouse and overheard him saying to his attendant *in Hebrew*, "Hand me the shampoo and pass me the comb...." Rabbi Zeira tells how he learned an important *halacha* from this, for since Hebrew is *loshon ha'kodesh*, the holy language, and since holy objects and words of Torah are not allowed in bathhouses where people are unclothed, one might assume that it is forbidden to speak Hebrew altogether in such a place. Yet Rav Yehuda had used Hebrew to ask for his shampoo and comb. From this Rabbi Zeira learned that one may use Hebrew to converse about secular subjects, even in a bathhouse. One can scarcely imagine the pleasure a Sage feels when he learns a new *halacha*. Rabbi Zeira grinned and declared, "If I had only just heard this, and didn't even speak to my teacher personally, my visit would have been worthwhile."

The anecdote of Rav Zeira crossing the Jordan River into Eretz Yisrael on a wobbly foot bridge (see beginning of Part II), aptly captures the enthusiasm with which he approached his goal of settling in the Holy Land. And living there actually deepened his already intense love of Torah and *mitzvoth*. He saw that whatever he had learned outside of Israel, no matter how deep and wise, was tinged with a slight impurity, the impurity intrinsic to *chutz l'aretz*. Therefore he fasted numerous times to be able to forget the Babylonian system of learning and so begin *anew* in the Holy Land. He said that "the air of Eretz Yisrael makes one wise."

His funeral was in Tiberias and his eulogy was as follows, "The land of Shinar conceived and bore him; the Land of the gazelle raised its beloved child. 'Woe unto me,' bereaved Rakkath (Tiberias), 'for I have lost my precious vessel.'"

A Four-Sided Coin

Among Early Authorities, there are four major positions concerning the commandment of *Yishuv Ha'Aretz*.

Opinion 1: It Is A Torah Commandment

Ramban includes the commandment of settling in Eretz Yisrael as one of the *Taryag* (613) *mitzvoth* and considers it fully applicable today. He develops his opinion through lengthy and thorough argument.

"We are commanded to possess the land which G-d gave to our forefathers, Abraham, Isaac, and Jacob, and not to forsake it to the nations, nor to abandon it. G-d commanded them as follows. 'Take hold of the Land and settle it. To you I have given the Land as a possession. You shall inherit the Land (Num. 33:53). Furthermore, at several points in Scripture G-d explicitly outlines the boundaries for them...

"Moses' recounting of the spy incident provides further proof that this is an actual commandment, for he says, 'Ascend, occupy it *as G-d told you to do*' (Deut. 1:21). And when they shrank from the original plan to enter the land immediately, Scripture condemns them, berating them with these words, You rebelled against the utterance of the L-rd' (Deut. 1:26). Thus Scripture clearly indicates that they were operating under the domain of an actual *mitzvah* which compelled them to enter Eretz Yisrael. The L-rd had not just warned them, or promised them, He had commanded them...

"It is clear to me that when the Sages speak so compellingly about the importance of living in Eretz Yisrael, and compare one who leaves the Land (without good reason) and dwells instead in *chutz l'aretz* to one who serves idolatry, they consider it an actual positive commandment. HaShem decrees that we should live there. This *mitzvah* is binding upon all Jews in every generation, even during the period of exile, and thus says the Talmud.

"The Midrash tells of a group of scholars who, for various reasons, left Eretz Yisrael to live in distant lands. At some point on their journey they suddenly realized how deep was their loss, how beloved was the Land of Israel. They raised their eyes to heaven and cried, tore their garments as a sign of mourning and recited aloud the verse, 'You shall possess it (Eretz Yisrael) and dwell in it. You shall observe all the statutes' (Deut. 11:31-32). They came to realize that 'Living in Eretz Yisrael is equal to all the other commandments,' and decided to return to Jerusalem....''

Many Later Authorities endorse Ramban's opinion, including Shelah, *Sefer Charedim*, Chatham Sofer, *Pe'ath HaShulchan*, and others.

Ramban's ruling applies only to individuals. It is not a call for all Jews to vacate their native lands and march to the Holy Land. Even Ramban agrees that the oath mentioned in Song of Songs is to remain in force until the Messiah himself calls for an ingathering of exiles. Some authorities even go so far as to explain that Ramban speaks only to those already in Eretz Yisrael, that he in no way implies that every Jew is under an absolute obligation to immigrate to Israel. Rather, he cautions those already there not to leave without proper license. For every minute that one resides in Eretz Yisrael, even as a temporary visitor, he is fulfilling the *mitzvah* of *yishuv ha'aretz* and must have good reason to leave, for in so doing, he actively stops fulfilling a Torah obligation.

Opinion 2: It Is A Rabbinical Ordinance

Rambam does not include this *mitzvah* in his list of the 613 Torah commandments. He concludes that there was never a Torah command of *yishuv ha'aretz*, not even in Temple times when most Jews were, in fact, living in the Land. He identifies, instead, two Rabbinical

Commandment of Yishuv Ha'Aretz / 165

ordinances, one which makes living in Eretz Yisrael a praiseworthy thing to do, and one which prohibits emigration *from* the Holy Land without proper license. Rashi, Rosh and *Or HaChayim* agree with this opinion.

They challenge Ramban's proofs point by point. When G-d charges them to "occupy the land and settle in it," He is *promising* the Jewish people that He will give them Eretz Yisrael as an inheritance which they will eventually possess. He is not *commanding* them to do so. They interpret the story of the Sages who wept and mourned their leaving Israel as a reaction to the Temple's desolation and not a call for *yishuv ha'aretz*. Furthermore, their statement that "living in Eretz Yisrael is equal to all the other commandments" refers to the greater reward one accrues by fulfilling commandments in Eretz Yisrael, for the value of serving G-d in the Holy Land is greater than performing these same commandments in *chutz l'aretz*. Also one can fulfill certain commandments only in Eretz Yisrael for they specifically apply to that Land within the boundaries designated Israel. Furthermore, Rabbi Yehuda's ban, based on Jeremiah's prophesy which forbade emigration from Babylonia to Eretz Yisrael, clearly indicates that during *galuth* there is no command of *yishuv ha'aretz*.

Others counter their critique of Ramban's position with further support for the idea that *yishuv ha'aretz* is in fact a Torah commandment. If, as those who uphold the second opinion argue, the exact halachic implications of the verse in Numbers is ambiguous, then other passages in Deuteronomy can be brought to substantiate the position that living in Israel is an actual precept. For example, "Ascend, possess it...You rebelled against the utterance of the L-rd." Furthermore, if the Sages were only weeping over the destruction of the Temple, why did they turn back and explain themselves with the statement that "*Yishuv ha'aretz* is equal to all the *mitzvoth*"? Finally, those defending Ramban's position note that Rabbi Yehuda's ban only prohibited emigration from Babylonia, but not from other countries. Therefore it says nothing about the larger question of whether the commandment applies during *galuth*. Moreover, the Talmud does not accept his decision, as indicated by Rabbi Zeira's uncensured departure from Babylonia to Israel. And we know that Rabbi Zeira was only one of many who emigrated from Babylonia during this period of history.

These viewpoints are themselves countered by those who defend the second opinion; and so each side challenges the other and the argument continues even today.

3

Prerequisites for Immigration

Torah Observance

An essential preparation for immigration to Israel is Torah observance. Although one need not achieve purity from sin like Rabbi Zeira—a compliance with Torah law is absolutely basic. Special emphasis should be placed on studying those laws pertaining to the Land, such as separation of tithes, the Sabbatical year, when to rend one's garment at the Western Wall, and so forth. Of the 613 commandments, 195 can be fulfilled only in Eretz Yisrael and another 78 commandments pertain to the land and other conditions.

Some believe that non-observant Jews should not settle in Eretz Yisrael. The presence of "rebels" in the courtyard of the King of Kings might incite His anger, provoking another tragic exile, Heaven forbid. The author of *Sefer Charedim*, offers an historical example. The Samaritans were never punished for their idolatrous misdeeds when living in their homeland, but once they came to the Land of G-d and continued those same activities *HaShem* sent lions upon them to kill them. Therefore, every person should be sure when coming to Eretz Yisrael to be full of trepidation over and above the measure of fear of Heaven he had in *chutz l'aretz* and realize that now he is standing in the courtyard of the King.

Today many rabbis rule leniently on this matter. They base their position on a statistical fact—more and more Jews are becoming

Torah observant *because* of their experiences in Eretz Yisrael. The spiritual power imbued inside the Wailing Wall and other holy sites, fans the fire of that inner spark of light hidden within each Jew. A dim flicker may suddenly burst into a flame of devotion and commitment to Torah Judaism.

The Scale of Merit and Sin

The Midrash brings a parable of a king who regularly visited a certain city, always bringing his children along with him. One time their behavior was so rebellious that he became angry and swore never to take them again. The next time he went alone, but found that he missed them greatly. "Oh, how I wish my children were with me," he lamented. This parable, concludes the Midrash, teaches about G-d's relationship to the Jewish people. Even when they lived in Eretz Yisrael, in G-d's company so to speak, they began to rebel and violate His commands. On account of this defiance, *HaShem* exiled them to foreign lands. Yet now He misses them, in spite of their imperfections, and bemoans their absence. "Oh how I wish My children were with Me in Eretz Yisrael, even if they do not properly respect the Land."

Although this Midrash may be understood at face value, some commentators prefer to direct its message toward religious Jews—teaching them not to be over-critical of themselves and so refrain from *aliyah* when they recognize and admit that their observance of Torah and devotion to G-d are flawed. In spite of these failings, G-d wants their return to Israel.

No One is Faultless

Similarly, Ramban writes that one of Moses' messages to the generation of the wilderness, communicated in his soliloquy which constitutes the Book of Deuteronomy, was a promise that G-d would always act mercifully with them. Therefore, they should not shy away from possessing the Land because of their transgressions and imperfections, for truly, "There is no man who is totally free of sin" (Prov. 7:20). This false modesty would bring harsh decrees upon themselves. Rather than forfeiting their claim to Israel because of these things, they should repent, trust in G-d's mercy, and come anyway to fulfill their mission of living in the Land of Israel.

Whereas the Talmud teaches that living in Eretz Yisrael atones for one's sins, Rabbi Moses Cordovero explains that this only applies to unintentional ones. Other sins are only pardoned through suffering or by remaining patient, compassionate and G-d-fearing when someone insults one's pride. Furthermore, atonement of intentional sins requires deep repentance and Torah study.

Means of Livelihood

A second condition for *aliyah* is livelihood. A person must be able to support his family in Eretz Yisrael. Though one need not maintain the standard of living to which he was accustomed in *chutz l'aretz*, nevertheless he should not fall into poverty. Economic insecurity breeds desperation which can undermine one's religious commitments and priorities, for a person might feel compelled to make certain compromises in *halacha* in order to acquire income. Furthermore, he may be forced to live in neighborhoods or send his children to schools which do not support a Torah outlook. Finally, it is not respectful to the King to enter His palace as an empty-handed beggar. Kol Bo writes that one's reward for immigrating to Eretz Yisrael is great, *provided* he has a means of livelihood.

On the other hand, various charitable organizations like *Rabbi Meir Baal HaNess* exist to assist Torah scholars and their families while they are living in Eretz Yisrael. Rabbi Chaim David Azulai, known as Chida, taught that when one helps support the needy Jews of Eretz Yisrael, it is considered in Heaven as if he, himself, were living there. Rabbi Israel of Shaklov, leader of the Vilna Gaon's disciples in Israel, spent several years in Europe organizing a charity fund for Ashkenazi Jews in the Holy Land.

Safety Factor

A third prerequisite to *aliyah* is some assurance of completing a safe journey. Until a century ago, travel from Europe was indeed perilous. Rebbe Nachman of Breslov, who came in 1801, encountered many dangers on his round trip journey from Russia to Israel. Were it not for the Almighty's providential care, who knows if he would have completed his trip. Perhaps the Vilna Gaon was obeying this *halacha* when he returned home in the middle of his aborted pilgrimage to the Holy Land.

Rabbi Jacob Emden discussed this condition as it applied to his generation (1740!). "What can we do, we who are spiritually impoverished? It is as if we were living at the North Pole where the light of the Divine Presence has never shone—so far away are we from the Holy Land and the holy tongue. How great should be our

The perils of sea voyages were many. This insert is from Jacob ben Abraham's 17th century map of Eretz Yisrael.

effort to immigrate! We should travel by wagon and cross rivers by ferryboat in order to reach the Pleasant Land. Rain or snow should not prevent us from coming to the place of Divine service. Potential dangers are not an excuse for inaction since in times of peace the hazards are minimal. The perils of crossing desert and sea are surely not treacherous enough to exempt one from this great *mitzvah*.

"If we are really honest with ourselves, we must admit that dangers threaten body and soul wherever we may be — even in the seeming complacency of our daily life. How can we compare the spiritual benefits of living in Israel — the pleasure the Almighty feels when a Jew settles in Israel, and the atonement of sin afforded by the Land — with the relatively trivial dangers of the road? It is like deciding not to embark upon his journey to Israel because of a thorn in his foot, or for fear of what the customs agents might find. How long will we languish in the bed of laziness? Let us each devise a strategy against these excuses and journey immediately to Eretz Yisrael, the only place where you can lodge in the shadow of the Almighty and be secure under the shelter of His wings."

Today's Predicament

There was a time when travel meant only travail and not pleasure for an observant Jew. Road conditions, Sabbath, care of infants, kosher food, and the like, greatly curtailed the wanderlust of the Torah community. Yet the comforts and sophistications of the modern world have eliminated many of these problems. Surprisingly (or perhaps not so) this has worked both for and against the probability of a religious Jew travelling to Israel. Affluence, leisure and the airline industry have turned travel into big business, inculcating the consumer with a fantasy notion that "anyone who's anyone has travelled the world." The lure and glamour of exotic places has seduced the Jewish heart away from its primal attachment to Eretz Yisrael. The Holy Land becomes just another speck on the globe—one of hundreds of picturesque places to visit, photograph, and say, "I've been there." Yet for one whose vision penetrates beneath the surface of things, none of these other places can compare with the virtue of Eretz Yisrael, which is singular and incalculable.

Education

These are the three primary conditions which must be satisfied before it is appropriate for one to consider living in Israel. Nevertheless, there are other relevant factors which should influence one's decision. For example, it is extremely important that one's children have a solid Jewish education, not only for their own sake, but also for the strength of the Jewish community as a whole. To compromise on this is not appropriate. Therefore, a promising job offer in a new settlement town in Eretz Yisrael which does not have adequate educational facilities must be weighed against the high standard of Torah education currently available in *chutz l'aretz*.

A Conducive Environment

Similarly, if one's observance might be compromised because of the non- or anti-religiosity of the town where he can find work and a place to live in Eretz Yisrael, it is wiser to remain in *chutz l'aretz* within a healthy religious environment. The criterion for evaluating whether such a danger exists in a particular place is whether or not the community has such things as a *shul* with a set and daily *minyan*, a *mikveh* for women, availability of kosher food, neighbors who keep the Sabbath, and so on.

The decision to live in Eretz Yisrael is not a simple one. A person must balance, on the one hand, a Jew's obligation to dwell in his homeland (if such exists) and the spiritual uplift afforded by such a move against, on the other hand, his responsibility to his own and his family's physical, material and psychological well-being. There is no blanket prescription. Each family is different. Therefore any serious-minded *oleh* should seek the advice of his rabbis before making such a move.

A Warning Not to Speak Disrespectfully of the Land and its People

Whether one lives in Israel or not, he should never make negative, slanderous statements about its land, produce, or people. Speaking disrespectfully of Eretz Yisrael not only violates the Torah's proscription against *lashon hora* (damaging gossip), but implies a lack of trust in G-d, for one is showing disdain for that which G-d considers a precious gift and His most valuable of inheritances. Both are epitomized by the spies who were sent to scout out the Land as the Israelites prepared to enter. Whereas G-d called the Land "good," they despised His gift and described it as a "land which consumes its inhabitants," thereby turning the people's enthusiasm into resistance. Consequently the Israelites wandered an additional forty years in the desert and all who believed the slander of the spies died before reaching the Holy Land.

Furthermore, the Talmud relates that throughout the Babylonian exile, Jews spoke disrespectfully of their homeland while Sennacherib (King of Babylon) never boasted that his country was superior to Eretz Yisrael. For this reason alone, the Sages praise him profusely. Another lesson can be learned from this as well. If such recognition is accorded Sennacherib, who refrained from glorifying his own country at the expense of disparaging Israel, how much more so is one deserving of merit for not only refraining from criticism, but actually speaking positive words of praise for his beloved homeland.

Why Torah Leaders Did Not Come

Although many Torah leaders did immigrate to Eretz Yisrael, the majority chose to remain in their native countries. Why didn't they, of all people, feel the spiritual calling to live in the Holy Land? They who are always running to do *mitzvoth*, to serve G-d in every possible way, why did they disregard the commandment of *yishuv ha'aretz*?

Several explanations are offered. All agree that whatever the basis of their reluctance, it was not related to their position on the question of whether the commandment of *yishuv ha'aretz*, as it applies today, is of Torah or Rabbinic origin.

Ever since the Babylonian Exile there have been leaders who, for various reasons, apparently shunned this *mitzvah*. As a result of this phenomenon, the main academies of learning remained in Babylonia until the the 10th century, at which point the population slowly shifted to Europe, and the centers of Torah learning moved with them. Until the 17th century, Torah was strongest in Europe, while only a smattering of sparks glistened from the Holy Land.

Dissemination of Torah Takes Precedence

Rabbi Meir of Rotenberg, one of the Early Authorities, attributes their reluctance to sink roots in Eretz Yisrael to their unwillingness to sacrifice the time it would take from Torah learning to support their families in the Holy Land, where survival and livelihood are infinitely more demanding. Since the Talmud even permits one *to leave* Eretz Yisrael for the purposes of Torah study, how much more so should one not reject his precious learning opportunities in *chutz l'aretz* to settle in Eretz Yisrael if it will entail a serious decrease in his study. He concludes that the importance of learning and disseminating Torah overrides the commandment of *yishuv ha'aretz*.

Rabbi Jacob Emden agrees. He explains that the Babylonian scholars remained in *chutz l'aretz* because the academies there had become the centers of Torah scholarship and legal research. Despite the number of Sages living in Eretz Yisrael, the quality and quantity of learning in the Holy Land did not compare to what was happening in Babylonia at that time. Clearly, this was their primary consideration for remaining in "exile" rather than abandoning their Babylonian residence and adventuring to the Holy Land.

Extenuating Circumstances

Of course there were also many forced to remain in Babylonia due to illness, poverty, national emergency, and so on. Had it been a time of affluence, they would surely have travelled to the Holy Land, despite the benefits provided by the Torah centers in Babylonia. They would have made the trip even though it was obviously not the time of Messianic redemption, the time when every Jew has no choice but to return to his homeland.

These extenuating circumstances take on different expressions for the would-be immigrant. Not all are relieved to learn that they are exempt. For instance, Rabbi Emden writes that he himself weighed the pros and cons of the situation and decided that, without making a vow, he would try, G-d willing, to disentangle from his native land and make the journey to Eretz Yisrael. "When the time comes that this is possible, I will not fear the perils and tribulations of travel, nor focus on my weak physical state (the consequence of my sins and the terrible hardships I have suffered since youth—Bless the L-rd who has never taken away His loving kindness from me). I will journey 'upwards' to His Chosen Land and achieve the perfection of my soul on that sacred ground.

"The L-rd knows the depths of my humbled heart and understands the reality of my situation. Though I live in *chutz l'aretz* amidst material security, and my home is filled with Torah and prayer, still I long for the Holy Land and search the sky hoping...expecting...to find Mount Moriah there. Yet the surrounding countries are at war making it impossible to cross by land or sea without placing oneself in great and certain danger. While my children are young, I cannot travel through the wilderness. Finally I have not yet accumulated sufficient material and spiritual resources such that I will not be entering the palace of the King empty-handed. Were it not for these reasons I would make haste in keeping His charge; I would set forth immediately.

"Yet my hope is from the L-rd and I will wait patiently for the time when I can ascend to the mountaintop where stands the House of G-d. Even this period of delay is for good. With each day of *mitzvoth* I grow more worthy of the privilege, and so do others like me."

Today's Reality

Since World War II, things have changed. Travel is not life-threatening, material survival in Eretz Yisrael is manageable, and the preeminence of Torah centers in *chutz l'aretz* is history. Why, then, do rabbinical leaders still refrain from *aliyah*? Certainly it is not from disdain for the sanctity of the Land.

A contemporary rabbi answers through a parable. If a captain were suddenly to desert his ship, the vessel would surely flounder and possibly even sink. This is because the passengers and crewmen lack the skills to cover in his absence. The helmsmen of world Jewry are the rabbis and sages who navigate for the masses of exiled Jews. Their responsibility to their communities does not permit them the luxury of personal, spiritual development in Eretz Yisrael. If they abandoned ship, their constituencies in *chutz l'aretz* would suffer greatly—their very survival would be endangered.

Chofetz Chaim wrote exactly this. He explained that one of his reasons for not living in Eretz Yisrael was his sense of responsibility to European Jewry. He was filling a role as spiritual and halachic authority of the generation and were he to abandon it, with no one to take his place, the entire structure of Jewish learning and culture would suffer. Nevertheless he thirsted for the Holy Land, and still planned to spend the last years of his life there. He even had a house built in Petach Tikva. But by the time he was ready to "retire his post" he was already too weakened by age to actually accomplish his dream.

Chofetz Chaim (1839-1933) of Radan, Poland, was the leader of world Jewry. His writings include both halachic commentaries and topical, moral issues. His love of his fellow Jew was proverbial.

More recently, the Chief Rabbi of an important American Jewish community came to Israel and asked the Steipler Rav, Rabbi Y.I. Kinefsky, *zatzal*, (among the greatest rabbis of this generation), if he was permitted to fulfill his lifelong dream and heart's desire of settling in Eretz Yisrael. The Steipler asked one question, "Would your departure endanger the level and quality of religious observance in your community?"

"Yes, I believe it would," answered the American rabbi sincerely.

"Then you must stay in America, for your only purpose in life is to serve the Jewish people. You must remain with your community and continue to guide them."

The Decree of *Galuth*

Another reason why some Torah leaders remain in *chutz l'aretz* is their belief that exile is a Divine decree, a bitter medicine which must be swallowed and not spit out by returning to Israel before G-d deems it appropriate. According to this opinion, only with the coming of *Mashiach* are Jews worthy of returning to their homeland. This idea is expressed in a Midrash which compares the expulsion of Adam and Eve to the exile of the Jewish people.

G-d said, "I brought Adam into the Garden of Eden, and commanded him to do certain things and to refrain from others. He violated My instructions and I punished him with expulsion. And so I did with his descendants as well, these being the Jewish people. I brought them into Eretz Yisrael and gave them special commandments to fulfill there. They transgressed My will and I repaid them with expulsion, exactly as I had warned them through My prophet Hosea, 'I will drive them out of My house'" (Hosea 9:15).

This punishment of exile scattered the Jewish people to all corners of the earth, including the remnant which remained in Eretz Yisrael. Though immigration by individuals thirsting for their homeland does not violate the Divine decree, a mass exodus would. Since where Torah leaders go, their communities follow, their immigration to Israel would precipitate a massive *aliyah* and this would force the Messianic era before the world was ready or worthy, and much unnecessary suffering would result. Therefore G-d warned His people not to return *en masse* to the Holy Land, further stating that disobedience to His word would carry disastrous repercussions. For this reason, many Torah leaders remain in *chutz l'aretz*, longing for the day when *Mashiach* announces that it is time to come home.

"Immigration" of the Spirit

The True Credentials

"Wherever wisdom and fear of sin reside, there is found Eretz Yisrael." These are the words of Meiri, a 12th century sage and commentator on the Talmud. These two strengths of character have sustained Jews throughout their long sojourn in *galuth* and have preserved their connection to the Land. "Wisdom and fear of sin," continues Meiri, "are realized in their highest degree, only in the actual Land of Israel. Nevertheless, *wherever* these attributes are cultivated, one reveals the glory of his Creator and merits to delight in the splendor of His Divine Presence, and *this* is the essence of Eretz Yisrael."

The Chazon Ish voiced this same idea. "Poland, with its many *yeshivoth* and its distinction as the dwelling place of the pious Chofetz Chaim as well as residence of the vast majority of Torah leaders, is considered *like Eretz Yisrael*, whereas other countries are still viewed as *chutz l'aretz*."

Rabbi Nathan Shapiro, in his book on Eretz Yisrael, takes Meiri's premise to its inevitable conclusion. He writes that Israel is a metaphor for holiness and the good inclination, whereas *chutz l'aretz* represents the opposite. Therefore, one living in Israel who lets his evil inclination govern his life and divert him from Torah and *mitzvoth* has alienated himself from Eretz Yisrael. Conversely, one living in *chutz l'aretz* who sanctifies himself and leads a godly life has *spiritually* transplanted himself to Eretz Yisrael, and on some level is credited with the merit of actually having made *aliyah*.

Prague, like many other European cities, was an old, established Torah center. Pictured above is the Altnueschul prior to WW II.

A Calamity Which Prompted a Vow

"One who determines to immigrate to Israel as soon as he is in a position to do so," writes Rabbi Jacob Emden at the conclusion of his essay on Eretz Yisrael, "may find that circumstances detain or prevent him from actualizing his plans. Nevertheless, his intention itself will benefit him, and his prayers will be accepted as if he stood in Eretz Yisrael in front of the gate of heaven."

It may happen that a person who actually initiated the process of immigrating to Israel—packed up and set out on his journey—is prevented from realizing his dream by circumstances beyond his control. One such case was Rabbi Abraham Dansig, author of *Chayei Adom*, an important Torah personality in Vilna.

In Kislev, 1804, a fire broke out in his neighborhood and, before anyone realized what was happening, the beams of his house caved

180 / COMMANDMENT TO SETTLE IN ISRAEL

in, nearly killing himself, his wife, and his daughter. All were injured yet managed to escape alive. "The L-rd, in His compassion, reckoned our spilt blood as that of a sacrificial animal and atoned our sins." The death toll that night was over thirty, and many more were wounded. Rabbi Dansig organized a communal fast and composed special prayers to the Almighty. He further made a personal vow that, G-d willing, he would move to Eretz Yisrael as soon as his children married. "I will go up to the Holy City of Jerusalem and spend the rest of my life in that blessed place, serving G-d...."

He was fifty-six at the time and a great proponent of the importance of knowing the details of practical *halacha*. Thus to prepare for his journey, as well as to keep his goal constantly before him, he began to study and codify all the laws pertaining to Eretz Yisrael. He eventually organized this information into a manuscript called *Shaarei Zeddek*. He introduced the book with a warning:

"Should a person enter the king's court ignorant of what constitutes proper and respectful behavior he is liable to insult the king and be severely punished. How much more so when the King is *HaShem*. Therefore, anyone desiring to settle in Israel must become

Left: cover page to the second edition of *Shaarei Zeddek*, 1864. *Right*: cover page to the first edition of *Admath Kodesh*, 1913, by Rabbi Isaac Goldhar. His findings concerning the historical boundary lines and ancient sites and towns are widely accepted today.

proficient in the laws of the Holy Land, else he insult His Creator and bring trouble upon himself. Thus spoke Isaiah, 'When you come to appear before Me, who permits you to trample My courts?' (Isa. 1:12).

"If I am unable, G-d forbid, to immigrate to my homeland, I will fulfill the commandments of Eretz Yisrael by studying them and compiling this work. I lift my hands heavenward, with pure motive and adept action. I am anxious to ascend to His holy place and perform the *mitzvoth* of the Land."

As time passed, however, his health deteriorated and he even had to accept remuneration for his work as judge, a service which he had insisted upon providing free of charge throughout his life. *Shaarei Zeddek* became the standard reference book on the laws of the Land, preparing pilgrims from generation to generation for their new life in Eretz Yisrael.

Rambam's Annual Party

The Jewish soul feels an innate longing to reside in the Holy Land. Rambam, who spent only a short while in Jerusalem and Hebron before settling in Egypt, would celebrate with great festivity the yearly anniversary of the day he set foot in Eretz Yisrael, and asked his children to continue the custom after his death.

A Prayer from *Chutz L'Aretz*

Rebbe Nachman of Breslov composed a number of prayers for those in *chutz l'aretz* aspiring to immigrate to the Holy Land. One reads: Make us worthy to come to Eretz Yisrael, our holy habitation, the headwaters of faith, prayer, and miracles — the true source of life. There lies the root of Israel's attachment to their Heavenly Father. We ask this not based on our merit but as an undeserved gift from Your great and pure generosity. You, in Your infinite kindness and compassion, make us worthy to immigrate to Eretz Yisrael, soon, and there to serve You in truth, fear and love. Quickly redeem us from the depths of *galuth*. We have been exiled from our Land for so many years. Bring us in peace from the four corners of the earth and lead us upright to our Holy Land.

rest. That person said, 'You have been stricken and healed.' I felt G-d's compassion and lovingkindness shine upon me in that moment, and I knew that myself, my grandson. and my daughter would be saved.

"I buried my dead and returned to the Galilee with the two of them. There I remarried and started a new life. Yet a year later the plague returned. My wife was stricken and on the brink of death when the Almighty hearkened to our prayers and accepted our tears, thank G-d.

"Year after year calamities fell upon us and the threat of death never disappeared completely. On Rosh HaShannah, eight years later, my beloved son, Shemuel Zev, and his infant brother, Menachem, both passed away.

"Health was not our only problem. I suffered enormously from the gentiles. The final straw was when they closed off the city of Acco and imprisoned me. It looked as if I would be put to a torturous death. Yet the Merciful One saved me, fulfilling the verse, 'For He has delivered me out of all trouble' (Psalms 54:9). 'My trust is in the L-rd, I shall not fear for what then can a man do to me?'" (ibid. 118:6).

Rabbi Israel of Shaklov was a paragon of humility and courage for the entire Jewish colony in Israel. His whole being was wrapped up in the Holy Land—caring for the needy, disseminating Torah, and officiating as a political leader. His masterpiece on the laws of Eretz Yisrael, *Pe'ath HaShulchan*, "The Corner of the Table," won fame for its depth of insight and clarity.

The Cause of Suffering

The history of the Jewish people in Eretz Yisrael is the history of their self-sacrifice to G-d and Torah. When they prospered, it was because they totally and faithfully surrendered to Him; and when they suffered, it was from their own rebellion. When Abraham asked, "Whereby shall I know that I shall inherit it (Eretz Yisrael)?" (Gen. 15:8), he was asking *HaShem* to indicate by what merit his descendants would inherit the Land. G-d answers that it is in the merit of their sacrifices which could mean either their Temple offerings or their self-sacrifice.

Joshua's war of conquest expressed ultimate patriotism and self-sacrifice by the entire nation. Each man was genuinely willing to die for the Land which the Almighty had given them. And so, in the second wave of settlement, when Ezra gathered the exiles from Babylonia, these pioneers encountered untold hardships. Yet it was exactly this investment in the Land, this suffering, which engendered in them a deeply rooted love of her soil.

Anyone who yearns for Eretz Yisrael must be willing to accept the suffering that may go along with that. He must remain faithful and devoted to his Creator in spite of any discomfort— realizing that whatever comes upon him is an expression of G-d's lovingkindness. To live in Israel is a great privilege and hardships should only make his homeland more beloved.

"The privilege of living in Israel is so dear," declares the author of *Sefer Charedim*, "that even when times grow hard, we should rejoice in the luxury of suffering in the Holy Land. This is why the Torah joins the passage on Amalek, the mythological archenemy of the Jewish people in every generation, with the section about entering Eretz Yisrael in the Torah (Deut., end of chapter 25).... What exactly is the source of this hardship? In fact, it is the age old battle with Amalek that every Jew in every generation must wage. Since the beginning of time Amalek has tried to block our entry into the Land, and even today we see his machinations.

"The section on entering Eretz Yisrael begins with the Hebrew word *veyahi*, 'it will be' (ibid. 26:1), which is spelled with the four letters of the holiest and unspeakable name of G-d, the Tetragrammaton. This proves that living in Eretz Yisrael brings one to union with G-d...."

4

Departure Visa

To gain entrance to the palace of an earthly king one must wrestle with bureaucracies, cajole officials, and otherwise finagle an opening. In contrast, one's exit is a simple process, requiring minimal protocol. Eretz Yisrael, the L-rd's palace, is exactly the opposite. Entrance is open to any Jew. There are no bureaucratic obstacles in one's path, at least in terms of Torah law. Departure, however, is not so easy. According to *halacha*, exit permits are only issued under certain strictly defined circumstances and only with good cause.

Grounds for Departure

The Talmud lists only four justifiable grounds for leaving Eretz Yisrael. One may move to *chutz l'aretz* in order to study Torah, get married, escape a famine (or for other health reasons), and finally to earn a livelihood. The Early Authorities supplemented this list with three more acceptable exemptions: honoring parents, saving someone's life (including one's own in a time of war), and taking a gentile to court in a foreign country. The Later Authorities add one more to the list and permit a person to visit the grave of a *tzaddik* who is buried in *chutz l'aretz*. For any of these reasons a "visa" will be issued, yet only on condition that the person intends to return as soon as possible.

According to *halacha*, neither vacationing in the Greek Islands, mountain climbing in the Swiss Alps, nor the allure of a higher standard of living in America are valid grounds for going overseas.

These restrictions serve to discourage a Jew from abandoning his responsibilities to his homeland, and breaking his precedent of performing the special commandments exclusive to Eretz Yisrael. There is not the same kind of pressure for one in chutz l'aretz to move to Israel for he has never actually demonstrated a commitment to the mitzvah of yishuv ha'aretz, and so no vow, of sorts, is being broken.

Studying Torah

Nevertheless one may leave the Holy Land to study Torah in chutz l'aretz despite the number of highly qualified teachers currently living in Eretz Yisrael. The halacha acknowledges that a person cannot learn from just anyone, no matter how brilliant his teacher may be. Each individual must find a rebbe whose mind, temperament and style are compatible with his own. So critical is this to the learning process, that the Sages decreed it sufficient grounds for leaving the Land. This applies even to kohanim, members of the priestly families, for whom the laws prohibiting yeridah (literally descent, meaning emigration from Israel) are even more stringent.

Similarly, one may go abroad to study secular subjects such as medicine and science, if one's intention is to acquire skills that will enable him to make a living in Eretz Yisrael.

Soul-Mate

Not everyone accepts the opinion that it is appropriate to leave Eretz Yisrael in order to study abroad. For example, the Talmud relates the story (cited earlier) of Rabbi Eliezar ben Shamuah and Rabbi Yochanan who were travelling to the city of Nitivim to study under the venerable Sage and saint, Rabbi Yehuda ben B'Seirah. When they reached Sidon and recalled Eretz Yisrael, they raised their eyes to the heavens and wept. They rent their garments and cried out the verse, "You will occupy it (Eretz Yisrael) and dwell in it. You shall observe all the statutes" (Deut. 11:31-32). They justified their decision to return home with these words, "Dwelling in Eretz Yisrael is equal to all other mitzvoth of the Torah."

This story raises certain questions. Why did they tear their garments? This is the traditional expression of mourning upon hearing that a close relative has died or upon seeing the Temple in ruins (even today). The 17th century Kabbalist, Rabbi Aaron Berachya, suggests another possible motive for their expression of grief and mourning. Tradition teaches that one who lives in Eretz Yisrael, it is as if he were granted an additional soul (i.e. a deepened potential to know G-d and draw close to Him). This incremental leap in spiritual consciousness is bestowed by the merit of being in the Land itself, and as soon as one leaves, he forfeits the gift. Thus the Sages mourned the loss of their additional soul, the awareness of G-d conditional upon their living in Eretz Yisrael. For this semi-death they grieved and tore their garments, as for one whose soul has left his body altogether (G-d forbid). They balanced the costs and benefits of studying abroad and decided to return to Eretz Yisrael, where they could reclaim their precious souls that only grace those who dwell in the Land.

Similarly, when Jacob lay on his deathbed in Egypt, he swore Joseph to bury him in the cave of Machpelah, near Hebron. Were Joseph to refuse his request, Jacob threatened that his soul would depart from him that very instant. Yet what was Jacob really saying, for clearly he was on his deathbed, which meant the soul was preparing to leave his body at any moment anyway?

The explanation is that Jacob feared the loss of his additional soul, acquired in the merit of his dwelling in Israel. When he left the Holy Land, it was a temporary sojourn with the expressed intention of returning at the earliest possible moment. Therefore his additional soul stayed with him. Now, if he died before completing his round trip, and was buried in Egypt, it would belie his original declaration retroactively, turning his temporary excursion into a permanent departure. At that point the soul, conditional upon his making residence in Israel, would immediately depart, only to be replaced by the equivalent, but lower soul associated with *chutz l'aretz*. "Act toward me with truth and kindness," Jacob implored. "I pray you, do not bury me in Egypt" (Gen. 47:29). If Joseph would guarantee that his body would return to Israel, then his special soul would remain with him until his death and he would not spend even one moment of his life without it.

In Search of a Marriage Partner

Another valid reason for leaving Israel is to search for a marriage partner. Since a person's soul mate is decreed at birth, he must be free to find his match no matter where he or she may be living. Torah not only commands marriage as an essential ingredient of a person's spiritual life, but also as his responsibility to the planet. "The world was not created for emptiness. (Rather) He formed it to be inhabited" (Isa. 45:18), a task which is only fulfilled through marriage and procreation. For this reason *halacha* gives top priority to finding a proper mate. Yet even so, it only permits a temporary sojourn.

Rabbi Abraham Isaiah Karelitz (1879-1954) immigrated to Eretz Yisrael at the age of 55 years old from Vilna and settled in Bnei Brak. His classic halachic work, the *Chazon Ish*, covered the whole *Shulchan Aruch* and, over the years, was published in 23 volumes. Thousands came to him with personal problems, health matters and Torah issues. All left with clear answers that helped guide them in life. Although childless he became the father of a whole generation.

The young man thought a minute and rephrased his question. "If I return to America, I can work in my father's business and am assured of making a living that will enable me to remain in a Torah learning environment. If I settle here, I have no such guarantee. The possibility of finding a livelihood that would allow for full or even part-time learning, is not likely."

"In that case," counseled the Chazon Ish, "you should return to America."

Honor of Parents

The Rabbis permit us to leave Eretz Yisrael for the purpose of visiting parents, but only on the condition that we return as soon as possible. The *halacha* is derived from the story of Rabbi Asi who sought permission to exit the borders of Eretz Yisrael and greet his mother who was travelling by caravan to the Holy Land. He wanted to escort her to Eretz Yisrael, and for this he was granted permission. Before he reached her, news arrived that she had passed away. Rabbi Asi reflected, "Had I known this unfortunate fact, I would not have left Eretz Yisrael." *Tifereth Yisrael* concludes from this anecdote that since the commandment to honor parents after their death is Rabbinic, it does not take precedence over the prohibition against leaving Eretz Yisrael.

The question of whether the commandment of *yishuv ha'aretz* can overrule a parent's objections to his child's making *aliyah*, is a delicate one. The Later Authorities debate the problem and no clear solution is presented. Each case must be studied on its own individual merits. For this reason, close consultation with a rabbinic authority is absolutely necessary.

Visiting the graves of the *tzaddikim* is praiseworthy. Today there is a growing interest in visiting the holy places and gravesites in Eretz Yisrael.

Travelling to the Graves of Tzaddikim

Finally, we may leave Israel to visit the gravesites of *tzaddikim*, especially on the *yartzeit* of their passing. The rabbis permit this because such a pilgrimage confers great benefit on both the living and the dead. Recently, there has arisen the possibility of organized tours to Eastern European cities for the express purpose of visiting the graves of *tzaddikim*. Another much frequented tomb is that of the renowned Sephardi Kabbalist, Jacob Abuchatzira in Egypt. Rebbe Nachman's gravesite in Russia is also the object of many a pilgrim's ventures. At one time people frequented the tombs of Ezekiel the prophet near Bagdad, and Ezra the Scribe in southern Iraq. This was before political upheaval and institutionalized anti-Semitism curtailed Jewish movement in these countries altogether.

The Eternal Dream—that came True

In every generation Jews have longed for Eretz Yisrael, they hungered to return to Zion. For most it remained a dream that would never materialize, a futuristic hope inseparable from the Messianic era. Even if it was a *mitzvah*, they reckoned that it was unfulfillable like many other commandments of the Torah. "When the time will come, then we'll go up...."

Yet from the depths of brutal darkness sprang the *reality* (and the *necessity*) of Eretz Yisrael. A young chassidic *rebbe* from Galicia had already been in the concentration camps for several years when a Nazi guard discovered him with a *machzor*, a prayerbook for the High Holy Days. It was a week before Rosh HaShannah and the *rebbe* had borrowed it to jot down key words and phrases so that his prayers would be in order on that holiest of days. The guard became infuriated and beat him mercilessly with a club until he collapsed unconscious on the floor. Miraculously he survived, but the blows had taken their toll...he would remain forever deaf.

In the midst of his beating he prayed to his G-d. "O L-rd, please save me from the hands of this Nazi. For Your sake save me that I may serve You. If You will let me live, I promise to build a *shul* with a *mikveh* in Jerusalem, Your holy city, Jerusalem, Your holy city, Jerusalem...."

Years passed and the *rebbe* started a new life in *chutz l'aretz*. After thirty years, circumstances finally permitted his immigration to Israel. Now he could fulfill his vow which had become, in many ways, his reason for being. Now his dream could become a reality. On a quiet knoll in the Holy Land he built a *shul* and *mikveh*—in Jerusalem, the Holy City, Jerusalem....

והיה באחרית הימים נכון יהיה הר בית ה' בראש ההרים ונשא מגבעות

זכור מרחוק את ה' וירושלם תעלה על לבבכם

Notes

Introduction
Tradition teaches. *Yalkut Shimoni, Ekev*, 860.
One eighteenth century commentator. author of *Kedushath HaAretz*.
The Talmud addresses. *Derech Eretz Zutta*, ch. *shalom*.
Rabbi Yoel Shwartz explains. *Tziyon Beth Chayenu*, I, pp. 78-82.
The Sages anticipate. Mechilta, Bo.
Rabbi Dessler. *Miktav m'Eliyahu*, vol. 3, p. 352.
Chazon Ish. *Peer HaDor*, vol. 4, p. 236.

Part 1: A Terrestrial Abode

Chapter 1: A Pilgrimage to the Holy Land

p. 19   **In the year.** Based on Shelah's letter to his family in Europe; cited in *Eden Tziyon*, pp. 103-106.

p. 21   **The Maggid of Dubno.** from his book of parables *Kol Yaakov*.

p. 22   **prohetic insights.** Cf. *Kuzari*, 2:14, 1:47; the Holy Spirit, however, was not limited by time and space. Cf. *Tziyon Beth Chayenu*, p. 37.

         The Midrash. Cf. *Shelah HaKodesh*.

p. 23   **Chofetz Chaim writes.** *parshath Bo*.

p. 24   **A person might wonder.** Cf. *Eretz Yisrael* (Waxman), no. 84.

         The Zohar. ibid.

Chapter 2: The Measure of Holiness

p. 25   **three dimensions.** Cf. *Sefer Yetzira* 1.

         A Midrash. Song of Songs *Rabba* 5:1.

p. 26   **were hidden from them.** They had been hidden away by King Josiah 40 years prior to the Babylonian conquest. *Yoma* 21b (Tos. *v'urim*); Cf. *Seder HaDoroth*, p. 133, who adds that the sacred vessels were sanctioned only when all the Jewish people lived in Eretz Yisrael.

expansive" but not "a land flowing with milk and honey." Three nations (Hivite, Canaanite and Hittite) are mentioned by the sending of the hornets, which Ramban contends were necessary to send because the majority of these peoples enclosed themselves in fortified cities rather than openly fighting on the battlefield.

Each of the ten nations. *Sefer HaMefoar* by Rabbi Shlomo Malko, cited in *Eretz Yisrael* (Waxman), pp. 227-228.

The sin of the golden calf. *Tuv HaAretz*, p. 11b.

p. 63 **The L-rd's states.** Cf. Malbim, Deut. 19:8, Cf. Rashi.

Chapter 3: The First Influx

p. 65 **includes the Sinai Desert until Eilat.** *Eretz Yisrael* (Tuk.), pp. 82-83.

while other. *Tivu'oth HaAretz* and *Admath Kodesh*.

p. 67 **Nevertheless.** *Tivu'oth HaAretz*, p. 4.

they forgot thousands of laws. *Temurah* 16a. Othniel retrieved them through his lucid and piercing logic (ibid.).

whatever remained. Cf. Rashi, Josh. 1:10 and Ex. 16:35.

At one point He gave Joshua. Rashi, Deut. 31:7; Cf. *Sanhedrin* 8a.

Moreover, G-d promised. Malbim, Josh. 1:5.

p. 68 **G-d averted their anger.** *Temurah* 16a.

First and foremost. *Sefer HaChinuch* (no. 425) asks: Why is this *mitzvah* applicable throughout all time, even though these nations no longer exist? Any *mitzvah* which is withheld from us to do for the simple reason that it is, in reality, impossible for us to do, although Scripture does not limit it in time, is not called a commandment which is no longer capable of being executed. This *mitzvah* and the command to detroy Amalek were close to entirely fulfilled by King David. Even so, they are included among the 613 commandments.

This was an obligatory war. Rambam, *Hilchoth Melachim* 5:1-2.

every man. Women did not fight. Their duty was to supply food, etc. Cf. *Sotah* 8:7 (*Tifereth Yisrael*).

one who evaded this issue. Rambam, ibid. Rahab, who made the spies swear to save her life when the Israelites detroy Jericho, was not from one of the seven nations (*Kaftor v'Ferach*, ch.11, p. 167). She was permitted to convert because her desire stemmed back to a time earlier than the military conquest.

even their "image. Cf. *Melechath Shlomo*, Mishna Oheloth 18:7, in the name of the *Ari Zal*. Cf. *Or HaChayim*, Gen. 28:5, who writes that their very souls did not contain a holy aspect, as verified by the fact that there was never a single instance of conversion by any of them.

p. 70 **Joshua sent a three-point.** Yer. *Shevi'ith* 6:1, Rambam, *Hilchoth Melachim* 6:4-5 (Ravad disagrees with Rambam).

(2) Anyone choosing. Once they accept the seven commandments of the children of Noah they are no longer considered one of the seven nations. Now they are like any other gentile nation (*Kesef Mishna, Hilchoth Melachim* 6:4).

seven Noachide laws. They are: (1) not to serve idolatry, (2) not to blaspheme the name of G-d, (3) not to kill, (4) not to commit adultery, incest, etc., (5) not to steal, including kidnapping, (6) not to eat a limb taken from an animal before it has completely died, (7) to establish laws and judicial procedures. Cf. *Sanhedrin* 56b.

The Gibeonites were afraid. Malbim, Josh. 9:3.

p. 71 **Yet in order that Gentiles.** *Gittin* 46a, Rambam, *Hilchoth Melachim* 6:5, Malbim, Josh. 9:15.

The Gibeonites. were known as *nathinim* ("donated" to the Temple service). King David forbade intermarriage with them because of their cruel ways (*Yevamoth* 78b).

were circumcised. *Kiddushin* 4:1.

or with their gods". The Mishna (*Zavin* 1:5) records a Canaanite idol called *gad yavan* which was shaped like a pigeon and was stationed about 100 meters from the spring of Shiloach south of the Temple Mount.

Yet G-d anticipated. This was predicted in Num. 33:55.

Therefore Scripture likens. *Or HaChayim*, Ramban.

p. 72 **The miracle had a dual objective.** Malbim, Josh. 3:7.

and to instill fear. Cf. Rabbenu Bachaya, Deut. 11:25.

Tuesday. *Seder Olam Rabba*, ch. 11; *Pirkei d'Rabbi Eliezer*, ch.5, claims it was a Thursday.

The miracles...were a sign. Rashi, Deut. 11:31. Cf. Rashi, Gen. 32:11: "for with my staff I have crossed the Jordan." Jacob put his staff on the Jordan and the river split. *Baal HaTurim* adds that the splitting of the Jordan in Joshua's time was in the merit of Jacob.

a number of changes. *Sotah* 34b.

the holy Ark...had followed. Num. 10:21.

Malbim compares. Josh. 3:9.

p. 74 **LAWS CONCERNING...A MIRACLE.** *Berachoth* 54a, *Orech Chayim* 218.

Upon visiting. photographs or a movie of the site is not considered "seeing" (*Maggid Ta'alumoth, Berachoth* ibid.).

Within that 30 day period. However, one may say the blessing without *shem u'malchoth* (Bach).

For other reasons. *Mishna Berura* discusses this in the *Biur Halacha, Kigon Mearvoth*.

the lion's den. Some authorities suggest making the blessing without *shem u'malchoth* at any lion's den or burning furnace (*Eliyahu Rabba*).

Yet today, the exact location. Seder HaDoroth brings this eye-witness report: I saw the lion's den where Daniel was placed and the burning furnace where the three righteous men were cast. The furnace was nearly half full of water and whoever suffers from high fever or malaria washes himself in the water and is instantly healed. (cited in *Chibath Yerushalayim*, p. 300).

204 / Notes

p. 75   **At that site.** In the *Travels of Rabbi Benjamin*, he records going to the Dead Sea and journeying 6 miles to the Pillar of Salt where he witnessed a phenomenal sight. After midnight the pillar was completely intact, and an hour before dawn barely two handbreaths remained standing. Hundreds of goats came during those night hours and licked up the pillar. From the stump of two handbreaths the pillar slowly regained its form during the day and by midnight it once again assumed its full stature, only to be licked away again by the goats. Today, no one has reported seeing this.

who remembers the righteous. "righteous" refers to Abraham in whose merit Lot was saved.

Any person who himself was saved. It is customary for him to give charity and to say, "Behold, now I am giving this charity. May it be His will that it should be considered for me in place of the Thanksgiving offering that I would be obligated to bring if the Temple was standing today." Then he should recite the passage concerning the Thanksgiving offering (Lev. 7:12-15). (*Kaf HaChayim, Orech Chayim* 218:39).

p. 76   **Rabbi Ishtori Haparchi, composed.** *Kaftor v'Ferach*, ch.7, p. 121.

And for Elijah, You divided it. II Kings, ch.2.

Joshua circumcised all the men. Josh., ch.5; *Yevamoth* 72-73.

the mild northern breeze. Cf. *Seder HaDoroth*, p. 92, *viyahi*, until the episode of the spies the northern wind blew.

p. 77   **holy water.** Ashes from the red heifer (Num. 19) are dissolved in a flask of spring water and are sprinkled on a person. Even one drop removes the strongest impurities from him.

according to Ramban. cited in *Eretz Yisrael* (Waxman), p. 188.

The foreskin. *Shelah HaKodesh*, beginning of *lech lecha*.

The first, entirely new. Based on commentary to Lev. *Rabba, Emor* 28, cited in *Eretz Yisrael* (Waxman) with supplementary material, pp. 238-243.

Sefer HaChinuch **writes.** no. 302.

p. 78   **The Midrash.** Lev. *Rabba, Emor* 28.

exempt from most commandments. such as bringing the first-fruits (Deut. 26:1), bringing sacrifices to the Temple (ibid. 12:9), keeping the Sabbatical year (Lev. 25:2), and so on.

When Scripture prefaces. *Kiddushin* 37a-b; Rashi, Deut. 26:2 (and *Sifthei Chachamim*), Ramban, Num. 15:2.

certain exceptions. Rashi, Lev. 15:18; *Kiddushin* ibid.

p. 80   **Also...orlah.** Mishna *Orlah* 1:2.

The Midrash points out. Lev. *Rabba* 25:3. Cf. *Sotah* 14a.

an earthly Garden of Eden. Cf. *Kuzari* 2:14.

Kabbalistic teachings. *Tuv HaAretz*, p. 22b; Cf. *Sotah* 9:12-13; See *Shaar HaChatzer*, no. 72 and no. 169.

Grace...instituted in stages. *Berachoth* 48b

p. 81   **this precious Land where.** *Shiboleth HaLeket*, cited by *Beth Yosef, Tur, Orech Chayim* 187.

two additional ideas. *Berachoth* 48b, *Orech Chayim* 187:3.

the Land prior to circumcision. Rabbi Yaakov Emden Siddur, *Birchath HaMazon*, p. 121; Cf. *Eretz Yisrael* (Tuk.) ch. 27 (4), p. 90.

p. 83 **The Talmud explains.** *Chullin* 91b.
This blessing was an essential. *Tuv HaAretz*, p. 33b.
Midrashic interpretation. Tanchuma, cited by Rashi and Rabbenu Bachaya.
Jericho. *Sifri*, Deut. 11:24; Cf. Rashi, Josh. 2:1.
even the locks. *Me'am Loez*, Josh. 6:4.
Each day...the Israelite army. Malbim places the soldiers of all the tribes at the front except for Dan who marched as a rear guard unit.

p. 84 **circumscribed...seven times.** This procedure is similar to circling the deceased before burial. See *Me'am Loez*, Josh. 6:4. Malbim writes that the number seven hints to the power of holiness: seven days, seven ram horns, seven priests, seven encirclements.
Later this prayer was fixed. *Me'am Loez*, ibid.; Cf. Chida, *Devash L'fi*, oth aiyn, 9.
declares the sovereignty of G-d. Just as "Hear O Israel" affirms this Oneness and has a large letter *aiyn* and *daleth*, so *Aleinu* begins with an *aiyn* and ends with a *daleth* (*Kaf HaChayim, Orech Chayim* 132:2, no. 15). Cf. Bach, *Tur Orech Chayim* 133.
Its truth stuns. Yesod v'Shorash HaAvodah, Gate 5, ch. 10.
Rabbenu Hai Gaon. cited in *Shaar HaChatzer*, no. 425, together with the responsas of Rif and Rabbenu Gershom on the topic of why *Aleinu* should be recited in *chutz l'aretz*.
tradition teaches. *Mishna Berura, Orech Chayim* 132:2 (8).

p. 85 **The phrase.** Rabbenu Bachaya, Ex. 13:5.
Joshua composed. *Seder HaDoroth*, p. 94.

p. 86 **Moses designated.** Rashi, Deut. 18:2.
This insured against. Rambam, *Hilchoth Terumah* 1:2.
by a shrub. *Babba Bathra* 56a.
"The totality. *Tuv HaAretz*, pp. 11b-12a.

p. 87 **but no one ever identified.** Cf. *Tziyon Beth Chayenu*, I, p. 88. The question of the Palestinian claim to Israel is not one based on religious, Divinely-ordained roots. It is merely a political maneuver. Similar claims were made in the time of Alexander the Great by a group of African settlers. Cf. *Sanhedrin* 91a.

Chapter 4: The Conquest of Suria

p. 89 **a national conquest.** Rambam, *Hilchoth Melachim* 5:
sole of (his) foot. This applied to Joshua. Moses, had he brought the Jewish people into Eretz Yisrael, would not have had to conquer the enemy through tactical warfare. For him the literal words, "every place that the sole of your foot shall tread I shall give to you," meant just by marching across the land the heathens would collapse dead (Malbim, Josh. 1:3). Thus, had Moses led them into Eretz Yisrael they would have possessed all of her territories and been at liberty to conquer *chutz l'aretz*.

206 / Notes

p. 90 **fear in the hearts of his enemies.** "David's renown went out into all the lands; and the L-rd brought fear of him upon all the nations" (I Chron. 14:17).
Before a king. or the leader of the generation. Cf. *Tosefoth Yom Tov*, Sanhedrin 2:4.
Before a king can annex. Rambam, *Hilchoth Melachim* 5:1-2; Sanhedrin 1:5.
according to the boundaries. *Sifri*, Deut. 51.

p. 91 **The *urim and tumim*.** According to Ramban it is one of the 613 Commandments to ask Divine permission before going to war. Cf. *v'Yoel Moshe, Maamer Yishuv Eretz Yisrael*, section 13.

p. 92 **When Yoab.** *Yalkut Shimoni*, Psalms 60:1.
Chushan-Rishathaim. Judges 3:8-10.
which Scripture records. II Sam. 8, I Chron. 18.
it never actually assumed this status. Gittin 8, Tos. Avodah Zorah 21a.
The Midrash explains. *Sifri*, Deut. 51 on verse 11:24.
Yebusites...on Mount Zion. According to this *Sifri* the Yebusites were one of the seven Canaanite nations. Cf. Rambam, *Hilchoth Terumah* 1:3 and Malbim, Judges 1;8. Rashi and Radak, however, hold that the people dwelling in the stronghold of Mount Zion were descendants of the Hittites and the oath of peace between them and Abraham was still binding. (Josh. 15:63, Deut. 12:17, and Judges 1:21).

p. 95 **One explanation.** *Mo'adim v'Zemanim*, vol 5, no. 345.
Rabbi Yoel Teitelbaum. *v'Yoel Moshe, Maamer Yishuv Eretz Yisrael*, sect. 20; concerning the Midrash cited above that Yoab and David asked the Sanhedrin, see sect. 24.
Elijah built an altar. I Kings 18.
If true. The *urim* and *tumim* likewise were not approached in order that the Divine agency should not have to approve something which under normal circumstances was against Torah law.

p. 96 **Suria...certain agricultural.** *Oheloth* 18:7, *Challah* 47.
In other areas. See *Kaftor v'Ferach*, ch. 13 and Gittin 8a.
a Jew in Israel may rent. *Avodah Zorah* 1:8.
nor show them any mercy". ibid. 20a, "any mercy (*tichanem*)" is interpreted, "Do not give them a resting place (*chaniya*) in Eretz Yisrael."

Chapter 5: The Second Influx

p. 97 **annulled the Yom Kippur fast.** Cf. I Kings 8:65-66 (Radak).
422 B.C.E. Some modern Jewish historians date it 586 B.C.E., and claim that the Second Temple stood nearly 600 years instead of the traditional 420.
The new borders created. *Seder Olam Rabba*, ch. 30; Cf. *Yevamoth* 82b. The whole question whether or not the first sanctification by Joshua was temporary or forever is disputed by Resh Lakish and Rabbi Yochanan.

p. 99 **Moses sang.** Whether they repeated word for word after Moses, sang just the refrain, or sang in unison is debated in *Sotah* 30b.

Your people. Berachoth 4a, *Sotah* 36a, *Sanhedrin* 98b. Cf. Maharsha.

Had the entire...with Ezra. *Torah Nation*, p. 54; not like Rashi, *Sotah* 36a, who explains the sin stemmed back to their forebears in the First Temple; *Reshith Chochmah*, Gate of Fear 3:14, holds the sin was intermarriage which was widespread at that time.

Both Joshua and Ezra...began counting. *Archin* 32b-33a, *Seder Olam Rabba*, ch.30; Cf. Rambam, *Hilchoth Shemitah v'Yovel* 10:2-8, 12:15-16.

Yet...the Torah requires that all Jews. Rambam, ibid. There were seventeen Jubilees in all (*Seder Olam Rabba*, ch.11). Cf. *Tos. Nida* 47a *lo*, who holds the Jubilee continued even after the Ten Tribes were exiled since there were residences from all the tribes living in Eretz Yisrael.

Resh Lakish. *Yoma* 9a; Cf. *Tziyon Beth Chayenu*, I, pp. 130-131, where Resh Lakish's apparent outburst of hatred is discussed. Cf. *Yevamoth* 82a, where they debate if the first sanctification was or was not forever.

p. 100 **based on a verse.** "If she be a wall, we will build upon her a palace of silver; and if she be a door, we will enclose her with boards of cedar" (Song of Songs 8:9). He interpreted the verse as follows: If your forebears had come in the time of Ezra in strength like a wall, all together, they would have been compared to silver which does not corrode with the passage of time, symbolizing the return of the *Shechinah*. Now, however, that you returned like wood doors which swing to and fro, indicating that the Influx was only partial, you are compared to cedarwood which is susceptible to decay, connoting that the *Shechinah* could not dwell in the Second Temple as it had in the First Temple.

his mentor disagreed. Cf. Rashi, Gen. 9:27.

One township, Vermizah. from *Seder HaDoroth*, cited in *Chibath Yerushalayim*, pp. 268-269.

On the other hand. Cf. *Torah Nation*, p. 54.

but delayed his departure. *Megillah* 16b. The Talmud offers this as a proof that studying Torah is greater than building the Temple.

Baruch ben Neriah. Seder HaDoroth, p. 128; Cf. Maharsha *Megillah* 16b, who suggests that Baruch died in the second year of Daryavesh's reign. If so, why did Ezra linger five more years before embarking to Eretz Yisrael?

p. 101 **Their five month procession.** Cf. *Me'il Tzadaka*, no. 26.

p. 102 **All this...at great disadvantage.** Cf. parable by the Maggid of Dubno, *Ohel Yaakov, parshath Emor*, pp. 127-128.

Generations passed...until a shepherd boy. *Seder HaDoroth*, pp. 128-129.

the town of Al Azair. where his tomb is located today. For generations it was a major pilgrimage spot for Sephardi Jews, especially during the period between Passover and Shavuoth.

p. 104 **The question of why Joshua's...has baffled.** *Yevamoth* 82a-b, Rambam, *Hilchoth Terumoth* 1:5.

One scholar suggests. *Tosefoth Yom Tov* on Mishna *Ediyoth* 8:6.

p. 105 **Another commentator.** *Moadim v'Zemanim*, vol. 5, beginning of no. 345.

p. 107 **oral proclamation.** Cf. Ridvaz, *Hilchoth Terumoth* 1:5.

but Ezra had intentionally forced. *Kiddushin* 69b.

p. 108 **Purposely he avoided.** *Yevamoth* 16a; Cf. *Kaftor v'Ferach*, ch.11, p. 274.

The borders...were smaller. Cf. Mishna *Shevi'ith* 6:1, 9:2, *Challah* 4:8, *Ediyoth* 8:6.

p. 109 **as dictated by law.** *Shevuoth* 2:2.

p. 110 **Rambam asks.** *Hilchoth Beth HaBichirah* 6:16.

the Talmud explains. *Megillah* 28a.

p. 111 **This sanctity is Rabbinically derived.** Rambam's view is that Ezra's sanctification gave it Rabbinical status and not full Torah status because not all Jewry returned with Ezra. *S'mag* holds that Ezra's sanctification was of Torah status until the destruction of the Second Temple and from then onwards was Rabbinical. *Tur* holds that it has full Torah status even today. Ridvaz (*Hilchoth Terumoth* 1:5) ponders: Ezra's sanctification was for all time because of the oral proclamation. If so, why did not Joshua sanctify it orally, too? Joshua foresaw that the Temple would be destroyed, and if he sanctified it eternally, there would be no way for the poor to support themselves during the Sabbatical year.

LAWS OF TITHES. *Yoreh De'ah* 331.

Rabbi Samson Raphael Hirsch writes. *Horeb*, ch. 42 and Deut. 14:22.

for human consumption. Animal food, as well as ownerless fruit, or food grown in Eretz Yisrael on property owned by a gentile, or grown in neighboring countries, are usually exempt from tithes, although a rabbinic authority should be consulted.

p. 114 **It is forbidden...on the Sabbath.** If accidently done, however, the tithed food may be eaten immediately, even by the one who did the separation.

10. Today after separating. *Terumah gedolah* is estimated while *terumath maaser* must be precisely measured.

one wraps the separated. Wrapping is necessary because of the sanctity of the *terumah* which may not be treated in a degrading manner.

the coin. and not paper-money. The coin likewise must have an engraving on it.

of local currency. which today includes the *shekel* in Israel and U.S. coinage in America.

fluctuates. One coin which contains fifty *perutoth* today may devaluate and be worth less in the course of time. Therefore, one should inquire from time to time the exact value of a *perutah*.

When it becomes "full". THE METHOD OF REDEEMING *MAASER SHENI* COINAGE: After the coin(s) is 'full' it may be redeemed (thus removing the sanctity of *maaser sheni* embedded in it) except for the *perutah chamorah*, on a second coin worth at least a *perutah*. While holding the 'empty,' second coin, one says: "The *perutah chamorah* of *maaser sheni* which is in the 'full' coin(s), set aside for the purpose of redeeming *maaser sheni* and *ravai*, should remain *maaser sheni* while the rest of the *maaser* within this coin(s), as well as *ravai*, should be profaned (become *chullin*), it and the 'fifth,' on this 'empty' coin." This second coin is then destroyed. Now the first coin is empty except for the *perutah chamorah*, and may be reused to tithe. In this way a "full" silver dollar can be emptied on a penny and reused again.

PERUTAH CHAMORAH: At any single tithing the portion of *maaser sheni* must be equal to one *perutah*. If not, the transference from the produce to the coin cannot take place. The *perutah chamorah* is the amount in the *perutah* coinage (in each coin if more than one coin is set aside) which without a doubt is sanctified with the holiness of *maaser sheni*. This allows one to redeem fruit which is worth less than a *perutah*. For example: if the food to be tithed is worth 11 *perutoth* (or less), it is certain that the *maaser sheni* (9%) is less than one *perutah*. Since the value of a *perutah* fluctuates, one should regularly ask the current value of a *perutah* in order to be sure that the coins in his possession have a *perutah chamorah* at all times.

need not be in one's possession. Therefore one living in Israel may have U.S. coins set aside in America for this purpose, and vice-versa.

p. 116 **the world divides into three.** Rambam, *Hilchoth Terumoth* and *Hilchoth HaChodesh* 5:11; Cf. *Kaftor v'Ferach*, ch.13, p. 336.

four separate empires. *Seder Olam Rabba*, ch.30.

p. 118 **The criteria.** This discussion is based on Rabbi Y.M. Tukashinsky's investigation in his book *Eretz Yisrael*, pp. 28-32, and begins only after the period of mountaintop fire signaling ceased (*Rosh HaShannah* 21a). This includes the present borders. Cf. *Eretz Yisrael* (Tukashinsky), p. 34, where Eilat is discussed.

Chapter 6: The Messianic Eretz Yisrael

p. 123 **Much discussion centers.** *Sifri* on this verse.

sin of the spies. Num. ch.13-14.

p. 124 **Jerusalem...between tribes seven and eight.** Malbim (Ezek. 48:2-7) explains that in one sense Jerusalem's portion is in the *middle* of the 12 tribes. Among the first seven tribes, Manasseh and Ephraim may be considered as one tribe since they are the sons of Joseph. Therefore, Jerusalem's portion begins the second half, with five more tribes lined up south of it. Jerusalem's placement in the second half is to counterbalance the fact that in the first half are situated the leader-tribes of the four encampments.

210 / Notes

allocates to each of the twelve tribes. Cf. *Tosefoth Yom Tov, Taanith* 1:3.

Malbim...solves these riddles. Ezek. 47-48. For details, see especially his commentary on 47:15-19. How Malbim pinpoints Zor and Sidon north of Mount Hor is not clear.

the language of Ezekiel's vision. 47:13, and Malbim on verse 14.

p. 125 **indefinitely beyond the Jordan.** Cf. Song of Songs *Rabba* 137, where "the eastern direction" is interpreted even further—unlimited to include the whole world.

p. 126 **the tribes will not atrophy into extinction.** There is a famous letter sent in 1646 by the king of the Lost Tribes to the leaders of world Jewry. Reprinted with commentary in *Even Sapir*, I, p. 296, and *Keter Shem Tov* (Rabbi Gagin), parts IV-V, in the section "The Jews of Cochin," pp. 10-15.

He will bring them back. Cf. *Tosefoth Yom Tov, Sanhedrin* 10:3, where he explains the Mishna, "the Ten Tribes will not return in the future," in light of this prophecy of Ezekiel which openly states that they will return. Cf. Rabbenu Bachaya, Deut. 30:2.

the Midrash asks. Song of Songs *Rabba* 1:37. Cf. *Yalkut Shimoni*, end of Ezek.

Another Midrash. *Pisikta Rabba* 1, cited in *Yalkut Eretz Yisrael, Shaar Atidoth HaAretz* 10.

best understood figuratively. *Yalkut Eretz Yisrael*, ibid., 23 in commentary *Eretz Yehuda*.

p. 128 **First...Later...Finally.** Author's humble opinion.

It was Passover Seder. *Kumi Ori*, ch.4, pp. 62-63.

Part 3: Beneath the Holy Altar

Chapter 1: Altar of Atonement

p. 131 **The Sages elaborate.** *Ketuboth* 111a.

his sins are forgiven. cited in *Me'am Loez*, Deut.32:43.

walk several strides and return. Cf. *Shaar HaChatzer* no. 57; some authorities hold this blessing applies only to one who dies in Eretz Yisrael, as Midrash Proverbs 17 brings in the name of Rabbi Yochanan: Everyone who walks even one hour in Eretz Yisrael and dies there is guaranteed the world-to-come. Cf. *Yalkut Eretz Yisrael*, p. 54.

Rebbe Nachman. *Rabbi Nachman's Wisdom*, p. 54.

p. 132 **Maharal of Prague.** Chidushei Aggadoth, *Ketuboth* 111a. For esoteric interpretations see *Shaar HaChatzer* no. 325, *Ben Yehoyada, Ketuboth* 111a, and *Tuv HaAretz*, pp. 27a-30b.

The venerable. *Zohar, Acharei*.

p. 133 **The Talmud.** *Ketuboth* 112a-b.

Rabbi Chanina. Tos. *Ketuboth* 112a.

Rather each illustrates. Cf. *Eretz Yisrael* (Waxman), pp. 91-93, in the name of *Yad Yosef*.

shade to sun demonstrates. Based on Rashi.

p. 134 **When Rambam.** *Hilchoth Melachim* 5:10.
Nevertheless, if one feels. in the name of Rabbi Moses Sternbuch and Rabbi Y.M. Zacharish, *shelita*. The author of *Shevat Mussar* writes that at first glance this act appears to condone the forbidden act of bowing to the ground. Yet since Eretz Yisrael is the primary resting place of the *Shechinah*, the Land has sanctity like the cover of a Torah scroll. Therefore kissing the stones of Eretz Yisrael is, metaphorically speaking, like kissing the Divine Presence which resides in them.
says the Zohar. *Acharei*.

p. 135 **This is a holy angel.** from *Sefer HaMaaloth*, cited in *Shaar HaChatzer*, no. 537.
by one commentator. ibid.
The words of the prophet. *Zohar, Terumah*.
The difference between. from *Sefer HaMaaloth*.
Burial of the dead. *Sanhedrin* 46b. Today due to insensitivity and the high cost of funerals, cremation is becoming more prevalent even in Jewish circles. Torah law forbids it. The caption in one advertisement reads: "CREMATION, Reduce the High Cost of Dying," and has a picture of a ship with a well-dressed man wearing a skipper's cap reciting something from a book, and a woman wearing white holding an urn containing the ashes. Hanging off the ship's railing is an American flag.

p. 136 **Interestingly.** Cf. *Tziyon Beth Chayenu*, I, pp. 58-60.
Rabbi Enan. *Ketuboth* 111a. Cf. *Avoth d'Rabbi Nathan* 26:2.
Similarly Maharsha explains. *Ketuboth* ibid.
One 17th century writer. Rabbi Azariya Pigo of Valencia, author of *Bina l'Itim*.

p. 137 **writes Malbim.** Gen. 23:20, *Torah Or*.

p. 139 **Even when someone is buried.** Rama, *Yoreh De'ah* 363:1.
A story is told. *Yer. Kelayim*, ch.9. See similar story in *Ketuboth* 111a. Cf. commentary of *Bina l'Itim*, cited in *Eretz Yisrael* (Waxman), p. 59.
A commentator. author of *Tuv Yerushalayim*, cited in *Shaar HaChatzer*, no. 454.
Rabbi Meir...Ulah. *Yer. Kelayim*, ch.9.

p. 141 **(a) spared.** called *chibut ha'kever*. Cf. *Reshith Chochmah*, Gate of Fear, end of ch.12.
The Talmud proves. *Sanhedrin* 90b.
Rabbi Shimon ben Lakish. *Yer. Kelayim*, ch. 9; Cf. *Yalkut Eretz Yisrael*, pp. 79-80. Similar story is found in *Ketuboth* 111a.
Just as Eretz Yisrael. Cf. *Adrath Eliyahu*, cited in *Shaar HaChatzer*, no. 119.

p. 144 **Over 600 years ago.** *Kaftor v'Ferach*, ch. 11, pp. 298-299.
The Talmud asks. *Sotah* 34b. *Tosefoth* explains that when an individual prays at a grave, the dead realize that they in turn are to pray before G-d.

212 / Notes

p. 145 **The prohibition of necromancy.** Cf. *Sanhedrin* 65, *Yoreh De'ah* 179.
The Zohar summarizes. Acharei, cited in Responsas of *Minchath Elazar*, part I, no. 68.

p. 146 **All agree.** Maharil, Bach, *Chayei Adom*.
Many authorities. summarized in *Gesher HaChayim*, ch. 26, no. 7, and *Minchath Elazar*, I:68.
One's manner. Gesher HaChayim, ibid. Cf. Responsas of Chatham Sofer, *Orech Chayim* 166.
The opportunity. Gesher HaChayim, 26:9.

p. 147 **Furthermore, the Talmud.** *Chullin* 7b.
Rabbi Abba. *Zohar*, cited in *Hilyulah d'Rashbi*, p. 43.
Sefer Chassidim. no. 450.

p. 148 **One incident.** Cited in *Toldoth Rabbi Shimon Lavi*, by Rabbi A.Z. Margoliyoth. Cf. *Seder HaDoroth*, pp. 127-128, for the story of an Assyrian king who forced the Jews to open the tomb of the prophet Baruch ben Neria, Ezra's mentor, and how the incident was an incentive for the king's conversion to Judaism.
"If one, passing. *Pesikta Rabbati*, 12.

p. 149 **We are taught.** Jer. *Shekalim*, end of ch.2.
mention of the author's name. Cf. *Amirath Devar b'Shem Omro*, by the author of *Kuntrath Aruuth* (Rabbi M. Rabinowitz).
redemption to the world. *Megillah* 15b.
traditionally described. *Yevamoth* 97a.
Midrash concerning King David. Yer. *Shekalim*, ch.2, *Yevamoth* 96b-97a and Tos.
Maharsha. *Yevamoth* 96b. Cf. another interpretation by *HaKotev, Ein Yaakov*, Yer. *Shekalim*, ch. 2.

p. 150 **Rambam died.** Cf. *Sifthei Tzaddikim*, p. 96, and *Seder HaDoroth*, p. 206.

Part 4: The Commandment to Settle in Israel

Chapter 1: Longing for the Land

p. 155 **HaShem's private garden.** Cf. *Kol Bo*, no. 127.
Yet even more so. The Sabbath envelopes one day a week, Passover and Succoth for the seven days of the festival, etc.

p. 156 **Rabbi Jacob Emden wrote.** Introduction to his *Siddur Beth El*, 6.
three hundred. Cf. *Tziyon Beth Chayenu*, I, pp. 153-154.

p. 158 **Second, the calendar.** *Sefer HaMitzvoth, mitzvah aseh*, 153.
The innate yearning...from Abraham. Midrash cited by *Sefer Charedim*, ch.59, p. 234. Cf. *Eretz Yisrael* (Tuk.), ch.27, "The Jews' bond to the Land of Israel."
forth on the very day. Cf. *Me'am Loez*, Gen. 12:4.
Isaac was a unique case. Cf. Rabbenu Bachaya, Gen. 26:3.

p. 159 **Jacob pondered.** Rashi, *Me'am Loez*.
One explanation. *Midrash Rabba* Gen. 96. Cf. *v'Yoel Moshe, Maamer Yishuv Eretz Yisrael*, no. 50, for another answer.
Moses, who pleaded. Cf. *Eretz Yisrael* (Tuk.), ch.27, p. 96.

Notes / 213

         the Talmud asserts. *Ketuboth* 110b; Cf. *Haflah*, brought in *Eretz Yisrael* (Waxman), p. 33. Rabbi Nathan Shapiro comments that this is referring to one who lives in Eretz Yisrael after the destruction of the Temple. And when the Temple was standing, he in fact (figuratively speaking) had G-d.

         The Sages derive. Rambam, *Hilchoth Melachim* 5:12.

         Chapter 2: The Commandment of Yishuv HaAretz

p. 161 **Rabbi Yehuda...subscribed to the opinion.** *Ketuboth* 111a, *Berachoth* 24a.

         emigration from Babylonia. but not from other countries to Eretz Yisrael. Rabbi Jacob Emden explains that Babylonia, like no other place in *chutz l'aretz*, is similar to Eretz Yisrael. First our ancestral roots go back to Abraham who was born in Ur Kasdim and there G-d revealed Himself to him. Second, when the Jews were exiled at the destruction of the First Temple, they were expatriated to their "mother's house" where the Aramaic language was close to their native Hebrew. Furthermore, in Rabbi Yehuda's time the Babylonian *yeshivoth* were the spiritual fountainheads of Torah erudition.

         transgressed the prophecy. Cf. Tos., *bavalah*, that although this verse concerns the Babylonian exile, it equally applies to the second exile.

         three times in Song of Songs. *Ketuboth* 111a; Cf. *Tziyon Beth Chayenu*, I, p. 134.

p. 162 **the Talmud states.** ibid.

         one night he dreamt. *Berachoth* 57a.

         Rabbi Zeira stopped one last time. *Shabath* 41a.

p. 163 **"the air of Eretz Yisrael.** *Babba Bathra* 158b.

         His funeral. *Megillah* 6a.

         four major positions. listed in *v'Yoel Moshe, Maamar Yishuv Eretz Yisrael*, nos. 55-68.

         Ramban included. *mitzvah aseh* no. 4.

p. 164 **Many Later Authorities...and others.** Rashbatz (a *rishon*), Tashbatz, *Terumath HaDeshen*, Maharit, *Pe'ath HaShulchan*, *Me'il Tzaddakah*, Chazon Ish, Avnei Nezer, Eved HaMelech (Rabbi S. Houminer).

         Some authorities even go so far. *Avnei Ezra*, cited in *v'Yoel Moshe, Maamer Yishuv Eretz Yisrael*, no. 55.

         Rambam...He concludes. according to *Pe'ath HaShulchan* 2:28.

p. 165 **Rashi, Rosh.** Also Rashbash and *Shiyorei Knesseth HaGedolah*.

         They challenge Ramban's proofs. *Megillath Ester*, countering Ramban's view, *mitzvah aseh* no. 4.

         Others counter their critque. view of *Pe'ath HaShulchan* 1:3.

p. 166 **This...is the opinion of Rambam.** *v'Yoel Moshe* says this is the opinion of Rabbi Meir of Rotenberg cited by Rosh at the end of tractate *Ketuboth*. According to *Yesh Seder l'Mishna* this is also the opinion of Rif and Tur.

         opinion of Rabbi Chaim HaKohen. Tos. *Ketuboth* 110b.

Similarly, when Jacob. Rabbi Chaim Palaji's commentary to the Midrash, cited in *Eretz Yisrael* (Waxman), p. 260.

then his special soul would remain. A "practical" difference is in the fact that when one dies in Eretz Yisrael he is taken by a holy angel of G-d and not by a destructive angel. The same is true of one who dies while on a sojourn to *chutz l'aretz*.

The search for a marriage partner. *Avodah Zorah* 13a.

p. 190 **might disagree about whether to make *aliyah*.** *Ketuboth* 13:11; *Even HaEzer* 75:3-4.

Finally in times of famine. *Babba Bathra* 91a-b; Rambam, *Hilchoth Melachim* 5:9.

by the letter of the law. ibid. 91b. Cf. *Eretz Yisrael* (Waxman), no. 78, pp. 192-195.

p. 191 **In the late 17th century.** *Midrash Eliyahu*, cited in *Shaar HaChatzer*, no. 220, p. 76a. Rabbi Elijah HaKohen is best known for his work *Midrash Talpiyot*.

The standard of living. Yer. *Yadayim*, cited by Rif at end of Tractate *Sanhedrin*; Rambam, *Hilchoth Melachim* 5:9.

The story is told. As told to the author by Rabbi Y.M. Zacharish, a disciple of the Chazon Ish.

p. 193 **the story of Rabbi Asi.** *Kiddushin* 31b.

Tiferith Yisrael. *Kiddushin* 1:7, no. 54.

The Later Authorities debate. *Shaarei Zeddek*, ch. 11:5 (*Binath Adom* 3), feels the parents' wishes prevail, while *Pe'ath HaShulchan* 2:21, disagrees.

to visit gravesite of *tzaddikim*. Cf. *Shaarei Teshuva, Orech Chayim* 568:11, note 20; *Sedei Chemed*, beginning of *Maarecheth Eretz Yisrael*.

Glossary

aliyah: immigration to Israel.

baal teshuva: repentant.
Baalei Tosefoth: 12th and 13th century talmudic scholars from France and Germany.

challah: portion of dough set aside for priest.
chassidim: disciples of Baal Shem Tov.
chayim: life, living.
chutz l'aretz: outside the Land of Israel.

Eretz Yisrael: Land of Israel.

galuth: exile, diaspora.
Gemora: Talmud.
g'vuloth ha'aretz: boundaries of the Land (of Israel).

halacha: Jewish law.
HaShem: G–d, lit. "the Name."

kelipoth: negative evil forces.
kibush yochid: conquest by an individual monarch.

lashon hora: slanderous words.

Mashiach: Messiah.
maaser: tenth of one's produce.
matzah: unleavened bread.
mikveh: immersion pool.
minyan: quorum of men praying together.
mitzvah (-oth): commandment(s).

oleh: immigrant to Israel.
Olei Bavel: influx of Babylonian Jews at the beginning of the Second Temple.
Olei Mitzrayim: influx of Jews from Egypt in the time of Joshua.
Omer: a measure of flour offering brought at the Temple on the 16th of Nisan.

perutah: ancient coin worth 1/40th of a gram of pure silver.

rebbe: chassidic leader.

Shechinah: Divine Presence.
Shema: The prayer, "Hear, O Israel..." recited twice a day.
shemitah: Sabbatical year.
shul: synogague.
succah: booth.

Taryag mitzvoth: 613 Torah commandments.
tefillin: phylactery.
terumah: priestly portion.
tzaddik(-im): righteous one(s).

urim and *tumim*: breastplate/oracle worn by the High Priest.

yartzeit: the anniversary day of someone's passing away.
yeshivoth: schools of talmudic study.
yishuv ha'aretz: settlement in the Land.

zatzal: abb. of "may the deeds of the righteous be remembered for a blessing."

Bibliography

Primary Sources:

Ben Shimon, Rabbi David, *Shaar HaChatzer*, Jerusalem, 1852.

Goldhar, Rabbi Isaac, *Admath Kodesh*, Jerusalem, 1913.

Goldstein, Rabbi Chaim, *Mikomoth HaKedoshim*, Jerusalem, Yeshivath Kodesh Hilulim, 1978.

Hagiz, Rabbi Moses, *Sefath Emeth*, Vilna, 1876.

Haparchi, Rabbi Ishtori, *Kaftor v'Ferach*, Jerusalem, Luntz ed., 1897.

Horowitz, Rabbi Chaim, *Chibath Yerushalayim*, Jerusalem, Mushkowitz ed., 1964.

Horowitz, Rabbi Isaiah, *Eden Tziyon*, Jerusalem, Masura, 1957.

Muzafi, Rabbi Solomon, *Sifthei Tzaddikim*, Jerusalem, 1981.

Sathon, Rabbi Chaim, *Eretz Chayim*, Jerusalem, 1908.

Shapiro, Rabbi Natan, *Tuv HaAretz*, Jerusalem, 1891.

Sizling, Rabbi Judah, *Yalkut Eretz Yisrael*, Vilna, 1899.

Shwartz, Rabbi Yoel, *Tziyon Beth Chayenu*, Jerusalem, Yeshivath Devar Yerushalayim, 1981.

Shwartz, Rabbi Joseph, *Tivuoth HaAretz*, Jerusalem, Luntz ed., 1900.

Teichtal, Rabbi Isachar S., *Em HaBanim Smecha*, Jerusalem, 1983.

Teitelbaum, Rabbi Yoel, *v'Yoel Moshe*, New York, Jerusalem Pub., 1961.

Tukatzinsky, Rabbi Yechiel, *Eretz Yisrael*, Jerusalem, Lewin-Epstein, 1956.

Tukatzinsky, Rabbi Nisan, *HaAretz l'Givuloteyah*, Jerusalem, 1980.

Waxman, Rabbi Chaim, *Eretz Yisrael*, Jerusalem, 1963.

Secondary Sources:

Azulai, Rabbi Abraham, *Chesed l'Avraham*, Levuv, 1863.

Bachaya, Rebbenu, commentary on the Torah, Mosad HaRav Kook ed., Jerusalem, 1982.

Ben Ish Chai, Rabbi Yosef Chaim, *Ben Yehoyadah*, Jerusalem, 1965.

Berachya, Rabbi Aaron, *Maavar Yabbok*, Vilna, 1896.

Culi, Rabbi Jacob, *Me'am Loez*, Jerusalem, 1968.

Dansig, Rabbi Abraham, *Shaarei Zeddek*, Jerusalem, 1864.

Dubno, Rabbi Jacob of, *Ohel Yaakov*, Warsaw, 1886.

Eisenstein, Rabbi J.D., *Otzer Masa'oth*, Tel Aviv, 1967.

Emden, Rabbi Jacob, *Siddur Beth El*, New York, 1911.

Goldberg, Rabbi Abraham Hillel, *HaAretz u'Mitzvotheyah*, Jerusalem, Tifutzah, 1986.

Hagiz, Rabbi Moses, *Elei Masa'ei*, Jeruralem, 1932.

Hen, Rav Yaakov, *Aliyoth Eliyahu*, Tel Aviv, Peer, 1985.

Hirsch, Rabbi Samson Raphael, commentary to Bible, London, 1960.

Horowitz, Rabbi Isaiah, *Shnei Luchoth HaBrith*, Jerusalem, 1972.
Karelitz, Rabbi A. I. (Chazon Ish), *Kovetz Igeroth*, Bnei Brak, Mesurah, 1976.
Malbim, Rabbi Meir Lebush, commentary to Bible, Jerusalem, 1978.
Margoliyoth, Rabbi Asher Zelig, *Hiluhah d'Rashbi*, Meron, 1981.
Miller, Rabbi Avigdor, *Behold a People*, N.Y., 1968.
———, *Torah Nation*, N.Y., 1972.
(Rabbi) Nachman's Wisdom, trans. by Rabbi A. Kaplan, N.Y., 1973.
Rambam, Rabbi Moses Maimonides, *Yad Chazakah*.
Ramban, Rabbi Moses Nachmanides, commentary to Bible, Mosad HaRav Kook ed., 1974.
Schepansky, Rabbi Israel, *Eretz Yisrael b'Sifroth HaTeshuvoth*, vol. 3, Jerusalem, Mosad HaRav Kook, 1978.
Shag, Rabbi Y.D., *Kedushath HaAretz*, Jerusalem, 1977.
Shapiro, Rabbi Chaim Elazar, *Minchath Elazar*, N.Y., 1946.
Tukatzinsky, Rabbi Yechiel Meir, *Gesher HaChayim*, Jerusalem, 1960.

ואלו יעמדו על הברכה

In memory of all those souls whom I helped
prepare for the world of life everlasting.

Rabbi Aharon Steinberg

for:

The Chevra Kadisha Mortuary
7836 Santa Monica Blvd.
L.A., CA. 90046
(213) 653-8886
654-8415

★

In honor of the Almighty's *chesed*
in granting us a return to His Land.
Reb Binyomin Falk

★ ★ ★

Mr. Asher Schapiro	Rav Yeshaya Scharman
לז"נ הוריו יעקב בן אשר ע"ה	לז"נ אביו ר' יצחק יהודה
ורייזל בת יוסף שלמה ע"ה	בן ישעי' שארמן ע"ה
ת. נ. צ. ב. ה.	נלב"ע כ"ג אדר תשל"ז
	ת. נ. צ. ב. ה.

★★   ★★   ★★   ★★

Reb Gershon Ginsburg
לז"נ האשה הצדקת
פריידא בת ר' שלום ע"ה
ת. נ. צ. ב. ה.

עה"ק צפת תוב"ק
Ansicht v. Zefath - der Tafed
מבצר
Citadelle